THE JOURNEYS OF CELIA FIENNES

The Journeys of
CELIA FIENNES

Edited and with an Introduction by
CHRISTOPHER MORRIS,
Fellow of King's College, Cambridge

With a Foreword by
G. M. TREVELYAN, O.M.

LONDON
THE CRESSET PRESS
MCMXLIX

TO THE MEMORY OF
SIR JOHN CLAPHAM

Published in Great Britain in 1947
by The Cresset Press Ltd., 11 Fitzroy Square, London, W.1.
Revised edition 1949
Printed by Latimer, Trend & Co., Ltd., Plymouth.

CONTENTS

PART I

THE EARLY JOURNEYS IN THE SOUTH (*c*.1685–96)

PART II

THE NORTHERN JOURNEY AND THE TOUR OF KENT (1697)

PART III

"MY GREAT JOURNEY TO NEWCASTLE AND TO CORNWALL" (1698)

PART IV

LONDON AND THE LATER JOURNEYS (c.1701–1703)

PREFACE TO SECOND EDITION

I AM most grateful to a number of friends and correspondents—the most learned of whom preserved his anonymity —and to one reviewer for drawing my attention to mistakes or lacunae in the first edition. Actual errors I have endeavoured to correct but, for technical reasons, it has hardly ever been possible to add new matter, although in several places I should have liked to do so.

C.M.

20 MARCH 1948.

FOREWORD

By Dr. G. M. TREVELYAN, O.M.,
Master of Trinity College, Cambridge

*

*It is now almost half a century since I first came across the
1888 edition of this work. I have always regarded it as a fascinating
book in which to browse, and I have increasingly thought of it and
used it as a valuable source of economic and social history, in the
same class as Defoe's Tour of a few years later. But, both for
pleasure and for historical use, a proper edition, with scholarly
notes and Introduction, was eminently desirable. And at last we
have got it. Mr. Morris's scholarship, his knowledge of the period,
and his knowledge of and interest in the localities described by Celia
Fiennes have all been needed and all have been forthcoming abun-
dantly. The value of the work is thereby greatly enhanced. We have
here got a correct text, an explanation of many obscurities both as
to place names and other matter, and excellent explanatory notes—
in short a definitive edition.*

ACKNOWLEDGMENTS

It is a pleasure to offer my thanks to all who have helped me in the preparation of this edition of Celia Fiennes.

In the first place I am deeply indebted to Lord Saye and Sele, not only for his courtesy in allowing me to use the manuscripts of her Journals, but for the interest which he and other members of his family have shown.

I need hardly say how much honoured I am to have a foreword written by the Master of Trinity. I owe much to Mr. John Hayward, who first suggested that I should undertake the work, and continually gave me good advice. Professor G. N. Clark generously gave me his expert opinion on certain problems presented by the manuscripts. My old Tutor, the late Sir John Clapham, was kind enough to read my introduction and to send me some valuable suggestions. Dr. J. H. Plumb has put ungrudgingly at my disposal a great deal of his time and all of his remarkable knowledge of the period.

I have had the privilege of seeing some notes made by the late Mr. H. Avray Tipping for an edition at one time projected by *Country Life*. These have often been useful, especially on points of architectural interest. Where, in my notes, I owe the information to this source, I have appended the initials H.A.T.

I am also indebted in several ways to Mr. John Saltmarsh and to Mr. Kenneth Harrison. I have been much assisted by several members of the staff of the Cambridge University Library, and, in particular, by Mr. H. L. Pink.

Above all I must record what I owe to my cartographer, my typist and my severest critic, in other words to my wife, who undertook these and many other thankless tasks. Without her aid this edition might never have been finished and would certainly have few of such merits as it may be thought to possess.

C.M.

INTRODUCTION

It was by a side entrance, unannounced and indeed masked, that Celia Fiennes slipped unobtrusively into the world of letters. In 1812 the poet Southey published a miscellany called *Omniana or Horae Otiosiores* which includes a description of a long distance foot race in Windsor Park between an Englishman and a Scot, together with an account of the funeral obsequies in 1695 of Queen Mary II. Both passages were quoted from "the manuscript journal of a lady who was one of the spectators".[1] The lady, although Southey did not say so, was Miss Celia Fiennes, granddaughter of the first Viscount Saye and Sele.

Southey's manuscript, after various changes of ownership, has come into the possession of the present Lord Saye and Sele. It is a small octavo volume with no title or signature, although the fly-leaf is stamped with a beautifully designed monogram "C.F.".[2] The manuscript has had its margins savagely cut by an early nineteenth-century binder and has suffered, at the hands of at least one owner or dealer, the further indignity of a false attribution. This is proved by a catalogue cutting now pasted inside. Because she speaks of "my brother Sir Edmund Harrison", the authoress appears to have been taken for some unknown Miss Harrison. There are, however, numerous clues as to who she really was; and "brother" was once a common abbreviation for "brother-in-law". This Southey manuscript is a draft for part of a longer manuscript which is actually signed. The fuller version, in large octavo, was acquired about 1885 by the 16th Baron Saye and Sele. He gave it to his daughter the Hon. Mrs. Emily Griffiths, by whom it was incompletely transcribed and published in 1888 under the title *Through England*

[1] *Omniana*, vol. i, pp. 88–90.
[2] See title page of this edition.

on a Side Saddle in the time of William and Mary. This time the name of Celia Fiennes appeared, in rather small letters, on the title-page, although no author's name was given on the cover.[3]

Since 1888 Celia Fiennes has had a modest *succès d'estime*. The book is now rare and is known almost solely to bibliophiles or to serious students of the social and architectural history of Restoration England. The standard histories of the period have quoted from her once or even twice, and happily she has supplied two footnotes for the most popular history book of our day.[4] In one book only, so far as I know, has she been treated at any considerable length and, in the ten or twelve consecutive pages which she there receives, she is referred to consistently as *Mrs*. Fiennes.[5] Presumably "my brother Sir Edmund Harrison" had ensnared another victim. Quite a different trap had been laid unwittingly by Mrs. Griffiths. Her edition has no notes and only a few words by way of preface, but in it she found time to say "the only date mentioned is 1695". Actually it is 1697. This, by the strangest mischance, was to catch, in a very small matter, two very eminent victims; for it led Sidney and Beatrice Webb to argue, from the signposts which Celia Fiennes had noted in Lancashire, that the county authorities must have anticipated the law of 1697 ordaining signposts.[6] Celia Fiennes in fact saw these signposts in 1698. It would seem that there is a *prima facie* case for a definitive edition of Celia Fiennes, if only that no more scholars shall be caused to stumble. The real case rests of course on the intrinsic merits of her character and writing and on the intrinsic interest of what she saw. The text printed in 1888 does her much less than justice and has made her seem unintelligent at times.[7] Her readers are likely to agree that she deserves a full transcrip-

[3] Published by the Leadenhall Press.
[4] G. M. Trevelyan, *English Social History*.
[5] Joan Parkes, *Travel in England in the Seventeenth Century* (Oxford, 1925).
[6] Sidney and Beatrice Webb, *English Local Government*: (Part V) *the Story of the King's Highway*, pp. 156–7.
[7] By the omission of a sentence from her account of Cambridge, for example, an apparent confusion is brought about between Trinity Library and King's College Chapel.

tion and a reasonably accurate statement of the few facts about her which are ascertainable.

Celia Fiennes was born on June 7th, 1662,[8] almost certainly in the manor house at Newton Toney near Salisbury, the home of her father Colonel Nathaniel Fiennes, second son of William 8th Baron and first Viscount Saye and Sele. Her mother was Frances daughter of Richard Whitehead, another Roundhead colonel and squire of West Tytherley in Hampshire. Colonel Nathaniel's first wife was a daughter of Sir John Eliot the Parliamentarian martyr. Celia's three uncles and her five uncles by marriage had all fought against the King, while her grandfather the Viscount had been one of the earliest and greatest of the opposition leaders. There is reason to think that the Civil War was virtually planned in secret meetings between Pym, Hampden, Vane, Lord Brooke and others at Broughton Castle the old Viscount's seat;[9] and he was reputed to have made of nearby Banbury the most Puritan town in England. Was not Ben Jonson's Rabbi Zeal-of-the-Land Busy called "a Banbury man"?[10]

We know little of "Old Subtlety", as the Viscount was named, except from the writings of his enemies, although one Puritan news-sheet says that he "sparkled many glimpses into the consciences of all that were near him, and enlightened more places besides Banbury". To the cavaliers he seemed "a seriously subtil peece, and alwayes averse to the Court wayes, something out of pertinaciousnesse", with a preference for going "contrary to the wind".[11] Anthony à Wood thought him "ill natur'd, choleric, severe and rigid, and withal highly conceited of his own worth", and attributed his opposition to pique at failing to gain advancement from the King.[12] Clarendon's analysis went deeper and

---

[8] See Memorial Inscription in Newton Toney Church.

[9] Wood, *Athenae Oxonienses*.

[10] Cf. 'To Banbury came I, O profane one,
Where I saw a Puritane one
Hanging of his cat on Monday,
For killing of a mouse on Sunday.'
Richard Brathwaite, *Drunken Barnaby's Four Journeys* (1638).

[11] Arthur Wilson, *Reign of King James I*, p. 162.

[12] Wood, op. cit.

was more subtly malicious. "Lord Say", he says, was "a man who had the deepest hande in the originall contrivance of all the calamityes which befell that unhappy kingdome, though he had not the least thought of dissolvinge the Monarchy, and lesse of levellinge the rankes and distinctions of men, for no man valewed himselfe more upon his title, or had more ambition to make it greater, and to rayse his fortune, which was but moderate for his title. He was of a prowde, morose, and sullen nature, conversed much with bookes, having been bredd a scholar, and (though nobly borne) a fellow of New-Colledge in Oxforde." Clarendon hastens to explain that the fellowship was only of the kind reserved for "Founder's Kin" and to suggest that the Viscount's pedigree was faked. "His parts were not quicke, but so much above those of his owne ranke, that he had alwayes greate creditt and authority in Parliament." The Viscount "had with his milke sucked in an implacable malice against the government of the Church . . . and from that tyme he gave over any pursuite in Courte", he had "lived narrowly and sordidly in the country, havinge conversation with very few, but such who had greate malignity against the Church and State."[13] Certainly the Viscount's dislike of "levellinge" is borne out. He thought once of seeking religious freedom in America, where he had financial interests, but gave up the project on finding that he could not establish a hereditary peerage in New England.[14] Moreover, he was to retire in disapproval during the Commonwealth from all political activity. He ended as a member of Charles II's first Privy Council and died, aged 80, in the year of his granddaughter's birth, a year which also ended his party's last hopes of capturing or leavening the Church of England.

Nathaniel Fiennes, described by Clarendon as "the darling of his father", was a man of learning and ability whose Puritan doctrines had been stiffened before the Civil War by

[13] Clarendon, *Rebellion,* ed. Macray, vol. i, pp. 333–5. He owed his Viscountcy to a temporary rapprochement with the Duke of Buckingham.
[14] *Cal. State Papers: Colonial* 1574–1660, p. 123; *Lismore Papers,* 2nd series vol. iv, p. 108; Hutchinson, *History of Massachusetts Bay,* vol. i, p. 492 (ed. 1865); Winthrop, *History of New England,* vol. ii, p. 333.

his travels to Geneva and to Scotland. Later he became more of an Erastian and refused to take the Covenant. As a soldier he was not successful and had to surrender Bristol to Prince Rupert. For this he was tried, disgraced and actually condemned to death. The sentence, however, was remitted and, after a few years abroad, he was exonerated and returned to political life. Although he was "purged" by Colonel Pride, he retained the confidence of Cromwell; he became a member of the Council of State and Keeper of the Great Seal and was summoned to "the Other House", that equivalent of a House of Lords in the last of Cromwell's constitutional experiments. He wrote many pamphlets, and the speeches of "Lord Fiennes", especially one in favour of Cromwell's becoming King, were described as very "scriptural" or even as "such stuff as is scarce imaginable by us who have heard the Beast himself speaking . . . a Hocus, a Cabal, mysterious and Jewish throughout".[15] It is pleasant to find him pleading for clemency in the case of James Nayler the Quaker saint who had his tongue pierced for "blasphemy".[16] That Nathaniel Fiennes was less outstanding as a man of action is probable enough. Once, when a pickpocket was thought to be under the table at a Parliamentary Committee meeting, "Colonel Fiennes drew his sword and vapoured hugely, how he would spit him; but the fellow escaped, if indeed there were any such."[17] Unlike his father, Colonel Nathaniel never made his peace with Charles II, but he died unmolested in retirement at Newton Toney in 1669 aged sixty-one.

With this family tradition behind her, Celia Fiennes was, naturally, a Nonconformist. In her travels she was scrupulous to record and to rejoice at the number of "Descenters" meetings she found in the provincial towns. Her political opinions were of course ardently, not to say disingenuously Whiggish. She could not pass through Warwick without relating that Guy of Warwick, supposedly a giant, was really "but a little man in stature", and then continuing "such will

[15] *Commons Journal*, vol. vii, pp. 582–7.
[16] Thomas Burton, *Diary*, vol. i, p. 90.
[17] Ibid, vol. i, pp. 336–7.

the account be of our Hero King William the Third tho'
little in stature yet great in atchievements and valour." She
died on April 10th, 1741[18] and should have been well satisfied
with the seemingly unbreakable Whig ascendancy of that
day. The reign of Sir Robert Walpole had still a year to run.

Celia Fiennes had lived through a social as well as a
political revolution, for it was the age in which the business
man became at last able to buy himself into "good society"
outright. He had crept in deviously for a century or more but
by the end of the seventeenth century the last barriers were
down and henceforward he could enter quickly and openly,
hardly troubling to ring the bell. A sub-aristocracy with a
frankly plutocratic basis was growing up. To this the family
connections of Celia Fiennes bear excellent witness. "Old
Subtlety" had married a Temple, his sister a Villiers and his
eldest son, James the second Viscount, a Cecil. His other
children had married scarcely less "well", for Celia's aunts
between them had married one peer, two baronets, a baronet's son and the son of one mere knight. Nearly all of the
next generation were to marry commoners, many of whom
had business connections. The marriage of Celia's own sister
Mary is an interesting example. She married in 1684[19] Edmund Harrison of London, a "Turkey merchant".[20] He was
knighted in 1698 and seems to have been a really great and
perhaps not over-reputable business magnate, with his eggs
in many baskets. He can be found lending money to Marshal
Schomberg for his campaign in Ireland,[21] and applying as
joint owner of "several great tracts of land in divers . . .
plantations in America" for recognition as a Corporation.[22]
He became governor of a company trading to Greenland[23]
and a director of the New East India Company.[24] The serges
which the agent met by Celia Fiennes was buying for him in

[18] Memorial Inscription, Newton Toney Church.
[19] *Marriage Licenses. Vicar General* 1674–1687, p. 170 (Harleian Society
Publications).
[20] Narcissus Luttrell, *Brief Relation*, vol. v, p. 33.
[21] *Calendar State Papers Domestic*, 1690–1691, p. 530.
[22] Ibid., 1691–1692, p. 379.
[23] Ibid., 1700–02, p. 269.
[24] Ibid., 1698, pp. 369–70. Cf. Luttrell. Op. cit. iv., p. 485.

Exeter he sold in the following year as far afield as Leghorn.[25] His financial interests in the privateering enterprise of Captain Kidd will probably not bear too close inspection. It was over this matter that a fellow investor, the Earl of Bellamont, wrote "When he had made me depend on him for advancing the money, and saw that I could not easily raise it, he then gave me a Presbyterian gripe and fettered me in the writings between us."[26] Sir Edmund's four daughters all married Londoners, two of whom lived at Hackney. This is of interest, because it was at Hackney—probably in the home of one of her nieces—that Celia Fiennes eventually died.[27]

Celia moved easily and freely between social spheres. At Newbury she "called on an old acquaintance marryed to a tradesman". An acute contemporary observer, the Frenchman Henri Misson, noted that "it is no derogation to a man in England to be a merchant; yet it is very rare for Peers to put their younger sons out apprentices, as 'tis said they used to do".[28] Possibly so, but their granddaughters could marry merchants freely. Certainly it was with the Harrisons that Celia Fiennes was most intimate. She is also to be found in company with the daughters of her cousin Susannah who had married a prominent London lawyer, Thomas Filmer. It was probably with one or both of the Filmer girls that Celia Fiennes made her Northern tour of 1697, for she started with some "gentlewomen" from Amwell where the Filmers then lived.[29] The relations she visited in her early south-western journeys were mostly of her mother's family and were nearly all country squires. She may have been "dropped" by her grand relatives the Earls of Lincoln, for she did not visit

[25] *State Papers Domestic*, 1699–1700, p. 151.
[26] Luttrell, *Brief Relation*, vol. v, pp. 32–3; Hist. MSS. Comm. Portland, MSS. vol. viii, p. 75.
[27] Memorial Inscription at Newton Toney. Sir E. Harrison died in 1712, Lady Harrison in 1737. Musgrave, *Obituary*, vol. iii, pp. 154 and 157. For the Harrison pedigree see *Familiae Minorum Gentium*, vol. iii, p. 1139 (Harl. Soc. Pub.).
[28] Misson, *Memoirs and Observations in his Travels over England*. Written 1697. I quote from the somewhat free and racy translation made in 1719 by John Ozell.
[29] See Victoria County History, *Hertfordshire*, vol. iii, p. 417; Clutterbuck, *History and Antiquities of Hertford*, vol. ii, pp. 10–11.

them. She stayed, however, with her cousin the baronet Sir Griffith Boynton of Burton Agnes; and more often in Staffordshire with her uncle the distinguished old Cromwellian Sir Charles Wolseley, one of whose daughters, we are told, was married to a Wedgwood. It seems too that Celia did not pass through Worcestershire without going to see the Foleys, the builders of Stoke Edith, a family whose fortunes were founded by the great ironmaster, "Tom of 10,000£", as she calls him, whose son was Speaker of the House of Commons and whose grandson was to be a peer.[30]

Celia Fiennes was clearly in sympathy with the new society that was coming into being. Her interest in mining, in drainage projects and in manufacturing processes was hardly surpassed by Defoe's, although she had not his contempt for other things such as "the wonderless Wonders of the Peak" or for "brilliant palaces and gew gaw gardens". She went, "for curiositys sake" to see "the Burning Well" near Warrington, whereas Defoe omitted it, not being "satisfied it was valuable".[31] Her omnivorous appetite for facts left her with little time for the preaching of economic sermons like Defoe's. She stopped, however, to attribute the poverty of Scotland to its people's "sloth" and to tell us that she regarded a debtors' prison as a place of refuge which they did not deserve. And of course she disapproved of men without property getting into Parliament. In everything her taste was for the modern and the "commodious", whether it was the new style in architecture known to us as "Queen Anne"— she had a special liking for sash windows—or whether it was the water closet just installed at Windsor Castle. The best that she would concede for anything old was that it might, like the front of Euston Hall, "look nobly tho' not just of the new modell'd way of building", or that it might be, like Lichfield Cathedral, "a stately structure but old". Usually, as with the Rows at Chester, which she called a "dissight to the grace of the streetes", the old was held merely to detract

---

[30] See Burnet, *History*, vol. iv, p. 191 (Ed., 1823).
[31] Defoe, *Tour of the Whole Island of Great Britain.* First published 1724. (Everyman Edition, vol. ii, p. 267.)

from the beauty or "convenience" of the place. At York the buildings were "very low", "indifferent" and "look no better than the outskirts off London". She disliked the continuance of feudal ceremonies such as the tenants of Lord Paget waiting upon him at table on feast days. She said next to nothing of rural customs or indeed of villages at all. Her interests lay in rich men's houses and in the towns where "big money" could be made. She was even less amused than was Defoe by anything savouring of "Merrie England".

Almost the only external evidence we have of Celia Fiennes' existence is her appearance as the holder of a mortgage upon a piece of land in Cheshire. This we know from a lawsuit, "Marbury v. Tarbock", which came twice before the House of Lords in the winter of 1705-6.[32] The land was the estate of a certain William Marbury near Northwich and its value lay in its containing the first rock salt to be found in England. This discovery had been made in 1670 and a company to exploit it was formed in 1694.[33] We have a description of the mine by Celia Fiennes herself. Salt was still very important and the country had had to depend hitherto on the boiling of brine in pans. Celia Fiennes' little investment may suggest that she or her advisers were attracted by the newer forms of industrial enterprise.

Nearly all that we know of Celia Fiennes must be deduced from her own writing. The memorial tablet in Newton Toney Church gives the dates of her birth and of her death at Hackney. It tells us also that her baptismal name was Cecilia; but she must have been so generally known as Celia that the stonemason was at first misinformed, for he had to insert the missing "CI" above the "CELIA" he had cut.[34] In 1709, when Newton Toney manor was sold, she signed her name to the deed after those of the 4th Viscount and of the Harrisons;

[32] Hist. MSS. Comm. New Series, vol. vi, *Manuscripts of the House of Lords*, 1704-06, pp. 313-4 and 351-2.

[33] *Social England* (ed. H. D. Traill), vol. iv, p. 453; W. R. Scott, *Joint Stock Companies to* 1720, vol. ii, p. 470; Hist. MSS. Comm. Report XII, Part VI, p. 110; *The Case of Rock Salt* (1702); Ormerod, *History of Cheshire*, vol. i, xlvi; Nef., *Rise of the British Coal Industry*, vol. i, p. 178.

[34] In one of the two occurrences of her name in *Marbury v. Tarbock* she appears as "Cecilia".

and she signed as "Celia". The rest would be silence if she herself had been less garrulous.[35] She has left clues, however, which enable the amateur detective to date nearly all her movements and also the actual writing of the journal.

Her early tours generally begin and end at Newton Toney where Celia's mother lived until she died in 1691. The trip to Bath cannot have been later than 1687, for the additions, made in honour of Queen Mary of Modena's visit in that year, to the Cross in the Cross Bath, were not then to be seen. Celia Fiennes' journey by coach into Somerset with her sister and a maid may even have been before her sister's marriage in 1684. The journey to London "after my Mother's death" was presumably in 1691. The visit to Oxford must have been at least two years later, since the relations who showed her round did not matriculate till the autumn of 1693[36] and neither Queen's College Library nor Trinity Chapel, which are described as finished, were complete before that year. The next journey—into Herefordshire—must have been in or before 1696, as her uncle John, who died in that year, was still alive.

After her mother's death most of Celia Fiennes' journeys begin and end in London and she speaks of it as "home". It is likely that she had gone to live with or near her sister. She was certainly in London for the coronations of James II, of William and Mary, and of Anne; also for the funerals of Mary (March 5th, 1695) and of William (March 30th, 1702) as well as for King William's formal entry after the Peace of Ryswick (November 16th, 1697). Her early journeys had been rounds of visits with a little sight-seeing thrown in, but in 1697 Celia Fiennes undertook her first Grand Tour to the North. Possibly it was this and the succeeding "Great Journey" that were "begun to regain my health". Her first Northern tour began in May 1697: it is the only date she ever gives, and internal evidence confirms it. The tour of Kent, she says, was made in the same year, presumably in the late summer as it was the hopping season and she visited a "Bartholomewtide"

---

[35] But see my Appendix on Celia Fiennes' Will. I was unable to obtain the Will till this Introduction was in proof.

[36] Foster, *Alumni Oxonienses*.

fair (August 24th). There is ample evidence that her "Great Journey to Newcastle and to Cornwall" was made in 1698. She ran into the parliamentary election of that year; the Peace of Ryswick had been concluded; the building of Stoke Edith had begun; the Earl of Peterborough was recently dead; and Mr. William Allen was the Mayor of Chester.

After the description of London, of royal funerals and coronations and of the Lord Mayor's Show, and after a workmanlike account of the English constitution, there come a few short journeys mostly in the Home Counties, although she goes once more to Wolseley and Stoke Edith. These journeys can hardly have been earlier than 1701, for Stoke Edith was finished, Speaker Paul Foley was dead (he died in 1699) and the West portico of All Saints Church, Northampton, which was finished in 1701, was now complete. The last journey of all—to Epsom, Windsor and Hampton Court—is likely to have been later still. It may even be a postscript describing a journey undertaken after the main account was written.[37] Certainly Lord Ranelagh has had time to make alterations at Cranborne Chase, which he had bought only in 1700; and certainly Queen Anne has had time to settle down at Hampton Court where the state apartments, which she inherited unfinished in 1702, are now fully furnished.

There can be little doubt that the main body of the journal was written in the year 1702. April 23rd, the date of the Queen's coronation, is referred to as though it were "April 23rd last". Marlborough is still an Earl which he was until December 1702.[38] In the account of London Sir James Bateman is "our last sheriff". Arlington House, demolished in 1703, is still standing on the present site of Buckingham Palace, although alterations have begun and are mentioned in a marginal addendum. The *Royal Sovereign* is said to have been built "last yeare"—she went into service when Admiral Rooke hoisted his flag in her on June 1st, 1702.[39] Nor is it

---

[37] The smaller manuscript, which is certainly the earlier, breaks off before this journey.

[38] A marginal note, added later, says "Now Duke".

[39] See *Cal. S. P. Dom.*, 1702–3. Cf. Sir George Rooke, *Journal*, Navy Records Soc., pp. 147 and 149.

likely that Celia Fiennes would have described the Eddystone lighthouse without mentioning its destruction in the Great Storm of November 1703 had that event already taken place.

Only the smaller manuscript, that once owned by Southey, is in Celia Fiennes' own hand. It contains running corrections which can only be an author's, not a copyist's. The word "yarn", for instance, is deleted and—in the same line, not above it—"serge" is written in its place. This manuscript begins with the "Great Journey" of 1698 and ends with the Wiltshire journey that immediately follows the account of London and the Constitution. There are indications of sustained and fairly rapid writing, for there are no breaks or headings, while the spelling is even more faulty and there is even less use of punctuation than in the fuller and fairer copy used by Mrs. Griffiths. The fuller version is probably not in the same hand but the work of an amanuensis, although Celia Fiennes herself has made a rough list of contents on the fly-leaf—together with a scribbled calculation as to the number of bishoprics in England. She has also written marginal notes and headings and inserted just a few corrections. It is likely that, although she was recollecting in tranquillity, she had before her some notes made while she was actually upon the road. Without them she could hardly have remembered the price of meat in Ripon five years before —and her writing is full of just such details. Moreover, a reference to a portrait of "the present King William" at Euston Hall may be a survival from some such earlier notes or diary.

In her foreword Celia Fiennes disclaimed any intention of publishing her journal. But if, as she said, it was so "little likely to fall into the hands of any but my near relations", why did she take such pains to state that various persons mentioned were "cousins" or "relations of mine" and sometimes to explain in detail how they were related? Besides, she calls it specifically a "book" and there is something about the remarks she addresses to her countrymen and to her sex in general which suggests that she may have had in mind a wider public. The keeping and even the publishing of diaries and travel journals was becoming fashionable—there were hosts of others besides Pepys and Evelyn and Defoe.

It must be remembered that a new discovery of England was in progress. Aristocratic house-parties would sometimes go to watch a river being made more navigable or a fen being drained.[40] Treatises were written on Stonehenge and poems on "the Wonders of the Peak". A new edition of Camden's *Britannia*, brought up to date by Bishop Gibson, seems to have lain on the parlour tables of most well-to-do people. It is one of the few books to which Celia Fiennes expressly refers. A devoted band of antiquaries and topographers were grubbing up the English past.[41] Ogilby's wonderful road-book had appeared in 1675 and there were also surveys, comparable with modern directories and gazetteers, such as Blome's *Britannia*, Adams' *Index Villaris* and Chamberlayne's *Angliae Notitia*. Statisticians like Gregory King and Sir William Petty were trying to estimate the population. The English were becoming highly immodest about their own political discoveries, their own great men or "worthies", their own architecture and landscape and, above all, their own prosperity. They would have shared Defoe's delight when the "foreign gentleman" observed to him "that England was not like other countries, but it was all a planted garden".[42] They would have accepted his own verdict upon London as "the most glorious sight without exception that the whole world at present can show; or perhaps ever cou'd show since the sacking of Rome in the European, and the burning the Temple of Jerusalem in the Asian part of the world". They might even have agreed with Defoe about the London suburbs whither the citizens resorted, he said, "to draw their breath in a clean air" before returning to "smoke and dirt, sin and seacoal (as it was coursly express'd) in the busy city". It was of these same suburbs that he wrote "all this variety, this beauty, this glorious show of wealth and

[40] Evelyn, *Diary*, July 22nd, 1670.
[41] For example, Dugdale, Plot, Thoresby, Ashmole, Strype, Wanley, Rymer, Wharton, Anthony à Wood, White Kennett and Hearne.
[42] Defoe, Op. cit., vol. ii, p. 8.

plenty, is really a view of the luxuriant age which we live in."[43]

The growth of wealth, comfort and leisure has often coincided with a growth of hypochondria; and in the seventeenth century there was general agreement that among the "Wonders" of England were her "Spaws" or mineral waters. There was a widespread belief in this form of "Nature Cure", which is understandable enough if the incompetence of seventeenth-century doctors and the revolting character of their prescriptions are remembered. The Seaside was not to be discovered until King George III began to bathe at Weymouth. The prevalence of an almost exclusively meat and wheat diet among the well-to-do would have made spa waters all the more advisable. One element in the cult was a lingering tradition of pilgrimage to holy wells; and certainly Celia Fiennes remarks on the number of Papists among her fellow visitors to St. Winifred's and to St. Mungo's Wells. It was one of the few Catholic customs which could not be stopped, for a shrine can be pulled down but a spring cannot easily be dammed. The cult, however, was mainly sheer fashion, a sop to hypochondria and an excuse for taking holidays. At the spas near London plenty of recreational amenities were to be had, as will be seen from Celia Fiennes' account of Epsom or of Tunbridge. Near Epsom there were the races on Banstead Downs and there was Box Hill, where it was "very easy", as a contemporary wrote, "for Gentlemen and Ladies insensibly to lose their company in these pretty labyrinths of Box-wood, and divert themselves unperceived . . . and it may justly be called the Palace of Venus".[44] At Tunbridge the amenities were mainly gastronomic, such as the Sussex wheatear called "the English ortolan, which is a very dear bit at the Wells, but is the most delicious morsel for a creature which is but one mouthful, that can be imagined", or the mackerel brought from Hastings "within three hours after their being taken

[43] Ibid., vol. i, p. 168.
[44] John Macky, *A Journey through England in Familiar Letters from a Gentleman Here to His Friend Abroad.* Written in prison in 1709 and first published 1714. 5th edition 1732, vol. i, p. 140.

out of the sea".[45] No wonder that Congreve could write "You would not think how people eat here; everybody has the appetite of an ostrich and as they drink steel in the morning so I believe at noon they could digest iron."[46]

The new fashion began soon after Dudley 3rd Baron North had discovered, as he claimed, the Tunbridge waters, finding them salutary after his potations at the Court of James I. After Queen Catherine of Braganza took to visiting Bath or Tunbridge, as a cure for her sterility, the vogue for "Spaws" became almost universal. Every rank was catered for, the rich at Tunbridge, the middle class at Epsom, and the poor at Hampstead, Dulwich, Barnet or the humbler establishments in the provinces.[47] Characteristically, Celia Fiennes sampled them all, some of them many times. Once, near Sheffield, she had to be restrained from tasting some water which the local people thought noxious. The watering places were fashionable enough: Rochester wrote a poem on Tunbridge and Shadwell a play called *Epsom Wells*. Yet most of them were still little more than villages and part of their attraction lay in their rusticity and in the fun of "camping out". At Tunbridge Celia Fiennes noted that "they have made the Wells very commodious by the many good buildings all about it", but she was given very uncomfortable quarters at Buxton and found them altogether unromantic. "We staid two nights by reason one of our company was ill, but it was sore against our wills". A generation earlier the young medical student Edward Browne, son of Sir Thomas, had complained of the fare provided in Buxton at his lodgings—nothing but "oatcake and mutton, which wee fancied to taste like dog".[48] Barnet was better equipped but Celia Fiennes had "little stomach" for the waters there, a

---

[45] Ibid, vol. i, pp. 120–1. Defoe lifts the whole passage without acknowledgment, Op. cit. vol. i, p. 126.

[46] Congreve, *Letters*, To Dennis the Bookseller, August 11th, 1695, in *Works* ed. Summers, vol. i, p. 95. Cf. the account of Tunbridge Wells given in *Grammont's Memoirs*, chap. x. I am also indebted to Margaret Barton's delightful history of Tunbridge Wells.

[47] Defoe, Op. cit. vol. i, p. 157.

[48] *Journal of a Tour in Derbyshire*, 1662. In *Works* of Sir Thomas Browne, edited S. Wilkin, 1831. Vol. i, p. 34.

distaste she shared with Pepys who had to make frequent and necessary stops on his way home and suffered from a bad nightmare when he got to bed.[49] Bath itself was still fairly primitive, for the reign of Nash did not begin there until 1705, and the houses when Celia Fiennes saw them were "indifferent". Even in Defoe's time Bath, he said, "scarce gives the company room to converse out of the smell of their own excrements."[50]

Celia Fiennes was an authority on all the "Spaws" and had theories as to which waters were "diaretick" or "spiriteous", which were "quick purgers" or "good for all scurbutick humours", which were "chalibiets" or sweet and which were "stincking spaws". She was always concerned that a spring should be "quick" and anxious to know whether it contained sulphur or alum or "steel". She was fussy about bathing as near as possible to the actual spring. Her exact procedure at St. Mungo's Well near Knaresborough is given in great detail. "I used my bath garments and so pulled them off and put on flannell when I came out to go into the bed which is best . . . but some will keep on their wet garments and let them drye to them and say its more beneficial but I did not venture it. I dipp'd my head quite over every tyme I went in and found it eased a great pain I used to have in my head and I was not so apt to catch cold so much as before which I imputed to the exceeding coldness of the spring that shutts up the pores of the body."

That Celia Fiennes was actually robust is clear from her energy and her endurance but she showed at times a hypochondriacal strain and complained that crossing a ferry or eating "rhye bread" always made her ill. Her journeys are punctuated by the taking of waters and it is clear that she visited the "Spaws" more often than she relates. She knows Epsom well enough to comment on the growth of the week-end habit there; and the Tunbridge waters, she says, "I have dranke many years with great advantage". She even states that she has been to St. Mungo's in "7 severall seasons". Her

[49] *Diary*, edited Wheatley, vol. iv, p. 168, July 11th, 1664.
[50] Op. cit., vol. ii, p. 168.

precautions seem to have been largely needless, for she was none the worse after riding into Okehampton soaked to the skin, nor for sleeping at Ely in conditions so damp that she "had froggs and slow worms and snailes" in her room, although she supposed they were "brought up with the faggotts". Nor was there much wrong with her appetite. At Woburn she "eate a great quantity of the Red Coralina goosbery". She was excited by the potted char of Windermere; the salmon which she bought so cheaply in Scotland she carried back across the border in order to get it appropriately cooked; and at Colchester she ate enough oysters to make a noticeable inroad upon her purse. She was a connoisseur of beer, which was still the universal English beverage for men, women and children. "There are", wrote Henri Misson, "a hundred and a hundred sorts of Beer made in England; and some not bad: Art has well supply'd Nature in this particular. Be that as 'twill; I'm for Nature against the World."[51] Celia Fiennes would probably have agreed, for she was delighted whenever she was near enough the coast for French wine to be obtainable,[52] as she was at Rye and in North Wales and again at Aitchison Bank where she found the other elements in Border hospitality so little to her liking. Tea, she observed, was on sale at Epsom and at Tunbridge but she passed no judgement on it; she would not have found it in less fashionable quarters.

The accidents by flood and field which befell Celia Fiennes left her singularly unmoved and suggest that there was little the matter with her nerves. She might easily have been drowned once on the flooded causeway south of Ely and her "horses feete could scarce stand" as she crossed the Sands of Dee. Her horse fell in the cobbled streets of Lancaster and again in a bad hole in the road near Fowey. Just outside Alresford she was actually thrown. Above all there was the very unpleasant encounter with obvious highwaymen in Cheshire on the road to Whitchurch. Highwaymen, it should

---

[51] Misson, Op. cit., p. 17.
[52] Some of it may well have been smuggled, since there was a tariff war with France even when actual fighting was not taking place.

be noted, were greatly on the increase during the period of Celia Fiennes' travels.[53] Some of these narrow escapes drew from her devout ejaculations of thanksgiving to her "speciall Providence" but nothing more.

The roads of England in Celia Fiennes' day were of course less dangerous to life and limb than they are now; but the discomforts of travelling were infinitely greater. A traveller could lose his way on the Great North Road itself or find himself riding with his saddlebags in flood water.[54] On parts of the London-Canterbury Road, as late as 1723, two horsemen could not pass one another, "or even so much as two wheelbarrows".[55] It was inadvisable to ride unaccompanied over Hampstead Heath or Shooters Hill for fear of robbery. Evelyn had learned to his cost that it was dangerous anywhere "to ride neere an hedge".[56] An old statute had ordained that 200 feet should be kept clear on each side of the highway but it had long since lapsed, for where the soil was fertile this land would become enclosed. "There is good land where there is foul way", wrote Cotton in his continuation of Walton's *Angler*. So little hedging and ditching was carried out that quite often a footman with an axe would be sent in front to clear the way for coaches.[57] The roads had actually deteriorated since the Middle Ages and the increase of wheeled traffic was rapidly making them worse still. The forced labour for their upkeep was always grudged and nothing effective was ever done so long as the government left things to the local magistrates. Turnpikes to finance road repair had been legalized as early as 1663 but in the time of Celia Fiennes the only tolls regularly enforced were those at Wadesmill.[58] Legislators, in despair, had often resorted to purely restrictive and quite futile acts setting limits to the

[53] Joan Parkes, *Travel in England in the Seventeenth Century*, pp. 156–7.

[54] Ralph Thoresby's *Diary* (ed. 1830), vol. i, p. 69 (October 21st, 1680) and vol. i. p. 295 (May 17th, 1695).

[55] *Journeys in England* by Lord Harley, afterwards Earl of Oxford, in Hist. MSS. Comm. Portland MSS. vi, 76.

[56] Evelyn, *Diary*, June 11th, 1652.

[57] Parkes, Op. cit., pp. 5–11.

[58] Sir H. G. Fordham, *The Roads of England and Wales and the Turnpike System*, in Historical Teachers' Miscellany, vol. v, pp. 5–6. Celia Fiennes, however, met with a toll-gate near Wymondham.

size and weight of vehicles or to their wheels. Wheeled traffic, however, was still rare, although the "Flying Coaches", that went (in summer) from Oxford to London in one day, had begun in 1669. Even in 1712 it took a coach six days to go from London to Newcastle. Carriage was almost always done by long strings of pack animals. "The reason", wrote Celia Fiennes, "is plaine, from the narrowness of the lanes where is good lands . . . and where its hilly and stoney no other carriages can pass." She saw them near Kendal carrying "everything they would use", on the road to Exeter laden with serges, in Cornwall bringing in the harvest loaded "from the neck to the taile and pretty high", and taking coal from the Kingswood mines into Bristol or Taunton.

Long after coaches became commoner there remained parts of the country where they were hardly serviceable. Squire Western's wife had "a coach and four usually at her command; though unhappily, indeed, the badness of the neighbourhood, and of the roads, made this of little use". The condition of the road depended wholly on the nature of the soil; and right up to the time of Telford and McAdam, roads in the clay country were liable to be unusable after heavy rain. London could be virtually cut off from the North by the belt of clays that stretch across the Midlands, and even the Great North Road held its terrors near Baldock, as did Watling Street at "Hockley-in-the-Hole" or Hockliffe where Celia Fiennes thought it "a sad road" which must be "impasable" in winter. There were winters in which London was kept short of meat as a result.[59] In Derbyshire or the far North the stony soil and steep gradients turned the roads into mere tracks; and she found the same in Devonshire and Cornwall where the lanes narrowed progressively all the way to Land's End and even single horses sometimes had difficulty in getting through them. Yet the worst horror was the liquid mud of Sussex where the Horsham assizes were held only once a year—at Midsummer—and where timber bound for London that was caught by the autumn rains would be

[59] See Defoe, Op. cit., vol. ii, pp. 117-8, 122-3, 127-8.

dumped by the roadside and left there till the spring. John Macky, the famous government spy, reports at second-hand that respectable Sussex women had to go to church in ox-drawn coaches;[60] and Defoe, who often borrows from Macky, claims to have seen it for himself.[61] It was even said that Sussex men and animals had grown long-legged through pulling their feet out of the clay.

Against this background the travels of Celia Fiennes acquire a certain heroism. Almost all of them were made on horseback and on the "Great Journey" of 1698 she travelled alone apart from servants; and of these no mention is made of more than two. Of course she took spare horses with her but she never states how many. She was concerned at their not getting proper diet in Cornwall; and in the Lake District she had to have them reshod every two or three days. In really difficult or dangerous country—in Derbyshire or in the "moorish" or marshy lands near Wigan, among the Fells or along the Scottish Border—she hired a guide. Between Durham and Darlington the guide was carrying some of her "nightcloths and little things" and contrived to lose the bundle. This may well mean the bed linen which she carried with her, not trusting to the cleanliness of such bedding as she would find at inns. She was certainly gratified when her hostess in the "poor cottage" where she put up in Halt-whistle "brought me out her best sheetes which served to secure my own sheetes from her dirty blanckets". At the hands of innkeepers she suffered many things. In Haltwhistle she had been forced to sleep in the cottage because at the one inn "they had noe hay nor would get none, and when my servants had got some else where they were angry and would not entertaine me"; and in the cottage she could not sleep because of the peat smoke. At Aitchison Bank conditions were such that, she declares, "I could not bring myself to sit down", and "I could have no stomach to eate any of the food". She was luckier in the West Country, especially in Truro, where her landlady was so full of "reall religion"; but

60 Macky, Op. cit., vol. i, p. 28.
61 Defoe, Op. cit, vol. i, p. 129.

it is not surprising that she preferred to stay as much as possible in the houses of relations or acquaintances. In 1698 she had peculiar trouble in finding accommodation; for at Durham, at Richmond, at Boroughbridge and once again at Worcester she ran into the "clutter" and "randan" of the election crowds, expressing their political opinions "much according to the good liquor's operation". At Flint, at Stafford, at Gloucester and at Wells she escaped the election only to fall in with the assizes. She was glad at times to be offered hospitality by the local squire, as happened at Shuckburgh in Warwickshire; or by the parson, like that clergyman at Hemsworth near Rotherham whom she found to be, unlike so many of his cloth, "a very genteele man".

Little else can be deduced about her equipment or her luggage, except that she wore a "dust-coat" which got soaked through and then dried by the wind along the shore near Penzance. Quite possibly she took her own greyhound with her, for near Ambleside, while riding through a "parke", she saw some hares and "by meanes of a good greyhound I had a little course". Only someone of the most assured social position could have risked this defiance of the new and savage game laws. It was of course an age in which the aristocracy were really privileged. When Celia Fiennes' kinsman the fat Earl of Lincoln made his servants beat a 'prentice boy to death "for gazing at him in the street",[62] the coroner's jury found that the boy "long before was sick of a consumption and died of that disease, by the visitation of God".[63] It is even said that the "Proud Duke" of Somerset had outriders to clear the roads of plebeians lest they should see him as he passed, although one farmer refused to be stopped from looking over his own hedge and held up his pig so that it should "see him too."[64]

Quite how adventurous it was for a woman to be travelling virtually alone we cannot tell. There are no records to enlighten us, although half a century earlier, in the narrative

---

[62] Luttrell, *Brief Relation*, vol. ii, p. 370.
[63] Hist. MSS. Comm. *MSS. of the House of Lords*, 1692–3, p. 82. This was the fat peer who was counted as ten in order to pass the Habeas Corpus Act.
[64] *Memoirs of the Kit-Cat Club*, 1821, p. 13.

of Lieutenant Hammond of Norwich, we catch one glimpse of a French girl riding towards Canterbury. She was "a light and sprightly Mademoiselle, who, being well mounted, would be sure to be alwayes on the front and a file leader, and to leave a whole cloud of choking dust behind her. . . . She fear'd not to ride in the darke, whether it were up hill or downe dale, it was all one". In the inn at Canterbury "this pretty she rider at that time held it no nicety, nor point of incivility, to disrobe and bed her little, tender, weary'd corps in our presence, which I understood afterwards is common and familiar amongst them of that nation."[65]

It can hardly be doubted that Celia Fiennes was a model of propriety. She is relieved to find that the yellow canvas bathing dress provided for her at Bath "is stiff and made large with great sleeves like a parsons gown; the water fills it up so that its borne off that your shape is not seen; it does not cling close as other linning which looks sadly in the poorer sort that go in their own linning". At St. Winifred's Well, she says, "I could not have been persuaded to have gone in unless I might have had curtains to have drawn . . . for the wet garments are no covering to the body." She noted in Lord Exeter's house at Burghley "very fine paint in pictures, but they were all without garments or very little, that was the only fault, the immodesty of the pictures, especially in my Lords appartment". Nor were the exorbitant charges of the inn at Carlisle her only complaint against "a young giddy landlady that could only dress fine and entertain the soldiers".

Celia Fiennes could be censorious enough. Of some cottagers just across the Scottish Border she says "I tooke them for people which were sick, seeing 2 or 3 great wenches as tall and bigg as any woman sat hovering between their bed and the chimney corner, all idle doing nothing or at least was not settled to any work tho' it was nine of the clock when I came thither haveing gone 7 long miles that morning." "These foolerys", she calls the splendours with which the French ambassador is received at Court. She thinks the

[65] *A Relation of a Short Survey of the Western Counties*, 1635. Edited L. G. W. Legg for the Camden Miscellany xvi, pp. 10-11.

country has a better Constitution, through "Gods providentiall care", than, for its "folly, faction and wickedness", it deserves. She is scarcely less enraged than Dickens at the delays and corruption of the Chancery courts and of course she speaks her mind about the laws which penalize "tender consciences" but leave unpunished "the enormous crimes" of the established clergy. Nor can she describe the function of the Lord High Steward, when the Lords sit in judgement, without saying "then he adds his own thoughts to the side he thinks best, but usually he is so crafty as to add to the side of the majority". She was more tolerant of Quakers than were most of her contemporaries and went to a meeting in Scarborough but notes a little acidly that "their prayers were all made on the first person and single". On Fulke Greville's tomb at Warwick he is called the friend of Sir Philip Sidney, "which is", writes Celia Fiennes, "but of poore availe to him now dead if he was not the friend of the great Jehovah". Even her approval sometimes has a sting in the tail. The "excellent minister" at Bakewell is of a kind "not very frequent in our dayes to be found"; and the poor cottagers in Cornwall are damned with faint praise when they are commended for being so much cleaner than the Border Scots.

Much of her primness has an engaging, childlike quality about it and is offset by her simplicity and zest. Near Rye she attended a fair, "the saddest fair I ever saw—ragged tatter'd booths and people". Nevertheless, she goes on, "the music and danceing could not be omitted". The herbal she was shown in the apothecary's house at Bury St. Edmunds "was a fine thing and would have delighted me severall dayes but I was passant". In the press at Oxford she could not resist printing her name "severall tymes". She bought souvenirs in Wigan made of the local jet or "cannell coale", "for curiositys sake", and in a Cornish stamping mill for tin she "had a piece poured out and made cold for to take with me". She was, however, less of a vandal than some other seventeenth-century travellers, for she did not carve her initials on the Glastonbury Thorn or bring away "many branches and leaves" as the Puritan Sir William Brereton had done.[66] Nor did she try, as Evelyn did, to break off fragments of Stonehenge with a hammer.[67]

In the fine arts her taste was unsophisticated. She liked the altarpiece at Lichfield, which was "drawn so well that it lookes like a reall cannopy" and the one at Gloucester which was "soe much to the life you would at least think it carv'd" and, no less, the one at Ripon which "looks so natural just like real crimson satten with gold fringe like hangings". At Woburn she was delighted with "a figure of stone resembling an old weeder woman, used in the garden ... which is done so like and her clothes so well that at first I took it to be a real living body". She was even better pleased with the "fine willow tree" at Chatsworth which turned out to be a fountain, "it being made of brass and pipes to each leafe but in appearance is exactly like any willow". She admired Antonio Verrio, whose saints seemed to Pope to "sprawl" over so many painted ceilings, and she called him "the best hand in England which did the painting at Windsor". No doubt she would have agreed with Evelyn in saying that "his figures move."[68]

The charm of her style is difficult to analyse but undoubtedly it owes much to her unappeasable craving for new facts. No one so universally observant can be a bore. She has perhaps little more than a very good eye, but did not one great painter say of another, "Monet ce n'est qu'un oeil"? In her foreword she is disarming. "As most I converse with knows both the freedom and easyness I speak and write as well as my deffect in all, so they will not expect exactness or politeness in this book, tho' such embellishments might have adorned the descriptions and suited the nicer taste." Her "freedom and easyness" appear in her almost total lack of punctuation and grammar. She rattles and flows breathlessly on like Miss Bates or Mrs. Flora Finching or indeed Mrs. Bloom. Capital letters occur quite at random and her spelling

[66] Sir William Brereton, *Travels* (1635). Edition in Chetham Society Publications, vol. i (1844), p. 174.
[67] *Diary*, July 22nd, 1654.
[68] *Diary*, June 16th, 1683.

knows no laws of any kind. All such things were highly
arbitrary at the time but her standard is a long way below
that of her contemporaries and lends support to Macaulay's
strictures upon the education of women in that age. Illiterate
she certainly was not, for she knew Camden and the Eikon
Basilike and Richard Gilpin's book of Puritan devotions.
When she finds at Hereford a history of the Popes "writt in
old English", she says, "I made a shift to read it". Here and
there, incidentally, she notes with approval one of the new
Charity Schools. Nevertheless she is often ill-informed, especially about history,[69] and it is unlikely that she resembled
the widow who broke the heart of Sir Roger de Coverley
and was described as "such a desperate scholar that no
country gentleman can approach her without being a jest".

Celia Fiennes' descriptive writing is quite unambitious and
is full of the conventional "prospects" and "vistos", while
almost her favourite term of praise is "neat". Yet now and
then, for all her matter-of-fact tone, through sheer directness
and simplicity, she becomes strangely effective or even
moving. Her artless enthusiasm has a most infectious quality
when she tells how she rode "11 mile all in sight of the lovely
Medway", or how she saw a view near Canterbury that "was
very delicate and diverting", or how in Staffordshire she
"went on the side of a high hill below which the River
Trent rann and turn'd its silver streame forward and backward into Ss which looked very pleasant circling about the
fine meadows in their flourishing tyme bedecked with hay
almost ripe and flowers". There is too a remarkable passage
on crossing Blackstone Edge into Lancashire through mist
and "small raine" until she descends into "the fruitful
valley" full of "the sunshine and singing of birds".

On birds she is enthusiastic if not always scientific. At
low tide on the sands in the Solway Firth she "saw a great
bird which look'd almost black picking up fish and busking
in the water; it look'd like an eagle and by its dimentions

---

[69] Her inaccuracy about rivers, and about county boundaries, can be put
down to lack of maps. Ogilby's *Britannia* was not an atlas but a Road Book,
and ignored the rest of the countryside.

could scarce be any other bird". She considered prolonging her stay in Cornwall to hear "the Cornish Nightingale" or chough; and she describes a most mysterious bird on Lundy Island of which "one foote is like a turky the other a gooses foote; it lays its eggs in a place the sun shines on and sets it so exactly upright on the small end and there it remaines till taken up and all the art and skill of persons cannot set it up soe againe to abide". The swans in the Fens near Ely inspired one of her most charming miniatures: "Here I see that many swans nests on little hillocks of earth in the wett ground that they look as if swimming with their nests; some were with their young signetts, 3 or 4 in heape with their damms hovering over them for their security."

Yet Celia Fiennes responded no less quickly to the works of man, to the shipping in the mouth of the Thames, to formal gardens or to spacious streets. Even the Gothic and the Tudor could interest her at times. "In the Minster", she writes of York, "there is the greatest curiosity for windows I ever saw", and of the Cross at Coventry she says "in my phancy it very much resembles the picture of the Tower of Babel". And much as she affected to despise all ceremonies, it is obvious that she enjoyed the royal funerals and coronations. She must have been excited to write as she did of Queen Anne's head-dress: "Her head was well dressed with diamonds mixed in the hair which at the least motion brill'd and flamed."

It is by the vitality of Celia Fiennes that our attention is chiefly held. We must remember that what we have may be only a fragment of her actual travels if, as she says, she visited St. Mungo's Well in Yorkshire seven times. In her recorded journeys alone she entered every English county and crossed the Scottish Border, if only to flee back in horror at the poverty which she found. She also entered Wales and might have gone further had she not again found the poverty depressing. "The inhabitants go barefoot and bare leg'd—a nasty sort of people." She was greatly interested in the annual mileage which she covered; but her computations should not be accepted because, except near London, there were many local variations of the "mile". The statute mile had been defined since 1593 but was first put, quite literally, on the map by John Ogilby's *Britannia* in 1675. In many parts of England, especially in the North, the "old British mile" of 2428 yards was still the usual measure.[70] Celia Fiennes constantly noted that the roads she took were measured in "Long Miles". John Taylor the boisterous "Water Poet" had already observed, "The further I travelled Northward the more the miles were lengthened, and the pots shrunk and curtald; but indeed what the liquor wanted in measure it had in strength, the power of it being of such potentie that it would fox a dry traveller, before he had half-quenched his thirst."[71] In Yorkshire the same phenomena were observed by Celia Fiennes.

Whatever her mileage, there can be no doubt that Celia Fiennes has given us the first comprehensive survey of England since Harrison's and Camden's in Elizabeth's reign. Unlike Defoe she saw at first-hand everything which she described. Nor was she, like Defoe and Macky, in anyone's employment. She was a wholly detached and independent witness with very little *parti pris*. Consequently her value to the social or economic historian is inestimable, for hardly anything escaped her eye. In her journal we can read of fens and meres which have long since been drained, of ports which are now silted up, of rivers which were becoming navigable for the first time. She is always noticing enclosures, chiefly in the East, West and North, in her time mostly made for tillage rather than for pasture. Her book is full of details about the cloth manufacture, still the country's main industry, which had grown up since the English ceased to export most of their raw wool, as they had done in the Middle Ages. "It turns the most money in a weeke", she

[70] See Sir H. G. Fordham, *John Ogilby* (1600–1676) *His Britannia and the British Itineraries of the* 18th *Century*, in Transactions of the Bibliographical Society, 1925; F. Seebohm, *Customary Acres and their Historical Importance*, Part II, *The Old British Mile*; the Rev. J. B. Pearson, *On the Table of Distances between different towns given by Holinshed in his Description of England*, in Cambridge Antiquarian Society's Communications, vol. iv, pp. 261–270, 1879.

[71] *Part of This Summers Travels* (1639) p. 8, in *Works* ed. Spenser Society, 1870. First Collection.

said, "of anything in England." She described how the wool was farmed out to workers in their cottages or in "hired rooms" by capitalist clothiers or middlemen. She spoke as with expert knowledge of serge and baize, "shalloons" and "callimancoes". Few industries, especially the newer ones, escaped her observation. She saw the silk and paper which the French refugees were making in Canterbury, "the makeing of the fine tea-potts" which had just begun in Staffordshire, the glass-blowers and stocking knitters of Nottingham, the Honiton lace and the Manchester "cotton-tickings". She saw the iron foundries still flourishing in the Weald, the flax still grown in the Midlands and the saffron of East Anglia. She observed the rye crops of the North, the wealth of corn and orchards in Herefordshire and the Vale of Evesham, the Kentish hops and cherries, the "very large fine sheep" of Leicestershire. She noted that Bristol had displaced Norwich as the second town of England. She commented on the decay of Lincoln and on the rapid rise of Liverpool. Only in London was she too busy with coronations and conventional sight-seeing to take much stock of economic matters. Her account has not the glow and glitter with which Defoe tells of the city's immense growth and humming commerce.

Perhaps it was her financial interest in rock salt which gave to Celia Fiennes her peculiar eye for mineral wealth. Her fullest descriptions are nearly always given to the mines, to the Cornish tin and copper, to lead in Derbyshire and, above all, to coal, whether it lay in the still prosperous Gloucestershire coalfields or in Durham and Newcastle. "Tho' the surface of the earth looks barren", she wrote of Derbyshire, "yet those hills are impregnated with rich marble, stone, metals, iron and copper and coale mines in their bowells from whence we may see the wisdom and benignitye of our greate Creator to make up the defficiency by an equivolent, and also the diversity of the Creation which encreaseth its beauty." The great age of coal had now begun. Timber could not be transported over seventeenth-century roads on a big enough scale to keep the hearths of London burning.

Moreover most of the forests near the coast or inland waterways had been cut down, while Evelyn[72] and many others before him, including the poet Drayton,[73] had been worrying about deforestation. London's newer chimneys were now better built, and near the Tyne and Severn coal lay ready for coastal transport to the Thames. It was the coal smoke of London which had made the asthmatic King William take up his abode at Kensington. Between the time of Queen Elizabeth and the time of Celia Fiennes the production of British coal had increased fourteenfold and the amount annually unloaded at the Port of London had risen from about 11,000 tons to 500,000 tons. The rebuilding of St. Paul's was largely paid for by a levy on the Londoners' coal. By 1695 the tonnage of colliers was reckoned more than a third of all British shipping.[74] Celia Fiennes saw them passing Scarborough in convoy some seventy strong; and, as she neared Newcastle, "a town of greate trade", she "met with and saw abundance of little carriages with a yoke of oxen and a pair of horses together, which is to convey the coales from the pitts to the barges on the river. . . . This country all about is full of this coale; the sulphur of it taints the aire and it smells strongly to strangers".

Despite her masculine interest in the national economy, Celia Fiennes' narrative gains much from her having been a woman. A mere man might have told us less about the making of soap or cheese or cider or potted char or the Lancashire "clap bread"; or of the Cornish "apple pye with a custard all on the top", and "clouted cream" on top of that, which was "the most acceptable entertainment that could be made me". We might also have been given less detail about the processes of spinning used in Norfolk or of dyeing serge in Exeter. There is, however, loss as well as gain; for had she been a man of the same social standing, we might have heard something of the Royal Society or of the

[72] Evelyn *Sylva* passim.
[73] Drayton, *Poly-Olbion*, Song xvii.
[74] See J. U. Nef, *Rise of the British Coal Industry*, vol. i, pp. 19–20, 156–164, 173, 239, and vol. ii, pp. 381–2.

Bank of England, of the horse racing that was becoming all the rage or of the spread of cricket from the Weald into the Home Counties and from the lower classes to the country gentry, a process which was just then taking place.

Celia Fiennes is most a woman when she is describing gardens or domestic architecture, and to this we owe an unrivalled panorama of the grounds and water works and furniture and pictures of so many great country houses as they then stood. In pursuit of these she was untiring and imperturbable. At Bretby the daughter of the house was being married, and "above, the drawing roome had company in it . . . to wish her joy; but", says Celia Fiennes, "I was in several bed chambers; one had a crimson damaske bed, the other crimson velvet . . . this best was the bride chamber." We are given, in bewildering elaboration, full-length accounts of Wilton, Coleshill, Up Park, Stoke Edith, Broadlands, Thorpe, Hinchingbrook, Burghley, Newby, Burton Agnes, Chatsworth, Euston, Bretby, Lowther Castle, Bishop Auckland, Mount Edgecumbe, Durdans and many more, quite apart from Hampton Court and Windsor.

It was the period in which such houses were being built or rebuilt all over England, since great wealth was now much easier to amass. Despite the land tax, landowning paid well; for there was a government bounty on corn, while enclosures facilitated large-scale and progressive farming. Even had it been less profitable financially, the ownership of land would have remained the only way into "genteel" society. And so into the land and into the great country houses was poured most of the money made elsewhere—from trade or manufacture, from London ground rents or from royalties on coal. It must be remembered that it was an age in which commerce could hardly fail to pay. Markets were expanding; Joint Stock Companies were lessening investors' risks; shipbuilding and navigation had lately taken great steps forward —partly because of Newton's mathematics. An East Indiaman or a ship full of furs from Hudson's Bay was now far more likely to come safe to port. It would no longer be plausible for a playwright to make a whole fleet founder, as

Antonio's did. A ship in Celia Fiennes' day had only to come home for its owners to make very handsome profits.

With this world Celia Fiennes was hardly less well-matched than was Defoe. She too had all the Nonconformist, unromantic tastes and virtues. She too admired what was utilitarian and up to date. She too was sober, matter-of-fact, plain-spoken, trenchant and direct. There is, however, a warmth and charm in her Puritan piety and in her Whig enthusiasm which keep her human and retain our sympathy. So do her gusto and her curiosity, her delight in all novelties and her pleasure in so many simple things. She could be adventurous although she was so circumspect. She could show animal spirits although she was staid and well past her youth. There is nothing jaded or disillusioned in the shrewdness or even in the sharpness of her running commentary. It is simply that she had seen a great deal of the world and possessed considerable native wit and a much more than considerable power of observation. Travel had made her a full woman, and she had kept a very clean palate and a very clear eye. Perhaps we may take more literally than we were meant to that sarcasm of her contemporary, the satirical Samuel Butler, at the expense of tourists, "For certainly there is a great virtue in highways and hedges to make an able man, and a good Prospect cannot but let him see far into things."

CHRISTOPHER MORRIS.

Cambridge, October 1946.

EDITORIAL NOTE

IN THIS edition I have followed the longer manuscript, that which was imperfectly transcribed by Mrs. Griffiths in 1888. It was probably not written by Celia Fiennes with her own hand, but must have had her approval, since it bears her signature and contains her marginalia. It differs only in minutiae from her own holograph draft (Southey's manuscript) where the two cover the same ground. The principal difference lies in the spelling and punctuation, which are even more deficient in the draft. The fuller version may safely be regarded as a fair copy. Nevertheless I have made constant reference to the smaller manuscript which has often resolved doubts and difficulties. The draft covers what I have called Part III for this edition, and the first five sections of Part IV.

I have of course transcribed the complete text, and almost all the marginal notes, except where these are mere indications of the content of a passage. Occasionally, where the text would otherwise be unintelligible, I have inserted in a square bracket something that seemed to be required. I have also added, in square brackets, the modern spellings of identifiable place names, of some personal names and of a few other words. It would not, for example, be self-evident to most modern readers that by "peaso" Celia Fiennes had meant "piazza". The original spelling I have left practically untouched. I have, however, expanded contractions such as "ye", "yt", "wch" or "parliamt"; I have written an initial "i" for Celia Fiennes' "j" in such words as "jron" and "Jreland"; and I have eliminated "ff" which was the old convention for "F". Within certain limits I have adopted a modern use of capitals, for the completely arbitrary manner in which Celia Fiennes used and failed to use them could only be a distraction to the modern eye. Her punctuation is virtually nonexistent, although she sometimes used a comma where we should end a sentence or indeed a paragraph. For the sake of the reader, therefore, I have introduced a moderate amount of punctuation: but I have been as sparing of it as I could be, for I was anxious to preserve the breathlessness of Celia Fiennes. I have tried to do this by making the fullest use of semi-colons. The original is almost without breaks or headings, but, for obvious reasons, I have broken up the text into paragraphs as well as into parts and sections.

Celia Fiennes is one of those authors who could be annotated without end, by genealogists, by local antiquaries, or by economic historians. I have endeavoured to confine my notes to what might help or interest the general reader. They are intended to identify persons and places, to elucidate obscurities and to correct mistakes. I have also tried to amplify the picture of her times which Celia Fiennes presents, and for this purpose I have drawn upon the works of other contemporary or near-contemporary writers. It has not been practicable to give the source for each single piece of information. Moreover, I have had to pretend to such omniscience that some errors are sure to have crept in. For these, of course, I accept full and sole responsibility.

C.M.

NOTE TO SECOND EDITION

By 1808 Southey had obtained (through Charles Danvers a connection of Celia's) both of the MSS. and contemplated publication because, although Celia "could neither write English nor spell it . . . she was a woman of great observation, and her journal contains more information . . . than is to be found in any other work of the time, or even to be gleaned from all". The MSS. fetched 7 guineas at Southey's death. (*Letters*, ed. Warter, 1856, vol. ii, pp. 84–5.)

In June 1715 the diarist Dudley Ryder dined at Epsom with Celia's sister and nieces. "Lady Harrison . . . is a woman of a great deal of polite breeding and endeavours to keep up the dignity of her ladyship by an appearing reservedness and something of a distance. As to the four young ladies her daughters, the two eldest seem to be persons of a very good sense and genteel and good-humoured, but not beautiful at all. . . . The two youngest, though women grown, seem to have a great awe of their mother . . . and don't seem to be so genteel." (*Diary*, ed. Matthews, 1939, p. 34.)   C.M.

THE FIEN

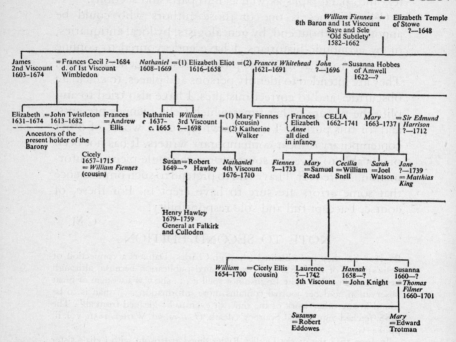

William Fiennes = Elizabeth Temple
8th Baron and 1st Viscount   of Stowe
Saye and Sele   ?—1648
'Old Subtlety'
1582–1662

James	= Frances Cecil ?—1684	Nathaniel = (1) Elizabeth Eliot = (2) Frances Whitehead	John = Susanna Hobbes
2nd Viscount	d. of 1st Viscount	1608–1669 1616–1658 1621–1691	?—1696 of Amwell
1603–1674	Wimbledon		1622—?

Elizabeth = John Twistleton   Frances   Nathaniel   William   = (1) Mary Fiennes   Frances   CELIA   Mary   = Sir Edmund
1631–1674   1613–1682   = Andrew   c 1637–   3rd Viscount   (cousin)   { Elizabeth 1662–1741 1663–1737   Harrison
                              Ellis   c. 1665   ?—1698   = (2) Katherine   { Anne   ?—1712
Ancestors of the   Walker   { all died
present holder of the   in infancy
Barony

            Cicely   Susan = Robert   Nathaniel   Fiennes   Mary   Cecilia   Sarah   Jane
            1657–1715   1649—? Hawley   4th Viscount ?—1733   = Samuel = William = Joel   ?—1739
            = William Fiennes   1676–1710   Read   Snell   Watson   = Matthias
            (cousin)   King

                                        Henry Hawley
                                        1679–1759
                                        General at Falkirk
                                        and Culloden

                        William = Cicely Ellis   Laurence   Hannah   Susanna
                        1654–1700 (cousin)   ?—1742   1658—?   1660—?
                                                  5th Viscount = John Knight = Thomas
                                                                              Filmer
                                                                              1660–1701

                        Susanna   Mary
                        = Robert   = Edward
                        Eddowes   Trotman

Characters mentioned in Celia Fiennes's journal are shown in italics
Many minor characters not mentioned either in Celia Fiennes's journal or in her will have been omitted

NES FAMILY

(continued below)

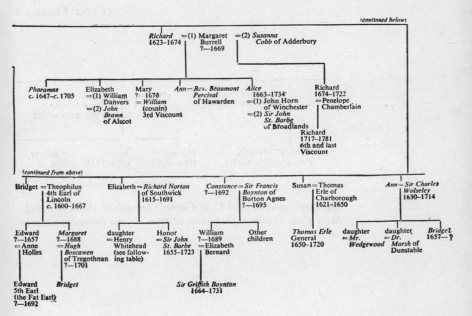

Richard = (1) Margaret = (2) Susanna
1623–1674   Burrell   Cobb of Adderbury
             ?—1669

Pharamus   Elizabeth   Mary   Ann = Rev. Beaumont   Alice   Richard
c. 1647–c. 1705   =(1) William   ? 1676   Percival   1663–1734   1674–1722
      Danvers   =William   of Hawarden   =(1) John Horn   =Penelope
      =(2) John   (cousin)   of Winchester   Chamberlain
      Brawn   3rd Viscount   =(2) Sir John
      of Alscot   St. Barbe
                                     of Broadlands
                                           Richard
                                           1717–1781
                                           6th and last
                                           Viscount

(continued from above)

Bridget =Theophilus   Elizabeth = Richard Norton   Constance = Sir Francis   Susan =Thomas   Ann = Sir Charles
c. 1600–1667   4th Earl of   of Southwick   ?—1692   Boynton of   Erle of   Wolseley
      Lincoln   1615–1691   Burton Agnes   Charborough   1630–1714
                                        ?—1695   1621–1650

Edward   Margaret   daughter   Honor   William   Other   Thomas Erle   daughter   daughter   Bridget
?—1657   ?—1688   =Henry   =Sir John   ?—1689   children   General   =Mr.   =Dr.   1657—?
=Anne   =Hugh   Whitehead   St. Barbe   =Elizabeth   1650–1720   Wedgewood   Marsh of
Holles   Boscawen   (see follow-   1655–1723   Bernard   Dunstable
        of Tregothnan   ing table)
        ?—1701

Edward   Bridget   Sir Griffith Boynton
5th Earl   1664–1731
(the Fat Earl)
?—1692

THE WHITEH

(Celia Fiennes's

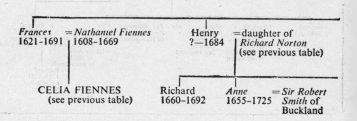

Frances = Nathaniel Fiennes   Henry   = daughter of
1621-1691 1608-1669   ?—1684   *Richard Norton*
                                             (see previous table)

        CELIA FIENNES   Richard   *Anne*   = *Sir Robert*
        (see previous table)   1660-1692   1655-1725 *Smith* of
                                                             Buckland

Characters mentioned in Celia Fiennes's Journal are shown in italics
Many minor characters not mentioned either in Celia Fiennes's Journal or

EAD FAMILY

maternal relatives)

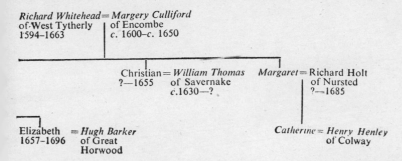

Richard Whitehead = Margery Culliford
of West Tytherly | of Encombe
1594–1663 | c. 1600–c. 1650

Christian = William Thomas   Margaret = Richard Holt
?—1655   of Savernake   of Nursted
                   c.1630—?   ?—1685

Elizabeth   = Hugh Barker   Catherine = Henry Henley
1657–1696   of Great   of Colway
                    Horwood

in her will have been omitted

TO THE READER

As THIS was never designed, soe not likely to fall into the hands of any but my near relations, there needs not much to be said to excuse or recommend it. Something may be diverting and proffitable tho' not to Gentlemen that have travelled more about England, staid longer in places, might have more acquaintance and more opportunity to be inform'd. My Journeys, as they were begun to regain my health by variety and change of aire and exercise, soe whatever promoted that was pursued, and those informations of things as could be obtein'd from inns en passant or from some acquaintance, inhabitants of such places, could furnish me with for my diversion, I thought necessary to remark: that as my bodily health was promoted my mind should not appear totally unoccupied, and the collecting it together remain for my after conversation (with such as might be inquisitive after such and such places) to which might have recourse; and as most I converse with knows both the freedom and easyness I speak and write as well as my deffect in all, so they will not expect exactness or politeness in this book, tho' such embellishments might have adorned the descriptions and suited the nicer taste.

Now thus much without vanity may be asserted of the subject, that if all persons, both Ladies, much more Gentlemen, would spend some of their tyme in Journeys to visit their native Land, and be curious to inform themselves and make observations of the pleasant prospects, good buildings, different produces and manufactures of each place, with the variety of sports and recreations they are adapt to, would be a souveraign remedy to cure or preserve from these epidemick diseases of vapours, should I add Laziness? It would also form such an Idea of England, add much to its Glory and Esteem in our minds and cure the evil itch of over-valueing foreign parts; at least furnish them with an equivalent to entertain strangers when amongst us, or inform them when abroad of their native Country, which has been often a reproach to the English, ignorance and being strangers to themselves. Nay the Ladies might have matter not unworthy their observation, soe subject for conversation, within their own compass in each county to which they relate; and thence studdy how to be serviceable to their neighbours especially the poor among whome they dwell, which would spare them the uneasye thoughts how to pass away tedious dayes, and tyme would not be a burthen when not at a card or dice table, and the fashions and manners of foreign parts less minded or desired. But much more requisite is it for Gentlemen in general service of their country at home or abroad, in town or country, especially those that serve in parliament, to know and inform themselves the nature of Land, the Genius of the Inhabitants, so as to promote and improve Manufacture and Trade suitable to each and encourage all projects tending thereto, putting in practice all Laws made for each particular good, maintaining their priviledges, procuring more as requisite; but to their shame it must be own'd many if not most are ignorant of anything but the name of the place for which they serve in parliament; how then can they speake for or promote their Good or redress their Grievances? But now I may be justly blamed to pretend to give account of our Constitution, Customs, Laws, etc., matters farre above my reach or capacity, but herein I have described what have come within my knowledge, either by view and reading or relation from others, which according to my conception have faithfully rehearsed, but where I have mistaken in any form or subject matter I easily submitt to a correction and will enter such Erratas in a supplement annext to the Book of some particulars since remark'd; and shall conclude with a hearty wish and recommendation to all, but especially my own Sex, the studdy of those things which tends to improve the mind and makes our Lives pleasant and comfortable as well as proffitable in all the Stages and

Stations of our Lives, and render Suffering and Age support-
able and Death less formidable and a future State more
happy.

Celia Fiennes

PART I

THE EARLY JOURNEYS IN THE SOUTH
(c. 1685-1696)

1. FROM NEWTON TONEY BY SALISBURY
AND WILTON TO THE ISLE OF PURBECK

THE ACCOUNT off severall Journies into severall parts of England with many Remarkes; some with my mother from Newtontony [Newton Toney] Wiltshire which is all on the downs a fine Champion[1] Country pleasant for all sports—Rideing, Hunting, Courseing, Setting and Shooteing. From Newtontony I went to Sarum 8 miles which is a Citty a Bishops Seate, pretty large town streetes broad but through the midst of them runs a little rivulet of water which makes the streetes not so clean or so easye to passe in,[2] they have stepp's to cross it and many open places for horses and carriages to cross itt—it takes off much from the beauty of the streets—the cause of it was from the burning of the old town called Salsebury [Old Sarum] which was on a hill about a mile off this and it was so drye and farre from springs that it was destroyed by fire and only the ruines of the Castle is to be seen like a high wall with fortifications: this town now stands low by the water by a great River. The houses are old mostly timber buildings there is a large Market House with the Town Hall over it and a prison just by, there is also a large Cross in another place and house over it for a constant Market for fruite, fowle, butter and cheese and a fish Market. The town is well served with all provissions, there is good

[1] Champaign or open, i.e. unenclosed, country.
[2] Lieutenant Hammond had approved. "Every street is here supplied . . . by pleasant little rivoletts which are knee deepe gliding sweetly through her bowells, to wash and cleanse them." (*Short Survey of Western Counties*, 1635, Ed. 1936, p. 60.) Defoe, however, thought "it keeps the streets always dirty, full of wet and filth, and weeds, even in the middle of summer". (*Tour*, Everyman Edition, i, 188.)

buildings in that part they call the Close both new built and the old good houses belonging to the doctors of the Church.

The Dean has a very good house and gardens so is the Bishop's Palace at the end of a row of trees, the roomes are lofty and stately.

All these houses are round the Cathedrall which is esteemed the finest in England in all respects it only lyes low in a watry meadow so that the foundations is in the water made of faggots and timber, yet notwithstanding its want of a riseing ground to stand on the steeple is seen many miles off the spire being so high it appeares to us below as sharpe as a Dagger yet is in the compass on the top as bigg as a carte wheele, its all stone and carved finely with spires and arches, there are severall doores into the Church, in the body of it stands the pulpet and seates on each side, there are two large Isle's runnes up on either side, the font stands below opposite to the quire that enters with 2 or 3 steps assent from a large Cross Isle that leades to the Cloysters in which is the Chapter house which is very large and supported only by one small stone Pillar in the middle, painted round the walls with figures carved the whole account of the book of Genesis, the Windows are painted very finely much of the history of the Bible: there is as many little Chappels in the Church as months in a yeare as many doores as weekes as many marble pillars as dayes as many windows as houres as many partitions in the windows as minutes in the year,[3] the roofe of the Church is very lofty and exactly neate in all things though not so large as some other Cathedralls: the top of the Quoire is exactly painted[4] and it lookes as fresh as if but new done though of 300 yeares standing: there is a very good organ and a deske for the reader raised so high even with the organ for the advantage of the voice to be heard, yet the Church is so lofty that the Ecco drowns the intelligableness of the voice. The Communion table hangings and the books are all of crimson velvet with gold fringe, 2

---

[3] Actually 12 doors, 365 windows and 8760 small pillars.
[4] The pictures were washed out in 1789. Defoe had already called them "mean, and more like the ordinary method of common drawing-room, or tavern painting than that of a church". (Ibid., i, 190.)

6

large Candlestickes gilt with great white tapers in them, a large gilt bason to receive the offerings in, there is many good monuments there: also there are the Statues of the 3 bishops that built the Church cut in stone, there are two large fine monuments above the rest, one all free stone for the Lord George [Sir Thomas Gorges] his Effiges and ladyes att length on a bed in their Robes and ruffs on pillows and the four pillars are twisted and over it Angels figures of birds beasts flowers and leaves very fine, there sits Justice with the ballance in her hand one scale laying over the other twisted lookes very naturall and well, with the wreathed work all in free stone with their Armes cut about in Escutheons all about: the other is a monument for the Duke of Summerset[5] all in marble, a large bed his Effigee in garment and ruff all in coullours, his lady the same only she is laid one step above him because she was daughter to the Dowager of France and sister to Henry the 7th of England by her second husband Charles Brandon Duke of Suffolk. There is the Effiges of their 2 sonnes, Lord Beachom at their head and Lord Seymour at the feete in armour on their knees and severall daughters on their knees at the bottom and 12 pillars of Irish gray marble, the Armes is cutt finely in Escutcheons and in figures with the supporters and severall sorts of beasts carved in a piramide fashion and on the top the Dukes Corronet, these 2 monuments are railed in with iron grates; there is the Effigee in stone off a doctor that starved himself to death attempting to imitate our saviour to fast 40 dayes, but at 17 dayes end he became sensible of his evil and would have retrieved his life by eateing againe, but then by the just judgment of god could not swallow any thing down his throate; there is a chaple or burying place of Judge Poppums[6] [Popham] that had two very wild sonnes, and by 2 pictures of his sonnes, pictured one with death the other with a skeleton, and set in the room they were to come

[5] Earl of Hertford, son of Protector Somerset.
[6] Sir John Popham, Chief Justice of King's Bench, died 1607. This reference is puzzling, since he is buried at Wellington, Somerset. One son is said by Aubrey to have "lived like a hog", the other merely to have been "a great waster".

into by their fathers order, it pleased God to bless as a meanes to reclaim them: ye pictures are there still.

The Windows of the Church but especially the Qoire are very finely painted and large of the history of the Bible, the tower for the bells are in the Yard at some distance from the Church.

There are 6 Churches in the town and subburbs and the County Goal at the end of the town called Fisherton just by the great river that runnes to Christ-Church. In Salsebury they keep the quarter session once in the yeare the other tymes are kept at Malbrough about 24 mile off and at the Devises [Devizes] about the same distance, which is a very neate little town with a very good market house and town hall sett on stone pillars; it is a bourrough and a very rich tradeing place for the clothing trade;[7] the fourth place the session is kept is Warminster about the same distance: its a pretty little town a good Market for corn and there is the Mindiffe [Mendip] Coale which is allmost as good as the sea-coale from New-Castle that is dugg out of the hills all about. But the Assizes is allways kept at Salsebury and is a Major [Mayor] town though Wilton about 2 mile off is the County town, and the knights of the shire are chosen there, though its now but as a little village as it were and only supported by the Earle of Pembrooke which lives there and has a very fine house[8] [Wilton] with large courts one within another: at the Entrance there is a lofty Hall with good pictures, 3 or 4 dineing roomes and drawing roomes of State with very good bed chambers and well furnished velvet damaske and tissue; one gallery and the dineing roome was all wanscoated with pictures of the family; there is a drawing roome and anti-roome the wanscoate is painted with the whole History of the Acardia romance made by Sir Philip Sidney brother to the then Countess of Pembrooke and composed by him in the fine woods above the house.

[7] The Somerset and Wiltshire woollen industry, described by Defoe as "this prodigy of trade", was extremely prosperous and famous. Devizes specialized in "druggets".

[8] Built mainly by Webb and famous for the "Double Cube" room by Inigo Jones

Another room is painted with all sorts of sports Hunting Hawking etc., they are all finely painted on the ceileing and very lofty: there is one dineing roome that the chimney is just under a window and the tunnells runnes upon each side: there is one chamber the chimney stands just by the window opposite to Salsebury and on the black marble chimney piece soe finely polished you may see all the Cathedrall as in a glass, I have seen it plaine: there are very fine marble chimney pieces in most of the roomes and marble windows.

The Gardens are very fine, with many gravel walkes with grass squaires set with fine brass and stone statues, with fish ponds and basons with figures in the middle spouting out water, dwarfe trees of all sorts and a fine flower garden, much wall fruite: the river runns through the garden that easeily conveys by pipes water to all parts. Grottoe is at the end of the garden just the middle off the house, its garnished with many fine figures of the Goddesses, and about 2 yards off the doore is severall pipes in a line that with a sluce spoutts water up to wett the Strangers; in the middle roome is a round table, a large pipe in the midst, on which they put a crown or gun or a branch, and so it spouts the water through the carvings and poynts all round the roome at the Artists pleasure to wet the Company; there are figures at each corner of the roome that can weep water on the beholders, and by a straight pipe on the table they force up the water into the hollow carving of the rooff like a crown or coronet to appearance, but is hollow within to retaine the water forced into it in great quantetyes, that disperses in the hollow cavity over the roome and descends in a shower of raine all about the roome; on each side is two little roomes which by the turning their wires the water runnes in the rockes you see and hear it, and also it is so contrived in one room that it makes the melody of Nightingerlls and all sorts of birds which engaged the curiosity of the Strangers to go in to see, but at the entrance off each room, is a line of pipes that appear not till by a sluce moved it washes the spectators, designed for diversion. The Grottoe is leaded on the top where are fish ponds, and just without the grottoe is a wooden bridge over the river, the barristers [balusters] are set out with Lyons set thick on either side with their mouths open and by a sluce spout out water each to other in a perfect arch the length of the bridge; there are fine woods beyond the house and a large parke walled in.

From thence I went to Blandford in Dorsetshire 18 miles through a haire waring [hare warren] and a forest of the kings [Cranbourne Chase]—Blandford is a pretty neate country town—thence to Merly [Merley] by Wimborn over a great river called the Stoure (a large arched bridge) to a relations house Sir William Constantines[9] house—thence to Poole a little sea-port town 4 miles off where was a very good Minister in the publick Church Mr. Hardy.

From thence by boate we went to a little Isle called Brownsea 3 or 4 leagues off, where there is much Copperice[10] made, the stones being found about the Isle in the shore in great quantetyes, there is only one house there which is the Governours, besides little fishermens houses, they being all taken up about the Copperice [Copperas] workes; they gather the stones and place them on ground raised like the beds in gardens, rows one above the other, and are all shelving so that the raine disolves the stones and it draines down into trenches and pipes made to receive and convey it to the house; that is fitted with iron panns foursquare and of a pretty depth at least 12 yards over, they place iron spikes in the panns full of branches and so as the liquor boyles to a candy it hangs on those branches: I saw some taken up it look't like a vast bunch of grapes, the coullour of the Copperace not being much differing, it lookes cleare like suger-candy, so when the water is boyled to a candy they take it out and replenish the panns with more liquor; I do not remember they added anything to it only the stones of Copperice disolved by the raine into liquour as I mention'd

---

[9] Sir William Constantine's second wife was a Collier of Puddletrenthide, and the Colliers were related by marriage to the Cullifords, i.e. to Celia Fiennes' maternal grandmother. For these families, see Hutchins' *History of Dorset*, iv.

[10] Copperas is green vitriol, used in dyeing, tanning and making ink. Copperas stone is iron pyrites or marcasite.

at first; there are great furnaces under, that keepes all the panns boyling; it was a large room or building with severall of these large panns; they do add old iron and nailes to the Copperass Stones. This is a noted place for lobsters and crabs and shrimps, there I eate some very good.

From Merly we went to the Isle of Purbeck. At Warrum [Wareham] we passed over a bridge where the sea flowed in and came by the ruines of Corffe Castle, which stands on a hill yet surrounded by much higher hills that might easily command it, and so in the Civil warrs was batter'd down with Granadeers, thence you rise a great ascent of hills called the Linch [Lynch], or rather the ridge, being so for 3 or 4 miles, rideing to Quare [Quar] which was 16 miles from Merly to a relations house Cos'n Colliers.[11]

From this ridge you see all the Island over, which lookes very fruitfull, good lands meadows woods and inclosures; there are many quarys in these hills of that which is called the free stone, from hence they digg it. The shores are very rocky all about the Island, we went 3 miles off to Sonidge [Swanage] a sea faire place not very big; there is a flatt sand by the sea a little way; they take up stones by the shores that are so oyly as the poor burn it for fire, and its so light a fire it serves for candle too, but it has a strong offensive smell. At a place 4 mile off called Sea Cume [Seacombe] the rockes are so craggy and the creekes of land so many that the sea is very turbulent, there I pick'd shells and it being a spring-tide I saw the sea beat upon the rockes at least 20 yards with such a foame or froth, and at another place the rockes had so large a cavity and hollow that when the sea flowed in it runne almost round, and sounded like some hall or high arch. In this Island are severall pretty good houses though not very large, att Kingston Sir William Muex [Meux] has a pretty house, and att Income [Encombe] Mr. Coliffords[12], Doonshay [Downshay] Mr. Dollings, and 7 mile off Quare att Tinnum [Tyneham] Lady Larences there is a pretty large

[11] John Collier, brother to Lady Constantine (see above).
[12] Robert Culliford (d. 1697) had married a sister of the first Earl of Clarendon. His son married a daughter of Sir Edward Laurence of Grange. The Dollings had twice married into the Culliford family.

house but very old timber built, there I eate the best lobsters and crabs being boyled in the sea water and scarce cold, very large and sweet; most of the houses in the Island are built of stone there is so many Quarryes of stone, this is just by the great cliffts which are a vast height from the sea; here is plenty of provision of all sorts especially of fish. From Tinnum we ascend a high hill of a great length till you are out of the Island, which does hardly appeare to be now an Isle, the tide haveing left it on this side that you passe only a little brooke—there is another Castle called Bindon, but that lyes low and appears not much—thence we came to Piddle [Piddletrenthide] 6 or 7 miles off where was a relation Mr. Oxenbridg[13] an old house which formerly was an abby; thence to Dorchester town 5 mile, it stands on the side of a hill, the river runns below it, the town lookes compact and the street's are very neatly pitch'd and of a good breadth, the Market-place is spaceious the Church very handsome and full of galleryes.

Thence we went to Burport [Bridport]—about 8 miles, the wayes are stony and very narrow, the town has a steep hill to descend through the whole place; thence to Woolfe 4 miles to a relations Mr. Newbery, a man of many whymseys would keep no women servants, had all washing ironing dairy, etc., all performed by men, his house look's like a little village when you come into the yard, so many little buildings apart from each other, one for a stillitory another for out-houses and offices another long building for silk wormes, and the dwelling house is but mean and spoyl'd by his fancy of makeing a hall up 3 storyes high, so lofty nothing suite-able to it; he had good gardens and orchards, much good fruite but all in a most rude confused manner. Thence we went to Colway neare Lime [Lyme] in Somerset-shire[14] about 8 miles to a relations house Mr. Hendlys,[15] from thence

[13] Robert Oxenbridge had married the widowed mother of Lady Constantine (see above).

[14] Lyme is not in Somersetshire. It will be found that Celia Fiennes is highly inaccurate, throughout the book, about county boundaries.

[15] Henry Henley of Colway married Catharine, daughter of Celia Fiennes' Aunt Margaret Holt (née Whitehead).

it is 2 mile to Lime, a seaport place open to the main ocean, and so high a bleake sea that to secure the Harbour for shipps they have been at a great charge to build a Mold from the town with stone, like a halfe moon, which they call the Cobb,[16] its raised with a high wall and this runns into the sea a good compass, that the Shipps rides safely within it; when the tide is out we may see the foundations of some part of it; that is the tyme they looke over it to see any breach and repaire it immediately, else the tide comes with so much violence would soone beate it down; there is some part of it low and only is to joyne the rest to the land, and at high water is all cover'd of such a depth of water that shipps may pass over it to enter the Cobb or Halfe Moone, which is difficult for foreigners to attempt, being ignorant, though its better then goeing round the other way, for those that know and do observe the tide; the Spring tides and on any storme does sometymes beate up and wash over the walls of the forte or castle into the court, and so runns into the town, though at other tymes when its the ordinary tide and calme sea, it is at least 300 yards from the banke on which the high wall is built.

In most parts of Sommer-setshire it is very fruitfull for orchards, plenty of apples and peares, but they are not curious in the planting the best sort of fruite, which is a great pitty; being so soone produced, and such quantetyes, they are likewise as careless when they make cider, they press all sorts of apples together, else they might have as good sider as in any other parts, even as good as the Herrifford-shire; they make great quantetyes of cider their presses are verye large, so as I have seen a Cheese, as they call them, which yeilded 2 hoddsheads; they pound their apples then lay fresh straw on the press, and on that a good lay of pulp of the apples, then turne in the ends of the straw over it all

---

[16] Roger North says "The Cob is a mole built in the sea . . . there is not any one like it in the world . . . for though it is an immense mass of stone . . . no one stone that lies there was ever touched with a tool, or is bedded in any sort of cement; but all, being pebbles of the sea, are piled up, and hold by their bearings only, and the surge plays in and out through the interstices of the stone, in a wonderful manner." (*Lives of the Norths*, ed. 1826, i, 244.)

round, and lay fresh straw, then more apples up to the top.

Just by Lime [Lyme] you cross a little brooke into Devonshire which is much like Somersetshire—fruitfull Country's for corn graseing, much for inclosures that makes the wayes very narrow, so as in some places a Coach and Waggons cannot pass; they are forced to carry their Corn and Carriages on horses backes with frames of wood like pannyers on either side the horse, so load it high and tye it with cords; this they do altogether the farther westward they goe for the wayes grows narrower and narrower on to the Lands End; they shewed me the Lizard Point[17] from Lime it was a good distance; the land grows narrower in a compass round, as it were round the sea.

From Lime [Lyme] the wayes are also difficult by reason of the very steep hills up and down, and that so successively as little or no plaine even ground, and full of large smooth pebbles that make the strange horses slip and uneasye to go; the horses of the country are accustomed to it and travell well in the rodes; in the opener wayes they use a sort of waine or carriage made narrower than our southern waggon but longer, and so load them high. From Lime to Burport [Bridport] is 12 miles, and so to Dorchester: thence to Blandford we pass over Woodbery Hill eminent for a great Faire that is kept there of all things; the road passed by Cherbery [Charborough], the foot of the hill; on the stop stands a pretty seate of Mr. Earles[18] my relation, the house is a new built house on the brow of the hill, whence you have large prospects of 20 mile round, you may see Shaftesbury thence 16 mile off; there is a good wood behind the house, good gardens wall'd with plenty of fruit, good fish and decoy ponnds, there is a very good hall at the entrance leads you to a large parlour and drawing room on the right hand that opens to the gardens, a very good little parlour on the left

[17] Impossible: Start Point must be meant.
[18] This is Thomas Earle or Erle (1650–1720), son of Celia Fiennes' aunt Susanna Earle (née Fiennes), later a General, who lost his hand at the battle of Almanza (1709). The Earles held Charborough by pouring water on the king's hands.

with servants room, and another parlour for smoakeing, all well wanscoated and painted, and the offices convenient; the chambers are good and lofty and sizeable good furniture in the best 2 Chambers; in an angle the staires leads up halfe way into the middle of the house and so divides in four parts and runnes to each angle a cross visto wayes through the house.

Thence 6 miles to Blandford, thence 18 to Salsebury and 8 mile to Newtontony which stands in the midst of the downs 8 mile from Andover a market town in Hampshire and the roade to London, it lyes 15 mile from Winchester, it is three mile from Amesbury.

2. STONEHENGE AND SOMERSET

[From Newton Toney its] 2 mile more to Stoncage [Stonehenge] that stands on Salsebury plaine—eminent for many battles being faught there, the many barrow or butts that are thick all over the plaine, and this of Stoneage, that is reckon'd one of the wonders of England how such prodigeous stones should be brought there; no such sort of stone is seen in the country nearer then 20 mile; they are placed on the side of a hill in a rude iregullar form, two stones stands up and one laid on their tops with morteses into each other, and thus are severall in a round like a wall with spaces between, but some are fallen down so spoyle the order or breach in the temple—as some think it was in the heathen tymes: others thinke it the trophy of some victory wone by one Ambrosious, and thence the town by it has its name of Amsebury; there is severall rows of lesser stones within the others set up in the same forme, of 2 upright and one lies on the top like a gate way, how they were brought thither or whether they are a made stone is not resolved; they are very hard yet I have seen some of them scraped, the weather seemes not to penetrate them, to increase the wonder the story is that none can count them twice alike, they stand confused, and some single stones at a distance, but I have told them often and bring their number to 91.[1]

This country is most champion and open, pleasant for recreations; its husbandry is mostly corn and sheep, the downs though short grass the feed is sweet, produces the finest wooll and sweet meat though but small; the little towns or villages lies in the valleys and runs along in the bottom and are called Bourns haveing water running in most of them.

From Stonidge I went to Evell [Yeovil] in Somersetshire thence to Meer [Mere] a little town about 15 mile; by the town is a vast high hill called the Castle of Meer, its now all grass over and so steepe up that the ascent is by footsteps cut in the side of the hill; I was on the top where some had been digging, and was come to a space that was arched and the walls plaistred and washed white and smooth, it was but a little roome; I tooke a piece of its walls and plaister; that shews there may be cells or vaults in the hill. From thence to Wincanton 7 miles which is on a steep hill and very stony; you go through the town all the way down as it were a steep precipice, all rocks; thence to Castle Cary 3 or 4 miles; its generally a good fruitfull country, much on inclosures as is most of Summersetshire.

Thence to Alford 2 mile where was a minerall water which Company resorts to for drinking, formerly it has been more frequented than of late; many now send for them severall miles and have Beer brewed of them, there being no good accomodation for people of fashion, the Country people being a clounish rude people; the waters are mostly from Alom [Alum], its a cleare little well and a quick spring, the bottom of the well has a sort of blewish Clay or Marle; its a quick purger good for all sharpe Humers or Obstruction. In three mile of this place is Queen Camell famous for a fine

---

[1] Lieutenant Hammond made it 90, Evelyn 95 and Defoe 72. There were many treatises on Stonehenge, including one by Inigo Jones. It was generally thought either Roman or pre-Roman; but Childry in *Britannia Baconica* (1661) proved to his own satisfaction that Stonehenge was a natural phenomenon "planted *ab initio*". Evelyn had found that "the stone is so exceeding hard, that all my strength with a hammer could not breake a fragment."

ring of bells and for the fine sort of brown thread called Nuns thread. As we returned from thence we came by Bruton a very neate stone built town, from it we ascend a very high steep hill all in a narrow lane cut out of the rocks, and the way is all like stone steps; the sides are rocks on which grow trees thick, their roots runns amongst the rocks, and in many places fine cleare springs buble out, and run a long out of the rocks, it smells just like the sea; we were full an hour passing that hill, though with four horses and a Chariot, my Sister self and maid; thence to Willding [?Wylye] which is a place of much water, so to Newtontony in all 30 miles.

3. BATH (IN OR BEFORE 1687)

ANOTHER JOURNEY to the Bath, from Newtontony to War-minster 18 mile, a good road town, and good way; thence to Breackly [Berkley] 5 mile a deep clay way; we passed over one Common of some miles length on a narrow Causy [Causeway] that a Coach can scarce pass, all pitched with slatts and stones, our Coach was once wedged in the wheele in the stones that severall men were forced to lift us out; its made only for Packhorses, which is the way of carriage in those parts; the Common is so moorish [marshy] their feete and wheeles would sinke in, so no going there.

Thence to Philip Norton [Norton St. Philip] 3 miles, a very neate stone built village; thence you pass a good way between 2 stone walls to the Bath 5 mile, down a very steep hill and stony a mile from the town scarce any passing and there descends a little current of water continually from the rocks; the wayes to the Bath are all difficult, the town lyes low in a bottom and its steep ascents all ways out of the town; the houses are indifferent, the streetes of a good size well pitched; there are severall good houses built for Lodgings that are new and adorned and good furniture, the baths in my opinion makes the town unpleasant, the aire thicke and hot by their steem, and by its own situation so low, encompassed with high hills and woods.

17

There is 5 baths: the Hot bath the most hot springs, its but small and built all round, which makes it the hotter: out of it runns the water into a bath called the Lepours: the third bath is called the Cross bath[1] which is something bigger then the former and not so hot; the Cross in the middle has seates round it for the Gentlemen to sitt and round the walls are arches with seates for the Ladyes—all stone, and the seate is stone and if you thinke the seat is too low they raise it with a coushon as they call it, another Stone, but indeed the water bears you up that the seate seemes as easy as a down coushon; before the Arch the Ladyes use to have a laced toilet hung up on the top of the Arch, and so to shelter their heads even to the water if they please; you generally set up to the neck in water;[2] this Cross bath is much the coolest and is used mostly in the heate of summer; there are Gallery's round the top that the Company that does not bathe that day walkes in and lookes over into the bath on their acquaintance and company. There are such a number of Guides to each bath, of women to waite on the ladyes and of men to waite on the gentlemen, and they keepe their due distance; there is a Serjeant belonging to the baths that all the bathing tyme walkes in galleryes and takes notice order is observed, and punishes the rude, and most people of fashion sends to him when they begin to bathe, then he takes particular care of them and complements you every morning, which deserves its reward at the end of the Season. When you would walk about the bath I use to have a woman guide or two to lead me, for the water is so strong it will quickly tumble you down; and then you have 2 of the men guides goes at a distance about the bath to cleare the way; at the sides of the Arches are rings that you may hold by and so walke a little way, but the springs bubbles up so fast and so strong and are

[1] Pepys bathed there in 1668 and met "very fine ladies; and the manner pretty enough, only methinks it cannot be clean to go so many bodies together in the same water".

[2] "The ladies bring with them japanned bowls or basons, tied to their arms with ribbands, which swim upon the surface of the water, and are to keep their handkerchiefs, nosegays, perfumes, and spirits, in case the exhalations of the water should be too prevalent."—Samuel Gale, *A Tour through Several Parts of England* (1705) in J. Nichols, *Bibliotheca Topographia Britannica III*, 22.

so hot up against the bottoms of ones feete, especially in that
they call the Kitching in the K[ings] bath, which is a great
Cross with seates in the middle and many hot springs riseth
there; the Kings bath is very large, as large as the rest put
together, in it is the hot pumpe that persons are pumpt at
for lameness or on their heads for palsyes; I saw one pumpt,
they put on a broad brim'd hatt with the crown cut out, so
as the brims cast off the water from the face; they are pumpt
in the bath; one of the men Guides pumps, they have two
pence I thinke for 100 pumps, the water is scallding hot out
of the pump, the armes or legs are more easyly pumped;
the Ladyes goes into the bath with garments made of a fine
yellow canvas, which is stiff and made large with great
sleeves like a parsons gown, the water fills it up so that its
borne off that your shape is not seen, it does not cling close
as other linning which lookes sadly in the poorer sort that
go in their own linning,[3] the Gentlemen have drawers and
wastcoates of the same sort of canvas, this is the best linning,
for the bath water will change any other yellow; when you
go out of the bath you go within a doore that leads to steps
which you ascend by degrees, that are in the water, then the
doore is shut which shutts down into the water a good way,
so you are in a private place, where you still ascend severall
more steps, and let your canvass drop of by degrees into the
water, which your women guides takes off and the meane-
tyme your maides flings a garment of flannell made like a
nightgown with great sleeves over your head, and the
guides take the taile and so pulls it on you just as you rise
the steps, and your other garment drops off so you are
wrapped up in the flannell and your nightgown on the top,
your slippers, and so you are set in Chaire which is brought
into the roome which are called slips and there are chimney's
in them, you may have fires; these are in severall parts of the

[3] Things were less decorous in 1634, for then "to see young and old, rich
and poore, blind and lame, diseas'd and sound, English and French, men and
women, boyes and girles, one with another, peepe up in their caps, and appear
so nakedly and fearfully, in their uncouth naked postures, would a little
astonish and putt one in mind of the Resurrection". (Hammond, *Short Survey
of 26 Counties*, ed. 1904, pp. 106–7.)

sides of the bath for the conveniency of persons goeing in
and out of the bath decently, and at the top of the staires
stands a woman that layes a woollen cloth for you to set
your bare foot, and also to give you attendance; the Chaires
you go in are a low seate and with frames round and over
your head, and all cover'd inside and out with red bayes and
a curtaine drawn before of the same which makes it close
and warme; then a couple of men with staves takes and
carryes you to your lodging and sets you at your bedside
where you go to bed and lay and sweate sometyme as you
please; your own maides and the maides of the house gets your
fire and waites on you till you rise to get out of your sweat.

All the baths has the same attendance, the Queens bath is
bigger than the other three but not a neare so big as the
Kings, which do run into each other and is only parted by a
wall and at one place a great arch where they run into each
other; the Queens bath is a degree hotter than the Cross bath,
and the Kings bath much hotter; these have all gallery's
round and the pump is in one of these galleryes at the Kings
bath which the Company drinks of; its very hot and tastes
like the water that boyles eggs, has such a smell, but the
nearer the pumpe you drinke it the hotter and less offencive
and more spiriteous; the baths are all emptyed as soone as
the company goes out, which is about 10 or 11 of the clock
in the morning, then by sluces they empty at once the bath,
so it fills againe, I have seen all the springs bubble up as
thicke out of the ground when the baths have been empty,
the bottom is gravell; so they will be full for the evening if
Company would go in againe, if so they empty them againe
at night, and they are filled against the morning; and there
will be such a white scum on the bath which the guides goes
and scimms off cleane before any Company goes in, if they
go in while this scum is on it gives them the bath mantle,
as they call it, makes them breake out into heate and pimples;
the like will be on them if they go into the bath before they
have purged, especially in the hotter bath.

The places for divertion about the Bath is either the walkes
in that they call the Kings Mead, which is a pleasant green

meaddow, where are walkes round and cross it, no place for coaches, and indeed there is little use of a coach only to bring and carry the Company from the Bath for the wayes are not proper for coaches, the town and all its accomodations is adapted to the batheing and drinking of the waters, and to nothing else, the streetes are well pitched and cleane kept and there are Chaires as in London to carry the better sort of people in visits, or if sick or infirme, and is only in the town, for its so encompassed with high hills few care to take the aire on them; there is also pleasant walkes in the Cathedrall in the Cloysters.

And that leades to the discription[4] of the Coronation in this place at the Bath the 23rd April which I recieved the ralation off, from a spectatrix, it being the day Queen Ann was crowned, and is never performed unless when a queen is the chiefe as Queen Elizabeth, etc., her Sister, our late Majesty's King William and Queen Mary because the queen was joyn'd in the throne as principle; they representing the Amazons consisting of the young Maids, the Companyes of the town being assembled at Mr. Majors [the Mayors] house begin to proceed with their officers masters and wardens and each Company with their flag; after marched in a troupe the Maides of the suburbs, each with their proper officers of themselves, as Captain Ensigne and Lievtenant with plummes of feathers; just before the Captain went her guard which was 6 young men drest in their holland shirts, with garters, and ribons in their hatts, and their swords drawn in their hands, then the Captain in her short wastecoate with gold lace, and their peticoates silke that were with furbellows one above another with ribons, with a trunchant in their hand with an inscription, god save queen ann; just behind their Captaines went two Maides with two scepters gilt, next them two more that bore the crown between them, which was gilt also; their Ensigne, their flag which holds the same inscription god save queen ann, was guarded by two young men drest as the others in their holland shirts, then the troupe followed in

---

[4] Although Celia Fiennes visited Bath in 1687 or earlier, this "discription" is of the rejoicings on April 23rd 1702, the year in which she is writing.

order in same dress as their officers with Crowns on their heads of guilded lauwrell, in number about 100; next came the Citty Maides with their Majoress [Mayoress] Generall with their plummes of feathers with a wreath of gilded lawrell like a Crown and on the top with all sorts of pretious stones the Jewellers shops could supply them with, and were guarded with young men as the others; behind the Majoress followed six all in white with a green cross swathe with this inscription in white, god save queen ann; each with their trunchant in their hand as the former and two carrying 2 scepters gilt and after them two more bore the Crown between them, which was very rich in pearles; then two more carryed the queens armes between them; their dress was just as the first were only much richer and finer and all of them gather'd up the upper peticoate in little scallops just to shew their underpeticoates which were white; the troupe of the amazans in order with their bows and arrows with crowns of gilded lawrel their officers had plumes of feathers and their Serjeants with their halberts; their number was also about 100.

Next after followed all the young men of the town form'd into a Company of Granadeers with their proper officers which had laced hatts and plumes of feathers; each soldier had a red cap with Cyphers and a Crown gilt with gold and furbelowed with blew round their head; and their hair was tyed back with scarlet ribon, they had scarlet garters and scarlet slings for their gunns, drest all in their holland shirts and white stockings and had a hanger by their sides; their number was about 30.

Next followed four couple of Maurice dancers with their pranceing horses, in holland shirts with laced hatts riboned, and cross swashes and garters with bells, with their two antiques drest in their formalityes, with hankershiefs in their hands danceing all the way.

Next walked the Clergy then next followed Mr. Major with two pages attending him followed by the Corporation, aldermen all in their scarlet gowns and the comon Councill in their gowns.

Next followed in the reare all the marryed men formed into a Company of Artilery their hatts laced with plumes of feathers, all in their own cloths, the Soldiers the same with swords and gunns with two blunderbusses; every Company both of men and women was attended by drums and all sort of Musick both wind and stringed instruments.

Thus they repaired to the Cathedrall; the granadeers salutes them just as they enter the Abby with a volly of shott and there they have a sermon and as they come out of the Cathedrall the Company of artillery salutes them againe with another volly; so in the same order they return to their Guild Hall where is a sumptuous feast with Musick and danceing which ends the solemnity with bonfires as is usual.

I now proceed to describe the rest of the town; there are green walkes very pleasant and in many places, and out of the Cathedrall you walk in to the Priory which has good walkes of rows of trees which is pleasant; there are the deans, prebends and doctors houses which stand in that green, which is pleasant, by the Church called the Abby which is lofty and spacious, and much Company walke there especially in wet weather; the Quire is neat but nothing extraordinary; in that Kings Mead there are severall little Cake-houses where you have fruit Sulibubs and sumer liquours to entertaine the Company that walke there.

The markets are very good here of all sorts of provision flesh and fish, especially when the season for the Company batheing and drinking lasts, great plenty and pretty reasonable; the chargeableness of the Bath is the lodgings and firing, the faggotts being very small but they give you very good attendance there.

4. BERKSHIRE AND OXFORDSHIRE

ANOTHER JOURNEY I went with my mother into Oxfordshire, by Barkshire to Hungerford 16 mile which is famous for Crawfish there being a good river and great quantetyes of that fish and large. This is in Barkshire, thence to Lamborn which is a woody country 7 miles, thence to Farington 7 mile, a pretty large place but lyes very watry, and so by Radcote 5 miles which is much the same deep countryes much on clay: by Farington is a fine house of Sir George Pratts called Coalsell [Coleshill];[1] all the avenues to the house are fine walkes of rows of trees, the garden lyes in a great descent below the house, of many steps and tarresses and gravel walkes one below another, and green walke with all sorts of dwarfe trees, fruit trees with standing apricock and flower trees, abundance of garden roome and filled with all sorts of things improved for pleasure and use; the house is new built with stone, most of the offices are partly under ground—kitchin pantry buttlery and good cellers—and round a court is all the other offices and out houses, this is all even with the back yards; the entrance of the house is an ascent of severall steps into a hall so lofty the rooff is three storyes, reaches to the floore of the gallery, all the walls are cutt in hollows where statues and heads carved finely are sett; directly fore-right enters a large dineing roome or great parlour which has a door thourough into the garden that gives a visto through the house, within that is a drawing roome, on the other side another roome of the same size, and backward is a little parlour all with good furniture tapistry damaske etc.; there runs up a pair of back staires at each end of the house quite to the top, to the gallery, which does make convenient all the Chambers; the great Staires goes out of the hall on each side, spacious and handsom, staires runs up and meetes on the landing place which is a passage, that runs on both sides to each end of the house but is made private by two doores on each side; on the top of the staires you enter in the midle into a dineing roome, within that a chamber on each side with two closets to each, bigg enough for a little bed with chimney's convenient for a servant and for dressing roomes, one of which has a doore also out into that passage and soe to the back staires, this is the same on the other end, and also two roomes on the other

[1] Built by Sir Roger Pratt, 1650–62, after consultation with Inigo Jones, for his cousin Sir George Pratt.

side each end of the hall which continues to run up even with the second story, which are all good chambers and one more here because the great staires goe but to the first story; they are all well and genteel'ly furnisht damaske chamlet[2] and wrought beds fashionably made up; over this runs a gallery all through the house and on each side severall garret roomes for servants furnished very neate and genteele; in the middle are staires that lead up to the Cupilow [cupola] or large Lanthorn in the middle of the leads, the house being leaded all over and the stone chimney's in severall rows comes up in them on each side; the Cupilow it shewes exact and very uniform, as is the whole Building. This gives you a great prospect of gardens, grounds, woods that appertaine to the Seate, as well as a sight of the Country at a distance; there was few pictures in the house only over doores and chimneys; the hall was paved with black and whyte marble and had seates round the roome cut in arches in the walls.

From thence, Oxfordshire we enter over the Vale of the White Horse which takes its name from a Ridge of high hills on which is cutt out the shape off a horse in perfect proportions, in broad wayes, and is seen a great distance very plaine, the hills being on chalke look's white and the great valley in the bottom is term'd the manger; it extends a vast way, a rich inclosed country, and we pass through some part of Glocestershire at Norton [Over Norton] where is another Seat of my Brother Says: thence to Broughton by Banbery [Banbury] which is 25 mile.

Broughton is an ancient Seate of the Lord Viscount Say and Seale;[3] its an old house moted round and a parke and gardens, but are much left to decay and ruine, when my brother came to it, he has two other houses in two or three miles; Shettford [Shutford] a little neate house and gardens, and Newton [Newington] but that is mostly pulled down.

From Broughton I went to see Edgehill where was the famous Battle fought in Cromwells tyme; its 10 mile off,

[2] Camlet, originally a costly Eastern fabric, subsequently imitated in England.
[3] Still the seat of Lord Saye and Sele and the present home of Celia Fiennes' manuscripts.

the Ridge of hills runns a great length and so high that the land beneath it appears vastly distant, its a rich ground full of inclosures and lookes finely, tho' formidable to look down on it and turnes ones head round, the wind allwayes blows with great violence there because of the steepeness of the hill, the top is a flatt full of Barrows and hills that are markes of a Camp and battles.

About 2 mile from Broughton is a great old house [Wykham Park] much like Broughton its Sir Robert Dashwoods —most of the great houses there about are old built; about three mile off at Adderbery which is a pretty neate vilage where are two or three good houses, one of Sir Thomas Cobbs and Lady Rochesters looks neate and well with good gardens.

There is about 2 mile off the Lord Guilffords[4] house Roxton [Wroxton] which is a good house within a parke, you enter a large hall, on the left hand leads to a little parlour down to the kitchins; the halfe pace att the upper end of the hall leads into dineing roome, drawing roome, and a large staire-case with good pictures, there you enter another large dineing roome with great compass windows, fine Pictures of the family; within is a drawing roome and chambers and closets well proportioned, little or no furniture was up, only in the worst roomes, in one closet att each doore was Queen Mary and Queen Elizabeths pictures to the foot in bibb and apron very pretty, in one roome was the Lord North and Ladyes picture, which was Lord Chiefe Justice, and their sonnes picture in the middle, all at length: many good pictures in most roomes, there was a part new built all the new fashion way, which was design'd for the present Lord Gilford [Guilford] and Lady, the gardens are very good the out houses and stables handsome.

Banbury is a pretty little town the streets broad and well pitched, the whole Country is very pleasant and the land rich, a red earth; they make some of their fences with stones dry walls without morter, it seemes much on a flatt and you have

[4] Francis North, 1637–1685, first Baron Guilford, Lord Chancellor, whose life by his son Roger comprises the first part of the *Lives of the Norths.*

a large prospect; from thence to London we go by Alesbury [Aylesbury] 20 mile, thence to London 30 mile.

5. INTO HAMPSHIRE AND ALONG THE THAMES (BEFORE 1691)

A JOURNEY my mother[1] went from Newtontony to Durly in the [New] Forest 15 miles; thence to Nursteed [Nursted] 15 nile to a relations house (Aunt Holts)[2] a neat new built house with brick and stone; a hall, little parlour on the left side and back door into a court built round with all the offices out to the stables barnes; on the right side a great parlour and drawing roome that opened into the garden, which were fine gravel walkes grass plotts and beyond it a garden of flower trees and all sorts of herbage, store of fruit, a free-stone broad walke in the middle to the house; the Chambers are very good and convenient, and in the front is a place walled in, beyond is a long ground sett with rows of trees; on the right side of the house is a large grove of firrs halfe scotts halfe norroway which lookes very nobly; the roades all about this country are very stony, narrow and steep hills, or else very dirty as is most of Sussex but good rich land; it is in 2 mile of Petersffield in Hampshire which is a good little neate town, in a mile of it is a Gentlemans house called Maple Duram [Mapledurham] which might now be new named into yew, for the great number of yew trees set thick in severall green walkes that grows high and is cutt close to the body, up almost to the top, and the tops are left in a great head that spreads and makes it very shady and pleasant.

From thence we went to Guilford which is a good town built with stone, the streetes are broad; thence to Kingston on the Thames 30 mile, thence to London 10 mile, from London againe to Colebrooke [Colnbrook] 15 miles, thence to Maidenhead 10, you go in sight of Winsor Castle on the

[1] Celia Fiennes' mother (née Frances Whitehead) died in December, 1691, aged 70. (See Memorial Inscription, Newton Toney.)
[2] Margaret, youngest daughter of Colonel Richard Whitehead, had married Richard Holt of Nursted near Petersfield.

left hand, and Eaton Colledge as you pass the bridge at Maidenhead, and on the right hand you see Cliffton house [Cliveden] a fine building of the Duke of Buckingams; thence to Redding [Reading] 5 miles which is a pretty large place, severall Churches, in one lyes buried one of my sisters that dyed at my Grandmothers there of the small pox, her monument of white marble stands up in the Chancell.[3]

From Redding to the Veale [Theale] 5 mile sad clay deep way, this is in Barkshire; thence to Newbury 8 mile all clay mirey ground; Newbery is a little town famous for makeing the best whipps, its a good market for corn and trade; thence to Newtontony over Way Hill [Weyhill] famous for a Faire[4] kept there on Michelmas day, 11 mile, thence 8 mile.

[3] In St. Giles' Church, Reading, is a memorial inscription to Ann Fiennes, third daughter of Colonel Nathaniel by his second marriage. She died in 1675. The two elder daughters, Frances and Elizabeth, had also died in childhood (see Mem. Inscr., Newton Toney). Celia was the fourth child and her sister Mary (afterwards Lady Harrison) the fifth. Mary was twenty-one when she married in 1684 (see *Marriage Licenses, Vicar-General*).

[4] The greatest sheep market in the country. It was alleged that 500,000 sheep were sold at one fair in Defoe's time. (Op. cit., i, 289.)

6. FROM NEWTON TONEY TO LONDON THROUGH HAMPSHIRE AND SURREY (1691)

My journey to London after my Mothers death was by Sutton [Sutton Scotney] 14 mile thence to Baseing-stoke 12 mile, a large town for to entertaine travellers and commodious, 2 mile beyond we pass by Basen [Basing] on the left side, a house of the Duke of Boltons with a large parke and gardens; the house is not fine being much demolished and spoyled after the Civil warres, it being a garrison held by the King; on the right hand at a mile distance is another good house and fine Parke of the Duke of Boltons called Hacket [Hackwood] you come in sight of, some little distance you come in sight also of a great building like a little town [Bramshill Park] the house of Sir Robert Hendlys [Henley]; so to Hartfford-Bridge is 8 mile more, thats only a place full of inns for the conveniency of the road; thence over a heath you go to Bagshott that is 8 mile all on a heavy sand,[1] where you come by a parke of the kings and in it is a pretty house; thence to Eggum [Egham] 8 mile, very heavy sand, so to Staines where you cross the Thames on a Bridge to Midlsex and so to Houndslow 4 mile, to Brandford [Brentford] 4 mile, to Turnumgreen [Turnham Green] 2, thence to Hammersmith 2 to Kensington 2 to London 2 miles.

[1] Bagshot Heath was regarded by Defoe as "a foil to the beauty of the rest of England; or a mark of the just resentment shew'd by Heaven upon the Englishmen's pride . . . a vast tract of land, some of it within 17 or 18 miles of the capital city, which is horrid and frightful to look on, not only good for little, but good for nothing; much of it a sandy desert, and one may frequently be put in mind of Arabia Deserta". (Op. cit., i, 143.)

7. FROM LONDON TO OXFORD AND THENCE INTO SUSSEX (c. 1694)

ANOTHER JOURNEY from London to Alsebury 30 mile, from thence to great Horrwood in Buckinghamshire 10 miles; from thence I went to Hillsdon [Hillesden] a house of Mr. Dentons 7 miles, which stands in the middle of a fine Parke; the house stands on a riscing in the middle and lookes very well, its not large, a good hall with 2 parlours and has a glide through the house into the gardens which are neately kept, the grass and gravel walkes with dwarfs and flower trees and much fruit; the prospect is fine all over the gardens and parkes and the river and woods beyond them; we went to Thorndon [Thornton] Sir Thomas Tyrrells, a good old house and very good gardens, some walkes like arbours close, others shady, others open, some gravel, others grass with Cyprus' trees, a fine river runnes all the back side of the garden, where is very good fish; the house is low but runnes much on the ground, so there are many roomes which are lofty but its not built in many storyes; thence we went 4 mile to Stow [Stowe] Sir Richard Temples new house,[1] that

[1] Stowe was still an old house. Celia Fiennes disliked it, though she liked the newly laid out grounds. By "new" she means "newly-inherited" (at the time she was writing). Temple acquired it in 1697.

stands pretty high; you enter into a hall, very lofty with a gallery round the top, thence through to a great parlour that opens in a bellcony to the garden, and is a visto thro' the whole house, so that on the one side you view the gardens which are one below another with low breast walls and taress [terrace] walkes, and is replenished with all the curiosityes or requisites for ornament pleasure and use, beyond it are orchards and woods, with rows of trees; on the other side you see the parke rowes of trees; the roomes are all lofty and good, the hall is not large, sutable to its height; a great many chambers and roomes of state, some the ground floores are inlaid fine pictures, a good staircase, a gallery which leads to the ledds through a large Cupelow which gives the prospect of the whole Country. We went to Horrwood 7 mile, by severall other seates of Sir Ralph Verny's[2] [Verney] who has most exact fine gardens; within two mile off Horrwood is a well of minerall waters from iron just like Tunbridg and as good, I dranke them a fortnight, there are severall of the same sort of springs all about that Country.

Thence I went to Buckingham town 7 mile, a very neate place, and we passed the river Ouise over a very high bridge, tho' the river seemed not then so very full, but it swells after great raines, which makes them build their arches so large. Thence to Banbury in Oxfordshire 13 miles, thence to Morton Hindmost [Moreton-in-the-Marsh][3] in Glocestershire 14 miles, thence to Hales [Hailes Abbey] 8 miles, over steep stony hills, a house of Lord Tracys where my brother Say lived, a good old house and there is a pretty Chappel with a gallery for people of quality to sitt in, which goes out of the hall, that is a lofty large roome; good parlour and severall good lodging roomes, you ascend into the house by severall stone stepps. Within 2 mile of this is a better house [Toddington] of the Lord Tracy with a very good parke,

[2] Middle and East Claydon.
[3] Moreton-in-the-Marsh, once known as Moreton Henmarsh (H.A.T.). Celia Fiennes' "Brother Saye" was her half-brother, William, who became third Viscount in 1694. It was her Aunt Susanna (née Cobb) widow of Richard Fiennes (1623–74) who lived at Moreton, and whom she visited there.

which stands so high that by the Lodge I rode up the banke I could see all the parke about and the deer feeding and running, there is a little river and large ponds, it gives you a good sight of the country about, which is pretty much inclosed and woods, a rich deep country and so the roads bad; there are severall high hills that I was on that gave a large prospect to the eye; I saw some of this land improved in the produce of woads which the dyers use; its ordered in this manner, all the summer season if drie for 4 or 5 months they sow it or plant it (but I thinke its sown) then its very clean wedd [weeded], when grown up a little out of the ground for it rises no higher than lettice, and much in such tuffts; the coullour off the Leafe is much like Scabins [scabious] and the shape resembling that; this they cutt off close to the ground and soe out off the same roote springs the Leafe againe; this they do 4 tymes, then in a Mill with a horse they grind the Leaves into a paste, so make it up in balls and drye them in a Penthouse, to secure it from raine, only the wind dryes it; this plantation of about 12 acres would employ 2 or 3 familyes men women and children, and so they generally come and make little hutts for themselves for the season to tend it.

Here I saw flax in the growth; the smell of the Woade is so strong and offencive you can scarce beare it at the Mill: I could not forse my horse neare it.

From thence I returned backe by a place where is a stone [the Four Shire Stone] stands to divide four shires, Worcester Oxford Glocester and Warwickshire; so I ascended there a high hill and travaill'd all on the tops of the hills a pleasant and good roade; I Came to Rowle Stone, where are many such greate Stones as is at Stonidge, one stands uppright a broad Stone called the King's Stone, being the place a Saxon King was secured against his enemies; thence to Broughton in all 26 miles; thence I went to Astrop where is a Steele water much frequented by the Gentry, it has some mixture of Allum so is not so strong as Tunbridge; there is a fine Gravell Walke that is between 2 high cutt hedges where is a Roome for the Musick and a Roome for the

Company besides the Private walkes; the well runnes not
very quick, they are not curious in keeping it, neither is
there any bason for the spring to run out off, only a dirty well
full of moss's which is all changed yellow by the water;
there are lodgings about for the Company and a little place
called Sutton, this is four mile; thence to Oxfford 14 mile all
in a very good road and an exceeding pleasant country; you
pass by many fine Seates Park's Woods: the land here and
in most part of this County is rich red mould and deepe so
as they are forced to plough their ground 2 or 3 tymes for
wheate and cannot use wheeles to their ploughs; its rich
land and produces plenty of all things.

Oxford opens to view 2 mile off, its scituation is fine on a
round hill, environ'd round with hills adorn'd with Woods
and Enclosures, yet not so neare as to annoy the town, which
stands pleasant and compact; there is a fine Causy for neare
two mile by the road for the Schollars to walke on; the
Theater stands the highest of all and much in the middle
encompass'd with the severall Colledges and Churches and
other Buildings whose towers and spires appeares very well
at a distance; the Streetes are very cleane and well pitched,
and pretty broad, the High Streete is a very noble one, soe
large and of a greate length; in this is the University Church,
called St. Maryes, which is very large and lofty but nothing
very Curious in it.[4]

The Theater[5] is a Noble Pile of building its paved with
black and white marble exceeding large and lofty built
round and supported by its own architecture all stone, noe
pillars to support it; itt has Windows all round and full of
Gallery's for the Spectators as well as Disputants when the
acts are at Oxford; over the rooff of this large roome are as
large roomes with severall divissions which are used for the

[4] The Virgin which had stood above the doorway was destroyed in the
first year of the Civil War, when Oxford was occupied by the troops of Celia
Fiennes' grandfather, "Old Subtlety" ("Lord Say's Bluecoats"). He had
done very little other damage.

[5] The Sheldonian, built by Wren 1663-8. Defoe thought it "infinitely
superior to anything in the world of its kind". (Op. cit., ii, 25.) It was one of
Wren's first two buildings, when he was still best known as Professor of
Astronomy.

dryeing the printed sheetes of bookes, and this has lights in
ovalls which is quite round the Theater, and in the midled
is a large Cupelow or Lanthorne whence your eye has a very
fine view of the whole town and country, this is all supported on its own work; under the theatre is a roome which
is fitted for printing where I printed my name severall tymes,
the outside of the theatre there is a pavement and spike of iron
in a raile round with pillars of stone to secure it from the
street.

Just by it is a little building which is full of Antiquityes
[the old Ashmolean Museum] which have many curiositys
in it of Mettles Stones Ambers Gumms; there is the picture
of a Gentleman that was a great benefactor to it being a
travailer, the frame of his picture is all wood carved very
finely with all sorts of figures leaves birds beasts and flowers,
he gave them 2 fine gold Meddals or silver gilt, with two
fine great Chaines off the same, one was all curious hollow
worke which were given him by some prince beyond sea;
there is a Cane which looks like a solid heavy thing but if
you take it in your hands its as light as a feather, there is a
dwarfe shoe and boote, there are several Loadstones and it
is pretty to see how the steele clings or follows it, hold it on
the top att some distance the needles stands quite upright
hold it on either side it moves towards it as it rises and
falls.

There are severall good Colledges I saw most of them;
Waddom [Wadham] Hall is but little; in Trinity Colledge is
a fine neate Chapple new made finely painted; Christ Church
is the largest Colledge, the Courts large, the buildings large
and lofty; in one of the Courts is a tower new-built for to
hang the Mighty Tom,[6] that bell is of a large size so great a
weight they were forced to have engines from London to
raise it up to the tower; there is a fine ring of bells in the
Colledge St. Magdalines its just by the river; there is to
Maudline Hall (which is a very large and good Cloyster) a
very fine gravell walk, two or 3 may walke abreast, and rows

[6] Tom Tower, built from Wren's design in 1684.

of trees on either side, and this is round a water which makes it very pleasant.[7]

St. Johns Colledge had fine gardens and walkes but I did but just look into it, so I did into Kings,[8] and Queens Colledges and severall of the rest I looked into; they are much alike in building but none so large as Christ Church Colledge; I was in New Colledge which is very neate but not large, the buildings good, the Chapple very fine; the Garden was new-makeing, there is a large bason of water in the middle, there is little walkes and mazes and round mounts for the schollars to divert themselves in.

Corpus Christus Colledge—which is but small—there I was entertained at supper, and eate of their very good bread and beare which is remarkably the best any where Oxford Bread is.

The Physick Garden[9] afforded great diversion and pleasure, the variety of flowers and plants would have entertained one a week, the few remarkable things I tooke notice off was the Aloes plant which is like a great flag in shape leaves and coullour, and grows in the form of an open Hartichoake, and towards the bottom of each leafe its very broad and thicke in which there are hollows or receptacles for the Aloes; there is also the Sensible plant [Mimosa], take but a leafe between finger and thumb and squeeze it and it immediately curles up together as if pained, and after some tyme opens abroad again, it looks in coullour like a filbert leafe but much narrower and long; there is also the Humble plant that grows on a long slender stalke and do but strike it, it falls flatt on the ground stalke and all, and after some tyme revives againe

[7] The cloisters and walks belonged to Magdalen College, not to Magdalen Hall. (H.A.T.)

[8] There is, of course, no King's College in Oxford, but if, as appears below, Celia Fiennes believed that King Alfred founded University College, the explanation may lie there. The fiction dates from a lawsuit of 1377 but was confirmed by the Court of King's Bench in 1726 and is still part of the law of England. But she may mean "King's Hall", i.e. Brasenose.

[9] The Physick Garden was much admired by most English visitors (e.g. Evelyn) but was despised by the Italians who reported the tour of Cosimo III, Grand Duke of Tuscany, in 1699. "From the smallness of its size, irregularity, and bad cultivation," they thought that it "scarcely deserves to be seen". (*Travels of Cosimo III*, by L. Magalotti, trans. 1821, pp. 262–3.)

and stands up, but these are nice plants and are kept mostly under glass's, the aire being too rough for them; there is the Wormwood sage called Mountaigne sage, its to all appearance like Comon sage only of yellower green, a narrow long leafe full of ribbs, in your mouth the flavour is strong of Wormwood to the taste.

The library is as large as 2 or 3 roomes but old, and a little disreguarded except one part, which is parted from the rest, wansecoated and fitted up neate and painted, which was done by King James the Second when he designed Maudling Colledg for his priests a seminary.

Here I met with some of my relations[10] who accompanyed me about to see some of the Colledges I had not seen before; St. John's Colledge[11] which is large and has a fine Garden at one entrance of it with large Iron-gates carved and gilt, its built round two Courts; the Library is two walks, one out of the other, the inner one has severall Anatomy's in cases,[12] and some other Curiosity of Shells Stone Bristol Diamonds Skins of fish and beasts; here they have the great Curiosity much spoken off, King Charles the Firsts Picture, the whole lines of face band and garment to the shoulders and arms and garter is all written hand and containes the whole Comon prayer, itts very small the caracter but where a straight line is you may read a word or two; there is another of Gustaus Adolphus whose portraiture is represented to the eye in writeing alsoe and contains his whole Life and prowess; there is alsoe the Lords prayer and ten Commandments in the compass of a crown piece, there are also severall books all of writeing on vellum leaves, and one book written in

[10] These relations were most probably: (1) Nathaniel Fiennes (1676–1710) who became fourth Viscount Saye and Sele in 1698, the son of Celia's half-brother William (third Viscount). He matriculated August 1693. (2) Richard Fiennes (1674–1722) son (by second marriage) of Celia's Uncle Richard. Her cousin Richard matriculated September 1693, became Rector of Akeley, Bucks., and was the father of Richard the sixth and last Viscount. (See Foster, *Alumni Oxonienses*.)

[11] The garden is that of St. John's, but the gates must be those of Trinity College gardens. (H.A.T.)

[12] Ralph Thoresby, the famous Yorkshire antiquarian and devout Nonconformist, records in his diary for May 24th, 1684, that "the skeletons and stuffed human skins in the Anatomy School suited my melancholy temper". (i, 174.)

F

the Chinease Caractor on the indian barks off trees, there is
alsoe a Book of the Genealogies of the kings since the Conquest to King Charles the Second with the severall Coates all
gilded very fresh till the two or three last, which is pretended
to be deficient from the art being lost of laying Gold so fine
on any thing to polish it, but thats a great mistake, for that
art is still in use in England, but the excuse served the negli-
gence or ignorance of the workman; there was alsoe one
book with severall Cutts in it off the Conception of Christ till
his Ascention; there was alsoe a fine Prayer book or Mass
book off Q. Marias; this was in the new part of the Library
which was neately wanscoated and adorned—there is a fine
grove of trees and walks all walled round.

Queens Colledge Library[13] is all new and a stately building
emulating that of Christ Church in Cambridge;[14] it is not so
large and stands on one range of Pillars of stone, the other
front being all with Statues in stone, in nitches and carved
adornements, and on the top figures and statues; the Staircase is pretty broad but not so finely wanscoated or carved
as that at Cambridge; the roome is lofty, but not so large,
well wanscoated, and there is good Carvings; its mostly full
of Books in the severall divisions and great Globes, its
boarded under foot, here is no ballcoany because the prospect
is but to a dead wall, its very handsom.

Trinity Colledge Chapple[15] which was not finish'd the last
tyme I was at Oxford, but now is a beautifull magnifficent
Structure, its lofty and curiously painted the rooffe and sides
the history of Christ's ascention and very fine Carving of thin
white wood just like that at Windsor, it being the same
hand,[16] the whole Chappel is wanscoated with Walnut-tree
and the fine sweet wood, the same which that the Lord
Orfford[17] brought over when High Admiral of England
and has wanscoated his hall and staircase with, it is sweet

---

[13] The Library, by Hawksmoor, was finished 1693–94.
[14] She means Trinity College.
[15] The new Chapel was built 1692–93 from designs by Aldrich, Dean of
Christ Church, who had consulted Wren.
[16] Grinling Gibbons.
[17] Edward Russell, first Earl of Orford, victor of La Hogue.

like Cedar and of a reddish coullour, but the graine much finer and well vein'd.

New Colledge[18] which belongs to the Fiennes's, William of Wickam the founder, so I look'd on my self as some way a little interested in that; here I was very handsomly entertained by Mr. Cross which was one of my Nephew Say and Seale's Tutors when at Oxfford: these Fellowships in New Colledge are about [£]100 say, and a very pretty appartment of dineing roome bed chamber and studdy and a room for a Servant, tho' the Serviteurs of the Colledge gives attendance, and here they may live very neately and well if sober, and have all their curiosityes; they take much delight in greens of all sorts Myrtle Oringe and Lemons and Lorrestine [Laurustinus] growing in potts of earth, and so moved about from placc to place and into the aire sometymes; there are severall New Lodgings added and beautifyed here, the Gardens also with gravell and grass walkes, some shady, and a great mount in the middle which is ascended by degrees in a round of green paths deffended by greens cutt low, and on the top is a Summer house, beyond these Gardens is a bowling-green, and round it a close shady walke, walled round and a cutt hedge to the bowling-green.

There are in Oxfford 18 Colledges and Six Halls viz. New Colledge, Christ-Church Colledge, Martin [Merton] Colledge, Corpus Christy Colledge, Magdalen Colledge, University Coll, Pembrooke Colledge, Linghorn [Lincoln] Colledge which is overlook't by the Devil, Brasen-nose Colledge, Wadham Colledge, Queens Colledge, Belial [Balliol] Colledge, Orrel [Oriel] Colledge, Trinity Colledge, Exccetter Colledge, All-Souls Colledge, Jesus Colledge, St. Johns Colledge. Halls 7, viz Alben Hall, Maudlin Hall, Newin [New Inn] Hall, Hart Hall, Glocester Hall, St. Mary Hall, and Edmond Hall.

[18] The Fiennes family was already "Wykeham-Fiennes", through descent from William of Wykeham's sister. In this way they had acquired not only Broughton Castle, which contains "William of Wykeham's Chapel", but rights as "Founder's Kin" both at Winchester and at New College. "Mr. Cross", who entertained Celia Fiennes, was Richard Crosse (1665–1732) Fellow of New College. His pupil, after becoming Viscount, made Crosse Rector of Broughton in 1704. (Foster, op. cit.)

There is a very odd custom in Queen Coll. for every new-years-day there is a certain sum laid out in Needles and Thread which was left by the Founder, and every Gentleman of that Colledge has one given him with these words: Take this and be thrifty.

In New Colledge Garden in the plott there is the Colledg Armes cutt in box and the 24 letters round it; next plott a Sun-dial cutt in box and true-lovers knotts; att the Entrance of the Colledge over the gate is the Fiennes's and the Wickams Arms cutt in stone, sett up there by my Nephew Say when he was at the Colledge before his travels;[19] there is a large stone statue in the middle of the first quadrangle of William of Wickhams the Founder, railed in with iron grates; in the Library are the pictures of some of the learned men which belonged formerly to the University.

From Oxford I went to Abington [Abingdon] and cross'd the River Thames on a bridge att the end of the town, and so entered into Barkshire and rode along by the Thames side a good way, which was full of Barges and Lighters,[20] its 6 mile to Abington. Before I proceed will insert the names of the Founders of the Halls and Colledges in Oxford—University Colledge was founded by King Alfred,[21] Baliol Colledge was founded by John and David Baliol, Merton Colledge by Walter De Mert [Merton], Excetter Colledge by Walter Stapleton, Oriel Colledge by King Edward the Second, Queen Colledge by Robert Egglesfield, New Colledge by William of Wickham, Lincoln Colledge by Richard Fleming, all Souls Colledge by Henry Chicklag [Chichele], Magdalin Colledge by William Wainfleet, Brason-nose Colledge by William Smith and Richard Sutton, Corpus Christy

[19] Her nephew Nathaniel was on his travels at the moment of his succession to the title in 1698 (see Luttrell, *Brief Relation*, iv, 460). Celia Fiennes is therefore describing the arms she had seen later, but not at this visit.

[20] The Thames had been made navigable as far as Oxford about the beginning of the seventeenth century. Indeed it is related of Robert Burton, the Anatomist of Melancholy, that in his old age "nothing at last could make him laugh but going down to the footbridge in Oxford and hearing the bargemen scold and swear at one another, at which he would set his hands to his sides and laugh most profusely". (White Kennet, *Register and Chronicle*, 1728, 320–321.)

[21] Here as elsewhere Celia Fiennes has fallen a victim to the mythological history of the Universities, which still had a wide currency.

Colledge by Richard Fox, Christ Church Colledge by Henry the Eight, Trinity Colledge by Thomas Pope, St. Johns Colledge by Thomas White, Jesus Colledge by Queen Elizabeth, Wadham Colledge by Nicholas and Dorothy Wadham, Pembrooke Colledge by Thomas Teisdale and Richard Whitewick.

Hart Hall by Walter Stapleton, St. Mary Hall by King Edward the Second, New In Hall by William of Wickham, Magdalen Hall by William of Wainfleet, Gloster Hall by Thomas White, Albon Hall by the abbess of Alban, St. Edmond Hall by the Arch Bishop of Canterbury.

From thence I went to Abington—Abington town seemes a very well built town and the Market Cross[22] is the finest in England, its all of free stone and very lofty, even the Isles or Walk below is a lofty arch on severall pillars of square stone and four square pillars, over it are large Roomes with handsome Windows, above which is some Roomes with windows a little like the Theatre att Oxford, only this is a square building and that round, it makes a very fine appearance.

From thence I went to Elsly [Ilsley] 8 mile farther, a little Market town, good Inns; thence Newbury; most of this way is much on Downs and good roads, its 7 mile to Newbury where I called on an old acquaintance marryed to a trades-man Mr. Every, who is so like the Minister his Uncle that was my acquaintance; here I staid an hour and then proceeded on to Basen stoke 12 long miles, being my ready road to Chichister and from Besen stocke [Basingstoke] to Alton 8 mile, and from thence to Petersffield and to Nurstead [Nursted] 11 long miles, this was in Hampshire so was Basen stoak; here I lay at a Relations House Mr. Holt that marry'd my Mothers Sister; from thence I went to Chichester through a very fine Parke of the Lord Tankervailes,[23] stately

[22] Celia Fiennes often uses "Market Cross" for market house or, as in this case, town hall. It was built 1678–82.

[23] Up Park, near Harting, where Mr. H. G. Wells's mother was once housekeeper; the house appears as "Bladesover" in *Tono Bungay*. It had just been built when Celia Fiennes saw it. Lord Tankerville (1655–1701) had been Ford Grey, Baron Grey of Wark. He was a prominent Whig and owed his new title to William III, in spite of having turned King's Evidence against Monmouth. His widow, later, married Richard Rooth, the house of whose first wife is described by Celia Fiennes in her account of Epsom.

woods and shady tall trees at least 2 mile, in the middle stands his house which is new built, square, 9 windows in the front and seven in the sides, brickwork with free stone coynes and windows, itts in the midst of fine gardens, gravell and grass walks and bowling green, with breast walls divideing cach from other and so discovers the whole to view; att the entrance a large Court with iron gates open, which leads to a less, ascending some stepps free stone in a round, thence up more stepps to a terrass, so to the house; it looks very neate and all orchards and yards convenient.

Thence I entered into Sussex and soe Chichester which is 12 miles; this is but a little Citty encompass'd with a wall, with 4 gates which casts the two streetes directly a cross each other and so lookes through from gate to gate, one Streete does; the other it seemes did so formerly, but in new building of some of their houses they have encroach'd into the Streete and so hinders the through visto, in midst of these 2 or 4 streetes divided by the Market place is a very faire Cross of Stone like a Church or greate arch, its pretty large and pirra-mydy form with severall Carvings.

The Cathedrall is pretty lofty, the painting on the roofe in the Quire and Isles lookes very fresh tho' 300 yeares old; there is in the Isle on the roofe the phancy of 6 faces joyned and 6 eyes and yet each face has two eyes and in another place the faces turned outward and so the 6 faces are 12 eyes; the Quire is good, there is a fixed pulpit in it overight the Bishops seate, which is not usual, I never saw it before, usually they have pulpits that are moveable; there is a faire Organ and another pulpit in the body of the Church; there is also an entire Church in the Cathedrall by it self which is the Parish Church, there are in all 6 parishes and so many Churches besides the Cathedrall; over the alter is painted glass chequer'd blew white and red so deepe the coullour is struck into the glass as makes it darkish; in one of the Isles is a square place on each side the wall is filled with the Kings pictures from the Conquest to their present Majestyes, there is also one Picture pretty large of a Saxon King in his Robes and an Abbott with his brethren petitioning to build

this Cathedrall which before belonged to the Isle of Ely[23a]
where was the Bishops See; there is also one large Picture of
another Bishop petitioning King Harry the 8th to finish and
paint the Church; on the other side the wall is filled up with
the severall Abbots and Bishops since the Conquest that have
been of Chichester—in their advancement they are brought
from Bristol to Chichester, and next advance is to Ely and so
on to greater revenues; the tower is 260 odd steps, from
whence you may see the whole town, there are 3 or 4 good
new houses (one is the Dean's Mr. Edds a very good man)
from thence I saw the Isle of Wight, Spitthead; the sea comes
within a mile of the citty, remarkable for Lobsters and Crabs
Chichester is; there is an Engine or Mill about a mile off
the town draws up salt water at one side from the sea and
fresh water from a little rivulet which descends from a hill,
and so supply's the town; halfe way off the tower you go
round the quire and looke down into it; there are severall
effigies of marble and allabaster of the Bishops of the place
and one of the Earle of Arrundell and his Lady.

Chichester is 50 mile from London the direct way by
Guildford, but I went through more of Sussex, which is
much in blind dark lanes and up and down steepe hills, to
Billinghurst [Billinghurst], and passed through Arundell
parke belonging to the Duke of Norfolke, this was 18 mile;
from whence I went to Dorken [Dorking] in Surry 15 mile
where are the best trouts in that river which runns by Box
Hill,[24] a remarkable diversion to people that go to Epsum:
the hill is full of box which is cutt out in severall walks,
shady and pleasant to walk in tho' the smell is not very
agreeable; the brow of the hill being such a height gives a
large prospect of a fruitfull vale full of inclosures and woods,
and this River runns twining it self about and is called the
Swallow,[25] and just about Dorken and Leatherhead 4 mile

[23a] Presumably Selsey.
[24] The walks on Box Hill had been laid out by the Earl of Arundel, the
great connoisseur of the arts, who had procured most of Charles I's pictures
for him. For an account of the "diversions" of Box Hill, by John Macky, see
Introduction, p. xxvi.
[25] The Mole is alleged to flow as an underground river here, but actually
becomes a chain of swamps.

thence, it sinkes away in many places which they call Swallow holes; this must be some quick sand but the Report of it is it sincks here and runnes underground a mile or two and rises about Moles [Molesey] and runs againe: Camden does credit this and repeates a tryal one made of forceing a Duck into one of those falls, which came out at the other side by Moles with its feathers allmost all rubbed off, which supposses the passage to be streight, but how they could force the Duck into so difficult a way or whither anything of this is more than Conjecture must be left to every ones liberty to judge.

From Darken [Dorking] its 10 mile to Kingston—a chalky hard road—which is in Surrey, this stands on the Thames; its a great Market for Corne, I was there on Satturday and saw great quantety's of Corn and Mault sold; thence I passed by Richmond Park wall a good way and came in sight of Hampton Court which is a noble Building; had the good Queen Mary lived to have finished it, it would have been the noblest palace in the Kingdom; I passed the end of Wanstead [Wandsworth] and Clapham and part of Lambeth, haueing Chealsey College[26] in view and the whole Citty's of Westminster and London, so thro' Southwark over London Bridge into Middlesex, 10 mile in all from Kingston; this little journey was 220 mile.

[26] Chelsea Hospital, built by Wren (1681–87) on the site of the old college, and traditionally assigned to Nell Gwyn's prompting of King Charles's generosity.

8. FROM LONDON INTO HEREFORDSHIRE, GLOUCESTERSHIRE AND BACK (IN OR BEFORE 1696)

ANOTHER JOURNEY into Herrifordshire from London: by Uxbridge to Islip 50 miles, that is 7 mile off Oxford; from Islip to Woodstock,[1] where remaines no footesteps of faire Rosomands Bower only the walls round the park and the little brookes that supply'd it with water for the baths and wells and ponds; thence to Morton Hindmost [Moreton-in-the-Marsh] in Glocestershire to a Relations house, My Uncle

[1] The old house, celebrated in Scott's novel, had been destroyed, but some walls of "Rosamond's Bower" still stood, until Marlborough removed them when he built Blenheim Palace.

Richard Fiennes widdow; a little neate stone built town, good Innes for the travellers, being the road from London to Worcester and Herrifford and Wales; thence over Broadway hills to Parshur [Pershore], in all 30 mile by 12 of the clock, thence to Upton where we pass on a large bridge over the fine River the Severn, which runs from Worcester and to Glocester Shrewsbury and to Bristol where it runns into the Sea: in some places its very broad some miles over, but here it was no broader than the Thames is at Staines, it affords good fish, Salmon and severall sorts besides; I think this River does not ebb and flow so farre into the land; here we enter into Worcestershire and ascend Mauborn [Malvern] hills or as some term them the English Alps—a Ridge of hills divideing Worcestershire and Herifordshire and was formerly esteemed the divideing England and Wales, Herriford Shropshire, etc., were Weltch Countys—they are at least 2 or 3 miles up and are in a Pirramidy fashion on the top; I rode up upon the top of one of the highest, from whence could discern the Country above 40 miles round, and noe hills but what appeared like Burrows or Mole hills; these being so high nothing could limitt the eye but distance. Just at the bottom stands Worcester town which lookes like a large well built town of brick and stone, I was not in it; on the one side of this high Ridge of hills lies Worcester Oxford Glocestershire etc., appears in Plaines Enclosures Woods and Rivers and many great Hills tho' to this they appeare low; on the other side is Herrifordshire which appear like a Country off Gardens and Orchards, the whole Country being very full of fruite trees etc., it lookes like nothing else, the apple pear trees etc., are so thick even in their corn fields and hedgrows.

The descent is as long and steep in some places as its riseing was; thence to a Relations house, my uncle John Fiennes[2]

[2] Colonel John Fiennes (d. 1696) third son of "Old Subtlety", fought at Naseby and won the esteem of Cromwell (see Carlyle's *Letters and Speeches of O.C.* App. vii) who made him a member of his "House of Lords". A Republican pamphleteer described him as "such a one as they call a sectary, but no great stickler" as he was said to be entirely under the influence of his brother Nathaniel. (*Harleian Miscellany*, iii, 486.) His son Laurence became fifth Viscount Saye & Sele in 1710. The house was New House, Stretton Grandison.

and his son, New House, 20 mile from Parshur, which I rode all in one day in June—and the miles are here very long so that at least it may be esteemed the last 20 mile as long as the 30 mile gone in the morning—my Cos'n Fiennes has made a very convenient habitation at this place, which contrary to its name was an old built house timber worke; but by his alterations and additions of good brick walls round the Court and 4 pretty gardens with good walks, grass platts, much good fruite of which the country does easily produce, and if persons are curious in planting may have the best, which my Cosen has here; and the walls some lower than other gives the sight of the garden at one view, severall large orchards behind the house with new Stables and offices which makes it look well; itts in sight of severall houses, but all old buildings Lady Hoptons [Canon Frome House] in a low meadow, there are woods by it and a little river parts them, called the Froomy [Frome], which gives name to severall little villages as Cannon Froom, Bishops Froom, Castle Froom; this runnes into another little river called the Lug [Lugg], and both runnes into the River Wye which is on the back side of Herriford town; this was 7 miles from us, its a pretty little town of timber buildings, the streets are well pitched and handsome as to breadth and length; the River Wye is as broad as the Thames is at Maidenhead bridge or hardly so broad, its a rapid river and seemed much disturb'd; there is very good fish in it; it did not looke cleare when I saw it, but was thick and yellow but that is against foul weather.

The Mount, which is the only thing of the Castle that remaines, commands the sight of the river and town; the Cathedrall is very neate but small, the Carving of the wood in the Quire was good; in the Library I was shown by the Dean of Herriford the History of Pope Joan with her Picture, it was printed in and with the history of all the popes in Rome successively, it was writt in old English but I made a shift to read it; there is the Bishops Palace and the Deanes and Doctors houses which are the best buildings but they are not very fine or large; a mile thence on a flatt is Mr. Paul

Folie's [Foley] Seate called Stoake[3] in whose parlour you see Herriford very plaine; its a very good old house of Timber worke but old fashion'd and good roome for Gardens but all in an old form and mode, and Mr. Folie intends to make both a new house and gardens; the latter I saw staked out, so it will be to no purpose to say any thing of it as its now, only the good Barns and Stables that are new covered with slate, the fine Bowling green walled in and a Summerhouse in it all new; there is beyond this fine woods and a delicate Parke above the house, pailed in, that is stored with deare both red and fallow and affords 12 brace in a season, there are also fine Coppices.

From thence to Newhouse againe, 7 mile hither; we went 5 or 6 tymes from Newhouse to Broughton; we went by Eshum [Evesham] and the Vale of the Red Horse, being a Vale of a great extent, the earth is all red, its a very rich Country for corn and fruites and woods; its called the Vale of Eshum or of the Red Horse from a red horse cut out on some of the hills about it, and the Earth all looking red the horse lookes so as that of the white horse vale, here is all very heavy way to Weston[4] [Weston-sub-Edge] 25 mile in Glocester to a Parsonage of my Cos'n Pheramus Fiennes, given him for his life by his and our Grandfather William Lord Viscount Say and Seale; its a neate building all stone, and the walls round court gardens and yards all are of stone.

A mile thence was one of his sisters marryed to a Parson Mr. Browne[5] that has a very neate and convenient little House and Gardens; a mile from thence is a very high hill

[3] Stoke Edith, completed about 1700, was built by Paul Foley, Speaker of the House of Commons, and a Tory, although his father the ironmaster had been a Noncomformist and a friend of Richard Baxter's. Celia Fiennes was to visit Stoke Edith at various stages of its construction. It was burnt down in 1927.

[4] Weston-sub-Edge, famous until the Puritan Revolution for the Dover's Hill Whitsun Games. Pharamus Fiennes, son of Colonel John, became Rector in 1685 (Foster, op. cit.). He was probably the "Dr. Fiennes" whom Evelyn heard preach before the King on November 30th, 1684, and wrongly called "son of Lord Say and Seale". He must have died before 1710 or he would have succeeded to the Viscountcy.

[5] Elizabeth Fiennes, daughter of Colonel John, married as her second husband John Brawn, or Brown, of Alscott, Glos.

from whence I could see a great distance, Warwick and Coventry and a large tract of Land all round; att the foote of this hill lyes Camden Town [Chipping Campden] which I went through; its built all of stone as is the Church which is pretty, for such a little town its large; I went to see the Effigie of the little Viscountess Camden that lived to a great age was Mother to the Earle of Gainsborough; its cut out in white marble and stands in an arch then the wall with two leav'd doores to it, to keep it from the dust; there were severall little Monuments besides in the Church; from thence to Brailes and thence to Broughton 19 miles, to my brother Say, which is 50 miles from London; I went by Alsbury [Aylesbury] 20, thence 30 to London.

9. THE NEW FOREST, WINCHESTER AND THE ISLE OF WIGHT

A JOURNEY I went into the New Forrest in Hampshire to Farnum [Farnham] 38 mile; there we go by Aberstone [Abbotstone] the Duke of Boltons house, stands on the side of a hill where are fine Gardens and much fruite; from Fernum you see the Castle which is the Bishops of Winchesters house, its a large building; thence you go to Alton 7 mile, thence to Alsford [Alresford] 7 mile more, you go along on the hills in sight of the River All which gives name to those places—its a good chaulky way—thence to Winchester 7 mile; in one mile off the town is Woolsey[1] that was formerly the Bishops house, a large rambling building like a little town, this is on Maudline Hill whereon a considerable Faire is kept neare Michelmas, the traffique mostly hopps which that Country produceth good and cheese; its noted for a vast many of waines from severall parts especially from the West Country.

Winchester is a large town was once the metropolis, there is a wall encompassing it with severall Gates, the streets are

[1] She is confusing the hospital of St. Mary Magdalen with Wolvesley Palace. (H.A.T.)

pretty good large and long, the buildings but low and old, only some few in the Close which are new built of the Doctors houses by the Colledge and the Church; the Dean's house is a good old house, timber buildings, there are some of the roomes lofty and large, a dineing drawing room and bed chamber very good, a long Gallery runns through the house and opens into the Garden by a descent of severall stone stepps; the Garden is but small, there are green and gravel walkes higher and lower but its all in an old fashion'd form, but neately kept and severall Curiosityes in potts of flowers and greens; the Bishops palace [Wolvesley Palace] stands in a low ground or watry meadow its a timber building but so unpleasant that the Bishop lives not at it but at Farly [Farnham] Castle about 20 mile off.

The Cathedrall at Winchester is one of the biggest in England and is to be admired for its largeness not its neatness or curiosity; there is an ascent of 20 steps up to the Quire that is finely carved in the wood and on the top all round stands in fine painted chests the bones of the Kings of England that were buried there, for Winchester was the Regal Citty, which now it has lost as also a peculiar art of dying the best purples; in the Church there are no good Monuments worth notice; the body of the Church is very large and all the Pillars the like, the Isle large, the Steeple lookes noble, but the Spire is not a neare so high as Salisbury; in the town is a new building begun by King Charles the Second for a Palace[2] when he came to hunt, and for aire and diversions in the Country, I saw the Modell of it which was very fine, and so would it have been if finished, but there is only the outside shell is set up; there were designed fine apartments and two Chapples but its never like to be finished now.

There is a good river runns thro' the town at the backside the Castle stood high but there now remains only the ruined walls and banks, on which they make gardens and hopp-

[2] The "King's House", designed by Wren, was begun in 1683 but discontinued by James II. (H.A.T.) The Duke of Bolton was allowed to remove some of the materials for his house at Hackwood. (*Portland MSS.*, vi, 174.)

yards which runnes a great length on the side of the brow of the hill that some part of the town is built on, it lookes pretty.

Here is a good Colledg; it is on the same foundation that New Colledg in Oxford are both built and endowed by Great William of Wickam an ancester of the Fiennes's and Lord Say and Seale; so all the founders kindred by his own Statutes are first to be chosen and have a right to many priviledges; its only in default or want of any of his kindred or of Such and Such Parishes which he names that any other person ought or can be chosen a Child of this Colledge; they have such a number above 100, they have their diet and a gown every year and so much money every quarter, and here they have their Learning till fitt for the University and then in their turns at the Elections are sent to New Colledg as they are fitt, where they have the continuance of their Learning and provision; there are also Fellowships which as they become vacant they who are fitt its bestowed on them, on which a young man may maintain himself well and so improve his Learning; these Fellowships at New Colledg are forfeited if they do not live there or for the most part, and also as soone as they are marryed they are put out in number, fellows master and warden; but at Winchester the Fellowships are of greater value and do appertaine to a person during life in case he comes and resides for the most part there, even when they are marryed; I thinke there are but 7 Fellowships here; there is a Warden of the Colledge and a schoolemaster and usher at Winchester.

The Colledge is a good pile of Building, there is a very pretty Chapple in it and a very fine Library which is in the Cloysters that are very good for walking; there is a large hall they eate in and have their exact Commons to every one, so have the fellows; their Lodgings are convenient and all their offices, the Warden has built a new appartment for himself which looks well.

About a mile or two beyond Winchester we go by St. Cross, a large hospitall for old men and I thinke most is for the decayed Scholars; the Masters place is worth 1000 pound a yeare, it used to be annexed to the Warden of the Colledges place; by their foundation they are to give reliefe to any Travellers that call there, so farre as a Loafe of bread, as big as our two penny bread is, and a Draught of beare and a piece of mony, I thinke its the value of a Groate.[3]

From thence I came to Redbridge, thence to Buckland in the New Forrest in all 20 mile; from Buckland—which was a Relations house Sir Robert Smiths[4]—its a mile to Limington [Lymington] a Seaport town, it has some few small shipps belongs to it and some little trade but the greatest trade is by their Salterns:[5] the Sea water they draw into trenches and so into severall ponds that are secured in the bottom to retain it and it stands for the Sun to exhale the watry fresh part of it, and if it prove a drye sumer they make the best and most Salt for the rain spoyles the ponds by weakning the Salt; when they think its fit to boyle they draw off the water from the ponds by pipes which conveys it into a house full of large square iron and copper panns, they are shallow but they are a yard or two if not more square, these are fixed in rowes one by another, it may be twenty on a side, in a house under which is the furnace that burns fiercely to keepe these panns boyling apace, and as it candy's about the edges or bottom so they shovell it up and fill it in great Baskets, and so the thinner part runns through on Moulds they set to catch it which they call Salt Cakes; the rest in the Baskets drye and is very good Salt, and as fast as they shovell out the boyling Salt out of the panns they do replenish it with more of their Salt water in their pipes; they told me when the season was drye and so the Salt water in its prime they could make 60 quarters of Salt in one of those panns which they constantly attend night and day all the while the fire is in the furnace, because it would burn to waste and spoyle the panns, which by their constant use wants often to be repaired; they leave off Satterday night and let out the fire

---

[3] Defoe alleges that the funds had been "embezzel'd and depredated by the rich, and turn'd to the support of luxury and pride". (Op. cit., i, 187.)

[4] Anne Whitehead (1655–1725) niece of Celia Fiennes' mother, had married Sir Robert Smith.

[5] Said by Defoe to supply all southern England with salt. (Op. cit., i, 206.)

and so begin and kindle their fire Monday morning, its a pretty charge to light the fire; their season for makeing Salt is not above 4 or 5 months in the year and that only in a dry Summer; these houses have above 20, some 30, others more of these panns in them, they are made of Copper; they are very carefull to keep their ponds well secured and mended by good Clay and Gravell in the bottom and sides, and so by sluces they fill them out of the sea at high tides and so conveyed from pond to pond till fit to boyle.

From Limmington [Lymington] to Lindhurst [Lyndhurst] is 6 mile, where is a house of the kings when he comes to hunt in the New Forrest and the Lord Warden of the Forrest is there when he comes to hunt and hawk, to whome comes all the Gentry of the Country to waite on him; he dines at Night from 7 to 12 of the clock, he is served in plaite, those that hunt with him all day comes and dines or supps with him; he has power to dispose and order the concerns of the Forrest for the timber for shipps and to have it cherrish'd and secured from spoyle, as also the Deare and Game to be preserved; the disposeing of the Lodges are in his power: there are 15 Lodges and these are disposed to Gentlemen that have under keepers that takes the care of it, and what is peculiar to the New Forrest and known no where else are these Brouce Deare; at these severall Lodges the Keepers gather Brouce[6] and at certaine tymes in the day by a call gathers all the Dear in within the railes which belongs to each Lodge and so they come up and feed upon this Brouce and are by that meanes very fatt and very tame so as to come quite to eate out of your hand; all the day besides they range about and if they meete any body, if it be their own keeper, without the pail of the Lodge they will run from him as wild as can be; these Lodges are about 4 miles asunder and its a great priviledge and advantage to be a Cheefe Keeper of any of these Lodges, they have venison as much as they please and can easily shoote it when the troop comes up with in the paile, for none are allowed to shoot out in the Forrest nor are allowed to go out with gun or dog, or to keep any, except

[6] Brouce, or Browse, the young shoots and twigs of trees or shrubs.

Gentlemen, and not they if they have been found shooteing in the Forrest; I think its Fellony for any to kill the kings dear; there are severall Rangers of the Forrest; and 6 Verderers that are their justices or judges of all matters relateing to the Forrest, these ought allwayes to reside in the Forest and are to attend the king when he comes into the New Forrest, clothed in green; they have a Buck and Doe every year for their fee besides being Masters; the under keepers are at their beck so that they can get as much venison as they want; there is also a Rider of the Forrest who is to see about that all things are secure and well done and the Timber kept and Deer, to see they are not spoyled or destroyed; his Right is to all the Deer that are hurt or maimed, as also he is to have the shoulder of the first Stagg that is hunted and killed in the season; there is a Bow man which is to provide the King with bow and arrow when he comes into the Forrest; they have some priviledge also, but the shooteing by bow and arrow being left off that office is not regarded.

From Lindhurst [Lyndhurst] about a mile is a parke called New Parke enclosed out of the Forrest with pailes, it belongs to the kings house, there is a house in it which was the Lodge, a large old timber house; from Limington to the Isle of Wight its about 4 leagues; to Yarmouth you go by Hurst Castle that runnes on a point of land into the sea just by the Needles, within a league of Yarmouth, and those Needles are severall Great Rocks on that side of the Island, craggy, and severall stand out into the sea which makes it very hazardous for shipps to pass there especially in a Storme, or for Strangers, the passage being narrow between the Needles and Hurst Castle can easily command any ship that would pass there; from Yarmouth which is a little Sea-port and has a little Castle that can annoy any Enemy that should pass by Hurst[7] so between them may well secure that part of the Isle, and all on the back side of the Island are

[7] Thomas Baskerville (1630–1720) whose *Travels* appear in the Portland MSS., describes the firing he saw against a suspected smuggler in the narrows here, "with bullets which kept a plaguey singing in the air". (*Hist. MSS. Comm., Portland MSS.*, ii, 288.)

those Needles that are a naturall fortification it being in-accessible; so at another part of the Isle there is Sandum Fort [Sandown] which is a pretty strong place; the Island is 10 mile in the breadth and 30 mile in length; upon most of the high hills you see the wall of the sea on both sides, if not all round you as in some places.

From Yarmouth to Newport is seven mile, a little town that the arm of the Sea comes up to, its one of the biggest town in the Island; in a mile off it is Casbrooke [Carisbrooke] Castle into which King Charles the first retired when he was worsted by the Parliaments forces; there are some good roomes still that remaine but the most part are destroyed and only ruined walls to be seen, there is a deep well of 40 fathom, they draw up the bucket by a great Wheele in which they put a horse or ass, a stone thrown down sounds a long tyme ere you hear it splash into the water; about seven miles thence is Cowes, both East and West, 2 ports for shipps to ride in, and be recruited with all sorts of provisions, which is done on very reasonable terms; the fertillity of the whole island produces corn of all sorts in great plenty, and all sorts of cattle and butter cheese as also great stores of fish and fowle; there is some little part forrest land, but for the most part are meddows and good downs.

The little ports are all fitted for the Seamen and their affaires—little houses, not but there are severall good old houses that are gentlemens Seats, as Sir Robert Dilington [Dillington] at Knighton and Sir John Oglander[8] at Nun-well, Sir Robert Worstly[9] and severall more; Sir Robert Holmes[10] has a good Estate there he was the Governour of the Island and of Yarmouth Castle, and there he is buried where is his Statue cutt in length in white marble in the Church and railed in with Iron-Grates, he was raised from nothing and an imperious Governor and what he scrap'd together was forced to leave to his Nephew and base

[8] The old Cavalier whose *Diary* has been published.
[9] The Worsleys were of Appuldurcombe.
[10] Sir Robert Holmes of Thorley, a famous admiral under Charles II, had died in 1692, leaving his estate to his nephew on condition that he should marry his uncle's bastard daughter.

Daughter, haveing no other, and they have set up this stately Monument which cost a great deal; there is one place called Mottstone [Mottistone] just by the sea side, the name comes from many Great Stones that stand up in the grounds not unlike the stones at Stonidge [Stonehenge] in Wiltshire, but this sort of Stone is in many places of the Island and most of the houses are built of Stone, some few Brick; from a hill just above Cowes that runns along by the Sea-side you may easily see Spitt-head and St. Hellens Point and all the Shipps that lay along the Road and that lay in Portsmouth Haven; from Ride [Ryde] is 3 leagues to Portsmouth I pass'd it in an hour; Portsmouth is a very good town well built with Stone and Brick its not a large town, there are Walls and Gates about it and at least eight Bridges and Gates without one another with Ditches which secures it very strongly to the Landward; to the Sea the fortifications are not so strong, there is a plattform with Guns and Pallisadoes; there is a good dock for building shipps, but about 6 mile off at Burston [Bursledon] and Red bridge are the best shipps built; there are most of the great shipps lye at anchor here.

I was a board the Royall Charles[11] and the Royal James which are fine shipps the Roomes spacious for length and breadth but not high, there was a large Chappel and Cabbin with damaske furniture; the Castle at Portsmouth is not great its rather called the Kings House where is a great deal of armes; I was in the Dineing Roome where King Charles the Second met Queen Katherine and was marryed to her and set the crown on her head; there from that roome out of double doores goes a long wooden bridge to the Plattforme; just by is South sea Castle which is wash'd round by the sea and pretty deep water att Spring tides, it looks very fine but think its but of little Strength or Service; above the town is a very fine down called Porchester [Portchester] Down very pleasant for Sports Hawking and Hunting: 6 mile over this down is Southwicke, Col. Nortons,[12] a good old house

[11] The *Royal Charles* had been captured by the Dutch in the Medway in 1667, perhaps the worst humiliation inflicted on that occasion.
[12] Colonel Richard Norton of Southwick (1615–91) had married Elizabeth

capable of being made fine large Garden room Woods and Grounds lying well about it and a good Warren Coppices and the stately'st Timber trees as may be seen; he was an old officer in the Long Parliament service.

This is 15 mile from Winchester, and from Winchester to South-hampton is ten miles—that is a very neat clean town and the Streets well pitch'd and kept so by their carrying all their carriages on sleds as they do in Holland, and permit no Cart to go about in the town and keep it clean swept, this was formerly more strictly observ'd when the town was full of trade for it is a good Port, but now the trade has failed and the town almost forsooke and neglected;[13] its a place of no strength now by reason of the Castle being ruined and the Fortifications neglected and the Gunns taken thence, tho' by most its thought the best scittuated port for shipps to ride and take their provision in, and so capable of tradeing, but the last 2 Reignes for near 40 year discourag'd it, being a proper place for the French to have seiz'd and secured for themselves; about 3 leagues off is Cashot [Calshot] Castle just out into the Sea, which does encompasse it all but a very little point of land called Horsy Beach that runnes out into the New Forrest by Bewly [Beaulieu] which was an Abby in the Forrest, for the extent of the Forrest is large miles long; all round Cashott Castle on the beach itts as full of fine Cockle shells so that they heap them up all round the Castle like a wall; it was at South-hampton King Philip landed when he came to marry Queen Mary.

From thence its 6 miles to Rumsey [Romsey] and the road runns just by a fine house of one of my Relations Sir

Fiennes, Celia's aunt. One of his daughters had married Celia's uncle, Henry Whitehead. Colonel Norton was a stalwart old Parliamentarian. In 1660 he had stood out for the recall of all "purged" members of the Long Parliament, regardless of how they might vote, saying "that freedom of Parliament was the just right and interest of the nation and if they thought it fit to bring in the Turk, they ought not to be imposed on the contrary". (*Verney Memoirs*, ii, 154.) He became Governor of Portsmouth and still held that important post at the time of the Revolution, during which he suffered from a highly diplomatic form of gout. (*Hist. MSS. Comm., Dartmouth MSS.*, iii, 135.)

[13] Southampton had lost its trade in French wine. (See Baskerville, op. cit., p. 287.)

John St. Barbe's,[14] the rows of trees in the avenues runns just from the road to the front of the house; you enter a Court thats wall'd in and blew iron gates, the Court has a round in the middle rail'd in, designed for a Bowling Green, and the Coaches drive round it to come to the Entrance which is severall stone stepps to a broad space that is railed with balls and banisters, the space is paved with broad free stone the stepps the same 8 or 10; the house is a halfe Roman H the hall is in the middle with double doores, its very lofty and large there's a Chimney just against the entrance, on the right hand runns in an entry through the house to the back yard where are the offices Stillhouse and Barnes and Coach houses and a very fine Stable built of brick, there are large partitions; in this entry you have the Pantry and Cellars and on the other side the Kittchin Larders and Pastry which is one wing of the house, and just behind the hall is the Servants hall and a little parlour just by the pantry and back staires, then the Great Hall is divided in halfe by the Staircase which hangs on its own work not supported of either side to the first half pace[15] and all the way up without support on the one side; they are of oake the railes and banisters are varnished; the halfe paces are inlaid with yew wood, which lookes a yellowish red, in squaires; they land on the next story with a space of this Inlaid worke of a good bigness the whole compass of the Staircase; the roof of the Staires is even with the roofe of the next Story; on the other side of the Staires are severall rows of Pillars of wood painted like marble for to walke between, and you pass quite under the Staires into a little Closet and a little farther into a back yard where is a Bathing house and other necessarys; there is a screen stands on the side of the Staires next the Chimney to make that part more private; the hall runns quite through to the Garden where there is a door with stepps down and so

[14] Sir John St. Barbe (1655–1723) who was made a baronet at the age of eight, married (1) Honor, daughter of Richard Norton (see above), (2) Alice, daughter of Celia's uncle John Fiennes, widow of John Horn of Winchester. (The "Mrs. Horn" visited by Celia Fiennes.) Sir John St. Barbe's seat was Broadlands, near Romsey, which was to be the seat of Lord Palmerston in later days.
[15] Half-pace, either a dais or a landing part-way up a staircase.

at this door you see thro' the house to that back yard I mention'd at the end of the entry; the other wing of the house is a large parlour and drawing roome this is out of the hall by the Garden, the hall is well painted and a carved Cornish [Cornice] round and pillars on the wanscoate round the room; the parlour is wanscoated and painted a cedar coullour; the next story you enter of [off] this large halfe pace on the right hand, into a door which leads fore right to a Balcony and on the left hand into a passage which leads to the chamber over the drawing roome and by it is a Servants roome even with the passage; on the right hand is a passage leads to another roome just over-against; open the doores and there is a perfect visto, so there is the other way and a Servants roome even with the passage; beyond this roome is a back Stair leads to the bath and by the Servants roome is a large back Staire that leads to the next story the Great Stairs ending here; and on the left hand they lead into a large dineing roome and then a drawing roome and next a bed chamber which has a back doore to the back Staires by the kitchin, these doores open through to the end one way the best bed chamber and quite to the balcony, the other side a visto.

Within the dineing roome on the left hand is a very large bed chamber which indeed is the best good tapistry hangings, here is design'd a velvet bed, its painted white, there are very good Pictures; here is a little back staires to the Servants hall; the dineing roome is wanscoated and varnish'd—the other roomes nothing done to, that is the drawing roome and chamber; with in there is damaske and camlet beds in the other roomes and off these back staires by the kitchin is a chamber anty-roome dressing roome 2 closets; these back staires goe up to the next story that leads to the roomes over this and to a long Gallery that is window all to the front and leads to all the Chambers; there is handsome roomes only those at the side and end are Garret fashion, between are Servants roomes and closets thence a little pair of staires leads up to the Gallery and thence up to the Cupilow which is in the middle of the house all Windows round, and on the top has a Gold Ball that holds severall gallons; on each Wing there are 2 little towers one has the Clock the other a Sun-dial and on the top two gold balls of a lesser size.

The Gardens are walled in, some with brest walls some higher with flower potts on them, severall places with open grates to look through with stone balls or figures on the pillars each side the Gates every way; there is a water house that by a Wheele casts up the water out of the River just by and fills the pipes to serve all the house and to fill the bason designed in the middle of the Garden with a Spout in the middle; the Gardens are not finish'd but will be very fine with large gates open to the Grounds beyond some of which are planted with trees; its a fine thing, but doubt its no very good aire, it stands in a low place near the River the hills all round on that side and the Mold and Soyle is black and such as they cut up for peate.

The road from hence to Salisbury is by White Parish and Juy [Ivy] Church and you come in sight of my Lord Coalrain [Coleraine] house [Longford House] that looks like a good Building of stone but its just so upon the great River [the Avon] that it looks like a little Castle or Shipp;[16] this river runns to Breamore from Salisbury just by a very fine Seat of the Lady Brooks which was Sir William Doringtons [Dodington] heir; the house stands finely to the River, a brick building, you enter into a walled Court low up 12 stepps at least into a noble hall, on the left hand was a parlour and on the right a large drawing roome a little parlour and large Staires up to severall very handsom Chambers furnish'd with good tapistry and damaske and some velvets which was new, because the fire had spoiled most of the goods but the house was built just in the same figure; the kitchins and offices are all under the Roomes of State and they go down steps to it under the arch of stepps that ascend to the hall; out of the drawing roome by Glass doors you enter the Garden on a terrass and that by stepps so to severall Walks of Gravel and Grass and to the Gardens

16 Longford House was built during Elizabeth's reign on a triangular plan with towers at each corner. (H.A.T.)

one below another with low walls to give the view all at once; here was fine flowers and greens dwarfe trees and oring and lemon trees in rows with fruite and flowers at once, and some ripe, they are the first oring trees I ever saw; here are stately woods and walks.

This River runns to Fording bridge a little place thence to Ringwood thence to Christchurch; it turns many great Mills and there have been great attempts to make it navigable which would be of great advantage but all charge has been lost in it; there is store of good fish in it, it runns to Christ-church and divides the New Forrest from Wiltshire; there is a large Bridge that crosses at Christchurch where it runns into the Sea; this is 18 miles from Salisbury; Southampton is 20 miles from Salisbury 20 miles from Newtontony over the down 6 to Rumsy [Romsey] 4 to Lockerly two to East Titherly [Tytherley] where Sir Francis Rowles [Rolle] has a fine House and Garden and Groves; one on the edge of the hill all in sight of the road looks finely of Scott and Norro-way firrs in rows looks very well; in 2 mile of this is Dean which was Sir John Evlings [Evelyn], now his Grandsons Lord Kingston, it seems to be a good lofty Building, its woody and very fruitfull; there is likewise a good old Seate of Mr. Whiteheads[17] my Grandfathers, Normans Court in West Titherly, its well wooded good Gardens but a very old House a fine grove of firs to the front; this is 7 mile from Newtontony and as much to Stockbridge which is the Road to London thence to Sutton [Sutton Scotney] 12 mile thence to Basin-stoake 12 mile—its a large town and has a good trade being a Road; a mile thence is Basin [Basing House] on the left hand which was a house of the Duke of Boltons[18] but being a Garrison in the Civil warrs was pulled down and

[17] Colonel Richard Whitehead (1594–1663) father, by his first wife Mar-gery Culliford, of Celia Fiennes' mother.
[18] Charles Paulet (1625–1699) formerly Marquis of Winchester, was created Duke of Bolton in 1689. He was an ardent Whig who, in conscious imitation of Junius Brutus under the Tarquins, feigned madness in James II's reign. He toured the country with four coaches and a hundred horsemen, sleeping by day and carousing or hunting by torchlight all night. (See Sir John Reresby, *Memoirs*, ed. 1904, pp. 292–3 and Burnet, *History*, ed. 1823, iv, 403.)

now only some part remaines, and the Gardens which are improved and new walls built fine fruit and vineyards a large parke to it; on the right hand about a mile off is Hackwood which is another Seate of the Duke of Boltons in a pretty parke it looks very pretty not large; Basinstoake lyes watrish but its on chalke; a little further on the left hand at some distance you see a fine Seate [Bramshill] of Sir Robert Henleys it looks like a little town its so large a building and they say its a noble thing finish'd and furnish'd very well with good Gardens.

To Harfordbridge 8 mile thence to Bagshott 8 mile a heavy sandy way and the same from thence to Egum [Egham] 8 mile, thence to Staines a mile where we cross the Thames on a bridge and enter Middlesex thence to London 15 miles.

10. HAMPTON COURT

I went to see Hampton Court 10 mile from London it looks like a little town the buildings runn so great a length on the ground, the old buildings and the new part which King William and Queen Mary built; the Queen took great delight in it, the new was but just the shell up and some of the Roomes of State ceil'd but nothing finished,[1] the roomes were very lofty round a large Court and all the appartments intire; the old buildings were on the other side the Privy Garden; there was the Water Gallery that opened into a ballcony to the water and was decked with China[2] and fine pictures of the Court Ladyes drawn by Nellor [Kneller]; beyond this came severall roomes and one was pretty large, at the four corners were little roomes like closets or drawing roomes one pannell'd all with Jappan another with Looking Glass and two with fine work under pannells of Glass; there was

[1] Hampton Court was still as it was when Queen Mary died in December 1694. Work on it was not begun again till 1699.
[2] Queen Mary had brought with her from Holland an interest in porcelain and other forms of "Chinoiserie", and had started an English fashion for such things.

the Queens Bath and a place to take boat in the house; the Gardens were designed to be very fine, great fountaines and grass plotts and gravell walkes and just against the middle of the house was a very large fountaine and beyond it a large Cannal guarded by rows of even trees that runn a good way; there was fine carving in the Iron Gates in the Gardens with all sorts of figures, and iron spikes round on a breast wall and severall rows of trees.

JOURNEYS
IN 1697

SCARBOROUGH
RIPON
BOROUGH-
BRIDGE
BURTON
AGNES
KNARESBOROUGH
HARROGATE
YORK
TADCASTER
HULL
PONTEFRACT
DONCASTER
ROTHERHAM
CASTLETON
BUXTON
LINCOLN
NEWARK
UTTOXETER
NOTTINGHAM
GRANTHAM
WOLSELEY
STAMFORD
PETERBOROUGH
COVENTRY
HUNTINGDON
WARWICK
NORTHAMPTON
CAMBRIDGE
BISHOPS
STORTFORD
AMWELL
ST. ALBANS
LONDON
ROCHESTER
CANTERBURY
MAIDSTONE
DEAL
TUNBRIDGE
WELLS
DOVER
RYE
WINCHELSEA

HELEN MORRIS
1946

PART II

THE NORTHERN JOURNEY AND THE TOUR OF KENT (1697)

1. FROM AMWELL BY CAMBRIDGE AND LINCOLN TO NOTTINGHAM

HERE BEGINS My Northern Journey in May 1697.

From London to Amwell Berry[1] in Hartfordshire 19 mile thence to Bishops Startford [Stortford] in Essex 13 mile which is a very pretty neat Market town a good Church and a delicate Spring of Water which has a wall built round it very sweet and cleare water for drinking, there is a little river runns by the town that feeds severall Mills.

Thence we went to Audlyend[2] [Audley End] 10 miles a house of the Earle of Sussex [Suffolk] which makes a noble appearance like a town, so many towers and buildings off stone within a parke which is walled round, a good River runs through it, we pass over the bridge; its built round 3 Courts, there are 30 great and little towers on the top and a great Cupilow in the middle, the roomes are large and lofty with good rich old furniture tapistry etc., but noe beds in that part we saw, there are 750 rooms in the house; the

---

[1] Amwell had come to Celia Fiennes' Uncle John through his wife, Susanna Hobbs. On his death in 1696 it passed to his son-in-law, Thomas Filmer, a well-known London lawyer, who had bought the reversion in 1693, (See Clutterbuck, *Hist. and Antiquities of Hertford*, ii, 11, and *Victoria County History, Hertfordshire*, iii, 417.) Celia Fiennes most probably travelled on this journey with one or both of Filmer's daughters, Susanna and Mary.

[2] Audley End was built by the Earl of Suffolk (not Sussex) between 1603 and 1616. Part of it, however, had already been demolished by 1662. Defoe spoke of it as "built by, and decaying with, the noble Dukes and Earls of Suffolk" (op. cit., i, 88) but Thoresby in 1680 had still found it "the greatest house in England . . . a vast building or rather town walled in". (*Diary*, i, 65.)

"The magnitude of this house is reported to be such, that it is a day's work for a running footman to open and shut the windows. . . ." (Edw. Ward, *Works*, vol. ii, p. 231–2.)

Cannall in the midst of the parke look'd very fine its altogether a stately palace and was built for one of the kings.

Thence to Little-berry [Littlebury] one mile where is a house with abundance of fine Curiosityes all performed by Clockwork and such like which appears very strange to the beholders but the Master[3] was not at home so I saw no more than the Chaire they set in when they are carryd about; all the Country is pleasant between this and Cambridge you go in sight of so many neate villages with rows of trees about them and very neate built Churches sometimes 5 or 6 of these are in view together in 3 or four mile of each other, the Churches are stone-work. We went to Babaram [Babraham] where was a house of Sir Richard Bennets in a pleasant parke prettyly situated only it is in a low ground but the fine rows of trees in the severall avenues came just down to the Road, thence to Bornbridge [Bourn Bridge] 5 mile,[4] thence to Hodmogoge [Gogmagog] hills 3 mile which looks at a distance like a long Barn, but when you approach near you see it a great fortification or ruines of a Castle with great trenches one within another, and all the buildings there is only a long string of Stables[5] to keep the kings hunting horses; the hill is of a great heigth from whence you have a great prospect of the whole Country and of Cambridge which is 3 mile off; the town which lyes in a bottom and marshy ground all about it severall miles which is garnish'd with willows; the Buildings are old and indifferent the Streets mostly narrow except near the Market place which is pretty spacious, there stands the University Church.

Trinity Colledg is the finest yet not so large as Christchurch College in Oxford; in the first Court there is a very fine fountaine in the middle of the Quadrangle with a carved

[3] Henry Winstanley, the builder of the Eddystone Lighthouse. His whimsical mechanical inventions brought many visitors to his house. The "Chaire" was one "which runs backward into the garden on a rail". Winstanley also had a "water theatre in which tea and coffee were laid on in pipes and cups presented to the company. At the close all the pipes threw jets of water". (Z. C. von Uffenbach's Travels in England in *Cambridge under Queen Anne*, ed. Mayor, pp. 355 and 373.)

[4] She had actually passed Bourn Bridge before she came to Babraham.

[5] The stables were built by James II.

top and Dyals round; there are large Cloysters [in] the Second and the Library[6] runns all the rang of building at the end and stands on 3 rows of stone pillars; it opens into the Gardens and Walk with 3 large Gates or doores of iron carv'd very fine with flowers and leaves; the river runs at the back side of most of the Colleges; they have fine stone bridges over it and gates that lead to fine walks, the rivers name is Cam; the Library farre exceeds that of Oxford, the Staires are wanscoated and very large and easye ascent all of Cedar wood, the room spacious and lofty paved with black and white marble, the sides are wanscoated and decked with all curious books off Learning their Catalogue and their Benefactors; there is two large Globes at each end with teliscopes and microscopes and the finest Carving in wood in flowers birds leaves figures of all sorts as I ever saw; there is a large Balcony opens at the end that answers to the Staires.

King's College Chapple is the finest building I have heard off; curious Carvings of Stone on the out side, 12 large windows and two at each end very large, all finely painted all over the history of the new testament;[7] its a hundred and twenty steps to the roofe and supported by noe pillars all arch of stone, you walke on the arch or cradle as its term'd, there is 32 little windows cut in stone just as you ascend to the cradle or arch which runns on either side, and a pair of staires of 8 stepps to every three windows which lead up to the arch; thence you ascend the Leads over all which are fine secured by battlements round, there are 4 large Spires, at each corner one: on these Leads you may see a vast Country round, you see Ely-Minster and the towers; this is a noble building and stands on so advantagious a ground and so lofty built that its perspicious above the town; this is in lieu of the theatre at Oxford there being none here.

St Johns College Garden is very pleasant for the fine

[6] Wren's Library, begun in 1676, was complete in 1690, all but the balcony which was put up 1693–5. By "the Second" Celia Fiennes means Neville's Court.

[7] The windows of King's Chapel were not universally admired in the seventeenth century. Peter Mundy, the great Cornish traveller, in 1639 had thought them "not soe artificiall, nett, and true as now adaies are made off that kind". (*Travels*, ed. Hakluyt Society, iv, 33.)

walks, both close shady walks and open rows of trees and quickeset hedges, there is a pretty bowling green with cut arbours in the hedges; Queens College is old but a stately and lofty building; Claire Hall [Clare College] is very little but most exactly neate; in all parts they have walks with rows of trees and bridges over the river and fine painted gates into the fields; Katherine Hall [St. Catharine's College] is new built the Chapple was not quite finish'd,[8] the apartments for the Fellows and Gentlemen Commoners are very fine, a large dineing-roome a good Chamber and good Studdy and this for 8£ a year; here we were entertained by some of our Companys acquaintance.

From Cambridge we go just by Peterborough we see the Minster and the town very plaine all built with Stone; the road is very pleasant to Fenistanton [Fenstanton] 8 miles, to Godmanchester 3 and from thence Huntington 1 mile; we cross the River Lin[9] over a bridge and so enter Huntingtonshire this river goes to Lin [Kings Lynn] in Norfolke; its a very pleasant country to travel in in the Summer but after raines its in some places deep but the prospects are delighting, little town and good Enclosures with woods and some open countrys; Huntington is but a small Shire town, just by it is a house [Hinchingbrooke] of the Lord Sandwitch, it is pretty large; we enter a good lofty hall, in it hangs the Ship in which he was lost that is the representation of it cut out in little and all things exactly made to it;[10] there is a good parlour and drawing roome, well proportion'd are the rooms with good old furniture and good pictures there is a large dineing roome above with good tapistry hangings and its ceil'd with Irish oake carv'd with points hanging down like fine fret worke, this wood no spider will weave on or endure; there are good bed chambers with good furniture and fine Pictures, over one of the Chimneys is a fine picture

[8] St. Catharine's College was rebuilt 1673–1704. Work on the Chapel was stopped temporarily in 1697 through lack of funds.

[9] Celia Fiennes more than once uses this name for the Ouse.

[10] Edward Montagu, First Earl of Sandwich, to whom Pepys was Secretary at the Admiralty. He was blown up at the Battle of Sole Bay in 1672, and his body, found afterwards near Harwich, was buried in Westminster Abbey.

of Venus were it not too much uncloth'd, the Gardens and Wilderness and Greenhouse will be very fine when quite finish'd, with the dwarfe trees and gravell-walks, there is a large fountaine or bason which is to resemble that in the privy garden at White hall which will front the house; the high terrass walks look out on the Road; all this Country is good land and fruitfull and much like Oxfordshire.

From Huntington we came to Stilton 10 mile and came in sight of a great water on the right hand about a mile off which looked like some Sea it being so high and of a great length, this is in part of the fenny country and is called Whitl-some Mer[11] [Whittlesey Mere], is 3 mile broad and six mile long, in the midst is a little island where a great store of Wildfowle breeds, there is no coming near it in a mile or two, the ground is all wett and marshy but there are severall little Channells runs into it which by boats people go up to this place; when you enter the mouth of the Mer it looks formidable and its often very dangerous by reason of sudden winds that will rise like Hurricanes in the Mer, but at other tymes people boat it round the Mer with pleasure; there is abundance of good fish in it[12] this was thought to have been Sea some tyme agoe, and choak'd up, and so remaines all about it for some miles a fenny marshy ground for those little Rivers that runns into the Sea, some distance of miles; from hence to Water Newton 5 miles; thence to Wansfford 2 miles thence to Stamfford 5 miles.

We pass over a down where is a Cross that directs three wayes York, London and Oatly [?] in Wales, and here we come in sight of a Gentlemans house that stands finely on a hill in a parke pretty high with fine groves about it; a little farther when we are pass'd the water att Wansford we enter Ruttlandshire which seems more woody than the others.

Stamfford town is as fine a built town all of stone as may be seen, its on the side of a hill which appears very fine in the approach; severall very good Churches with high Spires

---

[11] The mere was drained c. 1851.
[12] Defoe relates that a flourishing trade was done by sending these fish alive in butts to London. (Op. cit., ii, 100–101.)

and Towers very ornamentall, its not very large but much finer than Cambridge, and in its view has severall good houses; on the right hand of Stamfford is a house of Mr. Neals, in a pretty neate parke pailed in, the house not very big but lookes well; on the side of the hill over against Stamfford and on the left hand overagainst the town stands my Lord of Exeters Burly [Burghley] House[13] eminent for its Curiosity; the Scituation is the finest I ever saw on the edge of the hill and severall rows of trees of severall acres above it quite to the Road, it stands in a very fine parke which is full of deer and fine rows of trees; you ascend to the house thro' the midst of rows of trees on either side a very broad Glide or visto that looks finely to the River and to the adjacent hills, a distance cloth[ed] with fine woods; the town of Stamfford appears very fine on the left hand and most noble woods on the right hand, the house looks very nobly, the Gardens very fine within one another with lower and higher walls deck'd with all sorts of trees and greens, very fine Gravel walks and Grass squaires with Statues and fine Grass walks, dwarfs and all sorts of green trees and curious things, very fine fountaines, there is one in the middle of the Garden thats just to the middle also of the house, that is of an exceeding great size; there is a fine Vineyard Warren and Groves which makes its prospects very delightful.

You enter a large Court walled, thence to a space of ground pretty large encompass'd round with a little wall of a yard high, of free stone very fine wrought, on which are to be iron railes and spires, that was not finish'd nor the space paved, which is design'd to be of broad stone; all before the house the little breast wall is in a Compass like a halfe Moone; the Sides up to the house are built in roomes for appartments, you ascend the house by stone steps about 12 that all turn round; the upper Stepp is at least 20 footsteps in compass, the door you enter is of iron carv'd the finest I ever saw, all sorts of leaves flowers figures birds beast

[13] Burghley House was built by Thorpe for the first Lord Burghley. It had just been altered by the fifth Earl of Exeter, who died of a surfeit of fruit at Issy in 1700.

68

wheate in the Carving; very large the doors are, there is an inside doore as case to it; on the other side of the house is such another door, that leads into a Court; the hall is a noble roome painted finely,[14] the walls with armory and Battles, its lofty and paved with black and white marble; you go thence into parlours dineing rooms drawing roomes and bed-chambers, one leading out of another at least 20 that were very large and lofty and most delicately painted on the top, each roome differing, very fine Carving in the mantle-pieces and very fine paint in pictures, but they were all without Garments or very little, that was the only fault, the immodesty of the Pictures especially in my Lords appartment; his bed chamber was furnish'd very rich the tapistry was all blew Silke and rich gold thread, so that the gold appeared for the light part of all the worke; there was a blew velvet bed with gold fringe and very richly embroidered all the inside with ovals on the head piece and tester where the figures are so finely wrought in satten stitch it looks like painting; there is also my Ladys appartment; severall roomes very richly furnish'd and very fine tapistry with silver and gold in most, there was at least 4 velvet beds 2 plaine and 2 figured crimson green severall coullours together in one, severall damaske beds and some tissue beds all finely embroydered; my Ladyes Closet is very fine the wanscoate of the best Jappan the cushons very rich work; there is a great deale of fine worke under glasses and a Glass-case full of all sorts of Curiosityes of amber stone, currall [coral] and a world of fine things. My Lord Excetter [Exeter] in his travells was for all sorts of Curious things if it cost him never so much, and a great many of my Ladyes fine things were given her by her Mother the Countess of Devonshire; there is a Chamber my Lady used to lye in in the Winter a green velvet bed and the hangings are all Embroydery of her Mothers work, very fine, the silk looks very fresh and figures look naturall.

[14] By Antonio Verrio (1639–1707) who was employed at Burghley for twelve years. "For the Bacchus bestriding a hogshead, he has, according to his usual liberty, borrowed the countenance of a dean with whom he was at variance." (Walpole: *Anecdotes of Painting*.)

There is a drawing room by that which has a great Curiosity that my Lord brought from beyond sea, on the Mantlepiece under a glass, its nunns work the finest Embroidery that it looks just like point or the finest linnen you can see, this cost a great Sume; there are fine Chimney-pieces of Marble and the windows the same; there are at least 20 rooms very large and lofty that are all painted on the top, there are at least 20 on the other side of the house all with different frett works on the Ceiling besides almost as many more roomes that are a building, some the floores not laid others not finish'd yet the house will be a vast thing when done, the floores were Inlaid in severall roomes, the Chapple is old and not to abide, the painting is good but the place is not suteable to any part else; the great variety of the roomes and fine works tooke me up 2 full hours to go from on roome to another over the house; the Bowling-green Wilderness nor Walke I was not in, being so great a tract of ground, but you see it all at a view on the top of the house, it is esteemed the finest house and scituation that is in England and will be very compleate when finish'd.

From thence we went to Streton [Stretton] 6 mile a little house of one Mr. Horsman, very good Plantations of trees about it stone building. Rutlandshire seemes more woody and inclosed than some others; thence to Colson [Colsterworth] where Lincolnshire comes in, 2 mile, thence towards Lincoln we go on a fine champion country much like Salisbury Plaine, and a large prospect all round at a distance; you see woods and towns, this is the best part of this shire, for most part is fenny; and we went twenty six miles all on such way quite to Lincoln town, we pass by Grantum [Grantham] which is a good town 16 mile from Lincoln, all built with Stone but lies down in a low bottom, the Church has a very high Steeple[15] its seen above a great hill that is by it of a great length, and 'tis a long tyme when you see a great part of the Steeple ere you come to see the Church or town, it lies so in a bottom.

Lincoln opens to view at least 6 miles off, it stands on a

15 280 feet.

very high hill and looks very fine at the entrance, the houses stand compact together the Streetes are but little, but its a vast hill to ascend into the town where the Minster stands, by that meanes its very perspicious and eminently in view a great many miles off; the tower that Great Thoms Nest is 250 steps up, 8 persons may very well stand up In the hollow of the bell together, its as much as a man can reach to the top of the bell with his hand when he is in the inside, its rarely ever rung but only by ringing the Clapper to each side— which we did—and that sounds all over the town; the houses are but small and not lofty nor the Streetes of any breadth; the Sea has formerly come up to the town and that has been very deep water where now great part of the town is built, so that what was the town formerly is that which stands upon a precipice as it were of a hill, the water is choaked up now and the Sea comes not near in severall miles and what water they have is called Lincoln Dike, you pass it over on a bridge.[16]

We went thence by many very fine Seates we pass by Sir John Brownlows [Belton Hall] and severall others thence to Newark 12 mile in Nottinghamshire; just by it you see a very pretty new house of brick building [Averham] of the Lord Lexingtons, with the walls and towers that looks very well; Newark is a very neate Stone built town the market place is very large and look'd fine, just by it is the Great Church which is large and with a very high Spire, there is prayers twice a day in it; there remaines the holes in the Church walls that the bullets made which were shott into the town in the Siege laid to it by the Parliament army in the Civil Warrs; the Castle was then demolish'd so that only the ruinated walls remaine which is washed by a very pretty river.

At this we enter Nottinghamshire and here I met with the strongest and best Nottingham ale that looked very pale but

---

[16] This was the canal on which Lincoln's trade had depended. It was rapidly falling into disuse in 1672 when the Frenchman, "Jorevin de Rocheford" published his *Description of England and Ireland*. (See Trans. in Grose, *Antiquarian Repertory*, 1809, iv, 617.) Defoe speaks of Lincoln as "an old, dying, decay'd, dirty city". (Op. cit., ii, 93.) Most contemporary writers quote a proverbial prophecy "Lincoln was, London is, York shall be".

exceeding clear, thence to Nottingham town, its 12 mile more and we fery'd over the Trent, which in some places is so deep but waggons and horses fords it; I rode along 7 or 8 mile by the Trent which is a fine River tho' not so broad as the Thames is at Kingston, but it look'd very pleasant to ride by its bancks for so many miles, and on the other side was a high Ridge of hills shaded over from the top to the bottom with fine trees and this for severall miles, when on the other hand you see a vast bottom called Note Vale, the wood belongs to one Mr. Heckam; you pass by severall pretty houses by the river side, stone buildings good gardens, and a little farther you see the Lord Kingstons house which is contigeous to Nottingham town called Home Peirpoynt [Holme Pierrepont] which looks finely in woods.

The town of Nottingham[17] is the neatest town I have seen, built of stone and delicate large and long Streetes much like London and the houses lofty and well built, the Market place is very broad—out of which runns 2 very large streetes much like Holborn but the buildings finer and there is a Pyaza all along one side of one of the Streetes, with stone pillars for walking that runns the length of the Streete, which is a mile long; all the streetes are of a good size all about the town and well pitch'd, there are severall good houses in the town, there are 3 or 4 large houses of the Duke of New-castles with the Castle,[18] which is a fine thing stands very high on a hill and when you come to the Castle you ascend 40 steps to the Court and Hall, the roomes are very lofty and large, 6 or 7 state roomes, and a long gallery hung with fine Pictures of the family, the wanscoate is most of Cedar; some roomes are hung with good tapistry, the Chamber of State is hung with very rich tapistry so much silver and gold in it that the 3 pieces that hung the roome cost 1500£; the bed

[17] Nottingham was Celia Fiennes' favourite town which she used as a standard of comparison. She was at one with Baskerville, who thought Nottingham "Paradise restored, for here you find large streets, fair built houses, fine women, and many coaches rattling about, and their shops full of merchantable goods". (Op. cit., 308.)

[18] The old Castle, pulled down at the Restoration (partly because it had been held against Charles I) was sold to and rebuilt by the Duke of Newcastle in 1674.

was rail'd in as the presence chamber used to be—the bed was damaske; the floore of the roome was inlay'd with Cyphers and the Corronet, here the Princess Ann lay when she fled in King James's tyme when the Prince of Orange was coming over; on the Leads you have a very fine prospect of the whole town and river, you see the Earle of Kingstones and Sir Thomas Willoughbys fine house [Wollaton] on the other side of the town, and at a distance we see Beavior [Belvoir] Castle the Earle of Rutlands house, and a prospect more than 20 mile about shewing the diversityes of Cultivations and produce of the Earth, the land is very rich and fruitfull, so the green Meadows with the fine Corn fields, which seemes to bring forth in handfulls, they sow most of Barley and have great encrease, there is all sorts of Graine besides, and Plaines and Rivers and great Woods, and little towns all in view.

They make brick and tile by the town; the manufacture of the town mostly consists in weaving of Stockings, which is a very ingenious art; there was a man that spunn Glass and made severall things in Glass birds and beasts, I spunn some of the glass and saw him make a Swan presently, with divers coulloured glass he makes Buttons which are very strong and will not breake; Nottingham is famous for good ale so for Cellars they are all dugg out of the rocks and so are very coole, att the Crown Inn is a Cellar of 60 stepps down all in the Rock like arch worke over your head, in the Cellar I dranke good ale; we were very well entertained and very reasonably att the Blackmoors Head.

2. THROUGH YORK AND HARROGATE TO HULL AND BURTON AGNES

THENCE WE went to Mansfield 12 mile and pass'd some part of the fine Forrest of Sherwood; Mansfield is a little Market town built with stone, there is a little river, they make and dye Tammy's here; there is one pretty stone built house just by the waterside of 40 stepps ascent into it; at the end of the town is an hospital built by a quaker for ancient people, its a good neat building they were to have 8 pound a year a piece and the roomes and gardens, but its chiefly for their friends; there is nothing remarkable here but the dearness of the Inns, tho' in so plentifull a Country.[1]

We went thence to Wursup [Worksop] and went through a parke of the Duke of Newcastles and by his house call'd Welbeake [Welbeck]; the house is but old and low buildings but the parke is the noblest wood I ever saw, fine and stately straight; a mile thence is a fine pile of Buildings of stone very uniforme and high called Worsup Mannour, built by a Coe-heir of the Devonshire house—3 sisters built 3 noble buildings, this and Ardeck [Hardwick] and Chattsworth;[2] a little beyond this is another Building the remaines of Worsup Abby.

All the way to Blith [Blyth] is a very heavy sandy way 12 miles; at Blith was a very sweete House[3] and Gardens and Grounds, it was of brick work coyn'd with stone and the Windows with stone all sashes, the building was so neate and exact, it was square with 4 juttings out at each corner; it stands high and commands the sight of the Country about,

---

[1] At Mansfield Baskerville had been better pleased. His Inn was kept by "persons well-bred" and he had been given "excellent claret, potted venison and other victuals well dressed". (Op. cit., 309.)

[2] Worksop, Hardwick and Chatsworth—as well as part of Welbeck and Bolsover—were, in fact, all built by the redoubtable "Bess of Hardwick" (1518-1608) gaoler of Mary Queen of Scots.

> "Four times the nuptial bed she warm'd,
> And every time so well perform'd,
> That when death spoiled each Husband's billing
> He left the widow every shilling.
> Sad was the dame, but not dejected;
> Five stately mansions she erected
> With more than royal pomp, to vary
> The prison of her captive Mary.
> When Hardwick tow'rs shall bow their head,
> Nor Mass be more in Worksop said,
> When Bolsover's fair fame shall tend
> Like Oldcotes, to its mould'ring end;
> When Chatsworth taste no Candish bounties
> Let fame forget this costly Countess."
>
> (*Letters of Horace Walpole*, ed. Toynbee, iv, 425.)

[3] Blyth Abbey, rebuilt *c.* 1684 by Edward Mellish, a London merchant in the Oporto trade; his operations included "cutting the river straight before the said house". (J. Raine, *History of Blyth*.) (H.A.T.)

the fine river by it with fish ponds and meadows and fine woods beyond makes it look very pleasant, the Gardens are very neate and after the London Mode of Gravel and Grass walks and Mount, and the Squaires with dwarfes and Cyprus firre and all sorts of greens and fruite trees; its very fruitefull I eate good fruite there; its just by the Church so that a large Arch which did belong to the Church is now made a shady seate to the Garden, with greens over it, under which is a Sepulchre for the family; it belongs to one Mr. Mellish a Merchant in London, its in all parts a most compleate thing and its scituation most pleasant.

Almost all the road between this and Doncaster is sandy way, to Rosdin [Rossington] 3 mile, thence to Doncaster 6 mile; here Yorkshire beginns and here the Musick well-com'd us into Yorkshire: Doncaster is a pretty large town of Stone Buildings, the streetes are good; there is a handsome Market Cross advanc'd on 20 steps at least, the Church is neate and pretty large, severall little Monuments; this town stands on the River Don which gives name to the town, here is also a good large Meeteing place; we were here the Lord's day and well entertained at the Angel, thence we went to Wentbridge and pass'd by woods belonging to Sir Went-worth;[4] by his house 7 mile to Wentbridge where had been a fire the night before caused by the Lightning and Thunder which was remarkably great, as we took notice of 2 barnes and a house was burnt.

Thence we ascended a very steepe hill and so to Ferry-bridge 3 mile, where we pass'd the fine River called the Aire, large for Barges as was most of those Rivers I have mention'd.

From thence to Todcaster [Tadcaster] 8 mile which is a very good little town for travellers, mostly Inns and little tradesmens houses; this stands on a very large River called the Whart [Wharfe]; just before you come to the town there is some of the water which on great raines are not to be pass'd, it was very deep when I went through;[5] thence we go

---

[4] Sir John Wentworth of Elmsall and Brodsworth.
[5] Even in the summer Defoe found "there was no passing it without a boat". (Op. cit., ii, 227.)

much on a Causey[6] to Yorke 8 miles more; it stands high but for one of the Metropolis and the See of the Archbishop it makes but a meane appearance, the Streetes are narrow and not of any length, save one which you enter of from the bridge, that is over the Ouise which lookes like a fine river when full after much raine—it is but low in comparison of some rivers—it bears great Barges, it looks muddy; its full of good fish we eate very good Cod fish and Salmon and that at a pretty cheape rate tho' we were not in the best inn for the Angel is the best, in Cunny [Coney] Streete; the houses are very low and as indifferent as in any Country town, and the narrowness of the streetes makes it appear very mean.

Nottingham is so farre before it for its size—its true Nottingham is not a quarter so bigg—else the Streetes and buildings are so much nobler as can be imagin'd, it looks better att the approach, because you see the towers off the gates and severall Churches in compassing the Minster and all the Windmills round the town, of which there are many; the River runns through the town and so its divided, the buildings look no better than the outskirts off London Wappen [Wapping] etc. The Bridg is fine arches and built on with houses, the Pavement which is esteem'd the chiefe part of town, where the Market house and Town hall stands, is so mean that Southwarke is much before it; there are a great many pretty Churches 16 in number, but the Minster is a noble building and holds in view at least 30 mile before you come to it; I saw it and also at that distance, and saw just by it a high hill or fortification it appeared to be, but when I came to York I found it to be only a very high hill [Heslington] with stately high trees on it as thick as could be, a noble Grove; the Minster is very large and fine of stone, carv'd all the outside 3 high towers above the Leads, I was in one of them, the highest, and it was 262 steps and those very steep steps;[7] there is a Gallery round the middle of the Church about halfe way that goes off these steps of the tower,

---

[6] The Roman road running along the York moraine.

[7] Baskerville found that they "made my thighs ache very much, and I fell that night into a fever". (Op. cit., 311.)

where you may go round and looke down into the body of
the Church and that was so great a distance that the Men and
Ladyes that were walking below look'd like Pigmyes and
very little to us above; on the Leads of the tower shews a
vast prospect of the Country at least 30 mile round, you see
all over the town that lookes as a building too much cluster'd
together, the Streetes being so narrow, some were pretty
long.

There is another river which fills the ditches round the
town called Fosse; in the Minster there is the greatest
curiosity for Windows I ever saw they are so large and so
lofty, those in the Quire at the end[8] and on each side that is
3 storys high and painted very curious, with History of the
Bible; the painting is very fine such as was in Kings Chapple
in Cambridge, but the loftyness of the windows is more than
I ever saw any where else, and by all accounts is peculiar;
there is such another Window at the end of the Cross Ilse
just by the Quire, all the other Windows are of the usual size
of other Cathedralls; the body of the Church is large and I
thinke larger than any Cathedrall I have seen, bigger than
Winchester Cathedrall; all these Isles are broad, the people of
fashion use them to walke in and on that account its much[9]
they keep it not cleaner; the Quire has very good Carving in
Wood about it, there is a very good Organ, the table cloth
and cushons and books at the Comunion table was crimson
velvet and hangings, and its embroyder'd very richly with
gold of a great depth and gold fringe at the bottom; this was
given the Church by Doctor Lamplue [Lamplugh][10] that
was the Archbishop whose Statue is in white marble in the

[8] The east window is about 75 feet high.
[9] Here the manuscript omits some such word as "pity". Lord Harley, in
1725, noted that "in the main aisle . . . the gentlemen and ladies walk after
the evening service in the summertime, for want of a convenience of a park
or gardens". (*Portland MSS.*, vi, 93.)
[10] Thomas Lamplugh (1615–91) was Bishop of Exeter when William of
Orange landed at Torbay. Lamplugh hurried to King James to attest his
loyalty, and was at once made Archbishop of York. The new Archbishop
promptly transferred his devotion to the new King. (See Sir John Branston,
Autobiography. Ed. Camden Soc., p. 333 and Luttrell, op. cit., i, 476 and 484.)
His monument is in the south choir aisle. The other "Effigy" is that of
Archbishop Hutton (1529–1606).

wall, with Mitre and shepherds crook; just by him is the
Effigy of another Bishop laying along cut in stone, and by
the aire and mien he looks more like a Soldier or Beau than
a Bishop, and so it seemes he was in humour; the Embroidery
at the table is almost yard deep, that was given by Lamplue.

In the vestry there is a well of sweet spring-water called
St Peter's well, the Saint of the Church, so it is St Peter's
the Cathedrall is; there is a large hunters Horne[11] tipt with
silver and garnish'd over and engrav'd finely, all double gilt
with a chaine, the same given by a Gentleman that also gave
his Estate to add to the revenues of the Church, on a dislike
to disobedient children, he used the horne when he hunted
and drank in it to. I saw there the fine tissue Cannopy that
was held over the head of King James the first when he came
into England and the head of 2 mace which were carry'd
before him then; there I saw a Chest that was triangular
fashion the shape of the Coapes when folded in the middle
and so put into this Chest; the Chapter house is very finely
carv'd and fine painting on the windows all round, its all
arched Stone and supported by its own work having no
pillars to rest on tho' its length and breadth be equal and at
least 24 foot each; here was a Mint[12] for Coyning the old
money and plaite into new mill'd money, I saw them at work
and stamp'd one halfe crown my self, they dispatch worke
very fast and have coyn'd several 1000£; I see all parts of the
work about, the pounding the boyling refineing and makeing
Barres and cutting out in the mill and bakeing and stamping,
all but Milling which art they are sworne to keep private.

The houses aboute the Minster were the Doctors; the
Bishops Seate [Bishopthorpe] was 4 or 5 mile out of town on
the River Ouise; from thence we went over a marshy Comon
to the Spaw at Knarsborough [Knaresborough] 12 mile; the
town is a pretty stone building, in it a large Market place,
there is a River—the water looks black, I fancy it runns off

[11] The Horn of Ulphus, dating from the tenth century.
[12] Minting in the provinces was a recent emergency measure to meet a
temporary shortage of currency. It will be noticed, when Celia Fiennes sees
the mint at Norwich in the following year, that the re-coining is then over.
(Cf. Misson, op. cit., 61–3.)

from the Iron and Sulpher Mines which changes the coullour
—we pass it over on a large bridge, tho' in some places they
may ford it, its all on a rock and the side of the hill by the
River is all rock, and the little houses are all built in the
rocks, there is a little Chapple cut out of the Rock and
arch'd and carv'd with figures of Saints I suppose, its called
St Robert Chapple; he was esteemed a very devout man, his
Effigee is carv'd at the entrance there is an alter that was
deck'd with flowers and the ground with rushes for the devout that did frequent it; severall Papists there about and
many that came to the Spaw and St Mongers [Mungo's] well
did say their prayers there;[13] there was a Manuscript with a
long story of this St Robert, there is also the ruines of an
abbey where there has been many bones taken up and some
preserv'd as Reliques; there was a papist Lady lodg'd where
we did, and our Land Lady at the Inn where we were treated
civily she told us she went with this Lady among these ruines
where the Lady would say her prayers, and one day some
had been digging and brought up the bone of a mans arme
and hand and the ligature of the elbow held the bones together, which by strikeing came asunder, and in the hollow
part of the joynt was a jelly like blood that was moist, this
Lady dipp'd the end of her handkerchief in it and so cut it
off and put it up as a Relique.

There are the ruinated walls of the Castle remaines but of
no use, but some part is made a prison and some vaults made
Cellars, I dranke very strong clear ale in one of those Cellars;
we were in a very pretty Garden of a Gentlemans of our
Landlady Mason's acquaintance, where was all manner of
Curiosityes of Flowers and Greens, great variety, there is
also a Cherry Garden with green walkes for the Company to
walk in, and a Great Seate in a high tree that gives a pleasant
prospect.

From thence we went over to Haragate [Harrogate] which
is just by the Spaw, two mile further over a Common that
belongs to Knarsborough, its all marshy and wett and here

[13] For the cult of Holy Wells, still observed by Papists, see Introduction,
p. xxvi.

in the compass of 2 miles is 4 very different springs of water:
there is the Sulpher or Stincking spaw, not improperly
term'd for the Smell being so very strong and offensive that
I could not force my horse near the Well, there are two Wells
together with basons in them that the Spring rises up in,
which is furr'd with a White Scumm which rises out of the
water, if you keep it in a cup but a few hours it will have such
a White Scumm over it, notwithstanding it rises out of the
Spring very cleare, and so being a quick Spring itt soone
purges it self cleare againe, it comes from Brimstone mines
for the taste and smell is much of Sulpher, tho' it has an
additionall offenciveness like carrion or a jakes; the Ground
is Bitumus or the like that it runns over, it has a quality of
changing Silver into the coullour of Copper, and that in a
few minutes, much quicker than the Baths in the West
County in Somersetshire; its a quick purger and very good
for all Scurbutick humours; some persons drink a quart or
two—I dranke a quart in a morning for two days and hold
them to be a good sort of Purge if you can hold your breath
so as to drinke them down—within a quarter of a mile is
the Sweete Spaw or Chalibiet [Chalybeate]; a Spring which
rises off Iron and Steele like Astrup [Astrop] or Tunbridge
and like the German Spaw, this is a quick Spring and the
Well made up with a bason, and a cover of stone over it like
an arch; this opperates as all iron springs does, tho I could
not find them so strong or spiriteous as those at Tunbridge;
one thing I observ'd of the Stinking Spaw tho' its taste and
opperation was like the Sumersetshire Bathes, yet this was
not warme in the least as those Bathes are. Just between these
two Spaws is a fine cleare and sweete Spring of Comon water
very good to wash eyes and pleasant to drinke; the fourth
Spring which is but two mile off these, is of a petrifying
quality, turnes all things into stone, it rises in a banck on the
top of a hill and so runns along in a little Channell about a
foote over, and all the ground it runns over is moorish and
full of holes, with water standing in it, which stincks just
like the Sulpher Spaw, and will turn Silver to the coullour
of Copper as that does, notwithstanding this clear spring

runns through it with a swift current to the brow of the hill
and then it spreads it self all round the hill, which is a Rock,
and so runns down all over the brow of the hill continually,
like a hasty shower of small and great raine, and so it meetes
in the bottom and runns all into the river Knarsborough;
and this water as it runns and where it lyes in the hollows of
the rock does turn moss and wood into Stone, or rather
crusts or candys wood; I saw some which had a perfect Shell
of stone about it but they tell me it does in tyme penetrate
through the Wood, I took Moss my self from thence which
is all crisp'd and perfect Stone; all the Grass Straws or any
thing that the water falls on it does convert to hardness like
Stone; the whole rock is continually dropping with water
besides the showering from the top which ever runns, and
this is called the dropping well; there is an arbour and the
Company used to come and eat a Supper there in an evening,
to have the pleaseing prospect, and the murmuring shower
to divert their eare; in a good space of tyme it will harden
Ribon like Stone or any thing else.

From Harragate [Harrogate] to Cockgrave [Copgrove] is
6 mile, where is a Spring of an exceeding cold water called
St Mongers [Mungo] Well, the Story is of a Child that was
laid out in the cold for the parishes care and when the Church
Wardens found it they took care of it, a new born Infant, and
when it was baptised they gave it the name of Amongust
because they said the Child must be kept among them; and
as the papist sayes he was an ingenious Child and so attained
learning and was a very religious man and used this spring to
wash himself; after sometymes that he had gotten prefferrment and so grew rich he walled the Spring about and did
many cures on diseased bodies by batheing in it, which
caused after his death people to frequent the Well which was
an inconveniency to the owners of the ground and so they
forbad people coming and stopped up the Well and, the
Story sayes, on that severall judgments came on the owners of
the ground and the Spring broke up all about his ground
which forced him to open it againe and render it usefull to
all that would come to washe in it—thus farre of the fable—

now the Spring is in use and a high wall round it; the Well is
about 4 or 5 yards square, and round the brimm is a walke of
broad stone round; there are 4 or 5 steps down to the bottom, it is no deeper at some places then a little above the
waste not up to the shoulders of a woman, and you may kneel
on a flatt stone and it comes to your chin, this the papists
made use of very much; at one corner the Springs rise they
are very quick and there is a Sluce that it continually runns
off so as to keep just at the same depth, and it runns off so
fast and the Springs supply so fast that it clears the Well
presently after any body has been in; I allwayes chose to be
just where the springs rise that is much the coldest and it
throws off any thing in the well to the Sluce.

Setting aside the Papists fancyes of it I cannot but think it
is a very good Spring, being remarkably cold, and just at the
head of the Spring so its fresh which must needs be very
strengthning, it shutts up the pores of the body immeadiately
so fortifyes from cold, you cannot bear the coldness of it
above 2 or 3 minutes and then you come out and walke
round the pavement and then in againe, and so 3 or 4 or 6
or 7 as many tymes as you please; you go in and out in Linnen
Garments, some go in flannell, I used my Bath garments and
so pulled them off and put on flannell when I came out to
go into the bed, which is best; but some came at a distance,
so did I, and did not go into bed but some will keep on their
wet Garments and let them drye to them and say its more
beneficial, but I did not venture it; I dipp'd my head quite
over every tyme I went in and found it eased a great pain I
used to have in my head, and I was not so apt to catch Cold
so much as before, which I imputed to the exceeding coldness of the Spring that shutts up the pores of the body; its
thought it runns off of some very cold Spring and from Clay,
some of the Papists I saw there had so much Zeale as to continue a quarter of an hour on their knees at their prayers in
the Well, but none else could well endure it so long at a tyme;
I went in 7 severall seasons and 7 tymes every season and
would have gone in oftener could we have staid longer.

We went back to Harragat [Harrogate] 6 mile and then we

went to Burrough Bridge [Boroughbridge] 8 mile, a famous
place for Salmon, but then we could not meete with any but
we had a very large Codfish there, above a yard long and
more than halfe a yard in compass very fresh and good and
cost but 8 pence; I saw as big a one bought then for 6 pence,
and six Crabbs as big as my two hands—the least was bigger
than one of my fists—all cost but 3 pence.

Thence to Harragate 8 mile, then we went and laid at
Knarsburough 2 mile, which was nearer to St Mungers Well;
for we went [to] it twice from Harragate and back which was
12 mile more, and found it too farre to go in an afternoone,
from Knarsburough it was but 4 mile; we went it four tymes
and back which was 16 mile, and we went afterwards to
Harraget 3 tymes and back 12 mile more.

From Knarsborough we went to Rippon [Ripon] a pretty
little Market town mostly built of Stone 8 mile, a large
Market place with a high Cross of severall stepps; we were
there the market day where provisions are very plentifull and
cheap; in the Market was sold then 2 good shoulders of Veal,
they were not very fatt nor so large as our meate in London
but good meate, one for 5 pence the other for 6 pence, and a
good quarter of Lamb for 9 or 10 pence and its usual to buy
a very good shoulder of Veale for 9 pence and a quarter of
Beefe for 4 shillings; indeed it is not large ox Beef but good
middleing Beasts; and Craw fish 2 pence a Dozen so we
bought them; notwithstanding this plenty some of the Inns
are very dear to Strangers that they can impose on; the town
stands on a hill and there is a good large stone built Church
well carved they call it a Minster; there is very fine painting
over the alter it looks so natural, just like real crimson satten
with gold fringe like hangings and severall rows of pillars
in isles on either side which looks very naturall; there are two
good Bridges to the town, one was a rebuilding pretty large
with severall arches called Hewet [Hewick] Bridge, its often
out of repaire by reason of the force of the water that swells
after great raines, yet I see they made works of wood on
purpose to breake the violence of the Streame and the middle
arche is very large and high.

There are severall good houses about the town and severall Gentlemens Seates about a mile or two distance; 2 mile off is a fine place of Sir Edward Blackets,[14] it looks finely in the approach in the midst of a good parke and a River runns just by it, it stands in the middle and has two large Gardens on each side; you enter one through a large Iron Barr-gate painted green and gold tops and carv'd in severall places, this is fine gravel walks between grass plotts 4 square with 5 brass Statues great and small in each Square, and full of borders of flowers and green banks with flower potts; on the other side of the house is just such a Garden, only the walkes are all grass, rowl'd, and the Squares are full of dwarfe trees both fruites and green, set cross wayes which lookes very finely, there is a Flower Garden behind the house, in it and beyond it a Landry Close with frames for drying of cloths, wall'd in, there are good Stables and Coach-house and all the offices are very convenient very good Cellars all arch'd and there I dranke small beer four years old—not too stale very clear good Beer well brew'd—their kitching pastry and pantry etc. all very convenient; in the pantry hangs a picture of the dimentions of a large ox that was fed in these grounds with the account of its weight, the quarters was 106 stone 1 [pound] and the hide was 12 stone and 8 pound, the tallow was 19 stone the head 4 stone the legs and feate weigh'd 3 stone 11 [pound]; this Gentleman breeds and feeds much Cattle in his grounds and has one of the largest Beeves in England.

His house is built with bricke and coyn'd [coigned] with stone, with a flatt Roofe leaded, with Railes and Barristers [balusters], and a large Cupelow in the middle; you may see a greate way round the Country; the front Entrance is 3 gates of iron barres and spikes painted blew with gold tops, and brick work between the gates and pillars, with stone tops carv'd like flower potts, the pillars all coyn'd with stone; the middle gate is made large in a compass like a halfe Moone;

14 Newby Hall, sometimes wrongly attributed to Wren; Celia Fiennes is wrong in saying Sir Edward's father was a Bristol merchant; he was a great mine-owner in Newcastle. (*Lives of the Norths*, i. 281.)

there are four more spaces in the wall open with iron barres and spikes, 2 of which are in each side, into the Gardens, and answers two like them on the other side of the Gardens; the two other are less and are at the end of a terrass walk just along the entrance which you ascend by steps from the middle gate, they are all adorned with brick pillars coyn'd with stone and stone heads, these are all painted blew and gold tipps, from the Tarress you have a Court that leads into the middle of the house into a large hall; over the doore at the entrance is a fine Carving of stone with leaves and flowers with fine stone pillars and the Armes cutt finely, there is a fine dyal and clock above all; the hall you enter is of a very good size and height, 2 dineing roomes and drawing roomes, one for the summer with a marble floore, 6 or 7 Chambers off a good size and lofty, so that most of the beds were two foote too low which was pitty they being good beds, one was crimson figured velvet, 2 damaske beds, the rest moehaire and camlet; the roomes were mostly wanscoated and painted, the best roome was painted just like marble, few roomes were hung, the furniture was very neatly kept, and so was the whole house; the roofe of the Staires was finely painted, there was severall pictures but not set up, the house being in mourning for his Lady and her mother the Lady Yorke which dyed in a month or two of each other, she left Sir Edward 10 Children, he has a great estate and will have the 2000£ per annum fall to him that is Lady Mary Fenwicks anuity, he was a merchants son at Bristol; the house is serv'd with water by pipes into a Cistern into the garden cellars and all offices; this was the finest house I saw in Yorkshire.

We returned to Knarsborough 9 mile and from thence we went to York againe 12 mile, this was the worst rideing in Yorkshire, then we pass'd thro' York town by another gate towards Hull and that Streete was larger and better buildings than what I saw before in Yorke, and here we pass over the muddy River called the muddy Fosse [Foss]; we pass'd over the river Derwent[15] that runns through the

15 She is confusing the Yorkshire with the Derbyshire Derwent.

middle of Derbyshire, to Born Bridge [?Barmby Moor] 9 mile, to Whitten [Market Weighton] 6 mile, a little neate Thatch'd town of a mile long, where we lay, and pass'd by Burlington Lord Cliffords house[16] that stood in a bottom amongst trees; it look'd well and they say is well painted and good furniture, but I saw not the inside, only pass'd by it; there we had a very large Salmon that cost and the sauce but 18 pence it was very fresh and good and above 3 quarters of a yard long; thence to Beverly [Beverley] 9 miles which is a very fine town for its size, its prefferable to any town I saw but Nottingham, there are 3 or 4 large Streetes well pitch'd, bigger than any in Yorke, the other lesser Streetes about the town being equal with them; the Market Cross is large, there are 3 markets one for Beasts another for Corne and another for Fish, all large, the town is serv'd with water, by wells walled up round or rather in a Square, above halfe ones length, and by a pully and weight letts down or draws up the bucket which is chained to the beame of the pully—there are many of these wells in all the streetes, it seemes its in imitation of Holland, they being supply'd with water soe—the buildings are new and pretty lofty.

The Minster has been a fine building all stone, carv'd on the outside with Figures and Images, and more than 100 pedastalls that remaine where Statues has stood, of angells and the like, the wood worke in the Quire is very fine, just by the Comunion table is the Sanctuary or place of Refuge, where Criminalls flee for safety, its a seate of stonework cut all in one; Earle of Northumberland's and Lady's Monuments: his is very plaine only a marble Stone raised up with stone about 2 yards high, his name (by means of his great atchievements in the Barrons warre) Great Percy Earle of Northumberland is monument enough to posterity; his tombe was a little fallen in and a hole so bigg as many put their hands in and touch'd the body which was much of it entire, of the bones the skull was whole and the teeth firme

[16] The house was Londesborough and the owner Charles Boyle, second son of the Earl of Burlington. He became Lord Clifford of Londesborough in 1696.

tho' of so many yeares standing; the Countess's monument is very fine its made of the same free stone the Church is built with but so finely polish'd that it looks like marble, and carv'd with figures birds leaves flowers beasts and all sorts of things and the armes is cutt out in severall places all about it; the top of the arch is one entire stone, as much as one can grasp and its all finely carv'd with all sorts of Curiosityes and adorn'd with gilding and painting; there are 4 good monuments all of marble of the Wharton family, in the middle of the Church is the tomb of St. John with a brass inscription on the pavement, and at a little distance they shew'd us the wearing of the pavement with the obeisance of his votarys this being St John of Beverly; at the end of the Church is the font the upper part of it that is the bason was of one entire marble of a darke coullour, the Cover was carved exactly and of a Piramidy form and very high; there is another Church called St Mary's that is very large and good, I thought that had been the minster at first entrance of the town; there is the prayers every day and its used on all accounts and so the other is neglected, this has a Quire in which they were preaching when we were there.

There is a very good free schoole for boys, they say the best in England for learning and care, which makes it fill'd with Gentlemens Sons besides the free Schollars from all parts; provision being very cheape here. I was offered a large Codffish for a shilling and good Pearch very cheape, we had Crabbs bigger than my two hands, pence apiece, which would have cost 6 pence if not a shilling in London, and they were very sweete.

From thence we went to Hull 6 mile all upon a Caussey secured with two little rivers running on each side, which is used to flow over their grounds it being a great flatt, severall miles, and the meadows are cloth'd with good Grass by that means; the River Hull runns from Beverly at the towns end, just by the Minster you cross it, this runns to Hull, the town is properly called so from that River, but its name is Kingston on the Hull being built on that River which runns into the Humber which is a noble river, the mouth of it opens just against this town; the buildings of Hull are very neate, good streets, its a good tradeing town by means of this great River Humber that ebbs and flows like the sea is 3 or 4 mile over at the least, it runns 20 mile hence into the Sea and takes in all the great Rivers, the Trent Ouise Aire Don the Derwent and the Hull, and carries much water that a man of warre of all sorts can ride; I was on board a new man of warre that belonged to the town and called the Kingston,[16a] it was but small well compact for provision and was built fit for swift saileing; the Humber is very salt allwayes it rowles and tosses just like the Sea, only the soile being clay turnes the water and waves yellow and soe it differs from the sea in coullour, not else; its a hazardous water by reason of many shoares the tides meete, I was on it a pretty way and it seemes more turbulent than the Thames at Gravesend.

We enter the town of Hull from the southward over two drawbridges and gates, there is the same entrance another part of the town by 2 gates and 2 drawbridges, there is also a third entrance by two gates and 2 drawbridges from Holderness, and so the ditches are round the town to the landward and they can by them floate [flood] the grounds for 3 mile round which is a good fortification; the Garrison and plattforme which is the fortification to the Sea is in a very uniforme figure and were it finished is thought it would be the finest fortification that could be seen, its wall'd and pallisadoed; I walked round it and viewed it and when I was on the water it seemes to runn a great length and would require many Soldiers to deffend the halfe moons and workes.

In the town there is an hospitall thats called the Trinity House, for Seamens widdows, 30 is their Complement their allowance 16 pence per weeke and fewell, they have a little Chapple to it for prayers; over this building is a large roome for cordage and sailes, where they make them and keep their stores; in the middle of this roome there hangs a Canooe to the roofe of the roome, just bigg enough for one man to sit in, and the Effigie of a Man that was taken with it, all his Cloths Cap and a large Bag behind him wherein his fish and

16a A fourth-rate, 64 guns, 365 men.

provision were, these were all made of the skin of fishes and were the same which he wore when taken, the forme of his face is only added and just resemble the Wildman that they took, for so the Inscription calls him or the Bonny Boatesman; he was taken by Captain Baker and there are his oars and spear that was with him—this is all written on the boate to perpetuate the memory of it—he would not speake any language or word to them that took him nor would he eate, so in a few dayes died.[17]

There is a good large Church in Hull, you enter a large isle just in the middle that runns quite across through the Church and divides the body of the Church, with the pulpet and pews on the one side with a partition of wood carv'd, and on the other side was such another partition for the Chancell, and I observ'd there their alter stood table-wise for the Comunion just in the middle of the Chancell, as it was in the primitive tymes before Popery came in; there was severall little monuments of marble in the walls.

From thence to Beverly againe 6 mile which is all a flatt, thence to Brance Burton [Brandesburton] 8 mile all likewise on a Levell which they call Loughs; here we could get no accomodation at a Publick house, it being a sad poore thatch'd place and only 2 or 3 sorry Ale-houses, no lodgings but at the Hall House as it was called, where liv'd a Quaker which were sufficient people, the rooms were good old rooms being the Lord of the Mannours house; these were but tennants but did entertain us kindly, made two good beds for us and also for our servants, and good bread and cheese bacon and eggs; thence we went to Agnes-Burton 7 mile, the miles are long and so they are in most part of these Northern County's, this is the East Rideing of Yorkshire and we saw the Session house at Beverly for this Rideing.

Agnes Burton [Burton Agnes] is a Seate of Sir Griffith Boyntons[18] grandson to Sir Francis which married my father's sister one of William Lord Viscount Say and Seales

---

[17] This was the Eskimo, captured in his kayak by Captain Andrew Barker in 1613.

[18] Sir Griffith Boynton (1664–1731) grandson of Celia's Aunt Constance (née Fiennes).

daughters; it looks finely in the approach; a mile or two off we pass by another of his houses which is newer built and very good Gardens, called Barmstone [Barmston], we eate some of the good fruite; the house is all built with Brick and so good Bricke that at 100 years standing no one brick is faulty; it stands on a pretty ascent, we enter under a Gate house built with 4 large towers into a Court, which is large, in the middle is a Bowling green palisado'd round, and the Coaches runns round it to the Entrance, which is by 10 stepps up to a Tarress, and thence a pav'd walke to the house, cut box and filleroy[19] [phillyrea] and lawrell about the Court, the front looks very uniform with severall round buildings on each side answerring each other, with Compass windows, and the middle is a round building and the door enters in in the side of that tower which was the old fashion in building, and is like my brother Say's house at Broughton; out of an entry you come into a very lofty good Hall, the Screen at the lower end (which divides it from the entry) is finely carv'd; the parlour and drawing-roome are well proportion'd roomes and the wanscoate is all well carv'd, in the moldings of the doores and chimneys are finely carv'd with staggs and all sorts of beasts woods and some leaves and flowers; and birds and angells etc.; there is beyond this a very good little parlour with plaine wanscoate painted in veines like marble dark and white streakes; there is a very good dineing-room over this and 5 very good Chambers some well furnished, all very neate and convenient with closetts to their own appartments, and anty-roomes; there is much of the same fine Carving in the dineing roome, the Chambers are all wanscoated and carv'd, there is a noble gallery over all with large windows on the sides, and at each end painted very curiously, out of which you view the whole Country round, and discover the shipps under saile though at a good distance; the Gardens are large and are capable of being made very fine, they now remaine in the old fashion, there is gravel

[19] Phillyrea, i.e. mock privet or jasmine box. The O.E.D. quotes Celia Fiennes as the authority for the spelling "fileroy" but gives her date as 1710.

walks and grass and close walks, there is one walke all the length of the Garden called the Crooked Walke, of grass well cutt and rowled, it is indented in and out in corners and so is the wall, which makes you thinke you are at the end off the walke severall tymes before you are, by means of the Codling hedge that is on the other side, this leads you to a Summer house that also opens to a large gravell walke that runns the breadth of the Garden to the house ward.

3. TO SCARBOROUGH AND PONTEFRACT AND THROUGH DERBYSHIRE TO WOLSELEY

FROM AGNES BURTON we went to Scarsbrough [Scarborough] 14 mile, we pass'd from this flatt to Boynton, thence ascended the wouls [wolds] or high hills so called in this country, and it prov'd misty, which made our observations to be fixed on it that the mist was thicker and more held in those high wouls as raine or mist is in thick trees, so the mist was much more there than in the plains, so thick in some you could not see the top; we descended these high wouls by a steep and hazardous precipice on one side and the way narrow.

Scarbrough is a very pretty Sea-port town built on the side of a high hill, the Church stands in the most eminent place above all the town and at least 20 steps you ascend up into the Churchyard; the ruines of a large Castle remaines, the Walls in compass severall acres of ground that feeds many beasts and milch cows, the hill on which the Castle stands is very steep and severall trenches over one another round the walls, all one side of the Castle stands out to the sea shore a good length, its open to the main ocean and to secure the harbour there is a mole or half moone, two, one within the other something resembling the Cobb at Lime [Lyme] in Sommersetshire; the sea when the tide is in is close up to the town and the bottom of a ridge of hills that runns from the town 5 or 6 mile in a compass, when its Ebb water it leaves the shore 400 yards all a flatt, and such good sand as you presently walke on it without sinking, the sand is so smooth and firme; and so you may walke 5 or 6 mile on the sand round by the foote of this ridge of hills, which is the poynt by which all the Shipps pass that go to Newcastle, or that way; I see 70 saile of Shipps pass the point and so come onward at some distance off from the Castle, supposed to be Colliers, and their Convoys;[1] on this sand by the Sea shore is the Spaw Well which people frequent,[1a] and all the diversion is the walking on this sand twice a day at the ebb of the tide and till its high tide; and there they drink, its something from an Iron or Steele minerall, but by means of the tide flowing on it every tyme, especially spring tydes, it covers the well quite and allwayes flowes up just to it, which leaves a brackish and saltness which makes it purge pretty much; but they say the Spring is so quick that it soone casts off the Sea water, but my opinion is that the whole spring and all the springs that bubble up all over the sands must be agreable and of the sort of water the Sea is, being so just on the sea side and so neare must be influenc'd by the salt water; it seems to be a pretty turbulent Sea, I was on it in a little boate but found it very rough even just in the harbour, I suppose the cause may be from standing so open to the Maine.

The town has abundance of Quakers in it, most of their best Lodgings were in Quakers hands, they entertain all people soe in Private houses in the town, by way of ordinary, so much a Meale, and their Ale every one finds themselves, there are a few Inns for horses only. I was at a Quakers Meeting in the town where 4 men and 2 women spoke, one after another had done, but it seem'd such a confusion and so incoherent that it very much moved my compassion and pitty to see their delusion and ignorance, and no less excited my thankfullness for the Grace of God that upheld others

[1] For the importance of the colliers taking Newcastle coal to London, see Introduction, p. xli. They were in convoy because the war with France was not yet concluded.

[1a] It was not until 3 years later that the first spa buildings were erected: even in 1732 Sarah Duchess of Marlborough found the accommodation very crude, especially the sanitary arrangements which were over-communal—"I came home as fast as I could for fear of being forced into that assembly." (*Letters of a Grandmother*, ed. Scott-Thomson, p. 46.)

from such Errors; I observ'd their prayers were all made on the first person and single, tho before the body of people, it seems they allow not of ones being the mouth of the rest in prayer to God tho' it be in the publick meetings; in this town we had good accomodations and on very reasonable terms; they drye a large fish like Codlings and salt them and, when you dress them, water them, then they string them on wire and so rost them before the fire and make good sauce for them, they eate very well and as tender as a fresh Codling and very sweete iff they were well cured when they were first taken, else they will taste strong.

Thence we went to Maulton [Malton] 14 miles which is a pretty large town built of stone, but poor, there is a large market place and severall great houses of Gentlemens round the town, there was one Mr Paumes that marry'd a relation of mine Lord Ewers [Eure's] Coeheiress[2] who is landlady of almost all the town, she has a pretty house in the place; there is the ruins of a very great house which belonged to the family but they not agreeing about it caused the defaceing of it, she now makes use of the roomes off the out buildings and gate house for weaving and linneing cloth, haveing set up a manuffactory for Linnen which does employ many poor people; she supply'd me with very good beer, for the Inn had not the best.

Thence to York 14 mile and so to Tadcaster 8 mile, thence to Aberfford 4 miles, all on a heavy bottom, these miles are long and I observe the ordinary people both in these parts of Yorkshire and in the northern parts can scarce tell you how farre it is to the next place unless it be in the great towns and there in their publick houses; and they tell you its very good gate [gait], instead of saying it is good way, and they call their gates yates, and do not esteem it uphill unless so steep as a house or precipice; they say its good levell gate all along, when it may be there are severall great hills to pass, but this account did encrease on us the nearer we came to

[2] This was Mary Eure, who married William Palmes of Lindley. She and her sister, unable to agree over the division of the estate, had the house pulled down and shared the stones exactly.

Darbyshire, but in generall they live much at home and scarce ever go 2 or 10 mile from thence, especially the women, so may be term'd good housekeepers.

To Aberford we came by severall pretty Seates in view, we lay at an acquaintances house Mrs Hickeringalls[3] [Hickeringhill]; thence we went to Castleton Bridge [Castleford] 5 mile where was a Glass house; we saw them blowing white glass and neale [anneal] it in a large oven by the heate of the furnace; all the Country is full of Coale and the pitts are so thick in the roade that it is hazardous to travell for strangers.

Thence to Pomffret [Pontefract] 3 miles which looks very finely in the approach; its built on a hill all of stone, its a very neate building and the streets well pitch'd[4] and broad, the houses well built and looks more stately than any in York, only its not the tenth part so bigg, its a neate little town as I have seen; there are severall very good houses in it, one Doctor Burgess has built a very good house which is call'd his Folly; there is a noble house at the entrance of the town of the Lady Grace Perpoynt [Pierrepont] and good Parke Gardens and Walks and a great revenue belonging to it, the daughter of the Marquis of Dorchesters;[5] there is a fine Church in the town and as spacious a market place as is at Salisbury, or as you shall see any where, and the buildings so even and uniforme as well as lofty that it appears very magnificent, its a Major [Mayor] town; we were in the chief Inn the Sunn, tho' there are many good Inns but this was a very good genteel Inn, and it happen'd the Landlord was then Major [Mayor] of the town.

Provisions are very easy here, we had 2 or 3 pound of Codffish for a small matter and it was a large dish; the town is full of great Gardens walled in all round, on the outside of

[3] Celia Fiennes' fellow-puritan, Ralph Thoresby, had stayed in the same house only three years before, "bargaining about rape and black wares" with Mr. Hickeringhill, whose brother was a well-known Evangelical parson at Colchester. (*Diary*, i, 250.)

[4] By "well pitch'd" Celia Fiennes means paved (cf. p. 251 below—"a naturall sort of paveing or pitching"). She does not mean cambering to provide drainage.

[5] Henry Pierrepont (1606–80) first Marquis of Dorchester, an old Cavalier who took up medicine in his old age, became F.R.C.P. and F.R.S., and hastened his end by taking his own prescriptions.

the town on the edge of the hill so the Gardens runns down a great way, you descend into them by severall stepps; its a fruitfull place fine flowers and trees with all sorts of fruite, but that which is mostly intended is the increasing of Liquorish [Liquorice], which the Gardens are all filled with, and any body that has but a little ground improves it for the produce of Liquorish, of which there is vast quantetyes, and it returns severall 100 pounds yearly to the towns;[6] the leafe is not much unlike a rose leafe, but somewhat narrower and longer, the coullour is something a yellower green, else the branches grow like it with double leaves on a stalke, and severall all down the stalke somewhat in the manner of Caliceily or Solomans Seale and much of that smoothness of leafe.

Thence to Hemsworth 4 mile where we could meet with no lodging, only little ale-houses to give one a pot of beer, and so we went 2 mile farther but found it the same, and it being too farre to reach Rothcram [Rotherham] we made use of the hospitallity of a Clergyman one Mr Ferrer which was a very genteele man and gave us a civil entertainment and good beds, he has a very good house and genteelly fitted, good Hall and Parlour, and the Garden very neate; its a very fruitfull Country, which encourages Industry and there is plenty of stone like free stone which makes fine houses and walls.

Thence to Rotheram 12 miles, its most in a deep clay ground, and now the wayes are more difficult and narrow. Rotheram is a good market town well built all of stone, the Church stands high in the middle of the town and looks finely, its all stone and carv'd very well all the outside; thence to Achington [Eckington] 8 mile, a very little place, its 3 mile from Shellton [Sheffield] town but that was thought out of our way so we lay here in a poor sorry Inn, there was one good bed for us Gentlewomen; its a pretty long Parish and through it runns a water which came down a great banck at the end of the town like a precipice with such violence that

[6] Pontefract had supplied England with liquorice for a hundred years. (H.A.T.)

it makes a great noise and looks extreamely cleare in the Streame that gushes out and runns along; it changes the ground and stone or wood [which] it runns on off a deep yellow coullour, they say it runns off of a poisonous mine or soile and from Coale pitts, they permitt none to taste it for I sent for a Cup of it and the people in the Streete call'd out to forbid the tasteing it, and it will beare no Soape, so its useless.

Here we entred Darbyshire and went to Chesterffield 6 mile, and came by the Coale Mines where they were digging; they make their mines at the Entrance like a well and so till they come to the Coale, then they digg all the ground about where there is Coale and set pillars to support it and so bring it to the well, where by a basket like a hand-barrow by cords they pull it up, so they let down and up the miners with a cord.

Chesterffield looks low when you approach it from the adjacent hill which you descend, but then you ascend another to it; the Coale pitts and quaraes of stone are all about even just at the town end, and in the town its all built of stone; the Church stands in a place of eminency, the town looks well, the Streets good the Market very large; it was Satturday which is their market day and there was a great Market like some little faire, a great deale of corne and all sorts of ware and fowles, there I bought my self 2 very good fatt white (pullings as they call them) pullets for 6 pence both, and I am sure they were as large and as good as would have cost 18 pence if not 2 shillings apiece in London, so said all my Company; in this town is the best ale in the kingdom generally esteem'd.

All Derbyshire is full of steep hills, and nothing but the peakes of hills as thick one by another is seen in most of the County which are very steepe which makes travelling tedious, and the miles long, you see neither hedge nor tree but only low drye stone walls round some ground, else its only hills and dales as thick as you can imagine, but tho' the surface of the earth looks barren yet those hills are impregnated with rich Marbles Stones Metals Iron and Copper and Coale mines in their bowells, from whence we may see the wisdom and benignitye of our greate Creator to make up the defficiency of a place by an equivolent as also the diversity of the Creation which encreaseth its Beauty.

We go from Chesterffield to the Duke of Devonshires house and ascend a high hill at least two or three miles long; we pass'd by a cavity in one great Banck or Rock called Stonidge Hall, all stone of about 12 yards long and about 4 or 5 broad, its all rock like an arch on the Roofe, but its not fenc'd, so but the beasts trample and fowle it you can scarce go into it; the same long steep hill we had to descend which comes to Chattsworth[7] ten mile; the Duke's house lyes just at the foote of this steepe hill which is like a precipice just at the last, notwithstanding the Dukes house stands on a little riseing ground from the River Derwent which runs all along the front of the house and by a little fall made in the water which makes a pretty murmurring noise; before the gate there is a large Parke and severall fine Gardens one without another with gravell walkes and squairs of grass with stone statues in them and in the middle of each Garden is a large fountaine full of images Sea Gods and Dolphins and Sea Horses which are full of pipes which spout out water in the bason and spouts all about the gardens; 3 Gardens just round the house; out of two of the Gardens you ascend by severall stepps into other Gardens which some have gravell walks and square like the other with Statues and Images in the bason, there is one bason in the middle of one Garden thats very large and by sluces besides the Images severall pipes plays out the water, about 30 large and small pipes altogether, some flush it up that it frothes like snow; there is one Garden full of stone and brass statues; so the Gardens lyes one above another which makes the prospect very fine; above these gardens is an ascent of 5 or 6 stepps up to green walk and groves of firrs, and a wilderness and close arbours and

[7] William Cavendish, fourth Earl of Devonshire (created Duke 1694) began to rebuild Chatsworth in 1687 as an excuse for staying away from James II's court; the work was nearly finished in 1700. Defoe was puzzled at Chatsworth being classed as one of the "Wonders of the Peak" except on the grounds that it was a wonder for such a house to be built in such a "houling wilderness". (Op. cit., ii, 176.)

shady walks, on each end of one walke stands two pira-
midies full of pipes spouting water that runns down one of
them, runns on brass hollow work which looks like rocks
and hollow stones; the other is all flatts stands one above
another like salvers so the water rebounds one from another,
5 or 6 one above the other; there is another green walke and
about the middle of it by the Grove stands a fine Willow
tree, the leaves barke and all looks very naturall, the roote
is full of rubbish or great stones to appearance, and all on a
sudden by turning a sluce it raines from each leafe and from
the branches like a shower, it being made of brass and pipes
to each leafe but in appearance is exactly like any Willow;
beyond this is a bason in which are the branches of two
Hartichocks Leaves which weeps at the end of each leafe
into the bason which is placed at the foote of lead steps 30
in number, the lowest step is very deep and between every
4 stepps is a half pace all made of lead and are broad on each
side; on a little banck stands blew balls 10 on a side, and between each ball are 4 pipes which by a sluce spouts out water
across the stepps to each other like an arbour or arch; while
you are thus amused suddenly there runs down a torrent of
water out of 2 pitchers in the hands of two large Nimphs cut
in stone that lyes in the upper step, which makes a pleaseing
prospect, this is designed to be enlarged and steps made up
to the top of the hill which is a vast ascent, but from the top
of it now they are supply'd with water for all their pipes so
it will be the easyer to have such a fall of water even from
the top which will add to the Curiositye.

The house is built all of stone that is dugg out of the hills,
its like free stone; a flatt Roofe with barristers and flower
potts; in the front is 7 large windows the glass is diamond
cutt and all off large Looking-glass, the panes bigg 4 in a
breadth 7 in height; to the garden ward was 12 windows of
the same glass 4 panes broad 8 long; the lowest windows
are made with Grates before them and are for birds an
Averye and so looking glass behind; the stepps out of the
Garden are on either side 20 steps and iron barrs painted
blew and tipt with gold, the steps meete on the top in a halfe

pace railed the same, but the front entrance is not finished; there is a large Court which is to be pav'd and so stepps on each side of stone with half paces up to a tarress walke, the large gates of iron barrs are 3 at the Court and from this tarress you enter.

The front is with severall large stone pillars carv'd at the entrance into another Court which the house is built about, and here are peaso's [piazzas] supported with stone pillars under which you pass from one place to another, out of it is the Chapple which is a very lofty building and supported by 4 large pillars of black marble two at the alter 2 just at the bottom to support the gallery for the Duke and Dutches to sitt in; the pillars are 14 foote and so bigg that I could not compass one with my arms; these 4, and 2 stepps by the alter was made out of one stone cut out of the hill just by, so is all the marble about the house and so finely polish'd like a looking-glass; the pavement is black and white marble vein'd lay'd longwayes in large stones all of the same; the painting is very fine on the top and on the sides the history of Christ and the New testament; there is a very fine Carving of wood and stone, the Dove at the alter the Angels and Cherubims with flowers leaves laurell etc., very curiously carv'd.[8]

The hall is very lofty painted top and sides with armory, and there is 18 steps on each side goes up as an arch, with iron barristers tipt with gold which meetes on the top, large steps of stone, thence you enter a dineing roome two drawing roomes a bed chamber and closet, which opens quite thro' the house a visto, and at the end of the dineing roome is a large door all of Looking-glass, in great pannells all diamond cutt, this is just opposite to the doores that runs into the drawing roome and bed chamber and closet, so it shews the roomes to look all double; the floores of the roomes are all finely inlaid, there is very curious carving over and round the Chimney pieces and round the Looking-glasses that are in the peers between the windows, and fine carv'd shelves or stands on each side of the Glass; every

---

[8] The painting was by Verrio and others, and the sculpture by the Dane Caius Gabriel Cibber, father of Colley Cibber the dramatist.

roome is differring work and all fine carving and over the doores some of it is of the naturall coullour of the wood and varnish'd only, others painted; the Duchess's Closet is wanscoated with the hollow burnt japan [lacquer] and at each corner are peers of Looking-glass, over the Chimney is Looking glass an oval, and at the 4 corners, after this figure ;O;, and hollow carving all round the glass; the roomes are all painted very finely on the top, all the windows the squares of glass are so large and good they cost 10s. a pannell; there was sweete tapistry hangings with small figures and very much silk, they look'd as fresh as if new tho' bought severall yeares, there were no beds up.

There was as many roomes on the other side which were not finished, they were just painting the cielings and laying the floores, which are all inlaid; these were the Duke and Dutchess's apartments besides which are a great number of roomes and severall offices; there is a fine grottoe all stone pavement roofe and sides, this is design'd to supply all the house with water besides severall fancyes to make diversion; within this is a batheing roome, the walls all with blew and white marble the pavement mix'd one stone white another black another of the red rance [9] marble; the bath is one entire marble all white finely veined with blew and is made smooth, but had it been as finely pollish'd as some, it would have been the finest marble that could be seen; it was as deep as ones middle on the outside and you went down steps into the bath big enough for two people; at the upper end are two Cocks to let in one hott the other cold water to attemper it as persons please; the windows are all private glass; [10] the Gallery we ascended out of the hall into, before we came to the dineing roome—which I should have spoken off then—was delicately painted over head, and round on the top was a raile and barristers [balusters] so naturally drawn just round the cornish [cornice] that you would take it for a railed walke round the top to looke down into the gallery; there is another fine staircase all stone and hangs on it self, on the outside, the

[9] Rance is a variegated marble, red with veins and spots of blue and white.
[10] Ground glass.

support is from the wall and its own building, the stone of the half paces are large and one entire stone makes each; on the top of the staires the space leading to the roomes are 3 large Stones, the Stones cost 20£ a piece, so large and thick, you would wonder how they should be raised up so high and be supported by its own arch without any pillars on the outside; this is all of stone cut out of the hills which looks like what we call free stone, the house is all off the same and all the marble in the windows chimneys and pavements is all marble dug out of the hill above the house, both black, white, rance and curiously veined and polished so fine as any I ever saw which came from beyond sea.

Thence we came to Bankwell [Bakewell] a pretty neate market town 2 mile, it stands on a hill yet you descend a vast hill to it, which you would thinke impossible to go down and we was forced to fetch a great compass, and by reason of the steepness and hazard of the Wayes—if you take a wrong Way there is no passing[11]—you are forced to have Guides as in all parts of Darbyshire, and unless it be a few that use to be guides the common people know not above 2 or 3 mile from their home, but they of the country will climbe up and down with their horses those steep precipices; there are many fine springs of water purling out of the rocks on these hills; at Bankwell there was an excellent Minister in the Publick who pray'd and preach'd very seriously and his Life and Conversation is suitable, not very frequent in our dayes to be found; we went 3 mile off in the afternoone to heare another that was in a Meeteing and so 3 mile home againe; the hills about the town and all about the town is rocks of the finest marble of all sorts, huge rock, I took some of it and shewing it to severall they think it comparable to any beyond sea.

Thence to Haddon Hall (for so all the great houses are called, as Chatsworth Hall so this Haddon Hall) the Earle

[11] For an account of the hardships of travelling in this "strange, mountainous, misty, moorish, rocky, wild country . . . the craggy ascents, the rocky unevenness of the roade, the high peaks and the almost perpendicular descents" see Edward Browne, son of Sir Thomas, *Journal of a Tour in Derbyshire*, 1662 (in *Works of Sir T. Browne*, ed. 1836, i, 26–31).

of Rutlands[12] house 2 mile from Bankwell; its a good old house, all built of stone on a hill and behind it is a fine Grove of high trees and good Gardens but nothing very curious as the mode now is, there is a large Parke upon a great ascent from the house, which is built round a Court, the Parke is one part of some of the highest hills which gives a great prospect over the Country—but indeed all Darbyshire is but a world of peaked hills which from some of the highest you discover the rest like steeples or tops of hills as thick as can be, and tho' they appear so close yet the steepness down and up takes up the time that you go it, as if so many miles, and were the ground measur'd would be in length as much as miles on a plaine.

Thence to Buxton, 9 mile over those craggy hills whose bowells are full of Mines of all kinds off black and white and veined marbles, and some have mines of Copper, others Tinn and Leaden mines in which is a great deale of Silver; I have some which looks full of silver its so bright just brought up out of one of the mines; they digg down their mines like a well, for one man to be let down with a rope and pulley and so when they find oar [ore] they keep digging under ground to follow the oar, which lies amongst the stone that lookes like our fire stones; in that mine I saw there was 3 or 4 at work and all let down thro' the well, they digg sometymes a great way before they come to oar; there is also a sort of stuff they digg out mixt with the oar and all about the hills they call Sparr [fluor-spar], it looks like Crystal or white Sugar-candy its pretty hard, the doctors use it in medicine for the Collick, its smooth like glass but it looks all in crack's all over; they wall round the wells to the mines to secure their mold'ring in upon them; they generally look very pale and yellow that work Underground,[13] they are forc'd to keep lights with them and some tymes are forced to use Gun-

[12] The Earl became a Duke in March 1703, a fact which may help to date the writing of Celia Fiennes' journal.

[13] These are symptoms of lead poisoning. Defoe too saw here a miner "pale as a dead corps, who worked sixty fathoms deep" which caused Defoe "to reflect how much we have to acknowledge to our Maker, that we were not appointed to get our bread thus". (Op. cit., ii, 164-5.)

powder to break the stones, and that is sometymes hazardous to the people and destroys them at the work.

Its very difficult to find the wayes here for you see only tops of hills and so many roads by reason of the best wayes up and down that its impossible for Coach or Waggon to pass some of them, and you scarce see a tree and no hedges all over the Country, only dry stone walls that incloses ground no other fence; Buxton we saw 2 or 3 tymes and then lost the sight of it as often, and at last did not see it till just you came upon it—that 9 mile we were above 6 hours going it.

The house thats call'd Buxton Hall which belongs to the Duke of Devonshire its where the warme Bath is and Well, its the largest house in the place tho' not very good, they are all Entertaining houses and its by way of an Ordinary, so much a piece for your dinners and suppers and so much for our Servants besides; all your ale and wine is to be paid besides, the beer they allow at the meales is so bad that very little can be dranke, you pay not for your bed room and truely the other is so unreasonable a price and the Lodgings so bad, 2 beds in a room some 3 beds and some 4 in one roome, so that if you have not Company enough of your own to fill a room they will be ready to put others into the same chamber, and sometymes they are so crowded that three must lye in a bed; few people stay above two or three nights its so inconvenient: we staid two nights by reason one of our Company was ill but it was sore against our wills, for there is no peace nor quiet with one Company and another going into the Bath or coming out; that makes so many strive to be in this house because the Bath is in it; its about 40 foot long and about 20 or 30 foote broad being almost square, there is 10 or 12 Springs that bubble up that are a little warme —its not so warme as milke from the cow—and not a quick spring so that its not capable of being cleansed after every body has been in, its warme enough just to open the pores of ones body but not to cause sweat; I was in it and it made me shake, its farre from the heate that is in the Somersetshire Baths;[14] its cover'd over the top, but not ceiled and

[14] Defoe could "hardly be persuaded to come out of the bath". (Ibid., 167.)

there is an open place in the middle like a tunnell, which pours the cold down on your head; it would in my thoughts be better if it were exposed all to the aire and sunn; there is a pavement of stone on one side at the brim to walke on with benches of stone to sitt on; you must have a Guide that swims with you, you may stand in some place and hold by a chaine and the water is not above your neck, but in other parts very deep and strong, it will turn you down; about 10 or 12 yards distant is a spring called St. Anns Well which is for drinking, they have arch'd it up that its much hotter, it heates the cup you take it up in, but not a near so hot as the Somersetshire Baths and Springs are, the taste is not unpleasant but rather like milk, they say its Diaretick I dranke a part of a cup full.

Another Wonder is that of Pooles Hole thats just at the towns end, a large cavity under ground of a great length; just at the Entrance you must creep, but presently you stand upright, its Roofe being very lofty all arched in the rocks and sound with a great Ecchoe, the rocks are continually droping water all about, you pass over loose stones and craggy rocks, the dripping of the water wears impression on the stones that forms them into severall Shapes,[15] there is one looks like a Lyon with a Crown on his head, the water trickling on it weares it into so many shapes another place lookes just like the shape of a large Organ with the severall keys and pipes one above another as you see in a great Cathedrall; there is also a great stone which looks white and in shape like a salted Flitch of Bacon which hangs down from the roofe of the arch which is very lofty in this place; there is another rock looks like a Chaire of State with the Canopy and all glistring like diamonds or starrs, thus does all the

[15] The "severall shapes" formed by the stone are celebrated in Charles Cotton's verse:

> "Propt round with *Peasants*, on you trembling go,
> Whilst, every step you take, your *Guides* do show
> In the uneven Rock the uncouth shapes
> Of *Men*, of *Lions*, *Horses*, *Dogs*, and *Apes*:
> But so resembling each the fancied shape,
> The *Man* might be the *Horse*, the *Dog* the *Ape*."
> (*The Wonders of the Peak*, 1681)

sides of the rock all shine like Diamonds; the rocks are very
large and craggy and indented, some looks like the outsides
of Cockle shells others are smooth, all caused I beleive from
the dripping of the water; I was as farre as the Queen of Scotts
Pillar, which is a large white stone and the top hangs over
your head like a cannopy, all great white stones and in spires
or large iceickles, and glistring as the other; they may go
farther but I had no such curiosity, I had the Light carry'd
that shewed me to St Anns Needle after which is only sand,
this white stone is very like Chrystall of which there is a
stone like a bason or large font, wherein drops continually
the water which runns over and trickling down does as it
were candy in iceickles and points, under which is a pillar
of this white stone; we had some broken off which looks like
the insides of oystershells or mother of pearle, some looks
like alabaster; as I went I clamber'd over the top of all the
stones and as I came back I pass'd under severall of the
arches like bridges; they are both wayes full of loose stones
and the water dropping makes them slippery, it being also
very uneven by reason of the craggs; how it should come
none can give any good account; its call'd Pooles Hole from
a man of that name that was a Robber and use to secure himself in that place like a house and so the country people
imagined he made it, but some think it was dug to find mines
or marble or chrystal etc., because the mettle mines are full
of stone as I said before, only this enters it in the side whereas
the mines they make now are as a well perpendicular for
severall yards before it spreads, and that not till they come
to find metal; but the difficulty appears as to this hole, how
so large a cavity should be left as in some places the roofe is
as lofty as you can see and all stone; now how it should be
fixt so as not to tumble in by the weight of the earth and
stone on the top, as to the waters dropping that is but what
is customary among rocks and stones, there are many
springs which run in the veines of the Earth and allwayes
are running in such subteraneus vaults in the Earth, which
gather together and runs in a little channel in the bottom of
this Cave as you may step over.

The 4th Wonder is that off Elden Hole[16] about 2 mile from Buxton; its on the side of a hill about 30 yards if not better in length at the brimm, and half so broad, and just in sight is full of craggy stones like a rock for about 2 or 3 yards down, which contracts the Mouth of the Hole to about 4 yards long and 2 broad or thereabouts, which Hole is suppos'd to run down directly a vast length and has been try'd with a line and plummet severall fathom and the bottom not sounded; tho' some are of opinion its because the hole runns aslant so the plummet and line could not pass, and what we observ'd gives some strength to this notion, for cast a stone down you hear it strike a long tyme at the sides of the hole and if you go down below 100 yards or more and lay your head to the ground you shall hear the stone ring much longer than those that stand at the Holes mouth, which must discover the ground to be hollow at least much farther in compass than the mouth of the Hole; but its certain it must be of a great depth by reason of the tyme you can hear a stone strike and ring in its descending and that which lessens the sound may be by its breaking against the sides; its a very hazardous place, for if man or beast be too near the edge of the bank and trip they fall in without retrieve; the beasts graze in the grounds and hills but it must be some great force that drives them near the Hole; there is a sort of instinct in Nature self preservation and a great sence of danger in beasts; its reported that severall attempts have been made to fence the whole round with a stone wall as the manner of the fences are all over that Country but that it has been all in vaine, what they built up in the day would be pull'd down in the night and so its vaine to trye the secureing it round from any falling in, this the people tell us; the Country hereabout is so full of moore or quagmires and such precipices that one

[16] In reality the hole was found to be about 76 feet deep by an F.R.S. in 1730 (H.A.T.) But according to Edward Browne "the greatest ingines and the boldest fellows that could bee found to goe down could never find any bottome . . . and anything once thrown in is as safe as if it were in the moon. One wretched villain confessed upon a time at the gallows that hee rob'd a gentleman and threw him in, together with his horse. Empedocles might have made himselfe immortall here without fear of the discovery of his slippers." (Op. cit., pp. 33-4.)

that is a stranger cannot travell without a Guide, and some of them are put to a loss sometymes.

The fifth Wonder is Mamtour[17] [Mam Tor] which is a high hill that looks exactly round but on the side next Castleton, which is a little town in the high peake, on that side its all broken that it looks just in resemblance as a great Hay-Ricke thats cut down one halfe, on one side that describes it most naturall, this is all sand, and on that broken side the sand keeps trickling down allwayes especially when there is the least wind, of which I believe this Country scarce ever is without, many places of the hill looks hollow and loose which makes it very dangerous to ascend and none does attempt it, the sand being loose slips the foote back againe.

The 6th Wonder is at Casleton 4 mile from Elden Hole, its a town lyes at the foote of an exceeding steep hill which could not be descended by foote or horse, but in a compass, and that by the Roads returning to and agen on the side of the hill at least 4 tymes before we could gaine the bottom or top of said Hill; this is what they call the Devills Arse a Peake,[18] the hill on one end jutting out in two parts and joyns in one at the top, this part or cleft between you enter a great Cave which is very large, and severall poor little houses in it built of stone and thatch'd like little Styes, one seemed a little bigger in which a Gentleman liv'd and his wife that was worth above 100£ a year which he left to his brother chooseing rather like a hermite to live in this sorry cell; one Mr Midleton who was with us said he had dined with them there on carrots and herbs, and that he was dead and his

[17] Mam Tor, or the Shivering Mountain, sheds sand, shale and grit stone after frost or heavy rain. The pious Thoresby thought that "it may well pass for the emblem of a liberal man, never impoverished by his well bounded and grounded charity, his expenses being resupplied by a secret Providence". (Op. cit., i, 90–1.) The comment is in character: it is, however, lifted verbatim from Fuller's *Worthies* (ed. Nuttall I, 368.)

[18] Celia Fiennes is less squeamish than Defoe, who thought that the only wonder lay in the coarseness of our ancestors in thinking of "so homely a sirname . . . but it seems they talked broader in those days than we do now". (Op. cit., ii, 172.) The Rev. James Brome, whose *Travels* appeared in 1700, contented himself with calling it "a dismal place both for its name and nature"; but Edward Browne, being a young medical student, indulged in scabrous and elaborate physiological analogies. (Op. cit., 32–3.)

wife a year or two since; now none but very poor people[19]
live there which makes some small advantage by begging
and by lighting the strangers into the Cave which beyond
this you enter; so straight a passage at the mouth you stoop
very low even upon your breast and creep in and when you
are in about a yard or two's length you stand upright it
being lofty in manner of Poole's Hole, only the rocks hangs
down in so many places that there is often cause of stooping
very low to pass by them and here the ground you tread on is
all sand and firme, only the rocks do drip water in many
places which makes it damp and strikes cold to you; but
excepting the pillars of rock in some places that hang down
the most of it is very lofty and a great ecchoe, like a Church;
you pass a good way by the light of many Candles haueing
lost the sight of day from the first stooping entrance; at
last you come to a River they call it, a great water it is and
very deep, they say its about 12 yards over and some do go on
it with a little boate to the other side but I would not venture.

There was one Gentlewoman in our Company said she had
once been carry'd over on 2 mens shoulders, but they waded
above their waste in water, so I would not bee for so dangerous I was sure it was a difficult enterprise, and when you
are over that side they go over but such places as was pass'd
before, which leads to another such a water which some men
have pass'd over and so have gone on to a third water, but
there the rocks hung so low as almost to touch the water
which hindred their proceeding; that water I saw was strange
so deep and large and look'd like a standing water but
whether it were or not could not tell, no doubt but it has a
passage thro' the veines of the Earth or else would swell so
as to cause a bursting out of the Earth; it seemed to have a
motion with it; all these things shewes the great wisdom and
power of our blessed Creator to make and maintaine all
things within its own Bounds and Limits, which have a
tendency to worke out ruine to the whole frame of the world
if not bridled by Gods Command.

[19] Defoe found a lead miner living here with his wife and five children
and earning from 5d. to 8d. a day. (Op. cit., ii, 161–3.)

The Seventh Wonder is a Flowing and Ebbing Well
[Tideswell] between this town and Buxton which ceases its
miraculous motion but on great raines which raises the
springs, and then the man which was with us told me he
had seen it severall tymes in the winter when the springs
were high to Ebb and Flow severall tymes in a hour, which
appear'd by the rise and fall of the water from the edge of the
well—and the man seem'd to be a good sober man Mr Middleton it was—so that its likely when the springs are high
the water from the sea may have a quicker flux and reflux
thro' the Channells of the Earth but this is a good distance
from the sea of ebbing and flowing rivers.

From Castleton to Buxton is 6 mile, but they are very long,
you might go 10 of miles near London as soon as you are
going halfe so many here.

Thence we went to Ashburn [Ashbourn] 16 mile, where I
saw some of their Copper mines, and here they dig them like
a well but secure the side with wood and turffe bound with
the wood like laths or frames across and longwayes, to
secure it; this is a pretty neate market town; thence to Uxeter
[Uttoxeter] 8 mile and we cross a River on a long bridge and
so we enter Staffordshire which has quite a different Soyle,
sand and gravell and some clay and very pretty sort of
pebbles in the ground, some of a bright green like an emer-
ald, others veined, some clear like christall; this country is
well wooded and full of enclosures, good rich ground, is
extreamely differing from Darbyshire; just before we came
to Uchater [Uttoxeter] we pass by a very exact House and
Gardens [Beresford Hall] of one Mr Cotten a Justice of
Peace, its brick and coyn'd with stone, the Gardens and
Courts very compleate, but it stands in a low moorish
ground; to show this worlds good is not perfect but has its
foull as well as faire side, and with all its conveniency's must
labour under some difficultyes, we pass thro' a deep and long
water just by, but the bottom was hard gravell, this supply's
severall mills which are used for their prepareing the metal
they take out of the mines, I had a piece of Copper given me
by one of the Managers of them.

Thence we came to Woolsley [Wolseley] 7 mile to a Relations house Sir Charles Woolsley[20] whose Lady was my Aunt, where we dined; the House stands in a fine parke, the House is an old building and but low, its built round a Court; there is a large lofty hall in the old fashion, a dineing and drawing roome on the one hand and a little parlour on the other; the best roomes were newer built with chambers over them and a very good staircase well wanscoated and carv'd with good pictures; the rest of the house is all old and low and must be new built; the Gardens are good both gravell and green walks, there is a good River runns by it which has dwarfe trees and honysuckles and binds on the bancks, there is a great deale of good fruite and there are severall walks, one shady with high trees which my Aunt told me my Mother liked to walke in and so was call'd her walke; I eate a sort of flatt strawbery like a button which grew in a second crop from the same strawbery's roote which produces its first crop a sort of large garden strawberries, and this sort afterwards; in this Country they burn all this tyme of the yeare, July, their fern and make the ashes up in balls and so keep them to make Lye for driveing their Buck of Cloth's, which whitens them much.[21]

Not farre from hence they have the mines of the fine sort of Coale, that is hard and will be pollish'd like black marble, for salts or boxes or such like, the only difference it will not bear the fire as marble does else it resembles it very much;[22] there were of these mines just by, but now they have come to the end of this veine and so there is none within 6 or 7 mile; this is the Pitt Coale thats cloven and burns like a candle and makes white ashes like the Scotch-Coale, the same sort is in Nottinghamshire.

[20] Sir Charles Wolseley (1630–1714) had married Celia's Aunt Ann Fiennes. Like so many of the family, he had sat in Cromwell's "House of Lords"; and was also the author of a book against atheism. For another contemporary account of the house and grounds at Wolseley, see the Diary of the Rev. Rowland Davies (ed. Camden Society), pp. 105–6

[21] Lye, the alkaline solution used for cleansing, was then made from vegetable ash; "driveing" meant fulling or dressing woven fabrics; a "buck" was a tub or vat in which to steep clothes in lye.

[22] Cannel coal, which can be cut and polished like jet.

4. FROM WOLSELEY THROUGH WARWICKSHIRE TO LONDON

FROM HENCE we went to Litchfield [Lichfield] 7 mile a sandy road full of fine pebbles; Litchfield stands low, there is a greate standing water as I have seen just by the town which does often flow the grounds after raines, so the Road is secured with a banck and a breast wall of a good length into the town; its as a long Causy or Bridge the Road is and there are some few arches here and there to carry off the water; the water has very good fish in it, but it must be muddy, its the privilige of the Magistrates only to have fishing or to go about it with a little boate; the town has good houses, the Close has the Bishops and Deanes and Prebends houses which are good, the streetes are very neate and handsome, the breadth and length very well and the building handsome; the Minster is a stately structure but old, the outside has been finely carv'd and full of Images as appears by the nitches and pedistalls which remaine very close all over the walls, and still just at the front remaines some statues of the Kings of Jerusalem[1] and some Angels and Cherubims; at the door is a large statue of King Charles the Second, and all about the door is fine carving of flowers leaves birds and beasts, and some Saints and Apostles statues; the inside of the Church is very neate being new, but there is but little painting; there are two Quires, one old one with organs and seates, the other new which is very large with organs and fine Carving in the wood, here are 2 organs; there is a painting over the Communion table of peach coullour satten like a cannopy with gold fringe, and its drawn so well that it lookes like a reall cannopy; there is some remaines of a Castle, the walls and some of the towers remaine, the wall that encompasses the town is what encompass's the Church and goes from thence.

[1] "But," wrote Defoe, "I cannot say they are all sufficiently distinguished one from another." (Op. cit., ii, 81.)

We went thence to Colehill [Coleshill] 12 mile and pass'd
by severall good houses; here I saw the way of makeing
Runnett [Rennet] as they do in Cheshire: they take the Reed
bag and Curd[2] and haveing washed it clean, salt it and breake
the Curd small about the bag, so drye them being stretched
out with sticks like a glove, and so hang them in a chimney
till you need it, then cut a piece off this as big as halfe a crown
and boyle it in a little water, which water will turn the milke
better than any made runnet and its freshe; this is a pretty
little market town and stands on a hill.

Thence to Coventry all on a levell 8 mile; I came by
severall pretty seates one [Wishaw] on the left hand of Sir
Andrew Hackets stands in a parke and good gardens walled
in, and on the right hand we came close to a very pretty new
built house with severall rows of firrs, the outward Court
came in a compass with open Barrgates just to the road, and a
brick bridge from the Court at one side quite cross the highway—we drove[3] under it—which leads to a parke that runs
along on the other hand; the house was brick and coyn'd
with stone and the windows the same, 8 windows in the
front and the lawrells and greens look't very pretty.

Coventry stands on the side of a pretty high hill and as you
approach it from the adjacent hill you have the full prospect;
the spire and steeple of one of the Churches is very high and
is thought the third highest in England, in the same Church
yard stands another large Church which is something un-
usuall, two such great Churches together,[4] their towers and
the rest of the Churches and high buildings make the town
appear very fine; the streetes are broad and very well pitch'd
with small stone, the Cross[5] is noted and the finest building
in England for such a thing and in my phancy it very much

[2] The calf's stomach and its contents.

[3] Within reasonable distances of Wolseley, Celia Fiennes sometimes drove
instead of riding. Presumably she used the Wolseley equipage. She says
however, when adding up her mileage for the year, that she "did not go
above a hundred in the coach". (See below, p. 132.)

[4] St. Michael's and Holy Trinity.

[5] Built 1541-4, pulled down in 1771. "A *reformed cross* . . . without any
cross thereon, being a master-piece, all for ornament, nothing for superstition; so that the most curious hath just cause to commend, the most con-
scientious to allow, none to condemn it.' (Fuller, *Worthies III*, 269.)

resembles the picture of the Tower of Babel, its all stone carv'd very curiously and there are 4 divisions, each being less than another, to the top, and so its Piramidy forme; in each partition is severall nitches for statues quite round it where are Kings and Queens, and just on each side before each statue is their arms and the arms of England and the arms of the town, and so its adorn'd with coullours and gilding in their proper places, as in the garments and Crowns or Coronets and finely carv'd with Angels and Cherubims and all sorts of beasts birds flowers in garlands and leaves, thus in every division, there is variety quite up to the top which is finely carv'd and gilt.

This is the biggest place in the town and the streete very broad and runs off a great length, and most of the streetes are very good; the buildings are most of timber work and old;[6] there is a Water house at the end of the town which from springs does supply by pipes the whole town with water, in the manner that London is, there is also a water which serves severall mills that belong to the town; it seemes to be a thriveing good trading town and is very rich, they have a great publick stock belonging to the Corporation above 3 thousand pound a year for publick schooles charity and the maintenance of their severall publick expences; of their Magistrates and Companyes, the majority of the heads are now in the sober men's hands, so its esteem'd a Fanatick town; there is indeed the largest Chapple and the greatest number of people I have ever seen of the Presbiterian way, there is another meeteing place in the town of the Independents which is not so bigg, but tho' they may differ in some small things in the maine they agree and seeme to love one another which was no small sattisfaction to me, Charity and Love to the brethren being the characteristicall marke of Christs true Disciples.

Coventry has one thing remains remarkable not to be omitted, the statue of a man looking out of a window with

---

[6] Edward Browne said "Most of the city is built the old wooden way" (op. cit. 40) and Defoe called it "the very picture of the capital city of London, on the south side of Cheapside, before the Great Fire". (Op. cit., ii, 83.)

his eyes out,[7] and is a monument as history tells us of some priviledges obteined by a Lady, wife to the Nobleman who was Lord of the town, and she was to purchase them by passing on horse back through the town naked, which he thought she would not do, but out of zeale to relieve the town from some hard bondage she did, and commanded all windows and doores to be shutt and none to appear in the streete on pain of death, which was obey'd by all, but one man would open a window and looke out and for his impudence had this judgment on him to be struck blind, this statue is his resemblance and one day in a year they remember the good Lady by some rejoyceing.

There are severall good walks about the town, a large parke above the town which most people walk in; thence we went to Warwick; Coventry is joyn'd to Litchfield under one Bishop and that which I wonder at, that the Bishop and most of the Dignatorys and abundance of Gentry rather chooses to live at and near all about Litchfield, tho' it stands so low and watrish, than at Coventry which is a pleasanter scituation and better buildings; there is Sir Thomas Nortons house at the end of the town and a large parke. From Coventry to Warwick going about to see an acquaintance of our Company we made it 10 mile, and went in sight of the Lord Liegh [Leigh] on the left hand which lay all along by the River Aven [Avon], it stands low very well wooded [Stoneleigh Abbey].

We ascended a very steep hill to take a view of the Country and so could see Coventry and were just by Killingworth [Kenilworth] Castle on the right hand, much of the Ruines of the walls remain still; and so enter Warwickshire; the town of Warwick by means of a sad fire about 4 or 5 year since [1694] that laid the greatest part in ashes, its most now new buildings which is with brick and coyn'd with stone and the windows the same; there still remaines some few houses of the old town which are all built of stone; the streetes are

---

[7] According to Misson, "whoever lives in that house, is obliged to new paint the statue every year, and to provide him with a perriwig and a hat". (Op. cit., 60.)

very handsome and the buildings regular and fine, not very lofty being limited by act of parliament to such a pitch and size to build the town; the ruines of the Church still remaines the repairing of which is the next worke design'd;[8] the Chancell stands still, in which was all the fine monuments that were preserv'd from the fire, there is one monument of the great Earle of Leisters [Leicester] and his Ladyes in stone curiously wrought with their garments, and painted and gilded; there is another in marble of the Earle of Warwick, the statue cut very finely, the face hands and form very lively and under his head is a role of straw matting as you would suppose, being exceeding naturall cut in stone; in the middle stands the monument of the Earle[9] that was Regent in France and dyed there and was brought and buried here, his statue at length in armour, but the lines of his face and hands with the veines and sinews were so finely cast and the very aire of his countenance much to the Life or like a liveing man, all cast brass and burnish'd very delicately that it looks like gold, all his armour very exact and his arms are cut finely at his head, and supporters at his feete, with figures and images to adorne it round the tomb-stone; on the one side and each end is 4 and 2: 2 at the end statues of the great men that were of his family, sons and grand children, and on the other side are 4 ladies of the family, all cast in the same burnish'd brass, they are in little and all in religious habits which formerly in the tymes of Popery and superstition most persons coveted to dye in, their garments are folded in differing shapes and with many wrinklings and gathers which is very exact and the more to be noted being all in such a stiff mettle as Brass, and yet it lookes easye and naturall.

On the other side the Church in a little Chapple is a large monument of black and white marble in manner of a bed with pillars, and its grated round the pillars, black marble of some Nobleman [Fulke Greville] with a large inscription round it, and one thing is noted of him there that he thought

[8] The rebuilding was complete in 1704. (H. A. T.)
[9] Richard Beauchamp, Earl of Warwick, Joan of Arc's opponent.

it his greatest character to be esteem'd a great Friend and Companion of Sir Philip Sidney's which is but of poor availe to him now dead, if he was not the friend of the great Jehovah, but such is the folly and vanity of the most of the world to be in esteeme with the wise and great men of this world; there is delicate carving about the walls and round the windows in stone all manner of birds, beasts, laurells, flowers etc., and cherubims and gilded and painted in severall parts.

Warwick Castle is a stately building its now the Lord Brooke's house, you enter thro' two large Courts into a noble hall, wanscoated, within it is a large parlour all wanscoated with Cedar, which is full of fine pictures of the family, and beyond that is a drawing roome and bed chamber with good tapistry hangings, they are old but so good worke and so beautifull the coullours still you would admire it, and the worke so Curious all of silk that the very postures and faces look extreame lively and naturall and the groves streames and rivers looks very well in it; there was good velvet chaires in the roomes and good pictures; within the bed chamber is closets, out of one you looke to the river Aven at the end window—there is so greate a levell you may see near 20 mile, Stowe in the Old [Wold] you see which is as farre, its all full of enclosures and woods most of the Country; all these roomes are very lofty and large and larger than most houses I have seen, the Gardens fine and many without each other with good gravell and grass walks, squares of dwarfe trees of all sorts and steps to descend from one walke to another, the whole of which I saw at one view on the top of the Mount, together with the whole town and a vast prospect all about, the Mount being very high and the ascent is round to an agen[10] secured by cut hedges on the side of the path; at the entrance of the first Court the porter diverts you with a history of Guy Earle of Warwick, there is his walking staff 9 foote long and the staff of a Gyant which he kill'd thats 12 foote long, his sword helmet and shield and breast and back all of a prodigious size, as is his wives iron

[10] To and again, i.e. to and fro.

slippers and also his horses armour and the pottage-pott for his supper, it was a yard over the top; there is also the bones of severall Beasts he kill'd, the rib of the Dun-Cow as bigg as halfe a great cart wheele;[11] 2 miles from the town is his Cave dugg out by his own hands just the dimention of his body as the common people say, there is also his will cut out on stone but the letters are much defaced; these are the storyes and meer fiction for the true history of Guy was that he was but a little man in stature, tho' great in mind and valour, which tradition describes to posterity by being a Gyant; such will the account be of our Hero King William the Third tho' little in stature yet great in atchievements and valour.

From Warwick we went towards Daventry all along part of the Vale of the Red Horse which was very heavy way and could not reach thither being 14 mile; about 11 mile we came to a place called Nether Shugar [Lower or Nether Shuckburgh] a sad village, we could have no entertainment; just by it on the top of a steep hill is Shuggbery Hall a seate of Sir Charles Shuggberys,[12] [Shuckburgh] who seeing our distress, being just night and the horses weary with the heavy way, he very curteously tooke compassion on us and treated us very handsomly that night, a good supper serv'd in plaite and very good wine, and good beds; my Lady Shuggbery was the Lord Leigh's Daughter[13] and that day dineing there her Coach drove by us when in distress enquireing for lodging, which caused Sir Charles to come out to meete us, shewed a generous hospitable spirit to strangers, and with a great deale of good humour my Lady entertained us; the house stands within a good parke, the deer so tame as to come up near the gate which ascends steps to a Court of broad stone; the house looks very handsome built of brick and stone, good hall and large parlour and drawing roome well wanscoated, neatly furnish'd and a little parlour on the

---

[11] Childrey, in *Britannia Baconica* (1661), calls it "the shield bone of a wild bore, far bigger than the greatest oxe bone (it is very likely to be an elephant's)". (Op. cit., 113.) Actually it is a whale's.

[12] Sir Charles was the grandson of that Sir Richard Shuckburgh who was found hunting between the two armies at Edgehill, not knowing of the war.

[13] Celia Fiennes is mistaken. She was the daughter of Lord Willoughby de Broke. (H.A.T.)

other side with good pictures; the butlery kitchen and offices very convenient, two good staircases and 3 or 4 good chambers very well furnish'd, tho' not very rich, but in the generall all things were very well as any private Gentleman has whatever; he has severall good houses; he ordered one of his Daughters to get me a Curiosity they dig up in most part of the hill thereabout, they call them Arms its just like Mullets that they have in an Eschuteon to difference the third son from the first and second in a family.[14]

Thence we went to Daventry 3 miles, a pretty large Market town and good houses all of stone, and so we enter into Northamptonshire; to Northampton town is 8 mile which opens a noble prospect to your sight a mile distant, a large town well built, the streetes as large as most in London except Holborn and the Strand, the houses well built of brick and stone some all stone, very regular buildings; the Town Hall is new built all stone and resembles Guildhall in little; tho' it is a good lofty spacious place there is two Barrs in it with the benches and seat distinct, over one of the Barrs is King William and Queen Mary's pictures at length; the Church is new built its very neate, there is two rows of stone pillars at the entrance of the Church on the outside, and it is to be paved with broad stone but that was not quite finished, they were at worke on some adornments at the front;[15] there is abundance of new building which adds to the beauty of the town; we enter the town from Daventry over a large Bridge, and the water runs twineing about the grounds with rows of willows on each side of it which looks very pretty.

The way out of town towards London you go by a Cross,[16] a mile off the town, call'd High-Cross—it stands just in the middle of England—its all stone, 12 stepps which runs round it, above that is the stone carv'd finely and there are 4 large

[14] The heraldic mullet is a star with five or more points; so presumably the fossil was some species of crinoid, or starfish.

[15] Northampton had been burnt down in 1675. The West Portico of All Saints' Church was not finished until 1701. Celia Fiennes was to note it on her second visit. (See *Victoria County History, Northamptonshire*, iii, 49.)

[16] Queen Eleanor's Cross. Celia Fiennes is confusing this with High Cross, near Hinkley further north-west along the Watling Street, which she noted on a later journey.

Nitches about the middle, in each is the statue of some queen at length which encompasses it with other carvings as garnish, and so it rises less and less to the top like a tower or Piramidy; thence to Stony Stratford so cross the river Aven [Ouse] again 12 mile, and enter Buckinghamshire; at Stony Stratford which is a little place built all stone they make a great deale of Bonelace and[17] so they do all hereabout, its the manuffactory of this part of the Country, they sit and worke all along the streete as thick as can be.

Thence to Great Horwood; this Country is fruitfull full of woods enclosures and rich ground, the little towns stand pretty thicke, you have many in view as you pass the Road; 6 mile to Horwood, thence we pass by a lofty pile of building called Salden a Gentlemans house, and by the rich Mrs Bennets House[18] remarkable for coveteousness which was the cause of her death, her treasures tempted a Butcher to cut her throate, who hangs in chains just against her house; she had 3 daughters the two youngest are living one married to a Benet the other the Earle of Salisbury and are great fortunes by their mothers penuriousness.

Thence to Ouborn [Woburn] and enter Bedfordshire 13 mile; the Duke of Bedfords house[19] we saw, which stands in a fine parke full of deer and wood, and some off the trees are kept cut in works and the shape of severall beasts; the house is an old building, low, there are very good stables and out offices, landry yard, etc.; the Gardens are fine, there is a large bowling-green with 8 arbours kept cut neately, and seates in each, there is a seate up in a high tree that ascends from the green 50 steps, that commands the whole parke

[17] Bonelace is pillow lace; the name comes from the carved bone spindles or bobbins used in making it. "Let it not be condemned for a superfluous wearing, because it doth neither hide nor heat, seeing it doth adorn . . . not expensive of bullion like other lace, costing nothing save a little thread descanted on by art and industry. Hereby many children, who otherwise would be burthensome to the parish, prove beneficial to their parents . . . not to say that it saveth some thousands of pounds yearly, formerly sent over seas to fetch lace from Flanders." (Fuller, *Worthies I*, 397.)

[18] Salden House belonged to the Fortescues; Mrs. Bennett lived at Calverton Manor. The murder is reported in Luttrell's *Brief Relation*, September 20th, 1694.

[19] The house at Woburn was still the Tudor building, but the gardens were more recent, which explains why Celia Fiennes preferred them.

round to see the Deer hunted, as also a large prospect of the Country; there are 3 large Gardens, fine gravell walks and full of fruite—I eate a great quantety of the Red Coralina goosbery which is a large thin skin'd sweete goosebery—the walks are one above another with stone steps; in the square just by the dineing roome window is all sorts of pots of flowers and curious greens fine orange cittron and lemon trees and mirtles strip'd filleroy [phillyrea] and the fine aloes plant; on the side of this pass under an arch into a Cherry garden, in the midst of which stands a figure of stone resembling an old weeder woman used in the garden, and my Lord would have her Effigie which is done so like and her clothes so well that at first I tooke it to be a real living body; on the other side of the house is another large Garden severall gravell walks one above another, and on the flatts are fish ponds the whole length of the walke; above that in the next flat is 2 fish ponds, here are dwarfe trees spread of a great bigness.

From thence we came to Dunstable 7 mile over a sad road called Hockley in the Hole [Hockliffe] as full of deep slows [sloughs], in the winter it must be impasable, there is a very good pitch'd Causey for foote people and horse that is raised up high from the Road, and a very steepe chaulky hill from whence it has its name the Chalk Hill just as you enter Dunstable; its a good town as you shall meete with on the Road, its full of Inns, there is a long large streete with a great water in the streete it looks like a large pond; here I went to see two of my Relations, Daughters to Sir Charles Woolsley, one marry'd there to a Doctor of Physick Dr Marsh with whom was a maiden sister my Cos'n Bridget Woolsly.

Thence to St. Albans and so we enter Hartfordshire 12 mile: there is a very large streete to the Market place, its a pretty large town takeing all, the St. Juliers and that at one end and the other end is St. Nicholas, where is a handsome Church; the great Church which is dedicated to St. Albans is much out of repaire; I see the places in the pavement that was worn like holes for kneeling by the devotes of the Religion, and his votery's, as they tell you, but the whole Church is so worn away that it mourns for some charitable person to help repair it; there are severall good houses about the town one [Holywell House] of the Earle off Maulberoug[20] [Marlborough] and one of Mrs. Gennings [Jennings] the Countess Mother.

Thence we came to Barnet 8 mile, which is in Middlesex and seemes to be a very sharpe aire, its a large place and the houses are made commodious to entertain the Company that comes to drink the waters,[21] which certainly if they be at the paines to go once and see would have but little stomach to drink them; the well is a large place walled in 8 square, its at least two yards over and built 2 or 3 yards up from the water and over it is lattices of wood round to looke down into it and so covered like a house above, below are staires down to a doore to go in to dip the water there; I stood at the lowest step above the water to look into it, its full of leaves and dirt and every tyme they dip it troubles the water, not but what they take up and let stand looks clear but I could not taste it; its very deep and not done at the bottom with a bason as Tunbridg, neither can you see the bottom, so that it appears not to be a quick spring as Tunbridg or the Spaw or Hamstead waters, which have all fine stone basons in which you see the springs bubble up as fast, and by a pipe runs off as clear and fast; it more resembles Epsom for which reason I dislike that; thence to Highgate 6 miles, thence to London 4 miles, where I returned and all our Company, Blessed be God, very well without any disaster or trouble in 7 weeks tyme about 635 miles that we went together.

[20] Here a marginal note says "now Duke of Marlborough". As the Dukedom was created on December 14th, 1702, this suggests that Celia Fiennes had written her account before that date.
[21] Pepys found the Barnet waters almost too efficacious. See *Diary*, July 11th, 1664.

5. THE DOVER ROAD

MY JOURNEY to Canterbery and Dover in Kent the same year from Amwell [Amwell Bury] in Hartfordshire.

I went to Royston [Roydon] 1 mile and Epin [Epping] in
Essex 9 mile, thence to Rumford [Romford] through lanes
and much wood—that part of Essex is full of woods—that
was 10 mile; thence to Abnife[1] 14 mile, thence to Tilbury 3
mile which is a fine fort, a great flatt to the land full of watry
ditches and may be flooded all over, here was the fight by the
parliament in 1640;[1a] there are severall Buildings by themselves of a triangular form of brick-work, in which the powder
and amunition is kept; here is a ferry over to Gravesend where
we enter Kent which lyes just over against it, a little snugg
town under a hill, the houses little and thick together fitt
only for seamen and soldiers that are employ'd in the water
or the fort; I saw severall Colliers pass by laden towards
London; the Thames here is very rough and deep so as we
ferry over in a boate like a Hoy.

Thence I went to Rochester 7 mile most in lanes; we enter
the town over the Medway, which is the finest River I ever
saw it runs thence to the sea and meetes the Thames at the
Boy in Nore and so they fall into the sea together, but it ebbs
and flows up a great way above Rochester and is very salt;
the Bridg at Rochester[2] is the finest in England, nay its said
to equal any in the world, it is not built upon with houses
as London Bridge, but its very long and fine iron spikes like
a grate is on the top of the wall, which is breast high, and
these irons on the top which are above a yard more; its indented at each arch as all bridges are, there are 9 large arches
with the middle one which is to be opened by drawing up to
give passage to barges and little vessells; when the tyde was
out I saw the worke of the arches is with wood cut hollow
and stands a good distance into the water, to keep the water
from bearing too hard against the Bridge.

The town is large includeing the suburbs and all, for there
is a large place before you pass the river, which washes quite

[1] Possibly Aveley.

[1a] This must refer to the capture of Tilbury by Fairfax in 1647.

[2] Every traveller admired the bridge at Rochester, which was built c. 1400
and pulled down in 1856. "Through eleven high and large arches", wrote
Baskerville, "'proud Neptune charges the sweet purling stream of Medway."
(Op. cit., 277.) Celia Fiennes nearly always differs from her contemporaries as
to the number of arches in the bridges they saw, and she was generally wrong.

round that side of the town to the Dock yards, that a mile from it, where are two large yards for building ships; I saw severall large shipps building others refitting; there was in one place a sort of arches like a bridge of brick-work, they told me the use of it was to let in the water there and so they put their masts in to season; besides this dock here are severall streetes of houses on this hill which is pretty high and is just against Rochester, and on the hill you have the best prospect of the town and see the severall good Churches in it, and the Castle which is a pretty little thing, just by the Medway, which runs along by it and so at foote of this hill in a round, and so onward to sea; there were severall shipps at anchor along the River; all behind the town is another hill which is covered with fine woods that looks very fine.

Thence to Sittingburn [Sittingbourne] 11 mile all in sight of the lovely Medway, this is a very good town for the road and travellers as you shall meete with, the Church is all built with flints headed so curiously that it looks like glass and shines with the suns reflection.

Thence to Canterbury 16 mile, we pass by great Hop-yards on both sides of the Road and this year was great quantetyes of that fruite here in Kent; we pass by Feversham [Faversham] just at the towns end, which is 9 mile from Canterbury, its a very large town and good buildings of bricke; Canterbury opens to view 6 miles distant, by the advantage of a high hill we pass over to it, its a noble Citty, the gates are high tho' but narrow, the streetes are most of them large and long and the buildings handsome, very neat but not very lofty, most are of brickwork; its a flourishing town, good tradeing in the Weaving of Silks:[3] I saw 20 Loomes in one house with severall fine flower'd silks, very good ones, and its a very ingenious art to fix the warps and chaine in their Loomes to cast their work into such figures and flowers, there stands a boy by every Loome and pulls

[3] Silk weaving in England began c. 1600, but these fabrics were less popular than those imported by the East India Company. By 1697 the native industry had been protected from this competition by legislation, and technically improved by Huguenot refugees. (See Misson op. cit., 302 and Defoe op. cit., i, 118.) Misson remarks on the excellence of English silk stockings.

up and down threads which are fastened to the weaving and so pulls the chaine to the exact form for the shuttle to work through.

There are also Paper mills[4] which dispatches paper at a quick rate; they were then makeing brown paper when I saw it; the mill is set agoing by the water and at the same tyme it pounded the raggs to morter for the paper, and it beate oat-meale and hemp and ground bread together that is at the same tyme; when the substance for the paper is pounded enough they take it in a great tub and so with a frame just of the size of the sheetes of paper, made all of small wire just as I have seen fine screens to screen corne in, only this is much closer wrought, and they clap a frame of wood round the edge, and so dip it into the tub and what is too thinn runs through; then they turn this frame down on a piece of coarse woollen just of the size of the paper and so give a knock to it and it falls off, on which they clap another such a piece of woollen cloth which is ready to lay the next frame of paper, and so till they have made a large heape which they by a board on the bottom move to a press, and so lay a board on the top and so let down a great screw and weight on it, which they force together into such a narrow compass as they know so many sheetes of paper will be reduced, and this presses out all the thinner part and leaves the paper so firme as it may be taken up sheete by sheete, and laid to-gether to be thoroughly dryed by the wind; they told me white paper was made in the same manner only they must have white woollen to put between; there is a great number of French people in this town[5] which are employ'd in the weaving and silk winding, I meete them every night going home in great Companyes, but then some of them were employ'd in the hopping, it being the season for pulling them.

[4] Paper-making was another industry which owed much to the Huguenots who fled to England after the Revocation of the Edict of Nantes in 1685. Previously the one large-scale English product had been the brown paper made at Dartford. (See *Social England*, ed. Traill, iv, 583.)

[5] It has been estimated that 80,000 refugees, mostly French, arrived in England between 1670 and 1690 (ibid., iv, 450) and more came during the next decade. The native population was between 5½ and 7 millions at this time.

Here is a Spring in the town that is dranck by many persons as Tunbridge and approv'd by them, but others find it an ill water; one Gentleman in the same house I was in complained of a numbness in his limbs after drinking it sometyme, which is quite contrary to Tunbridge waters whose property is to retrieve lost limbs that are benumbed, and it comeing from steele should have that effect, it raiseing the blood and gives it a new circulation; the taste of the spring in this town seemes to be from a mixt soyle and bears a likeness to the Sulpher Spaw Epsome and the Iron springs too which are at Tunbridge: what its operation is I cannot tell only tasteing halfe a glass of it which I did not like; the well is walled in, and a raile round with stepps down and paved aboute for the Company to stand just at the head to drink, but I like no spring that rises not quick and runs off apace; that must have most spirit and good off the minerall it comes from.

There is fine walks and seates and places for the musick to make it acceptable and comodious to the Company; there is a large Market house and a town Hall over it in the town, but the Cathedrall is the finest sight there, the carving of stone is very fine on the outside, as also within; but its not so large as Salisbury; its a square tower no spire running up from it but the small ones at each corner of the tower for ornament; there are two large Isles in the middle of the Church which leads to open gates of iron barrs and spikes, thence is an ascent of 20 steps, as Winchester Church is, up to the Quire, where is a fine large organ; so is the font well carv'd and painted and gilded, the bottom is white and grey marble with white marble statues round the stem to the foote, the top is made in a pirimidy carv'd and painted; the windows in the Quire are most delicately painted as ever I saw, the Curiosity of the worke and coullours beyond others, but the size of the windows much inferior being very small for a Church; the Glass is very thick and the coullours laid on it strikes through the glass, its coullours tinctures all the glass, an art which now is lost amongst us; at the alter is a Cloth and Coushons of purple figured velvet the books the same, there is a broad tissue border of orrace work gold and silver, and at the edge is a fine knotted fringe of purple silk and gold, the Bishops seate and Cushon the same, which was given by our good Queen Mary King Williams Queen when she was at Canterbery [1693].

The Chapter house is pretty lofty supported by its own worke with out pillars, its ceiled with Irish oake; there are severall good monuments of the Kings and Queens and great men, and severall Bishops; there is one Bishops[6] statue that was at the paines to divide the Bible into Chapters which makes it more commodious to the reader, and was a good employment for him, it being the proper subject of such a person of the Church to studdy the holy scriptures which gives the truest wisdom; there is the Chaire that all the Arch Bishops are inaugurated in when made Arch Bishops, its wood with elbows; there is another statue of a Bishop cut out in wood his robes and all well carv'd and is firm and solid still except some small deffaceing by the soldiers in the warre tyme, and this has stood some 100 of yeares; there is a Chapple called Thomas of Beckets Crown, the roofe being carv'd in the form of a crown and painted; there is also a pavement which is much worne by the feete and knees off this Saints votarys that came to do obeysance to his Shrine; there is one brass statue in armour,[7] but its not so bright being less regarded than that at Warwick; under the Cathedrall is a large Church just like St. Faiths under St. Pauls in London; this is given to the French protestants in the town for the worshipping God; it holds a vast number of people, its as full of seates as can thrust by each other; it seemed a little darkish but they say when the doores are open its light enough, its so well arch'd that they cannot hear them in the Cathedrall when singing, at least no wayes to disturb them.

I went out another part of the town thro' a good gate and so to Dover 15 mile, much up hill and down, it was a good Road and sort of champion country, yet at a distance you see

6 Stephen Langton's, in St. Michael's Chapel.
7 The Black Prince.

many good woods and pretty houses with rows of trees; the
Castle at Dover[8] is discover'd five mile off standing on the
edge of a very steep high hill, on which you ascend up to
the tower 120 steps up, whence you discover Callice [Calais]
in France; I saw the clifts and hills plaine, but in some cleer
dayes towards the evening you may see the towers and
buildings of Callice; you likewise see a vast way on all sides
sea ward, and to the land; the Castle is left much to decay
and ruinated, only a small appartment for the Governour of
three or four roomes, else the whole is spoyl'd, the floores
taken up and wanscoate pulled down; I was in the roome
Queen Elizabeth was kept prisoner in till the Death of Queen
Mary, the balcony just by in which she saw the Messenger
coming which she supposed was of Death to take off her
head, but proved the Messenger that brought the news of
the Crown and Kingdoms falling to her by the death of her
sister;[9] she afterwards repaired the Chapple but now its
quite out of use the roofe and side being mouldred down in
many places.

There is a fine dry well in the Castle walled curiously of
a vast depth, the use of it was to discover the work of the
miners in tyme of a siege, whereabout they were at worke,
going down into this well discovered the working by the
shaking the earth at what side they were at worke, and so
might defeat them by a countermine; there is also a great
well of 60 fathom deep the water is drawn up by a great
wheele with a horse; notwithstanding its so deep yet its also
wide and exactly down right that I could see the water at
the top, and when I flung a stone which was a pretty while
descending I saw when it plashed into the water; there is on
the Plattform guns mounted which being so high commands
the Road so as no ship durst saile under it; its a mighty steep
Clift at the poynt which makes ones head giddy to look
down to the sea; there is one Gun of cast brass of a great
length finely carv'd and adorn'd with figures, this carrys

a ball a great way, tho' the bore or muzzle of the Gun be not bigger then my fist so the Ball its charged with cannot be bigg but it will do execution a great way off; this was made at Utriche [Utrecht] in Holland and presented to Queen Elizabeth, its worth a great sum of money for its curiosity; there is a little Cannon of the same worke which I have seen in the Tower at London, there is a great inscription on it; there are Gunns also planted in a little fort at the foote of this steepe clift to secure the Road from Pirates, for as to Dover town it looks like a place of no deffence, its a little place, the houses are little and looks thrust together; there is a market house and town hall, its well enough for the accomodation of the seamen and to supply the shipps with anything; it seems where the town stands the sea formerly came in, and was cover'd under water severall fathom deep so as the shipps ride there in harbour and the town was only within the limits of a wall which encompass's the Castle of which small matters appears, only of a great Banck and some parts of the ruines of the foundation, but the sea leaving the shore so farre they have built this town which has no gates.[10]

Thence we went to Deale 7 mile all by the sea side which is called the Downs, which sometymes is full of shipps all along the Road but now there were not many; the Downs seemes to be so open a place and the shoar so easye for landing I should think it no difficulty to land a good army of men in a little tyme, there is only 3 little forts or Castles they call them, about a miles distance one to another Warworth [Walmer] at Deal and Sandwich, which hold a few Guns but I should think they would be of little effect and give the enemy no great trouble; Deale looks like a good thriveing place the buildings new and neate brickwork with gardens, I believe they are most masters of shipps houses and seamen or else those that belong to the Cordage and saile makeing, with other requisites to shipping, all this Country about

[10] Misson thought it "surprising that Dover should be one of the Cinque Ports, when it cannot properly be said to have any port at all, but only an entrance for small barks". (Op. cit., 68.)

seemes to be a very fruitfull soyle and full of woods; you
see a many pretty towns altogether almost, neate Churches
and towers all the way you travell from Dover to Deale on
your left hand, but beyond Deale you go a very deepe heavy
sand for 4 mile to Sandwich; you go along by the Sea side
in sight of the Isle of Thannet which is just over against
Sandwich, and is so neer it you see the land and inclosures
and woods and houses—I suppose its not a quarter of a
league from Sandwitch—this is a sad old town all timber
building, you enter by a gate and so you go out of it by a
gate, but its run so to decay that except one or two good
houses its just like to drop down the whole town.[11]

Thence to Canterbery ten mile most thro' Lanes, we come
by my Lord Winchelseas house [The Moat] gardens and
parck, the house is an old building; and so I entered Canterbery another way through another gate, and observ'd all
wayes to the town being from hills gives the prospect of the
town very finely to the eye, and indeed it lookes like a good
Citty altogether which way ever you looke on it in the approach; from thence to Maidstone I went 9 mile back the way
I came, and on the hill 6 mile off which gave me so fine a
sight of Canterbury as I came did likewise present a pleaseing
prospect as I returned, it being a very high hill commands
the view of the Country a vast way, and with such variety
of woods rivers and inclosures and buildings that was very
delicate and diverting; when I turned off the road to Maidstone I travell'd through lanes and woods which were very
fine but hid the sight of the Country about, being so close
that it was the privatest Road I have travell'd, indeed about
10 mile short of Maidstone you ascend a very steep hill which
discovers the whole Country at one view 40 mile off backward from whence we came, and a few paces on the top of
the hill the descent of the hill on that other side is so great
a fall that gives you as full a discovery of the Country all
forward, both which shew the variety of grounds intermixt
with each other and lesser hills and plaines and rivers which
such advanced grounds present the travellers at one view;

11 The decay of Sandwich was due to the silting up of the harbour.

this is called Boxlye [Boxley] Hills and is part of the same Ridge of hills which runs along by Epsome.

From Canterbery its 30 mile to Maidstone; Maidstone town is a very neate market town as you shall see in the Country, its buildings are mostly of timber worke the streets are large the Market Cross runs down in the middle of the greate streete a good way, there being three divisions in it one good Cross for fruite another for corne and another for all sorts of things, 2 of which is built over for the Town Hall and publick use; there is also a large Goal; this streete, notwithstanding the hall and cross stands in the midst, is yet a good breadth on each side and when it comes to meete in one is very broad and runs down a great length, quite to the bridge cross the Medway, which is not very broad here yet it beares Barges that bring up burdens to the town; it seemes to divide the town for beyond the Bridge are buildings whole streetes which runs along the river, there are very pretty houses about the town look like the habitations of rich men, I believe its a wealthy place, there are severall pretty streetes;[12] this was Market day being Thursday and it seemed to be well furnish'd with all sorts of commodityes and I observed there was great quantety's of Leather but could not learn what particular thing that was their staple Comodity or tradeing in, but in generall it seemed to be like a little faire for the variety of wares tho' they told me that was not so full a Market as some dayes, because the Country people were taken up aboute their hopping so could not bring things to Market.

Thence to Rochester 8 mile, I came by a great many fine hopp-yards where they were at work pulling the hopps, I came into Rochester at the other side thro' the wood on the hill I mentioned before, from whence the town and the dock yards washed by the Medway, with the shipps at anchor, was as acceptable a prospect and diverting as was the other on

[12] Defoe called Maidstone "a town of very great business and trade, and yet full of gentry, of mirth, and of good company". (Op cit., i, 115.) The "staple commodity" which Celia Fiennes could not discover was the making of linen thread.

the other side; I went through the town just by the great
Church which is a good building but nothing curious, also
I went by the Castle wall which is but small what remaines
of it, thence over the fine bridge; and as I travell'd all along
in sight of the Medway to Rochester, so next day I went in
sight of the Thames, but from Rochester I went that night
to Gravesend which is all by the side of Cherry grounds that
are of severall acres of ground and runs quite down to the
Thames, which is convenient for to convey the Cherries to
London; for here the great produce of that fruite is, which
supplyes the town and country with the Kentish Cherrys,
a good sort of Flemish fruite;[13] I went 2 mile beyond Gravesend—which made it in miles 9 from Rochester—to a little
place called Northfleete, its much in the woods.

Thence I went to Dartfford, much on the hills and all in
sight of the Thames and see the shipps saile along to Dartfford 6 mile, a little neate town; thence to Shutershill
[Shooter's Hill] 2 mile, on the top of which hill you see a
vast prospect exactly round about it being a great height of
ground and such a descent every way that commands the
sight of a vast tract of ground, which appeares in the greatest
variety some lands clothed with trees others with grass and
flowers, gardens, orchards, with all sorts of herbage and
tillage, with the severall little towns all by the river, Eariff
[Erith], Leigh [Lee], Woolwich, etc., quite up to London,
Greenwitch, Deadford [Deptford], Black Wall, the Thames
twisting and turning it self up and down bearing severall
vessells and men of warre on it, and some under saile; on
this part of the River I have seen 100 saile of shipps pass by
in a morning which is one of the finest sights that is;[14] added
to this you view all Black Heath, the Kings Parke att Greenwitch and a vast Country on that side, besides the places
whence I came; by turning about I could view at least 20

[13] The Kentish cherry orchards were first stocked in the early sixteenth
century from Flanders. Kent was already the Garden of England and gave
the best wages to agricultural labourers—4 to 5 shillings an acre in harvest
time, plus 2 shillings a day food allowance. (See Baskerville, op. cit., 280.)
[14] A few months after Celia Fiennes passed, Peter the Great borrowed
John Evelyn's house at Deptford to study the Thames shipping.

mile; this is esteemed as a noted Robbing place;[15] on this hill are severall springs of water which comes from allum which are a very quick purger, much like Epsome and Dullage [Dulwich], but I thinke farre exceeds either in strength and opperation, thence to Greenwitch 2 mile where I ferry'd over, and observ'd one little shipp passed by me, which I observ'd was farr behind me in the morning at Gravesend and sailed along in sight all the tyme and was gotten before me; I ferry'd to Popler [Poplar] and Stepney, so to Hackney 3 mile, thence to Tatnum [Tottenham] 2 mile, thence to End-field[16] [Enfield] 5 mile, which is all in Middlesex ever since I ferry'd over out of Kent; thence to Amwellbery 10 mile in Hartfordshire which I compleated in 5 days and went 184 miles which, added to severall journeys I went in Hartford-shire and twice to Amwell and to London againe which is 76 mile alone, and the severall journeys at London and in Hartfordshire, comes to 150 more miles—besides the little rideings to take the aire at the parke or else which were severall miles more if added together—which I have gone this year, but without that it is 226 miles so add these to my Northern Journey this yeare makes about 1045 miles of which I did not go above a hundred in the Coach.

[15] It was here that, even a hundred years later, Don Juan was to meet with highwaymen (Byron, *Don Juan*, Canto xi, 8–17.)

[16] According to Macaulay Enfield Chase "was a region of five and twenty miles in circumference, which contained only three houses and scarcely any inclosed fields. Deer, as free as in an American forest, wandered there by thousands." (*History*, i, 311.) Unfortunately the reference Macaulay gives for this statement does not appear to exist. It is, however, confirmed by Thoresby (*Diary*, ii, 163.)

6. TUNBRIDGE WELLS AND SUSSEX

I BEING in Kent this year shall insert something of Tun-bridge[1] the waters I have dranke many years with great

[1] Tunbridge Wells was at this date the most fashionable of the "Spaws". Hamilton in his *Memoirs of Count Gramont* relates that "the Company, though always numerous, is always select; since those who repair thither for diversion ever exceed the number of those who go thither for health". Misson agreed: "The pretence of these waters brings together vast numbers of people, of

advantage, they are from the Steele and Iron mines, very quick springs especially one well, there are two with large basons of stone fixt in the earth with severall holes in the bottom by which the springs bubble up and fill it, so as it alwayes runns over notwithstanding the quantety dipp'd up in a morning—which is the usual tyme the Company comes —and the nearer they drink it the spring the better, it being a spiriteous water that is ready to evaporate if carry'd any way, as has been try'd by weighing the water by the Well and carrying them but to the middle of the Walks it has lost of the weight, and much more the end of the whole Walke; notwithstanding, many has it brought to their lodgings a mile or two off and drink them in their beds, nay some have them brought to London which is near 40 miles; they have the bottles filled and corked in the well under the water and so seale down the corks which they say preserves it.

They have made the Wells very comodious by the many good buildings all about it and 2 or 3 mile round, which are Lodgings for the Company that drinke the waters, and they have encreased their buildings so much that makes them very cheape; all people buy their own provision at the Market which is just by the Wells and furnish'd with great plenty of all sorts flesh fowle and fish, and in great plenty is brought from Rhye and Deale etc., this being the road to London, so all the season the water is drank they stop here which makes it very cheape, as also the Country people come with all their back yard and barne door affords, to supply them with, and their gardens and orchards which makes the markets well stored and provision cheape, which the Gentry takes as a diversion while drinking the waters to go and buy their dinners it being every day's market and runns the whole length of the Walke, which is between high trees on the market side for shade and secured with a row of buildings on the right side which are shopps full of all sorts of toys, silver, china, milliners, and all sorts of curious wooden ware, which this place is noted for the delicate neate and thin ware

both sexes, that are in very good health." (Op. cit. 330.) See also Introduc tion, p. xxvi. (Cf. Macky i, 117-121 and Defoe, i, 126.)

of wood both white and Lignum vitæ wood;[2] besides which there are two large Coffee houses for Tea Chocolate etc., and two roomes for the Lottery and Hazard board; these are all built with an arch or pent house beyond the shops some of which are supported by pillars like a peasa [piazza], which is paved with brick and stone for the drye walking of the Company in raine, else they walke with out which is a clay and sand mixed together—they have been intending to make it gravel which would be much better—all those conveniency's are added by the Companyes contributions every year, what has been and so what will be.[3]

There is at the lower end of the Walke, which is a broad space before you come to the walls of the Wells, where is a large sun dial set up on severall steps of stone; thence you go straight along to a Chapple[4] which has been built by the severall collections of the Company every year; its a pretty place and cost a great deal of money and every year there is a contribution for the maintenance of a minister; there are severall buildings just about the Well where are severall apothecary's shops there is also a roome for the post house; the Post comes every day and returns every day all the while the season of drinking the waters is, from London and to it, except Mondayes none comes down from London, so on Satturdayes non goes up to London; you pay a penny Extraordinary for being brought from Tunbridge town which is 4 mile distance, that being a post town, you likewise have the conveniency of Coaches every day from London for 8 shillings apiece dureing the whole season and Carriers twice a week.

There are severall bowling-greens about the Wells one just at it on Mount Sion, and another up the hill called Mount

[2] "Tunbridge Ware" was made from beech or sycamore inlaid with other woods. It was first made c. 1685 by a Mr. Wise. Harriet Smith preserved Mr. Elton's discarded 'court-plaister' in "a pretty little Tunbridge-ware box".

[3] The Pantiles were not yet constructed. The young Duke of Gloucester, the one surviving child of Princess Anne, fell over the bank here while playing soldiers in 1697—he was top-heavy, being hydrocephalous—and the Princess ordered proper paving to be laid.

[4] The Church or Chapel of King Charles the Martyr.

Ephraim, where is also a large Chapple, where the Presbi-
terians have preaching; they have a minister which by the
collections of the Company is also maintained all the winter
to preach, as is the publick Chapple at the Walks, there is
severall other bowling greens at a distance off a mile or two
fitted for the Companys Lodging, there, as Rust Hall and
Southborough; they have all houses to the greens so the
Gentlemen bowle the Ladies dance or walke in the green in
the afternoones, and if wet dance in the houses there being
Musick maintained by the Company to play in the morning
so long while they drink the waters and in the afternoon for
danceing; there are severall good taverns at the Walks and all
about to supply good wine, and Brew houses for beer and
Bakers for bread, but some of them come from London and
spoyle the market by raiseing the price, so the higlers and
hucksters in a great measure;[5] this whole Country is full of
stone and iron the earth is clay and sand.

About 3 mile off there is a good seate of the Lord Lesters
[Leicester's] Spenshurst [Penshurst Place] which stands in a
very good parke; the house is but old, large roomes and
stone staires and windows, a good hall and gallery full of
good old pictures, and other roomes of State, no furniture
but old tapistry hangings; you have a most pleasant prospect
as you go to it and from it, of valeys cover'd with woods [of]
great length and hills beyond on the other side; about three
or 4 [miles] off is a seate [Eridge] of the Lord Abergauneys
[Abergavenny], which is Lord of the Manour, in a parke
and fine woods all about it; the most of the Country is
woody; there is 4 or 5 mile off a place they cast Gunns[6] there

---

[5] "You engage with the Ladies at play without any introduction . . . every
Gentleman is equally received by the Fair Sex upon the Walks. This indis-
tinction is attended with one inconvenience, that Sharpers, whose trade is to
go Genteel . . . mix themselves in all the diversions. . . . They are the first that
bid you beware of Sharpers, when they design themselves to pick your
pocket. All Shopkeepers are in fee with these fellows." (Macky, op. cit., i,
119.)

[6] Iron-smelting in the Weald was still going on. It had arisen because
water-power, oak woods for charcoal, and iron-stone near the surface were
all found here together. It was very soon to cease, as the forests were giving
out and as coal-smelting was about to come in.

being a great store of oare [ore] all over the Country, its a great charge and continuall attendance; when they have lighted the fire for to cast bells or guns they must be cautiously blowing and the mettle will be apt to fall down on the nose of the bellows and harden that if it be not still ·cleared off would quickly damm up the fire and put it out; there are severall good houses all about and a pleasant place to ride in in the summer and dry weather but a sad deep unpassable road when much raine has fallen; as I was rideing about I took a view of the country in many parts; there is a little rivulet just by the Wells which divides the Countys so that the buildings are some in Kent and some in Sussex.

About Faint [Frant] 4 or 5 mile off is a house of Lord Abergauny [Abergavenny] and parkes and much woods about it; another way by Lakington Green [Langton Green] and Groombridge about 4 mile off is an old house in a parck, pretty large, called Ashurst which they say belonged to alderman Ashurst family, but hurst which signifies grove or wood is a name all here about as Spenshurst [Penshurst] Lord Lesters house 4 mile another way in a good parke, and Speldhurst another parish 2 or 3 mile off and Good-hurst [Goudhurst] about 12 mile off the Wells; I went by Calvery [Calverley] Plaine and Woodsgate [Woodgate] and so to a little market town called Branklye [Brenchley], the way is much thro' lanes being an enclosed Country for the most part, which is the cause of these names, as is much of Sussex which joyns to Kent, there are places called Billingshurst and Medhurst and Pendhurst etc.; this Goodhurst [Goud-hurst] I went to, stands on a great hill and is seen severall miles, 2 mile from the first ascent, which is at a little village belonging to it, and to the top of the hill which is the middle of the place; its a pretty large place, old timber houses, but the extent of the parish is neare ten mile, they are a sort of yeomanly Gentry, about 2 or 3 or 400£ a year and eate and drink well and live comfortably and hospitably; the old proverb was a Yeoman of Kent with one years Rent could buy out the Gentlemen of Wales and Knight of Scales and a Lord of the North Country, his Estate was so much better.[7]

All in these parts are the same Minerall waters being much on iron mines; I returned again to Tunbridge Wells the 12 mile, then I went from thence to Suṁerhill [Somerhill] about 4 or 5 mile of; thro' much woods and lanes and some pleasant shades of lofty trees, this is a seate of the last Viscount Purbecks[8] stands on a hill in a good large parke, built of stone and lookes in good repair for the most part, and good large roomes and staircases and abundance of good sizeable roomes leading one out of another in visto's thro' the house, something like our new way of building, and lofty enough; its capable of being very fine with little charge; the parke is fine with visto's of walks cut through and across, a great many which delights the rider or walker being so shady with lofty trees; there is remains of a bowling green which is an advanced piece of ground above all the rest, and discovers the Country a great circuite round; then we returned to the Wells againe 5 mile.

Then I went from the Wells to Rye 31 miles, by Ambursly [Lamberhurst] 8 mile, this was good way being a drye summer, otherwise its deep being clay for the most part; I pass'd much through lanes and little villages and near Rhye [Rye] I went thro' a coṁon full of bushes and furze and heath, its a pretty steep hill I ascended which is called Beggars Hill, and being Bartholomew-tide [August 24th] here was a faire which was rightly called Beggar-Hill Faire being the saddest

---

[7] These clothiers and farmers, said Defoe, "for the plainness of their appearance are called the gray coats of Kent; but are so considerable that who ever they vote for is always sure to carry it, and therefore the gentlemen are very careful to preserve their interest among them". (Op. cit., i, 115-6.) "Scales" means Cales, i.e. Cadiz. The Earl of Essex was held to have cheapened knighthood by creating 60 new knights on his expedition against Cadiz in 1596. See Fuller, *Worthies II*, 121.

[8] Somerhill had been built in 1613 by the Earl of Clanricarde. Later it passed to Lady Muskerry, now "Lady Purbeck", who had no right to that title, as her husband was only the son of a bastard son of a real Lady Purbeck. "Lady Purbeck" was deformed and very ugly, but had a passion for dancing in public. She was called "the Princess of Babylon" for reasons which will be found in *Gramont's Memoirs*. After "Lord Purbeck" was killed in a duel in 1684 she married the Jacobite "Beau" Feilding. She died in 1698 and her husband was later tricked into marrying a prostitute, and also tricked the sixty-four-year-old Duchess of Cleveland into a bigamous marriage with himself. It is surprising that Celia Fiennes should have recognized the title, or brought herself to visit the house of such raffish people.

faire I ever saw, ragged tatter'd booths and people, but the musick and danceing could not be omitted; this hill on the top gave the view of the sea and a great tract of land on each side that is choak'd up with sand, which formerly was a good haven for shipps; the sea does still come up to Rhye town as yet but its shallow, and the Castle which stands a little distance a mile is also left of the sea at least 4 mile; this is Winchelsea Castle but all between it and Winchelsea is nothing but quagmire and marshes draned in some places by ditches, and this is at least 4 miles to the town which was all flowed up to the town; I did go to it but first ferry'd over a little arm of the sea which still finds a current up to some of the land between Rhye and Winchelsea; then I rode round the marshes on the side of a hill in narrow foote paths and passed over a Bridge cross another little arme of the sea, near it is a gate on the Bridge and enters you into the Libertys of the town, which stands on a pretty high hill from it and lookes not of any great circuite of ground by the first view, being high, but in the middle you see it has been a fine place for there were 36 large squares of buildings; the remaines of pieces of walls in most places you see or else a hedge supplys that you see the streetes were very broad and long and divided these squares, the cross streetes the same; I rode up a middle streete and saw the others run across of equal breadth, remaines of Churches and halls are to be seen, but else grass grows now where Winchelsea was, as was once said of Troy;[9] there are but a very few houses now but the Corporation still continues and the major and aldermen which 13 makes most of the inhabitants; Mr. Majors [Mayor's] house look'd neate as did the parsonage; they elect two Burgesses to it in the parliament and its the ancientest Corporation in England, so that should Lord Major of London meete Mr. Major of Winchelsea he must give him place; it was a flourishing place before the sea left it [as any] that was in England, but now lost as Rhye [Rye] will be in a little tyme if the sea

[9] Unexpectedly, Celia Fiennes is quoting Ovid (*Heroides* I, i,53). Lieutenant Hammond had written in 1635, "Surely this towne was formerly of great note, when (as they say) 50 brave taverne signs shin'd in her, now scarce one signe for a cup of good beere." (*Short Survey of Western Counties*, p. 28.)

leaves it, which is in a very fair way to do, and men now apply to quite drane the marshes for corn and grass rather then endeavour to cleare the channell of the sand, which if it were done would be the best harbour for shipps as formerly was; there are great vaults in Winchelsea which was the merchants cellars and ware houses; there was some few brass and marble statues in the Church but much demolished as was the Church.

Rhye [Rye] town is not very bigg a little market place, this is famous for fish, from hence all the good Turbutt Pearle[9a] and Dorea and all sort of sea fish comes to supply the Wells and London, but I could get little, the faire took up the fishermen; indeed here I dranke right French white wine[10] and exceeding good, and then returned to the Wells 38 miles; in the Road from thence to London you go either by Fairlane [Fairlawn] and so come just by Sir Harry Vaines [Vane's] house (now Lord Barnett [Barnard])[11] which lookes very fincly with the rows of trees about it; or else you go by Sevenoake [Sevenoaks] a sad deep clay way after wett; you come in sight of a great house on a hill called Summerly [Somerhill] looks like a little town it runs on so much ground, it was the Lord Purbeckes.

You also come in sight of Nonsuch[12] which was a great house of the kings built by Charles the Second; you pass on to the River head [Riverhead] as they call it, a fine spring of cleare water that runs thence in a little river; this is at the foote of a great hill called Madam Scott [Madamscourt] Hill so steepe as seldome is either rode down or up, and few coaches but gaines the top of it by a compass round it, which is steep enough; this is 15 mile from the Wells; thence to Farnburough [Farnborough] about 8 mile, thence to Brumley [Bromley] and to London 15 mile more.

[9a] Pearle and Dorea are Brill and John Dory.

[10] The French wine was very likely smuggled. Celia Fiennes rarely obtained it except near the coast.

[11] Fairlawn, near Shipbourne, now belonged to Christopher Vane, son of Sir Harry. He was made Lord Barnard in 1699.

[12] She may mean Knole, but certainly cannot mean Nonsuch, which was near Ewell and had already been pulled down by the Duchess of Cleveland, to whom Charles II had given it.

THE
'GREAT JOURNEY'
OF 1698

AITCHISON BANK
NEWCASTLE
CARLISLE
HALTWHISTLE
DURHAM
PENRITH
LOWTHER
RICHMOND
KENDAL
LANCASTER
HARROGATE
LEEDS
PRESTON
MANCHESTER
LIVERPOOL
FLINT
CHESTER
DERBY
SHREWSBURY
WOLSELEY
LEICESTER
NORWICH
PETERBOROUGH
ELY
SOUTHWOLD
HUNTINGDON
BURY
STRETTON GRANDISON
WORCESTER
IPSWICH
STOKE EDITH
COLCHESTER
GLOUCESTER
AMWELL
BRISTOL
WINDSOR
LONDON
BATH
LUNDY ISLAND
WELLS
NEWTON TONEY
TAUNTON
SALISBURY
WINCHESTER
EXETER
DORCHESTER
LAUNCESTON
PLYMOUTH
PENZANCE

HELEN MORRIS
1946

PART III

"MY GREAT JOURNEY TO NEWCASTLE AND TO CORNWALL" (1698)

1. FROM LONDON THROUGH EAST ANGLIA TO ELY

MY GREAT Journey to Newcastle and to Cornwall, the account of many journeys into most parts of England what observation and distance of one place to another in my travels.[1]

From London to Albins [Albyns] in Essex 17 mile, Sir Robert Abdys,[2] whose house stands very pleasantly in a park full of deer; the house on an advanced ground appeares to view at the entrance, but its old building large roomes, some rows of trees lead up to it; thence I return'd home 17 mile more; from London to Bednal-green [Bethnal Green] twice and back again 16 mile, from London to Highgate 4 miles to Mr. Thomas's[3] house, where is a most exact garden, with all sorts of greens and flowers and fishponds its all but little; there my Nephew Fiennes Harrison[4] with Mr. Showers went to fish with me, thence we went to Hampstead[5] so made it 5 mile home againe; I went from London

---

[1] It is with this heading and at this place that the smaller and earlier manuscript (Southey's MS.) begins.

[2] Sir Robert Abdy, a London merchant, was brother-in-law to Sir John Bramston, in whose *Autobiography* he frequently appears. The Home Counties were filling up with the country residences of such business men.

[3] Probably William Thomas, of Gray's Inn, widower of Celia's Aunt Christian (née Whitehead) who had died in childbirth in 1655.

[4] Fiennes Harrison, son of Celia's sister Lady Harrison (see Introduction p. xviii) died unmarried in 1733.

[5] Celia Fiennes probably went to Hampstead for its mineral waters. It was still a "village" in 1709 when Macky complained that "its nearness to London brings so many loose women in vampt-up old clothes to catch the City apprentices, that modest company are ashamed to appear here . . . it seems to me to be overstock'd with Jews and sharpers". (Op. cit., i, 88–9.) Defoe thought Hampstead "so near heaven" that it was not "a proper situation for any but a race of mountaineers, whose lungs had been used to a rarify'd air". (Op. cit., ii, 4–5.)

twice and back againe from Kensingston, in all 8 mile—this I put in only to know the number of miles that I went in one yeare.

From London to Amwell bery [Amwell Bury] which is in Hartfordshire 19 mile, where I staid a day or two, thence to Bishopstafford [Bishops Stortford] in Essex 13 mile, thence to Dunmew [Dunmow] 8 long miles thro' severall little villages, its very deep way especially after raines; this is a little Market town, they are altogether taken up about the spinning and prepareing for the Bayes [baize]: all along between that and Colchester you pass but halfe a mile ere one comes to two or 3 houses all along the road, its from Dunmow to Collchester 22 miles, and mostly clay deep way.

Colchester is a large town in the compass of ground, formerly there was 16 Churches tho' now much of it is ruinated;[6] a mile before you come to the new town one enters a little village which still is in the limits of the Citty and Majors [Mayor's] jurisdiction, there is a pretty good house of the Lord Lucas: you enter the town by a gate there are 4 in all, there is a large streete which runs a great length down to the bridge near a mile long, about the middle of it runs another broad streete and near its length, in which is the Market Cross and Town Hall and a long building like stalls on purpose to lay their Bayes [baize] when exposed to saile, great quantetyes are made here and sent in Bales to London that is 44 miles distant, the whole town is employ'd in spinning weaveing washing drying and dressing their Bayes, in which they seeme very industrious; there I saw the Card they use to comb and dress the Bayes, which they call them testles[7] [teasels] which are a kind of rush tops or something like them which they put in frames or laths of wood; the town looks like a thriveing place by the substantiall houses, well pitched streetes which are broad enough for two Coaches to go a breast, besides a pitch'd walke on either side by the houses, secured by stumps of wood and is

6 The ruination was caused by the siege in 1648.
7 The "fuller's teasel" or teazle has hooked prickles which were used for "teaseling" or dressing cloth so as to raise a nap.

convenient for 3 to walke together; their buildings are of timber of loame and lathes and much tileing, the fashion of the Country runs much in long roofes and great cantilivers and peakes; out of these great streetes runs many little streetes but not very narrow, mostly old buildings except a few houses builded by some Quakers that are brick and of the London mode; the town did extend it self to the sea but now its ruines sets it 3 mile off; the low grounds all about the town are used for the whitening their Bayes for which this town is remarkable, and also for exceeding good oysters, but its a dear place and to grattifye my curiosity to eate them on the place I paid dear; its a town full of Dessenters 2 meeteings very full besides Anabaptists and Quakers, formerly the famous Mr. Stockton was minister there till he dyed.

From Colchester to Ipswitch is 18 mile and thence to Dedom [Dedham] 9 miles,[8] the way pretty good except 4 or 5 miles they call the Severalls, a sort of deep moore ground and woody; at this place I passed over a wooden bridge pretty large with timber railes of which make they build their bridges in these parts; and now I go into Suffolk which is not so rich land as that part of Essex I passed through which was meadows and grounds with great burdens of grass and corn.

So I went to Ipswitch 9 mile more, this is a very clean town and much bigger than Colchester is now, Ipswitch has 12 Churches, their streetes of a good size well pitch'd with small stones, a good Market Cross railed in, I was there on Satturday which is their market day and saw they sold their butter by the pinte, 20 ounces for 6 pence, and often for 5d. or 4d. they make it up in a mold just in the shape of a pinte pot and so sell it; their Market Cross has good carving, the figure of Justice carv'd and gilt, there is but 3 or 4 good houses in the town, the rest is much like the Colchester buildings but it seems more shatter'd, and indeed the town looks a little disregarded, and by enquiry found it to be thro' pride and sloth, for tho' the sea would bear a ship of 300 tun up quite

---

[8] It is more likely that Celia Fiennes went first to Dedham *en route* for Ipswich.

to the key and the ships of the first rate can ride within two mile of the town, yet they make no advantage thereof by any sort of manufacture, which they might do as well as Colchester and Norwitch, so that the shipps that brings their coales goes light away; neither do they adress themselves to victual or provide for shipps, they have a little dock where formerly they built ships of 2 or 300 tun but now little or nothing is minded save a little fishing for the supply of the town.[9]

There is one pretty good house [Christ Church Manor] of the Earle of Herriford [Hereford] that marry'd one of Mr. Norborns Daughters that was killed by Sir Thomas Montgomery; you enter thro' two Courts walled and divided by a breast wall on which are iron spikes pallasadoes, the middle is a broad gravell walke fenced in with stone balls on each side, 3 or 4 steps up into the other Court, and so many steps more thro' an arch into a third Court, this arch joyns a low building which are the offices and leaded on the top and rail'd round, and each end enters into chambers joyning to the house that is built round this last Court, from whence you enter the porch; the house is handsome all brick worke and brick pillars, a good hall parlour and drawing roome and large closet, 2 or 3 other roomes left answereing it and a Billyard Roome above with as many roomes of State all furnish'd with good old things; a pretty staircase but its all little; there are 3 gardens on the one side with grass and gravell walks all kept neate and good fruite; on the other side is one large garden with a sumer house in which stands a large statue, black of a gigantick form and proportion, this answeres the fine green house on the other side; this town has many Dessenters in it.

Thence I went to Woodbridge 7 mile, mostly lanes enclosed countrys; this is a little Market town but has a great meeting for the Dessenters; thence to Wickham 5 mile more —but these are all very Long miles.

[9] Defoe attributed the decay of Ipswich to unfair competition from captured Dutch "flyboats" put by the Government into the coal-carrying trade. (Op. cit., i, 41.)

Thence to Saxmunday [Saxmundham] 8 miles more, this is a pretty bigg market town, the wayes are pretty deep, mostly lanes very little commons; I pass'd by severall Gentlemens seates—one Mr. Dormers which stands in a fine parke the entrance from the Road thro' rows of trees discovered the front and building very finely to view, being built with stone and brick and many sashes lookes like a new house, with the open iron barr gates between pillars of stone the breadth of the house; so to Bathfort [Blyford] 8 miles where is the remaines of the walls of an Abby and there is still a very fine Church, all carv'd in stone hollow work one tire [tier] above another to the tower that ascends not very high but finely carv'd also; hence I descended into lower grounds banck'd on each side with a brick wall but low, and so a walk on it for foote people and severall arches here and there to draine off the water, so that those bancks are to secure the Road from the marshy fenny water that oft a great extent on both sides is subject to; thence I passed by some woods and little villages of a few scattered houses, and generally the people here are able to give so bad a direction that passengers are at a loss what aime to take, they know scarce 3 mile from their home, and meete them where you will, enquire how farre to such a place, they mind not where they are then but tell you so farre which is the distance from their own houses to that place; I saw at a distance as I descended some of their hills a large place that look'd nobly and stood very high like a large town; they told me it was called either Stowle [Southwold] or Nole I cannot tell which.

I rode in sight of St. Georges Channell in the way from Colchester and Ipswitch and so to Norwich, sometymes it was in view then lost againe; to Beckle [Beccles] is 8 mile more which in all was 36 miles from Ipswitch—but exceeding long miles—they do own they are 41 measured miles; this is a little market town but its the third biggest town in the County of Suffolke, Ipswitch, Berry [Bury St. Edmunds] and this; here was a good big Meeteing place at least 400 hearers and they have a very good Minister one Mr. Killinghall, he is but a young man but seemed very serious, I was there the

Lords day; Sir Robert Rich is a great supporter of them and contributed to the building the Meeteing place, which is very neate, he has a good house [Roos Hall] at the end of the town with fine gardens; there are no good buildings the town being old timber and plaister-work except his and one or two more, there is a pretty bigg Market Cross and a great market kept, there is a handsome stone built Church and a very good publick Minister whose name is Armstrong he preaches very well; they say notwithstanding the town is a sad Jacobitish town; this chooses no parliament men.[10]

At the towns end one passes over the River Waveny [Waveney] on a wooden bridg railed with timber and so you enter into Norfolk, its a low flatt ground all here about so that the least raines they are overflowed by the River and lye under water, as they did when I was there, so that the roade lay under water which is very unsafe for strangers to pass, by reason of the holes and quick sands and loose bottom; the ordinary people both in Suffolk and Norfolk knitt much and spin, some with the rock and fusoe as the French does,[11] others at their wheeles out in the streete and lanes as one passes; its from this town to Norwitch 12 miles and its 10 to Yarmouth, where they build some small shipps and is a harbour for them, and where they victual them,[12] also Harwitch about 12 or 14 miles also, but the miles are here as long again as about London, and pretty deep way especially after raines, these miles are much longer than most miles in Yorkshire.

Norwitch opens to view a mile distance by the help of a hill whereon is a little village; as I observe most of the great towns and cittys have about them little villages as attendants or appendix's to them which are a sort of subburbs, there being stragling houses for the most part all the way between that and the gates; you pass over a high bridge that leads on

[10] I.e. was not a Parliamentary Borough.
[11] A "rock" was a distaff and a fuseau or fusee a kind of spindle.
[12] "The colliers of Newcastle generally put in here, to take in refreshments." (Misson, op. cit., 336.)

over a high Causey of a pretty length which lookes somewhat dangerous, being fenced with trenches from its bancks
pretty deep thats on both sides to secure it from the water,
and these trenches runns in many places round the low
grounds to drain them, which are employ'd to whiten and
bleach their woollen stuff the manufacture of the place; this
long Causey brings you to the large stone bridge over the
river into which those trenches empty themselves.

Then you proceed to the Citty which is walled round full
of towers, except on the river side which serves for the wall;
they seeme the best in repaire of any walled citty I know,
tho' in some places there are little breaches, but the carving
and battlements and towers looks well; I enter'd the West
gate, there are 12 gates in all and 36 Churches which is to
be seen in a clear day altogether, on the Castle walls I told
30 myself; there they are built all of flints well headed or cut
which makes them look blackish and shineing; the streetes
are all well pitch'd with small stones and very clean and many
very broad streetes; that I entred in first was very broad for
2 Coaches or Carts to pass on either side and in the middle
was a great Well house with a wheele to wind up the water
for the good of the publick; a little farther is a large pond
walled up with brick a mans height with an entrance on one
end, a little farther was a building on which they were at
work design'd for a Water house to supply the town by
pipes into their houses with water, at a little distance was
another such a pond walled in, as I described before; these
things fill up the middle of this spacious streete which is for
use and also ornament, the spaces each side being so broad;
this brings you into a broad space called the Hay market
which is on a hill a very steep descent all well pitch'd as
before, this comes to another space for a market to sell hoggs
in and opens farther into divisions of buildings that begins
severall streetes that runs off good lengths and are of a
tollerable size; one runs along behind, which is all for
stalls for the Country butchers that bring their meate for
the supply of the town, which pay such a rent for them to the
town, on the other side are houses of the Town butchers the

Inhabitants,[13] by it is a large market for fish which are all at a little distance from the heart of the Citty so is not annoy'd with them, there is a very large Market place and Hall and Cross for fruite and little things every day, and also a place under pillars for the Corn market.

The building round here is esteemed the best and here is the Town Hall but all their buildings are of an old form, mostly in deep poynts and much tileing as has been observ'd before, and their building timber and they playster on laths which they strike out into squares like broad free stone on the outside, which makes their fronts look pretty well, and some they build high and contract the roofes resembling the London houses, but none of brick except some few beyond the river which are built of some of the rich factors like the London buildings; there is in the middle of the town the Duke of Norfolks house of brick and stone with severall towers and turrets and balls that looks well, with large gardens but the inside is all demolish'd, only the walls stand and a few roomes for offices, but nothing of state or tollerable for use.

On the Castle hill you see the whole Citty at once, being built round it, its a vast place and takes up a large tract of ground its 6 miles in compass; here is the County hall and Goale where the asizes are held and the sessions; nothing of the Castle remaines but a green space and under it is also a large space for the beast market and 3 tymes in the year is there very great faires kept, to which resort a vaste concourse of people and wares a full trade; the whole Citty lookes like what it is, a rich thriveing industrious place; Satturday is their great market day; they have beside the Town hall a hall distinct which is the Sealeing hall where their stuffs are all measured, and if they hold their breadth and lengths they are sealed, but if they are deffective there is a fine layd on the owner and a private marke on the stuff which shews its defficiency.

[13] Baskerville called it "the greatest shambles for butchers' meat I had ever yet seen"; he found some of the fish expensive: "They asked me for one pike under two foot 2s. 6d., and for a pot of pickled oysters they would have a shilling." (Op. cit., 269.)

Here was also the Mint which they coyn'd at, but since the old money is all new coyn'd into mill'd money, that ceases: here there is a fine large Cathedrall and very lofty but nothing remarkable of monuments or else; by it is 3 Hospitalls for boys girls and old people who spinn yarne, as does all the town besides for the Crapes Callimanco [Calico] and Damaskes which is the whole business of the place; indeed they are arrived to a great perfection in their worke so fine and thinn and glossy their pieces are 27 yards in length and their price is from 30 shillings to 3 pound as they are in fineness; a man can weave 13 yards a day, I saw some weaveing; they are all employ'd in spinning knitting weaveing dying scouring fulling or bleaching their stuffs; their hospitalls are well provided for there are 32 women in one as many men in the other, there is also a good free schoole; there is a great many Cerimonyes in the choice and swearing their major [mayor] they elect him the first of May and then prepare for his being sworne on Holly [Holy] Thursday; they new washe and plaister their houses within and without which they strike out in squares like free stone; all the streete in which this major elects house is very exact in beautifying themselves and hanging up flaggs the coullours of their Companyes and dress up pageants and there are playes and all sorts of shows that day, in little what is done at the Lord Major of London show; then they have a great feast with fine flaggs and scenes hung out, musick and danceing; I was in the hall they keep their feast in and saw some of their preparations for that day being about a fortnight to it.[14]

The town is a mile and a halfe from the North to the South gate, just by one of the Churches there is a wall made of flints that are headed very finely and cut so exactly square and even, to shutt in one to another, that the whole wall is made without cement at all they say, but it appears to be very little if any morter, it looks well very smooth shineing and black; a great many Descenters are in this Citty; the Gentlewoman that was my acquaintance there dyed 10 dayes before I came thither so I made no great stay there but

[14] Holy Thursday is Ascension Day, June 2nd in 1698.

to see about the town; there are besides severall common cunduits.

Thence I went to Windham [Wymondham] a little market town 5 miles, mostly on a Causey the country being low and moorish and the road on the Causey was in many places full of holes, tho' its secured by a barr at which passengers pay a penny a horse in order to the mending the way, for all about is not to be rode on unless its a very dry summer; thence we went mostly through lanes where you meete the ordinary people knitting 4 or 5 in a company under the hedges; to Attleborough 5 mile more which is such another little market town, then over an open down like Salisbery Plaine 4 mile more to a little village, still finding the country full of spinners and knitters; thence to Thetford 6 miles more, which was formerly a large place but now much decay'd and the ruines only shews its dimentions; there is a very high hill quite round stands up on one side of it and can scarcely be ascended so steepe; here I lay which is still in Norfolk.

Next day I went to Euston Hall which was the Lord Arlingtons and by his only daughters marriage with the Duke of Grafton is his sons by her, its two mile from Thetford; it stands in a large parke 6 miles about, the house is a Roman H of brick, 4 towers with balls on them, the windows are low and not sarshes else the roomes are of a good size and height; a good staircase full of good pictures, a long gallery hung with pictures at length—on the one side the Royal family from K. Henry the 7th by the Scottish race his eldest daughter down to the present King William and his Queen Mary, the other side are forreign princes from the Emperour of Moroccoe the Northern and Southern princes and Emperour of Germany; there is a square in the middle where stands a billiard table hung with outlandish pictures of Heroes, there is Count Egminton Horn [Counts Egmont and Hoorn] etc., at the end of the roome is the Duke and Dutchess of Graftons pictures at length also; thence I enterd into dineing and drawing roome and bed chambers of a very good size and good fretwork on the cieling, in one of the roomes was the Dutchess of Cleavelands picture in a

Sultaness dress—the Duke of Grafton being King Charles the Seconds base son by her—there was also another picture of the Royal family King Charles the Firsts 5 Children altogether, I have often seen 3 which was King Charles the Second King James and the Princess of Orange, but here was also the Lady Elizabeth and the Duke of Glocester a little Infant on a pillow; in another place there is the Queen Mothers picture and Lady Heneretta drawn large;[15] there is a fine hall and parlour below pav'd with free stone, there are good gardens with fountaines and some stone statues, a Cannall by the side, a large Court at the entrance with 3 iron barr gates which open to the front divided with stone pillars and balls; the Court without is walled round and the wall is carry'd a great length round the back yards, within this is another Court with iron spike pallasadoes divided every 2 or 3 yards by little stone pillars with balls; there are severall rows of trees runs of a great length thro' the parke a visto to the front of the house, which lookes nobly tho' not just of the new modell'd way of building; at the back gate I crossed over the river Waveny which is the division of the two County's and enter'd Suffolk, and pass'd over perfect downs champion country just like Salisbery Plaine, and the winds have a pretty power here and blows strongly in the winter not well to be endured.

So to St. Edmunds-bury [Bury St. Edmunds] 8 mile—but as has been often observ'd before the miles are very long—I pass'd by two or 3 little villages and about 2 mile off there is the town of St. Edmunds Bury which appeares standing on a great hill; the towers and buildings look so compact and well together with the trees and gardens thick about it the prospect was wonderfully pleasant; a mile off by a little village I descended a hill which made the prospect of the town still in view and much to advantage; its but two parishes; the Market Cross has a dyal and lanthorn on the top, and there being another house pretty close to it high built with such a tower and lanthorn also, with the two churches towers and some other buildings pretty good made it appear nobly at a

[15] The pictures of the royal family were by Van Dyck.

distance; this high house is an apothecarys,[16] at least 60 stepps up from the ground and gives a pleaseing prospect of the whole town, that is compact severall streetes but no good buildings; except this the rest are great old houses of timber and mostly in the old forme of the country which are long peaked roofes of tileing; this house is the new mode of building, 4 roomes of a floore pretty sizeable and high, well furnish'd, a drawing roome and chamber full of China and a Damaske bed embroyder'd, 2 other roomes, Camlet and Mohaire beds, a pretty deale of plaite in his wives chamber, parlours below and a large shop; he is esteem'd a very rich man; he shewed me a Curiosity of an Herball all written out with every sort of tree and herb dryed and cut out and pasted on the leaves—it was a Doctor of Physicks work that left it him as Legacy at his death, it was a fine thing and would have delighted me severall dayes but I was passant; there was two streets were broad and very long out of which run a cross 5 or 6 streetes more, which are as good as in most country towns, they were well pitch'd with small stones; there are many Descenters in the town 4 Meeteing places with the Quakers and Anabaptists, there is only the ruines of the Abby walls and the fine gate at the entrance that remaines stone well carv'd; it seemes to be a thriveing industrious town 4 gates in it.

There are a great deale of Gentry which lives in the town tho' there are no good houses but what are old rambling ones, they are in that they call the Green, a space by the Churches [St. Mary's and St. James'] which are pretty near together, they are pretty large but nothing curious in them, stone buildings no monuments worth notice; they keep them very clean and neate and have a moveable scaffold to clean the roofe and windows and walls; its a very dear place so much Company living in the town makes provision scarce and dear, however its a good excuse to raise the reckoning on strangers.

[16] The "Cupola House" belonging to Thomas Macro, the apothecary who built it. The initials "T.M." and the date 1693 are to be seen on the vane of the "lanthorn". (H.A.T.)

Thence I went to Admiral Russells who is now Lord Orford,[17] a long 10 mile and loseing my way made it 12 mile,
its pretty good way; I passed by a village or two and in a
mile of Lord Orffords house [Chippenham Park] I enter
Cambridgeshire; it stands 3 mile from New Market you ride
in sight of New Market Heath where the races are, its good
road; here are severall good gardens well kept good gravell
and green walks with fine greens and flowers walled in and
all the outhouses very handsome; a coach yard and stables
in the middle of which is a large gate into the ground and
built over with a high lanthorn where hangs the clock and
bell, this stands higher than the house like a tower, the house
being a flat roofe leaded and railed round full of chimneys,
but this tower I saw 10 mile off; all the out offices built round
a court very handsome; the hall is very noble paved with
freestone a squaire of black marble at each corner of the
freestone; there are two fine white marble tables veined with
blew, its wanscoated with Wallnut tree the pannells and
rims round with Mulbery tree that is a lemon coullour and
the moldings beyond it round are of a sweete outlandish
wood not much differing from Cedar but of a finer graine,
the chaires are all the same; its hung with pictures att full
proportion of the Royal family, all in their coronation robes
from Charles the First to his Majesty with the Queen also,
and at the end is Prince George and Princess Ann, in their
robes of crimson velvet and Dukel coronet as Duke and
Dutchess of Cumberland; the whole house is finely furnish'd
with differing coulloured damask and velvets some figured
and others plaine, at least 6 or 7 in all richly made up after
a new mode; in the best drawing roome was a very rich
hanging gold and silver and a little scarlet, mostly tissue and
brocade of gold and silver and border of green damaske
round it; the window curtain the same green damaske and
doore curtaines; there was no looking-glass but on the

[17] Edward Russell (1653–1727) created Lord Orford in 1697, was the
victor of La Hogue. "No gentleman was ever better loved by the English
sailors than he, when he had the first command of the fleet, but he soon lost
all by his pride and covetousness." (Macky, *Memoirs of the Secret Services*,
ed. 1733, p. 76.)

chimney-piece and just opposite in the place a looking glass used to be was 4 pannells of glass in length and 3 in breadth set together in the wanscoate; the same was in another drawing roome which was for my Lord; the dineing roome had this looking glass on the two peers between the three windows it was from the top to the bottom 2 pannells in breadth and 7 in length, so it shews one from top to toe; the roomes were all well wanscoated and hung and there was the finest carv'd wood in fruitages herbages gemms beasts fowles, etc., very thinn and fine all in white wood without paint or varnish, the severall sorts of things thus carv'd were exceeding naturall all round; the chimney pieces and the sconces stand on each side the chimneys and the glasses in those chambers where were loose looking-glasses, which were with fine carv'd head and frames some of the naturall wood others gilt, but they were the largest looking-glasses I ever saw; there was a great flower pott gilt each side the chimney in the dineing roome for to sett trees in; the great curiosity of this wood carving about the doores chimneys and sconces together with the great looking glass pannells is much talked off and is the finest and most in quantety and numbers thats to be seen any where; there is very fine China and silver things andirons and jarrs and perfume pots of silver; the common roomes are all new convenient and neate with double doores lined to prevent noises; the staircase is wanscoated, very noble fine pictures, there is the battle at La Hogue a large sea piece with an inscription of the Admiralls valour when the great ship the Gunn was burnt, mightily valued by the French King.

From thence I went 8 mile to Ely which were as long as the 12 I came from St. Edmundsbery, the wayes being very deep its mostly lanes and low moorish ground, for 4 miles together I passed over a low ground on each side deffended by the fendiks which are deep ditches with draines; the Fens are full of water and mudd; these also encompass their grounds, each mans part 10 or a dozen acres a piece or more, so these dicks are the fences, on each side they plant willows so there is 2 rows of trees runns round the ground which looks very finely to see a flatt of many miles so planted, but it must be ill to live there; all this while Ely Minster is in ones view at a mile distant you would think, but go it is a long 4 miles; a mile distant from the town is a little hamlet from which I descended from a steep hill and so cross a bridge over water which enters into the Isleand of Ely, and so you pass a flatt on a gravel Causey which way the Bishop is at the charge to repaire else there would be no passing in the summer; this is secured by some dikes which surround more grounds as the former, full of rows of trees, willows round them which makes Ely looke finely through those trees, and that stands very high.[18]

In the winter this Caussey is over flowed and they have no way but boates to pass in; they cut peate out of some of these grounds; the raines now had fallen so as in some places near the Citty the Caussey was covered and a remarkable deliverance I had, for my horse earnest to drinke ran to get more depth of water than the Caussey had, was on the brinke of one of these diks but by a speciall providence which I desire never to forget and allwayes to be thankfull for, escaped; that bridge was over the River Linn[19] which comes from Norfolke and does almost encompass the Island of Ely, which is 20 mile in bigness in which are severall little towns as Wisbech and many others.

There is another river that joyns with the Linn which composes this land into an Island; at this bridge is a gate but by reason of the great raines the roads were full of water even quite to the town which you ascend a very steep hill into, but the dirtyest place I ever saw, not a bitt of pitching in the streetes so its a perfect quagmire the whole Citty, only just about the Palace and Churches the streetes are well enough

---

[18] Celia Fiennes was lucky to see Ely clearly, as fogs so often lay upon the undrained Fens, "so that when the Downs and higher grounds of the adjacent country were gilded by the beams of the sun, the Isle of Ely look'd as if wrapp'd up in blankets, and nothing to be seen but now and then the lanthorn or cupola of Ely Minster". (Defoe, op. cit., i, 79.)

[19] The Ouse. Even after a dry winter, Baskerville in May 1681 was alarmed at crossing "the rotten bridges with our horses, being glad to alight for fear they should break through and stick in the rotten bogs under them". (Op. cit., 271.)

for breadth but for want of pitching it seemes only a harbour to breed and nest vermin in, of which there is plenty enough, so that tho' my chamber was near 20 stepps up I had froggs and slow-worms and snailes in my roome—but suppose it was brought up with the faggotts—but it cannot but be infested with all such things being altogether moorish fenny ground which lyes low; its true were the least care taken to pitch their streetes it would make it looke more properly an habitation for human beings, and not a cage or nest of unclean creatures, it must needs be very unhealthy, tho' the natives say much to the contrary which proceeds from custom and use, otherwise to persons born in up and dry countryes it must destroy them like rotten sheep in consumptions and rhumes.[20]

The Bishop does not care to stay long in this place not being for his health; he is the Lord of all the Island, has the command and the jurisdiction: they have lost their Charter and so are no Corporation but all things are directed by the Bishop and its a shame he does not see it better ordered and the buildings and streetes put in a better condition; they are a slothful people and for little but the takeing care of their grounds and cattle which is of vast advantage: where the yeares prove drye they gaine so much that in case 6 or 7 wet yeares drown them all over the one good yeare sufficiently repaires their loss.

There is a good palace for the Bishop built of stone, but it was unfurnished; there are two Churches, Ely Minster is a curious pile of building all of stone the outside full of carvings and great arches and fine pillars in the front and the inside has the greatest variety and neatness in the works; there are two Chappels most exactly carved in stone all sorts

[20] Lieutenant Hammond in 1635 found the Fen people drinking "unwholesome Crowland sacke . . . which they hold highly convenient and necessary to avoyd the divellish stinging of their humming gnatts, which is all the towne musicke they have . . . I think they be halfe fish, halfe flesh, for they drinke like fishes, and sleep like hogges". At Ely "most of her inhabitants have butt a turfy sent and fenny posture about them, which smell I did not relish at all with any content". (Op. cit., 89–91.)

There are people still living who have seen opium pills on sale in large baskets in Cambridge market place to comfort the victims of the Fenland agues.

of figures cherubims and gilt and painted in some parts; the roofe of one Chappell was one entire stone most delicately carved and hung down in great poynts all about the Church; the pillars are carv'd and painted with the history of the Bible especially the New Testament and description of Christs miracles, the Lanthorn in the Quire is vastly high and delicately painted, and fine carv'd worke all of wood in it, the bells used to be hung five, the dimention of the biggest was so much when they run them it shooke the Quire so and the carv'd worke that it was thought unsafe, therefore they were taken down; its 80 odd steps to the top of the Lanthorn and 160 steps round in compass.

There are very good monuments and abundance of niches in the walls where statues have been, there is one of white marble laying at length and so exactly cut that the hand lookes extreamely natural the sinewes and veines and very turn of the fingers so finely done as to appear very proper; there is another that was a Bishop [Cox] made by Queen Elizabeth, whose garments and all are marble and so finely embroydered carv'd and painted and gilt, and a verge all down before and round the neck with the figures of the apostles done in embroydery as it were, all marble very fine; there was 4 or 5 more good marble statues; there was on one of the pillars the shape of the seameless coate which Christ wore, in another place there is a great red cross very high on some of the arches and its very dangerous to go or climb round the pillars to it being of a vast height, and this used to be a pennance to the people in the tyme of Popery; there is one Chappel for Confession with a roome and Chaire of State for the priest to set to hear the people on their knees confess into his eare through a hole in the wall; this Church has the most Popish remaines in its walls of any I have seen, there still remaines a Cross over the alter the Candlesticks are 3 quarters of a yard high massy silver gilt very heavy.

The Font is one entire piece of white marble stemm and foote, the Cover was carv'd wood with the image of Christs being baptised by John and the holy Dove descending on him, all finely carved white wood without any paint or varnish; they draw up the Cover by a pully and so let it down again which shutts close unless against rains then it swells open as it did now, and I believe in that Citty its usually annoy'd with wet.

This Cathedrall was much frequented by the priests in King James the Seconds tyme and many of their Relicts washed faire to be seen and the woman told me the priest use to shew here where every thing was and they hoped quickly to be in possession of it, and made many promises how kind they would be to them their retainers to the Church, but blessed be God that put a tymely stop to the Protestants utter ruin and the hopes of the Papists; when I was upon the Tower I could see Cambridg and a great prospect of the country which by reason of the great rains just before laid under water, all the fenny grounds being overflow'd which I could see for a huge tract of ground being all on a flatt, unless it be one side of the town which is all the high dry grounds into which they drive up their cattle to secure them in the wet seasons; there is no tradeing in the town, their maine buissiness and dependance is on draining and fencing their grounds and breeding and graseing cattle; there is a fine gate of stone arch'd like a church which is called the Abbey but no remaines of the Abby left only as its built into houses for the Doctors and Clergy, within which is the Palace for the Bishop which is their temporall as well as spiritual prince or lord.

2. THROUGH PETERBOROUGH AND LEICESTER TO WOLSELEY

FROM THIS Citty I passed over those higher grounds on which was some good corn but mostly is for grass for their cattle, you see many pretty little towns 4 or 5 in view together 2 or 3 mile distant; I went to Sutton one of them 6 miles off the Citty, this was a little Market town; thence on

the fenn banks on the top of which I rode at least two miles
with the fenns on both sides which now were mostly under
water, a vast tract of such grounds which are divided by the
Dikes without trees as those I observ'd before, and these
high banks are made to draine and fence out the water from
the lower grounds and so from one banck to another which
are once in many acres of land 100, so that at length it does
bear off the water; but in the winter it returns, so as they are
forced to watch and be allwayes in repaireing those bancks,
and considering the vast allowance yearly for draining those
fenns at least 3000£ per annum I wonder they have not perfectly runn off the water, and so barracadoed it as not to
soe it often overflows it againe as it does in many places—
but they are all a lazy sort of people and are afraid to do too
much; here I see the many swans nests on little hillocks of
earth in the wett ground that they look as if swimming with
their nests, some were with their young signetts 3 or 4 in
a troope with their damms hovering over them for their
security; this brought me to the Armitage[1] along 8 mile in
all from Ely town and here I repass'd the River Lin [the
Ouse] on a wooden bridge and so went out of the Island
of Ely which was in Cambridgshire and entred into Hunting-
donshire.

There was another bridge over a deep place of the river
under which the boates and barges went, and this bridge was
in the water, one must pass thro' water to it, and so beyond it
a good way, and the road was so full of holes and quick
sands I durst not venture, the water covering them over, and
a stranger then cannot easily escape the danger, tho' I see the
Carryers went that way to save the expence of the ferry, but
I rather chose to ride round and ferry over in a boate (2 pence
a horse) to a little town; this river runs along by St. Ives
which was an old monastery and a rich one; from this ferry
its 8 mile to Huntingdon town, one goes much in sight of
the river and the severall places built on its bancks which
looks well, these are pretty long miles.

From Huntingdon town I went to Stillton 9 mile more,

[1] Hermitage, in Haddenham Fen.

and thence I went to the Citty of Peterborough in Lincoln-shire which was 5 long miles, the wayes deep and full of sloughs; it stands very high and to be seen at a great dis-tance, the towers of the Minster being all in view one would think it but a quarter of a mile when you have a mile or two still to it; the whole Citty looks very well and handsomely built but mostly timber worke; you pass over a long stone bridg; the streetes are very clean and neate well pitch'd and broad as one shall see any where, there is a very spacious Market place a good Cross and Town Hall on the top; the Cathedrall is a magnificent building standing in the midst on advanced ground all stone the walls very neately wrought, the front is in 3 great arches full of small stone pillars smoothly turn'd and halfe paces as it were in the 2 side arches; the head is with no high tower but 5 little ones 3 of which in the middle are higher and bigger than the other, between each are 3 pcakes like great Canteliver windows but all finely carv'd in stone; the middle arch is the entrance which is exceeding lofty as is the roofe of the whole and so well painted that it appears to be hollow carving, this seems to be the two remarkable things in the whole; its a spacious place but one large Isle which is in the middle leading up to the Quire where I observ'd they put the seate of any of their deceased dignatorys of the Church in black with an Es-cutcheon, here was one so now; here was the statue of the person that was last Abbott and first Bishop of the place, there was also the 2 monuments of 2 Queens that of Cather-ine of Spain King Harry the 8ths Queen and also the statue of the Queen Mary of Scotts[1a] that was both beheaded and buried here, and there is also the picture of an old man with the inscription of the whole matter which was the Sexton and dugg both their graves; here is a Pallace for the Bishop of stone building very neate, and the Doctors houses all in a space called the Colledg very neate but nothing curious, the river Linn[2] washes the town almost round it; looks like

[1a] The body of Mary Queen of Scots was removed to Westminster by James I. The sexton who buried her (as well as Katherine of Aragon) was called "Old Scarlet".
[2] Here the Linn stands not for the Ouse but for the Nene.

a very industrious thriveing town, spinning and knitting amongst the ordinary people.

I went thence to Wansford and passed by Mr. St. Johns house[3] [Thorpe Hall] son to Oliver Lord St. John which stands on a hill a mile from the town in a fine parke; there was no gates to Peterborough town, and as I pass'd the road I saw upon the walls of the ordinary peoples houses and walls of their out houses the cow dung plaister'd up to drie in cakes which they use for fireing—its a very offensive fewell but the country people use little else in these parts; Wansford is 5 mile from Peterburough, where I passed over the Bridge which entred me into Northamptonshire, the town being part in that shire which is towards London, the other in Lincolnshire which a mile or two farther joyns with Rutlandshire at Stamford (which town stands in the 3 Countys) where I lay at the Swan in Wanstead-in-England [Wansford], being a jest on a man makeing hay fell a sleep on a heap of it and a great storme washed the hay and man into the River, and carry'd him to the Bridge, where he awoke and knew not where he was, called to the people in the grounds and told them he liv'd in a place called Wanstead in England, which goes for a jest on the men of Wanstead to this day.

Thence I went to Durant [Duddington] 5 miles and passed over a very good stone bridge; here we are neare the quarrys of stone and all the houses and walls are built of stone as in Glocestershire; this river and bridge enter'd me into Leicestershire which is a very rich country, red land, good corne of all sorts and grass both fields and inclosures; you see a great way upon their hills the bottoms full of enclosures woods and different sort of manureing and herbage, amongst which are placed many little towns, which gives great pleasure of the travellers to view; the miles are long but hitherto pretty hard good way to Coppingham [Uppingham] 5 mile more, which is a neate markct town; Satturday is their market which is very good affording great quantetys of corn leather yarne and cattle, such a concourse

[3] Thorpe Hall, built by John Webb. Celia Fiennes corrected this to "Mrs St. John".

of people that my Landlord told me used to have 100 horse set up at his inn, and there were many publick houses here; you see very large fine sheep[4] and very good land but very deep bad roads; from hence to Leister [Leicester] which they call but 13 mile but the longest 16 I ever went and the most tiresome, being full of sloughs, clay deep way, that I was neer 11 hours going but 25 mile[5]—as they reckon it—between Wansford and Leicester town, a footman could have gone much faster than I could ride; their fewell here is, as I said but now, cowdung, or coale which they are supplyed with out of Warwickshire.

Leicester town stands on the side of a little riseing ground tho' at a distance from the adjacent hills it looks low, but its a good prospect; it has 4 gates, the streetes are pretty large and well pitch'd,[6] there are five parishes, the Market place is a large space very handsome with a good Market Cross and Town Hall; the river Sow [Soar] which runs into the river Reeke [Wreak] and both empts themselves into the Trent; I went to the Bow Bridge which is one arch over into the Priory, which King Richard the Third pass'd over out of the Priory when he went to fight in Bosworth field with King Henry the Seventh, but the Stone he struck his heel at, and against which his head was struck at his return when brought athwart the horse dead, I could not see, it being removed; but I saw a piece of his tombstone he lay in, which was cut out in exact form for his body to lye in, that remains to be seen at the Grey-hound in Lecester but is partly broken; there I saw a piece of the Jury [Jewry] wall as its called being in arches and was a place where the Jews burnt their sacrifices.[7]

There are two Hospitalls [Holy Trinity and Wigston's] one for old men the other women 24 in number, they are

---

[4] The Leicestershire sheep were "without comparison, the largest, and bear . . . the greatest fleeces of wool on their backs of any sheep of England". Their wool had too "the longest staple". (Defoe, op. cit., ii, 89.)

[5] It is 33 statute miles. The local measure was evidently the "Long Mile". See Introduction, p. xxxix.

[6] Celia Fiennes differed from Evelyn, who had called it an "old and ragged Citty . . . despicably built". (*Diary*, Aug. 9, 1654) and from Baskerville who, in 1675, reported it "an old stinking town". (Op. cit., 308.)

[7] Actually the Roman Forum.

allow'd 2s. 8d. per weeke, candle, fewell, oatmeale, butter and salt; I saw the Library which is pretty large there was two large Divinity Books the Arch-Bishop gave them lately, and the names of all their Benefactors, there was one book all written hand by a scribe before printing was found out, it was a fine vellum; and there was another Book of the New Testament in Chineaze Language and Caractour; the town is old timber building except one or two of brick; there is indeed that they call the Newark[8] which is encompass'd with a wall off a good thickness and two great gates with towers as the town gates are, in which they keep their arms and ammunition; the walls now are only to secure gardens that are made of the ruin'd places that were buildings of strength; in this Newark which is a large space of ground are severall good houses some of stone and brick in which some lawyers live franck [free], there is also a new pile of building all of brick which is the Guild Hall[9] where the Assizes are kept twice in the yeare and the session quarterly.

St. Martins Church which is one of the biggest (there is none very big and none fine) but here I saw Hyricks[10] [Heyrick] tomb who was Major of the town and was married to one wife 52 years, in all which tyme he buried neither man woman nor child tho' most tymes he had 20 in his family, his age was 79 and his widdow 97 at her death, she saw 142 of her posterity together. They have a water house and a water mill to turn the water into the pipes to serve the town, as it is in London, it comes but once a day so they save the water in deep leaden tubbs or cisterns for their use, there are wells in some streetes to draw water by a hand wheele for the common use of the town; the major and alderman goes about in procession on Holy Thursday which was the day I was there;[11] here are a great many Descenters in this town.

[8] The Newarke was the Hospital, or New Work, founded in 1321 but replaced by Tudor buildings. (H.A.T.)

[9] This was the old Castle, refaced in the reign of William III. (See *Transactions of the Leicester Antiquarian Society,* 1942-3, p. 160.)

[10] Robert Heyrick, or Herrick, a connection of the poet's, was an early seventeenth century alderman and ironmonger. Thoresby adds one more to Heyrick's "posterity". (*Diary,* ii, 166.)

[11] June 2nd, 1698.

This Country as I said was all rich deep land and they plough their land all with ploughs without wheels as they do in Oxfordshire and other deep lands; from thence I passed to Bosworth [Market Bosworth] 8 miles and went by a Gentlemans [Mr. Dixie's] house [Bosworth Hall] and thro' a little parck where the deer were very tame, and passed through Bosworth and over the ground where was the battle between King Richard that lost his life by the hand of the Earle of Richmond, afterwards King Henry the Seventh, who was crown'd in this Bosworth Field with the Crown taken off from King Richards head, who being dead was ignominiously cast across a horse and carried to Leicter [Leicester] and buried there as a just judgment of God for killing his two nephews and reigning in their stead.

This is a great flatt full of good enclosures; near this is Narsby[12] [Naneby] where was the great battle fought between King Charles the First and the Parliament of England; from thence I went to Fallmouth [? Fazeley] 7 miles more and so into Warwickshire over a bridg; this is a little market town; thence 3 miles more to Tamworth a neate town built of brick and mostly new—in sight at its approach it look'd like Litchfield but not a quarter so big a market town, it stands halfe in Warwickshire and halfe in Staffordshire— and so to Litchfield over a large stone bridg that crosses the Tamworth river that gives name to the town; to Litch- field is 5 mile more, all very good way mostly gravel I went it in an hour; this side entring the town I came by a large good Almshouse which I saw not before; they have in this town a custome at Whitsontide the Monday and Tuesday call'd the Green Bower feast by which they hold their Charter; the Bailiff and Sheriff assist at the Cerimony of dressing up Baby's with garlands of flowers and greens and carry it in procession through all the streetes and then as- semble themselves at the Market place and so go on in a solemn procession through the great streete to a hill beyond the town where is a large Bower made with greens in which

[12] Naseby is twenty-five miles to the south-east, in Northants; Celia Fiennes was probably thinking of Naneby, near Market Bosworth.

they have their feast; many lesser Bowers they make about
for the conveniency of the whole company and for selling
Fruite Sweetemeetes and Gingerbread which is a chief entertainment.

Thence I went to Woolsely 7 mile farther to Sir Charles
Woolsley where I staid 6 weekes, it being my Aunt his Lady
who engaged my stay; his Seate stands very finely by the
river Trent, there is also a moate almost round the house;
the house is old timber building only a large parlour and
noble staircase with handsome chambers Sir Charles has new
built; its built round a Court with a gate house which leads
to the outward court that has a paved walke broad stone the
same as the first court is paved with; there are green spaces
and a fine green banck with box or philleroy [phillyrea]
hedge cut round, there are very good gardens abundance of
fruite of all sorts and the finest dwarfe trees I ever saw, so
thick like a hedge and a huge compass every single tree and
very full of fruite of apples pears and cherries; there are fine
flowers tuber roses white and yellow, there was a fine sena
tree that bears a great branch of yellow flowers; the ground
lyes all well about the house, and a fine park by the end of it
part of which is on a high hill the side of which the deer
sports themselves, which looks just on the house and is
wonderfull pleasant; its a large parke 6 miles round full of
stately woods and replenish'd with red and fallow deer, one
part of it is pretty full of billberryes which thrives under the
shade of the oakes, its a black berry as big as a large pea and
are ripe about harvest; there is a very ill Custome amongst
them, now not to be broken, when they are ripe the Country
comes and makes boothes and a sort of faire the outside of
the parke and so gather the berries and sell them about the
Country; the greenes they call Wissums and on these Wissums the deer browse in the winter and on holly of which
there is great quantetys.

In Kank wood [Cannock Wood] just by there is also great
quantetys of ferne, which tho' it overuns their ground and so
spoiles the grass where its much, yet the usefullness of it
renders it necessary to be preserv'd; when its at its maturity

which happens just before harvest or hay tyme the whole Country are employ'd in cutting it up and burning it in heapes for the sake of the ashes, which they make fine and rowle them up in balls and so sell them or use them all the year for washing and scouring, and send much up to London, the ashe balls being easily sent about; without which they would have no ashes in the country for such uses, for their fewell is altogether coales which indeed are very good and plenty, you might have a load for 3 or 4 shillings brought home that would serve a poore mans familly the winter; its in great pieces and so cloven burns light, so as the poorer sort works by it and so it serves for heate and light; its very shineing coale all about this country tho' they complaine they have lost the vein of the best sort which they call Channell [Cannel] Coale, and is the sort they have still in Wales and Lancashire, which burnt much lighter and less waste, but this I thought to be very good no better than it, I have in London given 40s for such a load.

In this parke is severall ponds which affords good fish, as does the moate and the Trent, as trouts eeles tench perch etc.—the largest perch I ever saw just caught and dress'd immediately which eates in perfection—the hill in the parck called Harts Hill is so high that from the top of it you see near 20 miles round, shews all the Country which in this part of Staffordshire is full of woods and inclosures and good land except the Kanck-wood [Cannock Wood], which is but a barren heath ground but good wood, its fine for Hawking in the heath, its full of little brookes and rivulets which abounds with crawfish and they were the sweetest and largest I have seen any where.

3. WOLSELEY AND ITS NEIGHBOURHOOD

FROM HENCE to Stafford town is 5 mile you go by the banck of the Trent most of the way and passing over two Rivers on stone bridges called the Sore [Sow] and the Pink [Penk] which both empt themselves into the Trent—and so enter the town through a gate; its an old built town timber and plaister pretty much in long peaked rooffes of tileing, 3 gates to the town, there was another which leads to the Castle which now is ruinated, and only remaines on a hill the fortification trenches that are grown over with green, the streetes are pretty large and well pitched, a broad space for the market place wherein is a good Market House on stone pillars with a handsome Town Hall over it; some of the houses are pretty good; this country is much for entertainments in every house you must eate and drinke.

From thence back to Woolsley againe 5 mile, from thence to Heywood [Haywood] Parke, which was 2 mile, where lived a Daughter of my aunt Woolsley marryed Mr. Wedgewood, a little neate box they live in; from thence back againe 2 mile, to the Kank wood [Cannock Wood] is pleasant rideing, its 20 mile long belongs to the Lord Paget, there are 4 lodges in it a great deale of wood and deer and goates; I went to Furnes Coppice which is 4 mile on, it a fine covert of tall trees on a hill and a mile farther was a fine wood called Hedgford; [a] poole a quarter of a mile long full of good fish, thence home 5 mile; another day I went to Stiles Coppice 3 mile off which is on a high hill and a fine tufft of trees, it looks but little at a distance but is a fine covert for the sheep and cattle, I went quite round it, from whence could see the Country a good distance and see into 7 Countys together, Warwickshire Leicestershire Gloucestershire Derbyshire Staffordshire Shropshire and Cheshire, so home againe by Ridgly [Rugeley] a mile aboute, so it was 4 mile.

Another day I went to Boudezworth[1] [Beaudesert] the Lord Pagets house, 4 mile off, and passed by the Coale pitts where they were digging, they draw up the coale in baskets with a little wheele or windless like a well, its very good; Lord Paget's house is old brick built, the front is uniforme and very handsome with towers but there is no good roome but a long gallery thats worth seeing; its a fine parke, just by it is a high hill on which is the remaines of an old fortifica-

---

[1] Beaudesert, built by Thomas Paget in Elizabeth's time, after many restorations has now been dismantled. (H.A.T.)

tion they call it the Castle Wall, its of very greate antiquity but now grown over with grass; from thence the prospect of the Country is great, this parke is of large extent and some of those pitts are in it, the Channell Coales; but the water has overflow'd some of them and spoyl'd their digging; thence I went home againe 4 miles.

Another day I went to Panckeridge[2] [Penkridge] Race over the Kankwood 7 mile, where were most of the Gentlemen and Ladies of the Country, severall coaches and six horses; indeed the miles are long and the wayes bad in the winter that obliges them to drive more horses, these were persons of good estates also, there appear'd only one horse to run for the plaite which was a salver;[3] thence to Woolesley again 7 mile more; its a fine country hereabout for rideing one has a pleaseing prospect every way, especially on any advanc'd ground.

I went to Brinsy Coppice [Brindley Heath] which was 4 mile thence; could see towards Shrewsbury and the high hill the Reekee [Wrekin] and in a cleare day could see something of Chester, and so home againe 4 mile more; another day I went upon Itching Hill [Etchinghill] 1 mile which is a sort of rock but the stone is of a red coullour and looks like a sandy stone by its moldring, but they tell me when its wrought in a wall and have been season'd with the weather it grows very hard and serviceable in building; from thence I went a compass round to Heywood Parke [Haywood] 4 mile off and then home againe 2 mile; and another day I went the same tour about to Heywood Parke and back which was 6 mile more; while I stay'd at Woolsley I went twice directly to Heywood Parke above what I mentioned before and returned home which was in all 8 miles, and another day I went to a poole in the Kanckwood 3 mile to fish and from thence to Heywood Parke thro' a very fine coppice of trees on a hanging brow of a hill which look'd very fine, and so home

[2] Penkridge, in a district then famous for horse-breeding, had "the greatest horse-fair in the world". (Defoe, op. cit., ii, 78.)

[3] After the Restoration the racing 'plate', suitable for display on gentlemen's sideboards, replaced the older and more picturesque bell formerly hung round the winning horse's neck.

2 mile more. I name the number of miles I went only to see the whole account of miles I travell'd this yeare. These coppices there are many of them which is a good shelter for the cattle.

4. INTO DERBYSHIRE AND BACK

ANOTHER JOURNEY to Darby town[1] from Woolsly by Colton and Blithbery [Blithbury] 3 mile, thence to Yoxwell [Yoxall] 3 mile over Nedwood [Needwood] Forest of the kings which is 40 mile in extent, all the way you have a fine prospect of the Country, enclosed good lands admirable corne of all sorts, good grass; I went in sight of Tedbery [Tutbury] Castle which is the kings, a great fortification but all decay'd, here 4 mile more and there it was that I pass the river Dove on a stone bridge called Dovebridge which enters me into Darbyshire and thence its 8 mile more to Darby town.

Darby town lies down in a bottom built all of brick or for the most part, in it are 5 Churches built of stone the biggest of which I was in[2] [All Saints] the tower was finely carv'd full of niches and pedistals whereon statues had been set, but nothing worth notice in the inside except a monument which was over the vault of the Duke [Earl] of Devonshire, on which stands 2 Effigys at length all of white marble the Earle and his Countess of Devonshire with an arch of cannopy of stone over their heads, this is rail'd in with iron grates, there is also another statue of marble painted and gilded lying at length which is also railed in; the River Derwent runs by the town and turns many mills and the water

[1] On page 51 of the smaller MS. a marginal note reads "Write this to Darbyshire in other booke page 195 and soeforth to 66 in this book". The fifteen pages in question comprise the journey into Derbyshire, and end when Celia Fiennes resumes her main journey northwards. Page 195 in the larger MS. is nowhere near this passage, which suggests that there was once another manuscript book.

[2] All Saints' Church was rebuilt some 20 years later by Gibbs. One monument was of the first Earl of Devonshire and his wife the other of his mother, Bess of Hardwick. (H.A.T.)

engine which turns the water into the pipes that serves the
town, the same wheele grinds also, but they do it for a half
penny a strike which is the same measure as our bushell, at
this Engine they can grind if its never so high a flood which
hinders all the other from working, at the flood they are
quite choaked up, but this they can set higher or lower just
as the water is; there are bay's which they make with stones
to keep the water to run to the mill and thence it falls againe
into the Derwent; there is also a fine stone Cunduite in the
Market place which is very spacious well pitch'd, a good
Market Cross; this is a dear place for strangers notwithstanding the plentyfullness of all provision my dinner cost me
5s. and 8d., only 2 servant men with me and I had but a
shoulder of mutton and bread and beer; here they make great
quantetys of gloves, I did not observe or learn any other
trade or manufacture, they had only shops of all sorts of
things; they carry much of their carriages on sledges to
secure their pitching in the streetes.

Thence I went to Chartly [Chartley] 6 mile Lord Ferrers
and thence Bradly [Bretby] Lord Chesterfields and passed by
a fine parke of some Gentlemans, in which was a summer
house on the side of the hill amongst fine tall trees which
look'd very well, and on the right hand I turned up to the
Earle of Chesterfields Parke full of fine rows of trees running
up the avenues to the house; one enters an outward court
and drives round a little pond, like a ditch all pav'd with
stone or great bason of stone, in which were two swans
swimming about in that little compass; the gates are all iron
barrs and the whole front of the house open iron pallasadoe
spikes in a compass round like a half moone answerable
to that beyond, the stable yard is another such a demy circle
of open pallasadoe that lets you out to the prospect of the
grounds beyond, full of regular rows of trees; the house has
a visto quite thro' by a glass bellcony, doors into the gardens,
and so to the parke beyond; on that side the front has something surpriseing in it its all of free stone which is dipt in oyle
that adds a varnish to its lustre as well as security to its
foundation; the roofe is not flatt as our modern buildings so

the garret windows come out on the tileing which is all of slatt; none of the windows are sashes which in my opinion is the only thing it wants to render it a compleate building; its halfe a roman H, there is an ascent of 5 or 6 steps all stone to the gates and so you proceed on a broad paved walke, which is divided by a cross walke of the same, towards the upper end, thence the ascent by as many more stone steps into a noble hall that has a row of white marble pillars at the upper end; the middle the little roome with a marble table in the middle, which is the balcony into the garden but thats without steps down into the garden; from these rows of pillars on the right hand runs a passage to the servants roome and all the offices, and at the end is a Chappell which was very neate, over the alter is a large ovall of glass of the sort of Private glass used in windows to obscure the sight from without, but hinders not the light within side—this look'd pretty as being particular and uncomõn.

There was a little organ, and closets for the Lord and Ladies to sitt in; from the hall on the left hand enters into a large roome with a billiard table; from thence into a large parlour and 2 drawing-roomes, there was a good dineing roome above; the drawing roome had company in it—the Earle having just marry'd his eldest Daughter Lady Mary to one Mr. Cooke,[3] a Gentleman of a good Estate hard by, so there was company to wishe her joy—but I was in severall bed-chambers, one had a crimson damaske bed, the other crimson velvet set upon halfe paces, this best was the bride chamber which used to be call'd the Silver roome where the stands table and fire utensills were all massy silver, but when plaite was in nomination to pay a tax, the Earle of Chesterfield sold it all and the plaite of the house, so that when the table was spread I saw only spoones salts and forks and the side board plaite, noe plaites or dishes and but few salvers; the pictures was all burnt by a fire and so there are only bare walls, one roome was painted over head, the others frettwork.

But that which is most admired—and justly so to be—by all persons and excite their curiosity to come and see is the

[3] Thomas Coke of Melbourne.

Gardens and Waterworks;[4] out of the billiard roome the first was with gravell walks and a large fountaine in the middle with flower potts and greens set round the brimm of the fountaines that are paved with stone; you see but one garden at a tyme; the pipes in the fountaines play very finely, some of a great height, some flushes the water about, then you come to a descent of severall steps which discovers another fine garden with fountaines playing through pipes, besett on the bancks with all sort of greens and flower trees dwarfes honeysuckles in a round tuft growing uppright and all sorts of flower trees and greens finely cutt and exactly kept; in one garden there are 3 fountaines wherein stands great statues, each side on their pedistalls is a Dial, one for the sun, the other a Clock which by the water worke is moved and strikes the hours and chimes the quarters, and when they please play Lilibolaro on the Chymes—all this I heard when I was there—on one side of this garden is a half compass with a breast wall on which are high iron pallisadoes divided with severall pillars, stone with images on their tops; about 2 yards distance this opens to view the parke and a sort of cannall or pond which is in it of a good bigness; beyond this garden is a row of orange and lemon trees set in the ground, of a man's height and pretty big, full of flowers and some large fruit almost ripe; this has a penthouse over it which is cover'd up very close in the winter; this leads on to a great wilderness and just by it is another square with a fountaine whose brim is deck'd with flower potts full of flowers and all sorts of greens, on either side is 2 or 3 rows of orange and lemon trees in boxes one below another in growth.

Just against this is a wall cover'd over with lawrell finely cutt and also in the middle is an arch, and on either side stone staires ascends it which terminate in a sort of half pace all cover'd over with lawrell, and this enters a doore into another garden through a little garden house; this also has a fine fountaine like the others only as most off the others

---

[4] The gardens, which were not yet completed, were designed by the Frenchman Grilly, who also worked at Chatsworth. Bretby was demolished in 1780. (H.A.T.)

was green walks this was gravell, so was the garden on the right side of the house; the front garden which has the largest fountaine has also a fine green house and very fine flowers, and the beds and borders are cut in severall formes, the greens are very fine and the hedges cut in severall formes; there was one tree not much unlike the cyprus green but the branches were more spread and of a little yellower green, the barke of the limbs yellow, it was the Cedar of Lebonus; there was also fine strip'd stocks double like a rose; there was a large Ewe tree in the middle of one garden cut in forms, fine firrs and cyprus and filleroy [phillyrea] of which some was striped like silver white others yellow like gold which gave them their different names, and fine gilded and striped hollys.

There was one green in a pott call'd St. John the Baptists herb, it was full of many leaves and the coullour not much unlike the green they call Solomons Seale but longer and bigger leaves, its an annual plant; here just by the wilderness is the Tulip tree which runns up of a great height and the flower is on the top it flowers in August; there is a great avery of birds which stands like a sumer house open, there is also many close averys of birds and severall green shady walks and close arbours, there are very fine wood bines grows like tufts all in flower red and white; there is some of the fountaines that have figures in them that throws up water a greate height, a cascade of water.

Then I returned into the hall and so into a coole roome in which was a fountaine, where I dranke a glass of wine, and so proceeded; this was 3 miles from Chartry, thence through a fine visto or glide of trees which runs along the parke, and so to Burton on the Trent 2 long miles; this is a pretty large town, here is a very long stone bridge over the Trent; the streetes are very well pitch'd and some very broad; thence over Nedwood [Needwood] Forest 6 mile and thence to Yoksell [Yoxall] which is 6 mile more to Woolsley and they are all long miles.

Then I went againe to Stafford town 5 miles and from thence to Instree [Ingestre] Mr. Shetwins [Chetwynd]; its bad way, you go by St. Thomas's which was some old abbey its still a good house; going along the side of the hill gives a great view of the country that is mostly on inclosures we passed between two parkes, the one is Lord Astons, and goe in sight of Tixall Hall which is his, a good house and looks handsomely of stone building; the other was Mr. Shetwins [Chetwynd] parke which has fine rows of trees firrs Scots and Noroway, and the picanther; the front lookes nobly; noe flatt roofed houses in this country but much in windows; two large bow windows on each side runns up the whole building, the middle the same, besides much flatt window between so that the whole is little besides window; its built brick and stone; the part to the garden ward is new building of the new fashion and sash windows; the court is 2 or 3 stepps up with open iron pallasadoes the breadth of the house, and a broad paved walk which leads up to the doore in the middle; the visto is quite through the house and so to the gardens and through a long walke of trees of a mile through the parke to a lodge or summer house at the end, which lookes very finely, it being a riseing ground up to the parke; there is a crosse paved walke in the Court which leads to a little house on each end like summer houses with towers and balls on the top, the one leads through to the Church yard which is planted with rows of Ewe trees very uniforme and cut neately.

The Church[5] is new and very handsome good fretworke on the top the wood worke well carv'd its seates good wanscoate and with locks, in the Chancell are two monuments of marble, one all white, the other white with a border black and with white pillars, the middle at the bottom is alabaster; the pillars of the Church is made of the red stone which is plenty in this country and they are all polished over, the font is all white marble, stem the same veined blew, the foote is black, the cover is wood carv'd very well; the porch is very high on which is a dyal, it almost breaks ones neck to looke up at it for thats the tower in which are 5 bells.

There is just against this a garden, on the other side the

[5] Rebuilt in 1673. (H.A.T.)

dwelling house which is severall steps up it, gravell walkes full of flowers and greens and a box hedge cut finely with little trees, some cut round, and another hedge of strip'd holly cut even and some of lawrell cut even likewise; out of this goes into a flower garden divided into knotts in which were 14 Cyprus trees which were grown up very tall some of them and kept cutt close in four squares down to the bottom, towards the top they enclined to a point or spire; thence into another garden with gravel walks and so into a summer house through which you enter a good bowling-green, which also goes out of another garden which takes in the whole breadth of the house and is full of flowers and greens and dwarfe trees and little borders of severall sorts of greens cut even and close, of tyme severall sorts and of savin[6] which is another coullour and of lavender cotten another coullour and rosemary and severall others.

From this bowling-green in the middle you descend 18 steps in a demi circle inwards halfe way, then the stones are set round and so the half pace is, and the other stepps are round turned outward and the lowest much the largest, as was the uppermost of the first; this leads to a place designed for ponds to keep fish in, but this place will not admitt of any water works altho' its a deep dirty country, they neither have good gravell or marle to make a pond secure to hold water nor are they near enough the springs, but are forced to be supply'd with water by pipes from the River Trent that is a mile off—and yet the whole place seems a quage when one is descended the hill—this seemes to be the only thing wanting for just by the bowling-green is a very fine wilderness with many large walks of a great length, full of all sorts of trees scycamores willows hazel chesnutts walnuts set very thicke and so shorn smooth to the top which is left as a tuff or crown, they are very lofty in growth which makes the length of a walke look nobly; there is also a row on the outside of firrs round every grove 2 yards or 3 distant some silver firrs some Norraway

---

[6] Savin is *juniperus sabina*, a small bushy evergreen shrub. Lavender cotton is ground cypress.

some Scotts and pine trees; these hold their beauty round
the groves in the winter when the others cast their leaves.
This was from Stafford 3 mile and to Woolsley was 3 mile
more through narrow stony lanes through Great Heywood
[Haywood].

Att Instree [Ingestre] Mr. Shetwins [Chetwynd] I saw
a fine pomgranate tree as tall as my self, the leafe is a long
slender leafe of a yellowish green edged with red and feeles
pretty thicke, the blossom is white and very double; there
was a terrass walke in one of the gardens that gave the full
prospect of the country a great way about, its a deep country,
you are going these 3 miles to Woolsly a great while; there
was at Sir Charles Woolsly's some of the best good land and
some of the worst as is the Kankwood [Cannock Wood] but
here the roads are pretty good and hard which makes it
pleasant; there is much fine fruite here, Sir Charles takeing
great delight in his gardens—I must say I never saw trees so
well dress'd and pruned, the walls so equally cover'd as there;
there is severall sorts of strawbery's but the vermillion is the
finest very large as any garden strawbery and of a fine
scarlet coullour, but its a later sort; there was a pretty almond
tree in bloome the flower not unlike a rosemary flower.

5. FROM WOLSELEY THROUGH CHESHIRE INTO WALES AND OUT AGAIN

FROM THENCE I tooke my progress northward and went
from hence to Newcastle under Line [Newcastle under
Lyme] through Stone which was 9 mile, and then to
Trentum [Trentham] and passed by a great house [Trentham
Hall] of Mr. Leveston Gore [Leveson Gower], and went on
the side of a high hill below which the River Trent rann and
turn'd its silver streame forward and backward into Ss which
looked very pleasant circleing about the fine meadows in
their flourishing tyme, bedecked with hay almost ripe and
flowers; 6 mile more to Newcastle Underline where is the
fine shineing Channell [Cannel] Coale, so the proverb to both

the Newcastles of bringing Coales to them is a needless labour, one being famous for this coale thats cloven and makes white ashes, as is this, and the Newcastle on the Tyne is for the sea-coale that cakes and is what is common and famillier to every smith in all villages; I went to this Newcastle in Staffordshire to see the makeing the fine tea-potts cups and saucers of the fine red earth, in imitation and as curious as that which comes from China, but was defeated in my design, they comeing to an end of their clay they made use off for that sort of ware and therefore was remov'd to some other place where they were not settled at their work, so could not see it;[1] therefore I went on to Betely [Betley] 6 miles farther and went by a ruinated Castle the walls still remaineing called Healy [or Heighley] Castle—this was deep clay way; this town is halfe in Staffordshire and halfe in Cheshire one side of the streete in the one and the other in the latter, so that they often jest on it in travelling one wheele goes in Staffordshire the other wheele in Cheshire; here is a great mer or standing water 2 miles compass great store of good fish, it belongs to one Mr. Egerton.

Thence I went to Nantwitch [Nantwich] 5 long miles; Nantwitch is a pretty large town and well built, here are the salt springs of which they make salt and many salterns which were a boyling the salt; this is a pretty rich land; you must travell on a Caussey, I went 3 miles on a Caussey through much wood; its from Nantwitch to Chester town 14 long miles the wayes being deep; its much on enclosures and I passed by severall large pooles of waters but what I wonder'd at was that tho' this shire is remarkable for a greate deale of greate Cheeses and Dairys I did not see more than 20 or 30 cowes in a troope feeding, but on enquiry find the custome of the country to joyn their milking together of a whole village and so make their great Cheeses and so it goes round.

[1] This kind of ware was first made by John Philips and David Elers at Fulham about 1690. Later Philips made it at Bradwell Wood, near Burslem. This reference to Celia Fiennes is used by Rackham and Read in their *English Pottery* (p. 68) to prove that Philips had worked at Newcastle before moving to Bradwell. (H.A.T.)

West Chester town lies in a bottom and runs a greate length and is pretty big there are 10 Churches; the Cathedrall is large and lofty, the quire well carv'd fine tapistry hangings at the alter, a good organ; the Bishops Pallace is on the right hand of it and the Doctors houses all built of stone, there is a new Hall building which is for the assize and it stands on great stone pillars which is to be the Exchange, which will be very convenient and handsome; the Hall is round, its built of bricke and stone coynes, there are leads all round with battlements and in the middle is a tower; there are ballconies on the side and windows quite round the Cupillow that shews the whole town round; there is another Town Hall a long lofty place and another by the side which is called the Councill Roome both for the Major [Mayor] and Aldermen to meete for the buissinesse of the Corporation; the town is walled all aboute with battlements and a walke all round pav'd with stone; I allmost encompass'd the walls; the streetes are of a greate breadth from the houses, but there is one thing takes much from their appeareing so and from their beauty,[2] for on each side in most places they have made penthouses so broad set on pillars which persons walks under covert, and is made up and down steps under which are ware houses; tho' a penthouse or pallasadoe be convenient and a security from the sun or weather and were it no broader than for two to passe one by the other it would be well and no dissight to the grace of the streetes, but this does darken the streetes and hinder the light of the houses in many places to the streete ward below; indeed in some places were it only before the chiefe persons houses it would be convenient where its flatt and even with the streetes; the town is mostly timber buildings, the trade and concourse of people to it is chiefly from the intercourse it has with Ireland,[3] most take this passage, and also the intercourse with Wales which is parted from it and England by the River Dee, which washes the Castle walls

[2] Defoe also thought that the Rows, now so much admired, "make the city old and ugly". (Op. cit., ii, 70.)

[3] Chester in the Middle Ages had been a considerable port, but was now rapidly silting up.

in which they keep their stores—but nothing fine in it—the walls and towers seemes in good repaire; at the end of the town just by the Castle you crosse over a very large and long Bridge over the River Dee which has the tyde comes up much beyond the town, its 7 mile off that it falls into the sea but its very broad below the town, when at high tyde is like a very broad sea; there they have a little dock and build shipps of 200 tunn I saw some on the stocks.

Cross this river by this bridge enters Flintshire and so crossed over the marshes, which is hazardous to strangers, therefore Mr. William Allen[4] (which was the Major [Mayor] of Chester that tyme and gave me a very civil treate being an acquaintance of my Brother Sir Edmund Harrison)[5] so order'd his son and another gentleman to ride with me to direct to Harding [Hawarden] which was 5 mile; just by that was a very fine new built house of brick and in the exact forme of the London architecture which was this Mr. Majors house and good gardens.

At Harding, where was my Relation, Dr. Percivalls wife,[6] who was Minister of that place; his parish was 8 miles in extent and 2 lordships in it and the ruines of two great Castles in it remaines, its good rich land here much on enclosures and woods; in a tarresse walke in my Relations garden I could very plainly see Chester and the River Dee with all its washes over the marsh ground which look'd very finely; here are sands which makes it very difficult for strangers to passe without a guide; from thence my Relation carry'd me to Holly Well [Holywell] and pass'd thro' Flint town which is the shire town, 5 mile from Harding; its a very ragged place many villages in England are better, the houses all thatched and stone walls but so decay'd that in many places ready to tumble down; there was a Town Hall such a one as it was; it was at a Session tyme when I was there which shew'd it at its prime; there is a Castle which

---

[4] He was Mayor 1697-8. (See Ormerod, *History of the County Palatine of Chester*, i, 183.)

[5] She means brother-in-law. See Introduction, p. xiii.

[6] Ann Fiennes, daughter of Celia's Uncle Richard, had married Dr. Percival.

still remaines with its towers built of stone, its down to the
water side; from thence to Holy well is 3 mile mostly by
the water side which is reckon'd the sea—here I went just
in sight of High Lake [Hoylake] where were many shipps
rideing along that harbour.

St. Winfreds Well[7] is built over with stone on pillars like
a tryumphall arch or tower on the gates of a Church; there
is a pavement of stone within ground 3 sides of the Well
which is joyn'd on the fourth side by a great arch of stone
which lies over the water that runs off from the Well, its
many springs which bubbles up very fast and lookes cleane
in a compass which is 8 square walled in with stone; in the
bottom which you see as clear as Chrystall are 9 stones layd
in an oval on which are dropps of red coullour some almost
quite covering the top of the stone, which is pretended to
be the blood of this holy saint whose head was struck off
here, and so where her body laid this spring burst forth and
remaines till now, a very rapid current, which runs off from
this Well under a barre by which there are stone stepps for
the persons to descend which will bathe themselves in the
Well; and so they walke along the streame to the other end
and then come out, but there is nothing to shelter them but
are exposed to all the Company that are walking about the
Well and to the little houses and part of the streete which
runs along by it; but the Religeuse are not to mind that; it
seemes the Saint they do honour to in this place must beare
them out in all things, they tell of many lameness's and aches
and distempers which are cured by it; its a cold water and
cleare and runs off very quick so that it would be a pleasant
refreshment in the sumer to washe ones self in it, but its

---

[7] The chapel near the Well was built by "the Lady Margaret", mother of
Henry VII. The spring was said to have gushed forth when Winifred's head,
sliced off by a disappointed seducer, rolled downhill and into the church.
James II had given the chapel to some Catholic fathers. (H.A.T.) Defoe re-
counted the legend, "of which", he said, "I believe as much as comes to my
share". The priests were "very numerous" but had to "appear in disguise".
(Op. cit., ii, 66.) John Taylor the "Water Poet" had written in 1652, "The hill
descending is plentifully furnished with beggars of all ages, sexes, conditions,
sorts and sizes, many of them are impotent but all are impudent and richly
embrodered all over with such Hexameter poudred Ermins as are called lice
in England." (*A Short Relation of a Long Journey*, p. 12, in *Works*, ed. 1870.)

shallow not up to the waste so its not easye to dive and washe in; but I thinke I could not have been persuaded to have gone in unless might have had curtains to have drawn about some part of it to have shelter'd from the streete, for the wett garments are no covering to the body; but there I saw abundance of the devout papists on their knees all round the Well; poor people are deluded into an ignorant blind zeale and to be pity'd by us that have the advantage of knowing better and ought to be better; there is some small stones of a reddish coullour in the Well said to be some of St. Winifreds blood also, which the poore people take out and bring to the strangers for curiosity and relicts, and also moss about the bancks full of great virtue for every thing—but its a certaine gaine to the poore people, every one gives them something for bringing them moss and the stones, but least they should in length of tyme be quite gather'd up they take care to replenish it dayly from some mossy hill and so stick it along the sides of the Well—there is good streames runs from it and by meanes of steepe descent runs down and turns mills; they come also to drinke of the water which they take up in the first square which is walled round and where the springs rise, and they say its of wonder full operation; the taste to me was but like good spring water which with wine and sugar and leamons might make a pleasant draught after walking amongst those shady trees of which there is a great many and some straight and tall like a grove but not very uniforme, but a sort of iregular rows.

From thence I went back to Harding [Hawarden] which is 8 very long miles; at Holly Well [Holywell] they speake Welsh, the inhabitants go barefoote and bare leg'd a nasty sort of people, their meate is very small here, mutton is noe bigger than little lamb, what of it there is was sweete; their wine good being neare the sea side and are well provided with fish, very good salmon and eeles and other fish I had at Harding.

This shire is improperly called Flintshire there being noe flints in all the country; there are great coale pitts of the Channell [Cannel] Coale thats cloven huge great pieces, they have great wheeles that are turned with horses that draw up the water and so draine the Mines which would else be overflowed so as they could not dig the coale; they have also engines that draw up their coale in sort of baskets like hand barrows which they wind up like a bucket in a well, for their mines are dug down through a sort of well and some-tymes its pretty low before they come to the coales; it makes the road unsafe because of the coale pitts and also from the slough and quick sands all here about being mostly near the bancks of the water.

In this country are quarrys of stone, copper and iron mines and salt hills, its a hilly place very steep descents great many very high hills, but I went not so farre as Pen ma mower [Penmaenmawr] but cross'd the River Dee haveing first went two mile by these coale mines at least 10 in a place; its a thing which holds neer 2 bushell that is their basket they draw up which is bought for 6 pence.

I forded over the Dee when the tide was out all upon the sands at least a mile which was as smooth as a die being a few hours left of the flood; the sands are here soe loose that the tydes does move them from one place to another at every flood, that the same place one used to foard a month or two before is not to be pass'd now, for as it brings the sands in heaps to one place so it leaves others in deep holes, which are cover'd with water, and loose sand that would swallow up a horse or carriages, so I had two Guides to con-duct me over; the carriages which are used to it and pass continually at the ebbs of water observes the drift of sands and so escape the danger; it was at least a mile I went on the sands before I came to the middle of the channell which was pretty deep, and with such a current or tyde which was fall-ing out to sea together with the wind the horses feete could scarce stand against it, but it was but narrow just the deep part of the channell and so soone over; when the tyde is fully out they frequently ford in many places which they marke as the sands fall, and can go near 9 or 10 mile over the sands from Chester to Burton or to Flint town almost; but many persons that have known the foards well, that have come a year or half a year after, if they venture on their former knowledge have been overwhelm'd in the ditches made by the sands, which is deep enough to swallow up a coach or waggon; but they convey their coales from Wales and any other things by waggon when the tyde is out to Chester and other parts.

From Burton which was on the side of England the shore I went to the ferry 9 miles to the River Meresy [Mersey], another great river indeed much broader and a perfect sea for 20 mile or more; it comes out of Lancashire from Warrington and both this and the Dee empts themselves into the sea almost together a few leagues from Leverpoole [Liverpool] which poole is form'd by a poynt of land that runs almost round the entrance from the sea, being narrow and hazardous to strangers to saile in in the winter, the mouth of the river by reason of the sands and rocks is a gate to the river; this I ferry'd over and was an hour and halfe in the passage, its of great bredth and at low water is so deep and salt as the sea almost, tho' it does not cast so green a hew on the water as the sea, but else the waves toss and the rocks great all round it and is as dangerous as the sea; its in a sort of Hoy that I ferried over and my horses, the boate would have held 100 people.

6. LANCASHIRE AND THE LAKE DISTRICT

LEVERPOOL[1] [LIVERPOOL] which is in Lancashire is built just on the river Mersy [Mersey], mostly new built houses of brick and stone after the London fashion; the first original was a few fishermens houses and now is grown to a large fine town and but a parish and one Church, tho' there be 24 streetes in it; there is indeed a little Chappell and there are a great many Dessenters in the town; its a very rich

[1] The population of Liverpool had doubled in the previous 25 years but was still only c. 6,000; and there was still no mole or quay. By Defoe's time a dock had been constructed and Liverpool could almost rival Bristol as a port. (Op. cit., ii, 256–8.) The Exchange dated from 1673. The street running "quite through" was Dale Street.

trading town the houses of brick and stone built high and even, that a streete quite through lookes very handsome, the streetes well pitched; there are abundance of persons you see very well dress'd and of good fashion; the streetes are faire and long, its London in miniature as much as ever I saw any thing; there is a very pretty Exchange stands on 8 pillars besides the corners which are each treble pillars all of stone and its railed in over which is a very handsome Town Hall; over all is a tower and cupillow thats so high that from thence one has the whole view of the town and the country round; in a clear day you may see the Isle of Man—which also was in view from out of Wales at Harding [Hawarden] on the high tarrass walke in my Cos'n Percivalls garden.

Thence to Prescote [Prescot] 7 very long miles but pretty good way mostly lanes; there I passed by Mosel [Knowsley], the Earle of Darbys house which looked very nobly with many towers and balls on them; it stands amongst tall trees and lookes like a pleasant grove all about it; its an old house runs a large compass of ground; the town of Prescote stands on a high hill, a very pretty neate market town a large market place and broad streetes well pitch'd.

Thence to Wiggon [Wigan] 7 long miles more, mostly in lanes and some hollow wayes, and some pretty deep stony way so forced us upon the high Causey many [times]; but some of the way was good which I went pretty fast, and yet by reason of the tediousness of the miles for length I was 5 hours going that 14 mile, I could have gone 30 mile about London in the time; there was pretty much woods and lanes through which I pass'd, and pass'd by a mer or lake of water; there are many of these here about; but not going through Ormskerk I avoided going by the famous Mer call'd Martin Mer[2] that as the proverb sayes has parted many a man and his mare indeed; it being neare evening and not getting a Guide I was a little afraid to go that way it being very hazardous for Strangers to pass by it; some part of that mer one Mr. Fleetewood has been at the expence to draine so as to be able to use the ground for tillage, having by trenches

---

[2] Soon afterwards the mere was drained.

and floodgates with banks shutt out the waters that still kept it a marsh and moorish ground, but it was a very great charge; however it shews by industry and some expence if Gentlemen would set about it most of the waste ground, thats now a fenny moor and mostly water, might be rendred usefull and in a few yeares answere the first great charge on it;

Wiggons [Wigan] is another pretty market town built of stone and brick; here it is that the fine Channell [Cannel] Coales are in perfection, burns as light as a candle—set the coales together with some fire and it shall give a snap and burn up light—of this coale[3] they make saltcellars standishes and many boxes and things which are sent about for Curiositys and sold in London and are often offer'd in the exchanges in company with white or black marble, and most people deceived by them which have not been in those countrys and know it, but such persons discover it and will call for a candle to trye them wheather marble or coale; its very finely pollish'd and lookes much like jett or ebany wood for which one might easily take it when in boxes etc.; I bought some of them for Curiosity sake.

2 mile off Wigon towards Warrington—which was some of my way back againe but for the Curiosity's sake I did—is the Burning Well which burns like brandy;[4] its a little sorry hole in one of the grounds 100 yards from the road that comes from Warrington to Wiggon, just by a hedge or banck, its full of dirt and mud almost but the water continually bubbles up as if it were a pott boyling which is the spring or severall springs in that place, nevertheless I felt the water and it was

[3] "Canell coal . . . will polish like alabaster; then a lady may take them up in a cambrick handkerchief and they will not soil it, though they are as black as the deepest jet." (Defoe, Op. cit., ii, 267.)

[4] A marginal note reads "Burning Well, it wil boyle egges or meat". According to Roger North, "When the show-company are come, a man takes up the turf, and, after a little puffing of a brown paper match, gives fire, and instantly the hole is filled with a blue spirituous flame like brandy. . . . They put water in the hole and the flame continued upon the water as if it had been spirits. . . . But I question, if the body were not fluid, but rigid, as glass, whether the vapour would so easily pass it. . . . And it is some demonstration how easily the effluvia of a magnet may permeate glass, metals, and every palpable substance we are acquainted with." (*Lives of the Norths*, ed. 1826, i, 295–6.)

a Cold Spring; the man which shewed it me with a dish tooke out a good quantety of the water and threw away and then, with a piece of rush he lighted by a candle that he brought in a lanthorne, he set the water in the well on fire, and it burn'd blewish just like spirits and continued a good while, but by reason of the great raines that fell the night before the spring was weaker and had not thrown off the raine water, otherwise it used to flame all over the well a good height now it burnt weaker; however at last the wind blew out the mans candle, and he severall tymes lighted the bitt of rush or splinter of wood by the flame that burnt in the well; this is a little unacountable I apprehend its a sort of an unctious matter in the earth and soe through its veines the springs run which causes it so to burn, for I observ'd when they dug into the banck and opened the sort of clay or mudd it burnt fiercer and more.

From the Well I returned againe to Wiggon two mile and thence to Preston, and passed by Sir John Bradshaws house [Haigh Hall] which stood on the declineing of a hill in the midst of a fine grove of trees; severall fine walkes and rows of trees thereabout; just in the road on the banck whereon the hedge stood was errected a high stone pillar carv'd and a ball on the top with an inscription cutt on it shewing the cause of it, being the Monument of an officer that in a fight just there—his horse takeing the hedge and ditch on some distaste he tooke at the gunns and smoake—flung out his sword out of the scabbard and flung his Master down on the poynt of it which run him through that he dyed and lyes buried on the spott.

Preston is reckon'd but 12 miles from Wiggon but they exceed in length by farre those that I thought long the day before from Leverpoole; its true to avoid the many mers and marshy places it was a great compass I tooke and passed down and up very steep hills and this way was good gravel way; but passing by many very large arches that were only single ones but as large as two great gateways and the water I went through that ran under them was so shallow notwith-standing these were extream high arches, I enquired the meaneing and was inform'd that on great raines those brookes would be swell'd to so great a heigth that unless those arches were so high noe passing while it were so; they are but narrow bridges for foote or horse and at such flouds they are forced in many places to boate it till they come to those arches on the great bridges which are across their great rivers: this happens sometymes on sudden great showers for a day or two in the summer, but the winter is often or mostly soe that there is deep waters so as not easily cross'd; but once in 3 or 4 yeares there is some of those very greate floods I mention'd before that they are forced to boate from bridge to bridge which is little enough then to secure them; I passed by at least half a dozen of these high single arches besides severall great Stone Bridges of 4 or 6 arches which are very high also over their greatest rivers.

Preston stands on a hill is a very good market town, Satterday is their market which day I was there and saw it was provided with all sorts of things leather corn coales butter cheese and fruite and garden things; there is a very spacious Market place and pretty Church and severall good houses; at the entrance of the town was a very good house which was a Lawyers,[5] all stone work 5 windows in the front and high built according to the eastern building neer London, the ascent to the house was 14 or 15 stone stepps large and a handsome court with open iron pallasadoes in the gate and on each side the whole breadth of the house, which discover'd the gardens on each side of the house neately kept flowers and greens; there was also many steps up to the house from the court it was a compleate building; there was 2 or 3 more such houses in the town and indeed the generallity of the buildings especially in 2 or 3 of the great streetes were very handsome, better than is most country towns, and the streets spacious and well pitch'd.

[5] Defoe wrote, "the town is full of attorneys, proctors and notaries, the process of law here being of a different nature than they are in other places, it being a county palatine. . . . The people are gay here, though not perhaps the richer for that; but it has by that obtained the name of Proud Preston". (Op. cit., ii, 268.) As late as 1745 Lady Oxford found Preston "a very clean, pleasant, town consisting of two large streets wherein many of the neighbouring gentry have good winter houses". (*Portland MSS.*, vi, 190.)

I was about 4 houres going this twelve mile and could
have gone 20 in the tyme in most countrys, nay by the
people of those parts this twelve mile is as long and as much
tyme taken up in going it as to go from thence to Lancaster
which is 20 mile; and I can confirme this by my own experience for I went to Gascoyne [Garstang] which is 10 miles
and halfe way to Lancaster in two houres, where I baited,
and here it was I was first presented with the Clap bread
which is much talked off made all of oates; I was surpris'd
when the cloth was laid they brought a great basket such
as one uses to undress children with, and set on the table
full of thinn waffers as big as pancackes and drye that they
easily breake into shivers, but coming to dinner found it to
be the only thing I must eate for bread; the taste of oate
bread is pleasant enough and where its well made is very
acceptable, but for the most part its scarce baked and full
of drye flower on the outside; the description of how its made
ought to come in here but I reserve it to the place I saw it
made at the best way.

As I come to this place which was much over Downs or a
Race ground I came along by some of the old Picts walls the
ruines of which here and there remaines in many parts of
the country; Gascoyn [Garstang] is a little market town, one
Church in it which is a mile off from the town, and the parish
is 8 miles long which discourag'd me in staying there being
Satturday night and so pressed on to Lancaster; I perceive
most of the parishes are a great tract of land and very large
and also as beneficial, for all over Lancastershire the revenues of the parsonages are considerable, 2 and 300£, 500 and
800£ apiece; the parson at Leverpoole has 1100£ a yeare
and its frequent every where 3 or 400£.

Thence to Lancaster town 10 mile more which I easily
reached in 2 hours and a halfe or 3 hours, I passed through
abundance of villages, almost at the end of every mile, mostly
all along lanes being an enclosed country; they have one
good thing in most parts off this principality (or County
Palatine its rather called) that at all cross wayes there are
Posts with Hands pointing to each road with the names of

the great town or market towns that it leads to,[6] which does make up for the length of the miles that strangers may not loose their road and have it to goe back againe; you have a great divertion on this road haveing a pleasing prospect of the countrys a great distance round and see it full of inclosures and some woods; three miles off the town you see it very plaine and the sea even the main ocean in one place an arm of it comes up within 2 mile of the town; the River Lieue [Lune] runs by the town and so into the sea.

The situation of Lancaster town is very good, the Church neately built of stone, the Castle which is just by, both on a very great ascent from the rest of the town and so is in open view, the town and river lying round it beneath; on the Castle tower walking quite round by the battlements I saw the whole town and river at a view, which runs almost quite round and returns againe by the town, and saw the sea beyond and the great high hills beyond that part of the sea which are in Wales, and also into Westmoreland to the great hills there call'd Furness Fells or Hills being a string of vast high hills together; also into Cumberland to the great hill called Black Comb Hill [Black Combe] whence they digg their black lead [graphite] and no where else, but they open the mine but once in severall yeares; I also saw into Yorkshire; there is lead copper gold and silver in some of those hills and marble and christall also.

Lancaster town is old and much decay'd; there has been a monastery, the walls of part of it remaine and some of the carv'd stones and figures, there is in it a good garden and a pond in it with a little isleand on which an apple tree grows, a Jenitin [Jenneting],[7] and strawberys all round its rootes and the banks of the little isle; there are 2 pretty wells and a vault that leads a great way under ground up as farre as the Castle which is a good distance; in the river there are great wires or falls of water made for salmon fishing, where they hang their nets and catch great quantety's of fish, which is neare the bridge; the town seemes not to

[6] Signposts had been ordered by statute in 1697. See Introduction, p. xiv.
[7] A Jenneting is a St. John's Apple, a kind of early apple.

be much in trade as some others, but the great store of fish makes them live plentifully as also the great plenty of all provisions; the streetes are some of them well pitch'd and of a good size; when I came into the town the stones were so slippery crossing some channells that my horse was quite down on his nose but did at length recover himself and so I was not thrown off or injured, which I desire to bless God for as for the many preservations I mett with—I cannot say the town seemes a lazy town and there are trades of all sorts, there is a large meeteing-house but their Minister was but a mean preacher: there are 2 Churches in the town which are pretty near each other.

Thence I went to Kendall in Westmoreland over steepe stony hills all like rocks 6 miles to one Lady Middleton; and by some Gentlemen which were travelling that way that was their acquantaince had the advantage of going through her parke and saved the going round a bad stony passage; it was very pleasant under the shade of the tall trees; it was an old timber house [Leighton Hall] but the family being from home we had a free passage through on to the road againe much of which was stony and steep far worse than the Peake in Darbyshire; this Lady Middleton was a papist and I believe the Gentlemen that was travelling were too; in this park is the 3 Brother tree which a little from the root measures 13 yards circumference; thence to Kendall ten mile more, most of the way was in lanes when I was out of the stony hills, and then into inclosed lands; here in 6 mile to the town you have very rich good land enclosed, little round green hills flourishing with corn and grass as green and fresh being in the prime season in July; there is not much woods but only the hedge rows round the grounds which looks very fine; in these Northern Countyes they have only the summer graine as barley oates peas beans and lentils noe wheate or rhye, for they are so cold and late in their yeare they cannot venture at that sort of tillage, so have none but what they are supply'd out of other countys adjacent; the land seemes here in many places very fertile; they have much rhye in Lancashire Yorkshire and Stafford and Shropshire and so

Herriford and Worcestershire which I found very troublesome in my journeys, for they would not own they had any
such thing in their bread but it so disagrees with me as
allways to make me sick, which I found by its effects when
ever I met with any tho' I did not discern it by the taste; in
Suffolke and Norfolke I also met with it—but in these parts
its altogether the oatbread.

Kendall is a town built all of stone, one very broad streete
in which is the Market Crosse, its a goode tradeing town
mostly famed for the cottons; Kendall Cotton[7a] is used for
blanckets and the Scotts use them for their plodds [plaids]
and there is much made here and also linsiwoolseys and a
great deale of leather tann'd here and all sorts of commodityes
twice a weeke is the market furnished with all sorts of things.

The River Can [Kent] which gives name to the town is
pretty large but full of rocks and stones that makes shelves
and falls in the water, its stor'd with plenty of good fish and
there are great falls of water partly naturall and added to by
putting more stones in manner of wyers [weirs] at which they
catch salmon when they leape with speares; the roarcing of
the water at these places sometymes does foretell wet
weather, they do observe when the water roares most in the
fall on the northside it will be faire, if on the southside of the
town it will be wet; some of them are falls as high as a house
—the same observation is at Lancaster at the wires [weirs]
where they catch salmon, against storms or raines it will be
turbulent and rore as may be heard into the town—there are
3 or 4 good houses in the town, the rest are like good
traders houses very neate and tight, the streetes are all pitch'd
which is extreame easy to be repair'd for the whole country
is like one entire rock or pitching almost all the roads.

At the Kings Arms one Mrs. Rowlandson she does pott
up the charr fish the best of any in the country, I was curious
to have some and so bespoke some of her,[8] and also was

[7a] Kendal Cottons were in fact woollen cloth generally dyed green. Cf.
Falstaff's "three misbegotten knaves in Kendal green".

[8] The potted char of Windermere was "sent far and near, as presents to
the best friends", and was called "very happily, the golden Alpine trout".
(Defoe, Op. cit., ii, 269.)

as curious to see the great water [Windermere] which is the only place that fish is to be found in, and so went from Kendall to Bondor [Bowness] 6 miles thro' narrow lanes, but the lands in the inclosures are rich; but here can be noe carriages but very narrow ones like little wheel-barrows that with a horse they convey their fewell and all things else; they also use horses on which they have a sort of pannyers some close some open that they strew full of hay turff and lime and dung and every thing they would use, and the reason is plaine from the narrowness of the lanes: where is good lands they will loose as little as they can and where its hilly and stoney no other carriages can pass, so they use these horse carriages; abundance of horses I see all about Kendall streetes with their burdens.[9]

This Kendall is the biggest town and much in the heart of Westmoreland but Appleby 10 mile off is the shire town where the session and assizes are held and is 7 miles to this great Lake Wiandermer [Windermere] or great standing water, which is 10 mile long and near halfe a mile over in some places; it has many little hills or isles in it, one of a great bigness of 30 acres of ground on which is a house, the Gentleman that is Lord of the Manour lives in it Sir Christopher Phillips [Philipson]; he has a great command of the water, and of the villages thereabout and many privileges, he makes a Major [Mayor] or Bailiff of the place during life; its but a small mean place, Mr. Majors was the best entertaining house where I was; the Isle did not looke to be so bigg at the shore but takeing boate I went on it and found it as large and very good barley and oates and grass; the water is very cleer and full of good fish, but the Charr fish being out of season could not easily be taken so I saw none alive, but of other fish I had a very good supper; the season of the Charrfish is between Michaelmas and Christmas, at that tyme I have had of them which they pott with sweete spices, they are as big as a small trout rather slenderer and

[9] From Kendal, said Roger North, "they could write to most trading towns, and have answers by the packs (for all is horse-carriage) with returns (time being allowed) as certain as by the post". (*Lives of the Norths*, i, 293-4.) See Introduction, p. xxxi.

the skinn full of spotts some redish, and part of the whole
skinn and the finn and taile is red like the finns of a perch,
and the inside flesh looks as red as any salmon; if they are in
season their taste is very rich and fatt tho' not so strong or
clogging as the lamprys are, but its as fatt and rich a food.

This great water seemes to flow and wave about with the
wind or in one motion but it does not ebb and flow like the
sea with the tyde, neither does it run so as to be perceivable
tho' at the end of it a little rivulet trills from it into the sea,
but it seemes to be a standing lake encompass'd with vast
high hills that are perfect rocks and barren ground of a vast
height from which many little springs out of the rock does
bubble up and descend down and fall into this water; notwithstanding great raines the water does not seem much
encreased, tho' it must be so, then it does draine off more at
the end of the Lake; these hills which they call Furness Fells
a long row continued some miles and some of them are
call'd Donum Fells and soe from the places they adjoyne to
are named, but they hold the whole length of the water
which is 10 mile; they have some parts of them that has wayes
that they can by degrees in a compass ascend them and so
they go onward in the countrys; they are ferried over the
Lake when they go to market; on the other side over those
fels there is a sort of stones like rubbish or broken pieces
of stones which lies about a quarry that lies all in the bottom
of the water; where its so shallow as at the shores it is and
very cleer you see the bottom, between these stones are
weeds which grows up that I had some taken up, just like
sampyer [samphire] and I have a fancy its a sort of sampire
that indeed is gather'd in the rocks by the sea and water,
and this grows in the water but it resembles it in coullour
figure and the taste not much unlike, it was somewhat
waterish; there was also fine moss growing in the bottom
of the water.

Here it was I saw the oat Clap bread made: they mix their
flour with water so soft as to rowle it in their hands into a
ball, and then they have a board made round and something
hollow in the middle riseing by degrees all round to the

edge a little higher, but so little as one would take it to be only a board warp'd, this is to cast out the cake thinn and so they clap it round and drive it to the edge in a due proportion till drove as thinn as a paper, and still they clap it and drive it round, and then they have a plaite of iron same size with their clap board and so shove off the cake on it and so set it on coales and bake it; when enough on one side they slide it off and put the other side; if their iron plaite is smooth and they take care their coales or embers are not too hot but just to make it looke yellow, it will bake and be as crisp and pleasant to eate as any thing you can imagine; but as we say of all sorts of bread there is a vast deale of difference in what is housewifely made and what is ill made, so this if its well mixed and rowled up and but a little flour on the outside which will drye on and make it mealy is a very good sort of food; this is the sort of bread they use in all these countrys, and in Scotland they breake into their milk or broth or else sup that up and bite of their bread between while, they spread butter on it and eate it with their meate; they have no other sort of bread unless at market towns and that is scarce to be had unless the market dayes, soe they make their cake and eate it presently for its not so good if 2 or 3 dayes old; it made me reflect on the description made in scripture of their kneeding cakes and bakeing them on the hearth when ever they had Company come to their houses, and I cannot but thinke it was after this maner they made their bread in the old tymes especially those Eastern Countryes where their bread might be soone dry'd and spoil'd.

Their little carts I was speakeing of they use hereabout, the wheeles are fast'ned to the axletree and so turn altogether, they hold not above what our wheele barrows would carry at three or four tymes, which the girles and boys and women does go about with, drawn by one horse to carry any thing they want; here is a great deal of good grass and summer corn and pastures its rich land in the bottoms, as one may call them considering the vast hills above them on all sides, yet they contain a number of lesser hills one below another,

so that tho' at one looke you think it but a little land every
body has, yet it being so full of hills its many acres which if
at length in a plain would extend a vast way; I was about a
quarter of an hour in the boate before I reach'd the island
which is in the midst of the water so by that you may guesse
at the breadth of the water in the whole; they ferry man and
horse over it, its sometymes perfectly calme.

Thence I rode almost all the waye in sight of this great
water; some tymes I lost it by reason of the great hills interposeing and so a continu'd up hill and down hill and that
pretty steep even when I was in that they called bottoms,
which are very rich good grounds, and so I gained by degrees
from lower to higher hills which I allwayes went up and
down before I came to another hill; at last I attained to the
side of one of these hills or fells of rocks which I passed on
the side much about the middle; for looking down to the
bottom it was at least a mile all full of those lesser hills and
inclosures, so looking upward I was as farre from the top
which was all rocks and something more barren tho' there
was some trees and woods growing in the rocks and hanging
over all down the brow of some of the hills; from these great
fells there are severall springs out of the rock that trickle
down their sides, and as they meete with stones and rocks in
the way when something obstructs their passage and so they
come with more violence that gives a pleaseing sound and
murmuring noise; these descend by degrees, at last fall into
the low grounds and fructifye it which makes the land soe
fruit full in the valleys; and upon those very high fells or
rocky hills its (tho') soe high and yet a moorish sort off
ground whence they digg abundance of peat which they use
for their fewell, being in many places a barren ground yield-
ing noe wood, etc.; I rode in sight of this Winander Water
as I was saying up and down above 7 mile; afterwards as I
was ascending another of those barren fells—which tho' I
at last was not halfe way up, yet was an hour going it up
and down, on the other side going only on the side of it
about the middle of it, but it was of such a height as to shew
one a great deale of the Country when it happens to be be-

tween those hills, else those interposeing hinders any sight but of the clouds—I see a good way behind me another of those waters or mers but not very bigge; these great hills are so full of loose stones and shelves of rocks that its very unsafe to ride them down.

There is good marble amongst those rocks: as I walked down at this place I was walled on both sides by those inaccessible high rocky barren hills which hangs over ones head in some places and appear very terrible; and from them springs many little currents of water from the sides and clefts which trickle down to some lower part where it runs swiftly over the stones and shelves in the way, which makes a pleasant rush and murmuring noise and like a snow ball is encreased by each spring trickling down on either side of those hills, and so descends into the bottoms which are a moorish ground in which in many places the waters stand, and so forme some of those Lakes as it did here, the confluence of all these little springs being gathered together in this Lake which was soe deep as the current of water that passed through it was scarce to be perceived till one came to the farther end, from whence it run a good little river and pretty quick, over which many bridges are laid.

Here I came to villages of sad little hutts[10] made up of drye walls, only stones piled together and the roofs of same slatt; there seemed to be little or noe tunnells for their chimneys and have no morter or plaister within or without; for the most part I tooke them at first sight for a sort of houses or barns to fodder cattle in, not thinking them to be dwelling houses, they being scattering houses here one there another, in some places there may be 20 or 30 together, and the Churches the same; it must needs be very cold dwellings but it shews something of the lazyness of the people; indeed here and there there was a house plaister'd, but there is sad entertainment, that sort of clap bread and butter and cheese and a cup of beer all one can have, they are 8 mile from a

[10] Hammond in 1634 noticed similar "poore cottages . . . I thinke the sun had never shone on them . . . sicke they were as we never saw before, nor likely ever shall see againe". (*Short Survey of 26 Counties*, ed. 1904, pp. 42–3.)

market town and their miles are tedious to go both for illness of way and length of the miles.

They reckon it but 8 mile from the place I was at the night before but I was 3 or 4 hours at least going it; here I found a very good smith to shooe the horses, for these stony hills and wayes pulls off a shooe presently and wears them as thinn that it was a constant charge to shooe my horses every 2 or 3 days; but this smith did shooe them so well and so good shooes that they held some of the shooes 6 weeks; the stonyness of the wayes all here about teaches them the art off makeing good shooes and setting them on fast.

Here I cross'd one of the stone bridges that was pretty large which entred me into Cumberlandshire:[11] this river together with the additional springs continually running into it all the way from those vaste precipices comes into a low place and form a broad water which is very cleer and reaches 7 mile in length, Ules water [Ullswater] its called, such another water as that of Wiander mer [Windermere], only that reaches 10 mile in length from Ambleside to the sea, and this is but 7 such miles long; its full of such sort of stones and slatts in the bottom as the other, neer the brimm where its shallowe you see it cleer to the bottom; this is secured on each side by such formidable heights as those rocky fells in same manner as the other was; I rode the whole length of this water by its side sometyme a little higher upon the side of the hill and sometyme just by the shore and for 3 or 4 miles I rode through a fine forest or parke where was deer skipping about and haires, which by meanes of a good Greyhound I had a little Course, but we being strangers could not so fast pursue it in the grounds full of hillocks and furse and soe she escaped us.[12]

I observed the boundaries of all these great waters, which are a sort of deep lakes or kind of standing waters, are those sort of barren rocky hills which are so vastly high; I call this a standing water as the other because its not like other great rivers as the Trent Severne Hull or Thames etc. to

---

[11] She had crossed the Kirkstone Pass.
[12] This was a defiance of the Game Laws. See Introduction, p. xxxiii.

appear to run with a streame or current, but only as it rowles from side to side like waves as the wind moves it; its true at the end of this being a low fall of ground it runs off in a little streame; there is exceeding good fish here and all sorts of provision at the market towns; their market town was Peroth [Penrith] 10 long miles, a mile or two beyond this Ulls water; Tuesday is the market day which was the day I came thither, its a long way for the market people to goe but they and their horses are used to it and go with much more facility than strangers; at the end of this Ulls water is a fine round hill look'd as green and full of wood, very pleasant with grass and corne very fruitefull, and hereabout we leave those desart and barren rocky hills, not that they are limitted to Westmorland only, for had I gone farther to the left hand on into Cumberland I should have found more such and they tell me farr worse for height and stony-nesse about White haven side and Cockermouth, so that tho' both the County's have very good land and fruitfull, so they equally partake of the bad, tho' indeed Westmorland takes it name from its abounding in moorish ground yet Cumberland has its share, and more of the hilly stony part; indeed I did observe those grounds were usually neighbours to each other, the rocks abounding in springs which distilling it self on lower ground if of a spungy soile made it marshy or lakes, and in many places very fruitfull in summer graine and grasse, but the northerly winds blow cold so long on them that they never attempt sowing their land with wheate or rhye.

The stones and slatt about Peroth [Penrith] look'd so red that at my entrance into the town thought its buildings were all of brick, but after found it to be the coullour of the stone which I saw in the Quarrys look very red, their slatt is the same which cover their houses; its a pretty large town a good market for cloth that they spinn in the country, hempe and also woollen; its a great market for all sorts of cattle meate corne etc.

Here are two rivers one called the Emount [Eamont] which parts Cumberland and Westmorland which bridge I should have passed over had I come the direct roade from Kendall to Peroth [Penrith], but strikeing off to Ambleside to Wiandermer I came another end of the town; in this river are greate falls of waters call'd cataracts by reason of the rock and shelves in it which makes a great noise, which is heard more against foul weather into the town tho' the bridge be halfe a mile out of the town; the other river is called Louder [Lowther] which gives name to Lord Landsdowns [Lonsdale] house call'd Louder-hall [Lowther Castle][13] which is four mile from Peroth [Penrith]; I went to it through fine woods, the front is just faceing the great road from Kendall and lookes very nobly, with severall rows of trees which leads to large iron gates, open barres, into the stable yard which is a fine building on the one side of the house very uniform, and just against it is such another row of buildings the other side of the house like two wings which is the offices; its built each like a fine house jutting out at each end and the middle is with pillars white and carvings like the entrance of a building, these are just equal and alike and encompass the two sides of the first court which enters with large iron gates and iron palasadoes in the breadth, and then there is an ascent of 15 stone steps turned round very large and on the top large iron gates and same pallisad of iron betweene stone pillars, which runs the breadth of the front; this court is with paved walks of broad stone one broad one to the house, the other of same breadth runs acrosse to the stables and offices and so there is 4 large squares of grass in which there is a large statue of stone in the midst of each and 4 little Cupids or little boys in each corner of the 4 squares; then one ascends severall more steps to another little court with open iron railes and this is divided into severall grass plotts by paved walks of stone to the severall doores, some of which are straight others slope, the grass plotts being seven, and in each a statue, the middlemost is taller than the rest; this is just the front of

---

[13] "Lowther, where Sir John Lowther is building such a palace-like fabric as bears the bell away from all." (Thoresby, *Diary*, September 24th 1694.) Sir John was created Lord Lonsdale in 1696.

the house where you enter a porch with pillars of lime stone but the house is the red sort of stone of the country.

Below-staires you enter a space that leads severall wayes to all the offices and on one side is a large parlour which lookes out on these green plotts with images; the staircase very well wanscoated and carv'd at the top; you are landed into a noble hall very lofty, the top and sides are exquisitely painted by the best hand in England [Antonio Verrio] which did the painting at Windsor; the top is the Gods and Goddesses that are sitting at some great feast and a great tribunal before them, each corner is the Seasons of the yeare with the variety of weather, raines and rainbows stormy winds sun shine snow and frost with multitudes of other fancyes and varietyes in painting, and looks very natural—it cost 500£ that roome alone; thence into a dineing room and drawing-roome well wanscoated of oake large pannells plaine no frettworks nor carvings or glass work only in chimney pieces; 3 handsome chambers, one scarlet cloth strip'd and very fashionably made up the hangings the same, another flower'd damaske lined with fine Indian embroidery, the third roome had a blew satten bed embroider'd, in this roome was very fine orris[14] hangings in which was much silk and gold and silver; a little roome by in which was a green and white damaske canopy bed which was hung with some of the same hangings—being made for the Duke of Lortherdale [Lauderdale] and had his armes in many places, by his dying were sold to Lord Landsdon [Lonsdale], they containe a Scottish story and garb of the 4 quarters of the yeare; the roomes are all well pitch'd and well finish'd and many good pictures of the family and severall good fancy's of humane and animals; a good gallery so adorn'd which leads to a closet that looks into the Chappell, all things very neat tho' nothing extraordinary besides the hall painting; the chimney pieces are of a dark coulloured marble which is taken out of the ground just by, its well polish'd, there was some few white marble vein'd but that is not dug out of this country.

[14] Orris, a name given to lace of various patterns in gold and silver or embroidery made of gold lace.

The house is a flatt rooffe and stands amidst a wood of rows of trees which with these statues and those in two gardens on each side (which for their walks and plantations is not finish'd but full of statues) which with the house is so well contrived to be seen at one view; the Lady Landsdown [Lonsdale] sent and treated me with a breakfast, cold things and sweetemeates all serv'd in plaite, but it was so early in the morning that she being indisposed was not up.

So I returned back 4 mile to Peroth [Penrith] and came in sight of severall genteele seates or Gentlemens houses, and came by a round green spott of a large circumfference which they keep cut round with a banke round it like a bench ["King Arthur's Table"]; its story is that it was the table a great Giant 6 yards tall used to dine at and there entertained another of nine yards tall which he afterwards killed; there is the length in the Church yard how farre he could leape a great many yards; there was also on the Church at Peroth a fine Clock which had severall motions, there was the starrs and signes there was the encrease and changes of the moone by a darke and golden side of a little globe.

A mile from Peroth [Penrith] in a low bottom a moorish place stands Great Mag and her Sisters,[15] the story is that these soliciting her to an unlawfull love by an enchantment are turned with her into stone; the stone in the middle which is called Mag is much bigger and have some forme like a statue or figure of a body but the rest are but soe many craggy stones, but they affirme they cannot be counted twice alike as is the story of Stonidge [Stonehenge], but the number of these are not above 30; however what the first design of placeing them there either as a marke of that sort of moorish ground or what else, the thing is not so wonderfull as that of Stonidge, because there is noe such sort of stone in 20 miles off those downs and how they of so vast a bulk and weight should be brought thither, whereas all this country abounds with quarrys of stone and its mostly rocks.

The wayes from thence to Carlisle over much heath where

---

[15] "Long Meg and her Sisters." See Wordsworth's Sonnet on this "family forlorn".

they have many stone quarrys and cut much peate and turff, which is their chief fuel; its reckon'd but 16 mile from Peroth [Penrith] to Carlisle but they are pretty long, besides my going out of the way above 3 or 4 mile, which made it 20; they were very long and I was a great while rideing it; you pass by the little hutts and hovels the poor live in like barnes some have them daub'd with mud-wall others drye walls.

Carlisle stands in view at least 4 mile distant; the town is walled in and all built of stone, the Cathedrall stands high and very eminent to be seen above the town; you enter over the bridge and double gates which are iron-grates and lined with a case of doores of thick timber; there are 3 gates to the town one called the English gate at which I entred, the other the Irish which leads on to White haven and Cokermouth [Cockermouth], the other the Scottish gate through which I went into Scotland; the walls of the town and battlements and towers are in very good repaire and looks well; the Cathedrall all built of stone which looked stately but nothing Curious; there was some few houses as the Deans and Treasurer and some of the Doctors houses walled in with little gardens their fronts looked gracefully, else I saw no house except the present Majors [Mayor] house of brick and stone, and one house which was the Chancellors built of stone very lofty 5 good sarshe [sash] windows in the front, and this within a stone wall'd garden well kept and iron gates to discover it to view with stone pillars; the streetes are very broad and handsome well pitch'd.

I walked round the walls and saw the river, which twists and turns it self round the grounds, called the Emount [Eamont] which at 3 or 4 miles off is flow'd by the sea; the other river is the Essex[16] which is very broad and ebbs and flows about a mile or two off; there remaines only some of the walls and ruines of the Castle which does shew it to have been a very strong town formerly; the walls are of a prodigious thickness and vast great stones, its moated round and with draw bridges; there is a large Market place with a good

[16] Celia Fiennes meant the Esk, but should have meant the Eden.

Cross and Hall and is well supply'd as I am inform'd with provision at easye rates, but my Landlady notwithstanding ran me up the largest reckoning for allmost nothing; it was the dearest lodging I met with and she pretended she could get me nothing else, so for 2 joynts of mutton and a pinte of wine and bread and beer I had a 12 shilling reckoning; but since, I find tho' I was in the biggest house in town I was in the worst accomodation, and so found it, and a young giddy Landlady that could only dress fine and entertain the soldiers.

7. ALONG THE BORDER TO NEWCASTLE

FROM HENCE I tooke a Guide the next day and so went for Scotland[1] and rode 3 or 4 mile by the side of this River Emount[2] which is full of very good fish; I rode sometymes on a high ridge over a hill sometymes on the sands, it turning and winding about, that I went almost all the way by it and saw them with boates fishing for salmon and troute which made my journey very pleasant; leaving this river I came to the Essex [Esk] which is very broad and hazardous to crosse even when the tyde is out, by which it leaves a broad sand on each side which in some places is unsafe—made me take a good Guide which carry'd me aboute and a crosse some part of it here and some part in another place, it being deep in the channell where I did crosse which was in sight of the mouth of the river that runs into the sea; on the sand before the water was quite gone from it, I saw a great bird which look'd almost black picking up fish and busking[3] in the water, it

---

[1] Here a guide was needed for physical protection. The Assize Judge was always provided with an armed guard by the tenants of each manor he passed through. He was also expected not to be "so much of a South Country judge" as to have scruples against hanging thieves on "a violent suspicion". (*Lives of the Norths*, i, 286–8.) According to Macaulay, "No traveller ventured into that country without making his will".

[2] Actually the Eden.

[3] "Busking" is not a corruption for "basking"; to busk meant "of fowls: to shift about restlessly or uneasily". (O.E.D.)

looked like an Eagle and by its dimentions could scarce be any other bird.

Thence I went into Scotland over the river Serke [Sark] which is also flowed by the sea but in the summer tyme is not soe deep, but can be pass'd over tho' pretty deep but narrow; it affords good fish but all here about which are called Borderers seem to be very poor people which I impute to their sloth; Scotland this part of it is a low marshy ground where they cutt turff and peate for the fewell, tho' I should apprehend the sea might convey coales to them; I see little that they are employ'd besides fishing which makes provision plentiful, or else their cutting and carving turff and peate which the women and great girles bare legg'd does lead a horse which draws a sort of carriage the wheeles like a dung-pott and hold about 4 wheele barrows; these people tho' with naked leggs are yet wrapp'd up in plodds a piece of woollen like a blanket or else rideing hoods, and this when they are in their houses; I tooke them for people which were sick seeing 2 or 3 great wenches as tall and bigg as any women sat hovering between their bed and chimney corner all idle doing nothing, or at least was not settled to any work, tho' it was nine of the clock when I came thither, haveing gone 7 long miles that morning.

This is a little Market town called Adison Bank,[4] the houses lookes just like the booths at a fair—I am sure I have been in some of them that were tollerable dwellings to these —they have no chimneys their smoke comes out all over the house and there are great holes in the sides of their houses which letts out the smoake when they have been well smoaked in it; there is no roome in their houses but is up to the thatch and in which are 2 or 3 beds even to their parlours and buttery; and notwithstanding the cleaning of their parlour for me I was not able to beare the roome; the smell of the hay was a perfume and what I rather chose to stay and see my horses eate their provender in the stable then to stand in

---

[4] Celia Fiennes probably meant the village of Aitchison Bank, some two miles across the Border, but may have confused it with the tollbar, on the Sark, at Allison's or Alanson's Bank.

that roome, for I could not bring my self to sit down; my Landlady offered me a good dish of fish and brought me butter in a Lairdly Dish with the Clap bread, but I could have no stomach to eate any of the food they should order, and finding they had noe wheaten bread I told her I could not eate their clapt oat bread, soe I bought the fish she got for me which was full cheape enough, nine pence for two pieces of Salmon halfe a one neer a yard long and a very large Trout of an amber coullour; soe drinking without eateing some of their wine, which was exceeding good Clarret which they stand conveniently for to have from France, and indeed it was the best and truest French wine I have dranck this seven year and very clear, I had the first tapping of the little vessell and it was very fine.

Then I went up to their Church which looks rather like some little house built of stone and bricke such as our ordinary people in a village live in: the doores were open and the seates and pulpit was in so disregarded a manner that one would have thought there was no use of it, but there is a parson which lives just by whose house is the best in the place and they are all fine folks in their Sundays cloathes; I observe the Church-yard is full of grave stones pretty large with coates of armes and some had a coronet on the eschutcheons cut in the stone; I saw but one house that look'd like a house about a quarter of a mile, which was some Gentlemans, that was built 2 or 3 roomes and some over them of brick and stone the rest were all like barns or hutts for cattle.

This is threescore miles from Edenborough [Edinburgh] and the neerest town to this place is 18 miles, and there would not have been much better entertainement or accomodation and their miles are soe long in these countrys made me afraid to venture, least after a tedious journey I should not be able to get a bed I could lye in; it seemes there are very few towns except Edenburough Abberdeen and Kerk which can give better treatement to strangers, therefore for the most part persons that travell there go from one Noblemans house to another; those houses are all kind of

Castles and they live great, tho' in so nasty a way, as all things are even in those houses, one has little stomach to eate or use any thing as I have been told by some that has travell'd there;[5] and I am sure I mett with a sample of it enough to discourage my progress farther in Scotland; I attribute it wholly to their sloth for I see they sitt and do little—I think there were one or two at last did take spinning in hand at a lazy way; thence I tooke my fish to carry it to a place for the English to dress it, and repass'd the Serke [Sark] and the River Essex [Esk] and there I saw the common people, men women and children, take off their shooes and holding up their cloathes wade through the rivers when the tide was out; and truely some there were that when they come to the other side put on shoes and stockings and had fine plodds [plaids] cast over them and their garb seemed above the common people, but this is their constant way of travelling from one place to another, if any river to pass they make no use of bridges and have not many.

I came to Long Town [Longtown] which is 3 long mile from Addison Bank and is called a Border and indeed is very like the Scots land; thence I cross'd over a tedious long heath to Brampton a mile over Lime [Lyne] river and here I had my dinner dress'd; thence to Mucks hall [Monk's Hall] 6 miles; here I pass'd by my Lord Carletons [Earl of Carlisle] which stands in the midst of woods [Naworth Castle]; you goe through lanes and little sort of woods or hedge rows and many little purling rivers or brooks out of the rocks.

At Muncks Hall I cross'd such another brooke and so out of Cumberland I entred Northumberland; this is the place the Judges dine its a sorry place for entertainment of such a company; here the Sherriffs meete them it being the entrance off Northumberland which is much like the other county; this it seemes Camden relates to be a Kingdom; this I am sure of the more I travell'd northward the longer I found the

[5] In 1701 Sir John Perceval met with butter "of twenty colours and stuck with hair like mortar". "I ate in gloves for fear of the itch"; and kissing the landlady "had certainly brought up my dinner had not the bread been as heavy as lead in my stomach". (H.M.C. *Egmont* MSS. II, 207.)

miles, I am sure these 6 miles and the other 6 miles to Hart-whistle [Haltwhistle] might with modesty be esteemed double the number in most of the countys in England, especially in and about 30 or 40 miles off London; I did not go 2 of those miles in an hour; just at my entrance into Northumberland I ascended a very steep hill of which there are many, but one about 2 mile forward was exceeding steep full of great rocks and stone, some of it along on a row the remainder of the Picts walls or Fortification[6] at the bottom of which was an old Castle [Thirlwall Castle] the walls and towers of which was mostly standing; its a sort of black moorish ground and so wet I observ'd as my man rode up that sort of precipice or steep his horses heeles cast up water every step and their feete cut deepe in, even quite up to the top; such up and down hills and sort of boggy ground it was, and the night drawing fast on, the miles so long, that I tooke a Guide to direct me to avoid those ill places.

This Hartwhistle [Haltwhistle] is a little town; there was one Inn but they had noe hay nor would get none, and when my servants had got some else where they were angry and would not entertaine me, so I was forced to take up in a poor cottage which was open to the thatch and no partitions but hurdles plaister'd; indeed the loft as they called it which was over the other roome was shelter'd but with a hurdle; here I was forced to take up my abode and the Landlady brought me out her best sheetes which serv'd to secure my own sheetes from her dirty blanckets, and indeed I had her fine sheete with hook seams to spread over the top of the clothes, but noe sleepe could I get, they burning turff and their chimneys are sort of flews or open tunnills that the smoake does annoy the roomes.

This is but 12 miles from another part of Scotland, the houses are but a little better built—its true the inside of them are kept a little better; not far from this a mile or two is a greate hill from which rises 3 rivers: the Teese [Tees] which is the border between Durham and York, the Ouse that runns to Yorke and the river Tyne which runns to Newcastle

[6] This was in fact the Roman Wall.

and is the divider of Northumberland and Durham: this river Tyne runns 7 miles and then joyns with the other river Tyne that comes out of Northumberland and so they run on to Newcastle; from Hartwhistle I went pretty much up hill and down and had the river Tyne much in view for 6 miles, then I cross'd over it on a large stone bridge and so rode by its bank or pretty much in sight of it on the other side to Hexholme[7] [Hexham] 6 mile more; this is one of the best towns in Northumberland except Newcastle, which is one place the sessions are kept for the shire, its built of stone and looks very well, there are 2 gates to it many streetes some are pretty broad all well pitch'd with a spacious Market place with a Town Hall on the Market Crosse; thence I went through the Lord Darentwaters [Derwentwater] parke just by his house which is an old building not very large [Dilston]; soe 3 mile in all to a little village [Corbridge] where I cross'd over the Tyne on a long bridge of stone with many arches; the river is in some places broader than in others—its true at this tyme of the yeare being midsumer the springs are the lowest and the rivers shallow and where there is any rocks or stones left quite bare of water.

Thence I went 4 mile along by the Tyne, the road was good hard gravelly way for the most part but very steep up hills and down; on one of these I rode a pretty while with a great precipice on the right hand down to the river, it looked hazardous but the way was very broad; the river looked very reffreshing and the cattle coming to its sides and into it where shallow to coole themselves in the heate, for hitherto as I met with noe raines (notwithstanding the great raines that fell the 2 dayes before I left Woolsley [Wolseley] and the little showers I had when I went to Holly Well [Holywell] I was not annoy'd with wet nor extream heate, the clouds being a shade to me by day and Gods good providence and protection allwayes; this after noon was the hottest day I met with but it was seasonable being in July.

[7] Roger North said of Hexham: "From the entertainment and lodging there, it might be mistaken; but whether for a Scotch or for a Welsh town may be a nice point for the experienced to determine." (*Lives of the Norths.* i, 289.)

As I drew nearer and nearer to Newcastle I met with and saw abundance of little carriages with a yoke of oxen and a pair of horses together, which is to convey the Coales from the pitts to the barges on the river;[8] there is little sort of dung-potts I suppose they hold not above 2 or three chaudron; this is the Sea-coale which is pretty much small coale though some is round coales, yet none like the cleft coales; this is what the smiths use and it cakes in the fire and makes a great heate, but it burns not up light unless you put most round coales, which will burn light, but then its soone gone and that part of the coale never cakes; therefore the small sort is as good as any, if its black and shineing that shews its goodness; this country all about is full of this Coale the sulpher of it taints the aire and it smells strongly to strangers; upon a high hill 2 mile from Newcastle I could see all about the country which was full of coale pitts.[9]

New-castle lies in a bottom very low it appears from this hill and a greate flatt I saw all by the river Tyne which runns along to Tinmouth [Tynemouth] 5 or 6 miles off which could see very plaine and the Scheld [North Shields] which is the key or fort at the mouth of the river which disembogues it self into the sea; all this was in view on this high hill, which I descended 5 mile more in all nine from that place.

New-castle is a town and county of it self standing part in Northumberland part in the Bishoprick of Durham, the river Tyne being the division; its a noble town tho' in a bottom, it most resembles London of any place in England, its buildings lofty and large of brick mostly or stone; the streetes are very broad and handsome and very well pitch'd and many of them with very fine Cunduits of water in each, allwayes running into a large stone Cistern for every bodyes use, there is one great streete where in the Market Crosse

[8] Celia Fiennes does not comment on the "railways", of wooden rails, from the pitheads to the river, which were seen by Roger North *c*.1680. (Op. cit., i, 281.)

[9] "The country hereabouts would be the worst and most steril that I have seen in England, were it not for its mines of sea-coal, which are here so plenty, that it may justly be called the magazine whence all Europe is furnished with that commodity." ("Jorevin de Rocheford", Op. cit., 609.)

there was one great Cunduit with two spouts which falls into a large Fountaine paved with stone which held at least 2 or 3 hodsheads for the inhabitants; there are 4 gates which are all double gates with a sort of bridge between each; the West gate which I entred I came by a large building of bricke within brick walls which is the hall for the asizes and session for the shire of Northumberland; this is Newcastle on the Tyne and is a town and county; there is a noble building in the middle of the town all of stone for an Exchange on stone pillars severall rows; on the top is a building of a very large Hall for the judges to keep the assizes for the town, there is another roome for the Major [Mayor] and Councill, and another for the jury, out of the large roome which is the hall, and opens into a balcony which lookes out on the river and the key; its a lofty good building of stone, very uniforme on all sides with stone pillars in the fronts both to the streete and market place and to the waterside; there is a fine clock on the top just as the Royal Exchange has; the key is a very fine place and looks it self like an exchange being very broad and soe full of merchants walking to-an-againe, and it runs off a great length with a great many steps down to the water for the conveniency of landing or boateing their goods, and is full of cellars or ware houses; the harbour is full of shipps but none that is above 2 or 300 tun can come up quite to the key, its a town of greate trade.

There is one large Church [St. Nicholas] built of stone with a very high tower finely carv'd full of spires and severall devices in the carving all stone; the Quire is neate as is the whole Church and curious carving in wood on each side the Quire, and over the font is a greate piramidy of wood finely carv'd full of spires; there was a Castle in this town but now there is noe remaines of it but some of the walls which are built up in houses, and soe only appears as a great hill or ascent which in some places is 30 or 40 steps advance to the streetes that are built on the higher ground where the Castle was; there was one place soe like Snow Hill in London with a fine Conduite; their shops are good and are of distinct trades, not selling many things in one shop as is the custom in most country towns and cittys; here is one market for Corne another for Hay besides all other things which takes up two or three streetes; Satturday was their biggest Market day which was the day I was there and by reason of the extreame heate resolved to stay till the sun was low ere I proceeded farther, so had the opportunity of seeing most of the Market which is like a faire for all sorts of provision and goods and very cheape: I saw one buy a quarter of lamb for 8 pence and 2 pence a piece good large poultry; here is leather, woollen and linnen and all sorts of stands for baubles; they have a very indifferent sort of cheese, little things looks black on the outside and soft sower things.

There is a very pleasant bowling-green a little walke out of the town with a large gravel walke round it with two rows of trees on each side makeing it very shady; there is a fine entertaineing house that makes up the fourth side before which is a paved walke under pyasoes [piazzas] of bricke; there is a pretty garden by the side shady walk, its a sort of Spring Garden where the Gentlemen and Ladyes walke in the evening; there is a green house in the garden; its a pleasant walke to the town by the walls; there is one broad walke by the side of the town runns a good length made with coale ashes and so well trodden and the raines makes it firm; there is a walke all round the walls of the town, there is a good free Schoole, 5 Churches.

I went to see the Barber Surgeons Hall which was within a pretty garden walled in, full of flowers and greenes in potts and in the borders; its a good neat building of brick, there I saw the roome with a round table in it, railed round with seates or benches for the conveniency in their disecting and anatomiseing a body and reading lectures on all parts; there was two bodyes that had been anatomised, one the bones were fastned with wires the other had had the flesh boyled off and some of the ligaments remained and dryed with it, and so the parts were held together by its own muscles and sinews that were dryed with it; over this was another roome in which was the skin of a man that was taken off after he was dead and dressed and so was stuff'd the body and limbs, it look'd and felt like a sort of parchment; in this roome I could take a view of the whole town, it standing on high ground and a pretty lofty building.

Just by is a very good Hospital [Hospital of the Holy Jesus] for 14 widdows off tradesmen of the town, 2 good roomes a piece; a walke under a pyasoe with pillars of brickwork as is the whole building; there is a large Fountaine or Cunduite of water for their use and an open green before their house all walled in, its in the Major and Aldermens disposition, there is 2 or 300 pound a yeare to it I thinke its 10 pound apiece; there is a very good fountaine belongs to it and there is a fine Bridge[10] over the Tyne river with 9 arches all built on as London Bridge is, which enters you into Durham, and on this side of the bridge are so many streetes and buildings just like Southwarke; its a little town [Gateshead] but all is in the liberty of the County town of Newcastle and soe called, but its all in the Diocess of Durham; through part of this you do ascend a greate height and steepness which is full of rocky stony stepps and afterwards the hill continues when out of the town till it has set you as high as on the former hill on the other side the town, which I entred out of Northumberland, and as that gave a large prospect of the town and whole country aboute on that side, soe this gives as pleasing a sight of it on this side, and the whole river and shipps in the harbour.

[10] As so often, Celia Fiennes differs from other travellers as to the number of arches. Defoe counted seven and Sir William Brereton eight. (Defoe, op. cit., ii, 250 and Brereton, *Travels*, 1635, ed. 1844, p. 85.)

8. THROUGH DURHAM, RICHMOND, MANCHESTER TO SHREWSBURY AND WOLSELEY

THENCE I proceeded a most pleasant gravell road on the ridge of the hill and had the whole country in view, which seemes much on a flatt to this place tho' there be a few little steep up hills and descents; but the whole country looks like a fruitfull woody place and seemes to equal most countys in England; 7 mile to Chester streete [Chester le Street] which is a little Market town and I rode neare Lumly [Lumley] Castle which give title and name to the Lord Lumly,[1] the building look very nobly, its in a 4 square tower running up to the top, with three round towers at the top between the windows lookes well its a front the four ways, its not finely furnish'd.

At this little Market town I pass'd over the river Weire [Wear] which runns to Durham, which is 7 mile farther over a pleasant road and country that resembles Black heath, you see the towns and country's round full of woods; one sees the Citty of Durham four mile off from a high hill, not but the Citty stands on a great rise of ground and is a mile and halfe in length; the river runs almost round the town and returns againe that casts the Citty into a tryangular, its not navigeable nor possible to be made so because its so full of rocks and vast stones makes it difficult for any such attempt.

Durham Citty stands on a great hill the middle part much higher than the rest; the Cathedrall and Castle (which is the Pallace) with the Colledge and all the houses of the Doctors of the Churches houses is altogether built of stone and all encompass'd with a wall full of battlements above the walke, and this is about the middle of the hill which is a round hill and a steep descent into the rest of the town, where is the market place which is a spacious place and a very faire Town Hall on stone pillars and a very large Cunduite; from this all the streets are in a pretty greate descent to the river which lookes very pleasant by meanes of its turning and winding to and agen; and so there are 3 large stone Bridges with severall arches apiece.

The Abbey or the Cathedrall is very large, the Quire is good but nothing extraordinary some good painting in the glass of the windows and wood carving; there is over the alter a painting of a large Catherine-Wheele which encompasses the whole window and fills it up; the Bishops seate has severall steps up (its called the throne) with a cloth of gold carpet before it, the seate was King Charles the First

---

[1] Lord Lumley, who had been Earl of Scarborough since 1691, was reputed to own the richest coal mines in England. His castle had not yet undergone its treatment at the hands of Vanbrugh.

of crimson damaske; a good organ and a fine clock in which is the change of the moone and the seven starrs and the signes [of the Zodiac] with chimes and finely carved with four pirramidy spires on each corner, a much larger and higher one in the middle well carv'd and painted; the font is of marble the top was carv'd wood, its let in an arch of fine carving of wood very high and terminates in a poynt, and resembles the picture of the Building of Babel, its not painted; the Cloysters are good; a Chapple called St. Marys now used for to keep their Spiritual Courts; in the Vestry I saw severall fine embroyder'd Coapes, 3 or 4, I saw one above the rest was so richly embroider'd with the whole description of Christs Nativity Life Death and Ascention; this is put on the Deanes shoulders at the administration of the Lords Supper, here is the only place that they use these things in England, and severall more Cerimonyes and Rites retained from the tymes of Popery; there are many papists in the town and popishly affected, and dayly encrease. There was great striveing in the choice of the parliament men, which I had the trouble of in most of my journey, the randan they made in the publick houses, indeed I happen'd to get into a quiet good inn, and good accomodation, two maiden sisters and brother kept it, at the Naggs Head.

The Castle which is the Bishops Pallace stands on a round hill which has severall green walks round it with high bancks to secure them one above another, and on the top are the towers; about the middle of the hill is a broad grass walk railed in and enters into a dineing roome; there are very stately good roomes parlours drawing roomes and a noble Hall but the furniture was not very fine, the best being taken down in the absence of my Lord Crew who is not only a Barron of England but is a great Prince as being Bishop of the whole Principallity off Durham and has a great royalty and authority, is as an absolute Prince and has a great command as well as revenue;[2] his spirituall is 5 or 6000£ and his

---

[2] The Bishop of Durham held special vice-regal powers as ruler of a County Palatine. Nathaniel, Lord Crew (1633–1721), a Jacobite, was Bishop of Durham for nearly half a century.

temporalls since his brothers death makes it much more; he comes sometymes hither but for the most part lives at another Castle [Bishop Auckland] which is a noble seate about 12 mile off which is very well furnish'd and finish'd; he is the Governour as it were of the whole province.

His Pallace here makes a good appearance with the severall walks one below another, with rows of trees three or four descents and the wall at the bottom; just by the Castle is a place for the assizes, 2 open barres lookes out into what is the space the College and Doctors houses are and there is in the middle a very fine large Cunduite, the water falling into the Cistern from 4 pipes which gives a pleaseing sound and prospect, it being arch'd with stone and stone pillars and carv'd and alsoe a high top arch ending in a ball; its the finest of this kind I have seen, and so I must say of the whole Citty of Durham its the noblest, cleane and pleasant buildings, streetes large well pitch'd, the Market Crosse is large a flatt rooffe on severall rows of pillars of stone, and here is a good Cundit alsoe of stone; the walks are very pleasant by the river side, I went by its banck of one end of the town to the Meeteing-house which stands just by the river, there was a company of hearers at least 300 which on the consideration of its being under the dropings of the Cathedrall its very well; they have a very good minister there (but its Newcastle that has the greate Meeteing place and many Descenters) they have two very eminent men one of their name was Dr Gilpin[3] whose book I have read in, but he not being at home could not have the advantage of hearing him.

In the evening I walk'd out at Durham to another part of the town by another turn of the river along by its banck, and the river here would meete were it not for a ridge of a hill runs between it, in which are buildings and ascends up a mile in length which is one of the Parishes; in walking by this river we came to Sir Charles Musgroves [Musgrave] House

---

[3] Richard Gilpin (1625–1700) was an eminent Nonconformist divine and also a lawyer and a physician of some distinction. His book was *Dæmonologia Sacra: a Treatise of Satan's Temptations*, published 1677—"the largest and compleatest of any extant upon that subject". (*Memoirs of Ambrose Barnes*, ed. Surtees Society, 1867, p. 145. Cf., pp. 141–6 and 443–4.)

[Kepier Hospital] which is now old and ruinous but has been good; the gardens are flourishing still with good walks and much fruite of which I tasted, its a place that is used like our Spring Gardens for the Company of the town to walk in the evening and its most pleasant by the river, which by means off severall bays or wires which is of rock the waters has greate falls from thence which adds a murmuring sound acceptable to the people passing; they have good fish in the river but its full of rocks—they talk much of makeing it navigeable, but I fancy the many rocks all along in it will render it a difficult work.

I went a mile to see the Spaw Waters and to see a salt Spring in the rock in the middle of the river; in halfe a mile I came to a well which had a stone bason in it and an arch of stone over it, the taste was like the Sweete Spaw in York-shire, the Tunbridge waters; about halfe a mile farther I came to a well which is like the Sulpher Spaw, taste and looke agreeing thereto, which is from brimstone, but its not quite soe strong for it was a longer tyme before the silver was changed in it; here I went a very bad and hazardous passage full of stones like stepps, the water trilling down them and a very narrow passage by the bushes and bancks, but when I was got in there was noe returning so on I went to the river which was a large step to goe down into, and all the river full of shelves and rocks; the Spring is in the cleft of the rocks which stands up in the river, and soe springs up, but when much raines falls it washes down soe fast upon it that weakens the taste; from this place I came back againe a mile; Durham has about 7 Churches with the Cathedrall, its a noble place and the aire so cleer and healthy that persons enjoy much health and pleasure.

From thence to Darlington which is 14 pretty long miles but good way, but by the way I lost some of my night-cloths and little things in a bundle that the Guide I hired carry'd; this is a little Market town the Market day was on Munday which was the day I pass'd through it; it was a great Market of all things, a great quantety of Cattle of all sorts but mostly Beeves, it seemes once in a fortnight its much fuller; two miles from Darlington I came to the ground the Hell Kettles[4] are they talk much off, its in grounds just by the road where cattle were feeding; there are 2 pooles or ponds of water the one larger than the other the biggest seemed to me not to be the deepest nor is it esteemed soe deep; there was some sedge or flaggs growing round that, but the farthermost which was not soe bigg looked a cross that had noe flaggs or sedge on its bancks, but yet it look'd to me to cast a green hew, roleing waves of the water just in collour as the sea, and as the wind moved the water it very much resembled the sea, but the water when taken up in the hand look'd white and the taste was not the least brackish but fresh; my conception of the cause of the greenish coullour was from the greate depth of water, for the reason they call them Hell Kettles is that there is noe sounding a bottom which has been try'd by plumet and line severall fathoms down; the water is cold and as any other water when took up, it seemes not to decrease in a tyme of drought nor to advance with great raines, it draines it self insensibly into the ground.

This leads me the farthest way to Richmond, it being but 8 mile the ready road from Darlington to Richmond, but this way it was 10 miles and very tedious miles; three miles off Darlington I passed over Crafton [Croft] Bridge which crosses the river Teess, which divides Durham from Yorkshire, and soe entred the North Rideing of Yorkshire in which is that they call Richmondshire a shire of 30 miles; the way was good but long, I went through lanes and woods an enclosed country, I passed by a house of Sir Mark Melborn[5] on a hill, a brick building severall towers on the top, good gardens and severall rows of trees up to the house, it standing on a hill the trees runns along on the ridge of the same looks very finely.

Richmondshire has in it 5 waking takes [wapentakes] as they call them answerable to that they call hundreds in other

4 Defoe thought them "nothing but old coal pits filled with water by the River Tees" (op. cit., ii, 248) but they are in fact unaffected by the level of the river and are not more than twenty feet deep.
5 Probably Sir Mark Milbanke of Halnaby or Hannaby Hall, M.P. for Richmond, who died this year (1698).

countys; each waking takes has market towns in them and are under a Baliffe each which are nominated by the Earle Holderness who is the sole Lord of the whole, its 30 mile in extent; Richmond town one cannot see till just upon it, being encompass'd with great high hills, I descended a very steep hill to it from whence saw the whole town which it self stands on a hill tho' not so high as these by it; its buildings are all stone the streetes are like rocks themselves, there is a very large space for the Markets which are divided for the fish market flesh market and corn; there is a large Market Crosse a square space walled in with severall steps up, and its flatt on the top and of a good height; there is by it a large Church and the ruines of a Castle the pieces of the walls on a hill.

I walked round by the walls the river [Swale] running beneath, a great descent to it, its full of stones and rocks and soe very easye to make or keep up their wires [weirs] or falls of water, which in some places is naturall, that the water falls over rocks with great force which is convenient for catching Salmon by speare when they leap over those bayes; all rivers are low and dryer in the summer soe I saw them at the greatest disadvantage being in some places almost drye and the rocks and stones appear bare, but by those high and large stone bridges I pass'd, which lay across the rivers, shewd the great depth and breadth they used to be the winter tymes.[6]

There was two good houses in the town, one was Mr. Dareys [Darcy] the Earle Holderness' brother, the other was Mr. Yorks, both stood then and were chosen Parliament men; they had good gardens walled in all stone as in the whole town, though I must say it looks like a sad shatter'd town and fallen much to decay and like a disregarded place.

I passed on towards Burrowbridge [Boroughbridge] and came not farre from Hornby Castle the Earle of Holderness and also Suddbery Hall [Sedbury] 2 mile off Richmond Mr.

---

[6] A marginal note here reads "In Yorkshire is the River of Racal that loses it self as Moles in Surry and several miles of[f] rises agane". Probably the Arkle is the river meant.

Darcys house; this road was much on lanes which were narrow but exceeding long, some 3 or 4 mile before you came to any open place, and then I came to a Common which was as tedious to me at least 5 or 6 mile before I came to an end of it; then I pass'd through a few little villages and so I came the 19 mile to Burrowbridge [Boroughbridge] in Yorkshire;[7] here I was the most sensible of the long Yorkshire miles, this North Rideing of that County is much longer miles than the other parts, which I had been in before;[8] at Burrowbridge I pass'd the River Lid [Nidd] or Ouse on a large stone Bridge,[9] this River affords very good fish salmon and codffish and plenty of crawffish; here I met with the clutter of the chooseing Parliament men; thence I went for Knarsebrough [Knaresborough] 5 mile more—this dayes journey was a long 24 miles indeed, the wayes were very good and drye being the midst of summer; here I came to my old Landlady Mason where I lay the yeare before to drink the Spaw, and from thence I went to Harragate [Harrogate] over Knarsbrough Forest,[10] to Leeds, 12 mile, and I went by Harwood [Harewood] Castle, the ruined walls some remaines; it was much in lanes and uphills and down hill, some little part was open Common on the hill that leads down to the town gives a pleaseing prospect of it.

Leeds is a large town, severall large streetes cleane and well pitch'd and good houses all built of stone, some have good gardens and steps up to their houses and walls before them; this is esteemed the wealthyest town of its bigness in the Country, its manufacture is the woollen cloth the Yorkshire Cloth[11] in which they are all employ'd and are esteemed very

[7] Here a marginal note reads "In Whitby in this North Riding are stones in form of serpents folded and wreathed up; at Huntly [? Hunley] are round stones like cannon balls that being brocke are full of such, only without heads". These fossils will have been ammonites.

[8] For "Long Miles" see Introduction, p. xxxix.

[9] Celia Fiennes often comments on the stone bridges of the North. It must be remembered that, apart from London Bridge, all bridges over the Thames were still wooden.

[10] Thoresby lamented the almost complete denudation of this forest in 1703. (*Diary*, i, 424.)

[11] Mainly Kerseys, cheaper than West Country broadcloth. They were sold by pedlars all over England and even in Holland and Germany. (Defoe, op. cit., ii, 206–7.)

rich and very proud; they have provision soe plentifull that they may live with very little expense and get much variety; here if one calls for a tankard of ale which is allwayes a groate—its the only dear thing all over Yorkshire, their ale is very strong—but for paying this groat for your ale you may have a slice of meate either hott or cold according to the tyme of day you call, or else butter and cheese gratis into the bargaine, this was a generall custom in most parts of Yorkshire but now they have almost changed it, and tho' they still retaine the great price for the ale yet make Strangers pay for their meate, and at some places at great rates, notwithstanding how cheape they have all their provision; there is still this custome on a Market day at Leeds the sign of the Bush just by the bridge, any body that will goe and call for one tanckard of ale and a pinte of wine and pay for these only, shall be set to a table to eate with 2 or 3 dishes of good meate and a dish of sweetmeates after;[12] had I known this and the day which was their Market, I would have come then but I happened to come a day after the Market, however I did only pay for 3 tankards of ale and what I eate and my servants was gratis; this town is full of Discenters there are 2 large Meeting places, here is also a good schoole for young Gentlewomen; the streetes are very broad the Market large.

Thence I went to Eland [Elland] 12 long mile more, pretty much steep up hills and down the same; I crossed over a river at Leeds on a large stone bridge; the Country is much on enclosures good ground; I goe by quarrey of stone and pitts of coales which are both very good, soe that for fewell and building as well as good grounds for feeding cattle and for corne they are so well provided that together with their

[12] Other travellers also noticed that Yorkshire ale was nominally dear but actually cheap because the measure was liberal and because food was sometimes thrown in. (See John Taylor, quoted in Introduction, p. xxxix.) Baskerville paid sixpence for a quart bottle of ale (reduced to fourpence for old custoners) and once he had cold meat in addition, all for fourpence. (Op. cit., pp. 310 and 312.) The market day custom at Leeds, described by Celia Fiennes, was called the "Bridge End Club"; but Lord Harley in 1725 found it "a very dear bargain" because the meal provided was "by far the meanest that ever occurred to me, and I have had opportunities of seeing very mean fare". (Op. cit., pp. 140–1.)

industry they must needs be very rich;[13] all the hills about
Eland [Elland] is full of inclosures and coverts of wood that
looks very pleasant; this town gives title to the Marquis
Hallifax son, as does Hallifax to the Marquis; this lyes but 5
or 6 mile hence, its a stony town and the roads to it soe stony
and difficult that I was discouraged in going, the town now
being almost ruined and come to decay, and the Engine[14]
that that town was famous for—to be head their criminalls
at one stroake with a pully—this was destroyed, since their
Charter or Liberty was lost or taken from them because most
barbarously and rigourously acted even with an absolute
power which they had of all the town; on these informations
I resolved not to goe to that ragged town tho' there are
many good people and a large Meeteing.[15]

From Eland [Elland] I went to the Blackstone Edge 8
mile; when I had gone 3 of the miles I came to a greate
precipice or vast descent of a hill as full of stones as if paved
and exceedingly steep, I take it to be much steeper than
Blackstone Edge tho' not soe long; the end of this steep was
a little village all stony alsoe; these parts have some resemblance to Darbyshire only here are more woody places
and inclosures: then I came to Blackstone Edge noted all over
England for a dismal high precipice and steep in the ascent
and descent on either end;[16] its a very moorish ground all
about and even just at the top, tho' so high that you travel
on a Causey, which is very troublesome as its a moist ground,
soe as is usual on these high hills they stagnate the aire and
hold mist and raines almost perpetually; as I ascended the

13 "The country", wrote Defoe, "appears busy, diligent, and even in a
hurry to work". (Op. cit., ii, 203.)

14 The "Engine", which worked like a guillotine, had been devised for
the summary execution of those caught red-handed stealing in the cloth
market. One head is reputed to have fallen into an old woman's hamper, and,
"the woman not perceiving it, she carry'd it away to the market". (See Defoe,
op. cit., ii, 200-203.) The Engine was abolished c.1650 but was the model
for the Scottish "Maiden" from which Dr. Guillotine borrowed his "inven-
tion".

15 Defoe found no less than 16 Meetings, excluding Quakers. Halifax
was in fact far from ruin and decay, as the population was increasing rapidly.
(Defoe, ibid., ii, 198.)

16 This same year, 1698, Thoresby had crossed Blackstone Edge in the
February snow, but his horse fell and crushed his leg. (Diary, i, 322.)

morning was pretty faire but a sort of mist met me and small
raine just as I attained the top which made me feare a wet
day and that the aire would have been so thick to have quite
lost me the sight of the Country, but when I attained the top
where is a great heap raised up which parts Yorkshire, and
there I entred Lancashire, the mist began to lessen, and as I
descended on this side the fog more and more went off and a
little raine fell, tho' at a little distance in our view the sun
shone on the vale which indeed is of a large extent here,
and the advantage of soe high a high which is at least 2 mile
up, discovers the grounds beneath as a fruitfull valley full of
inclosures and cut hedges and trees; that which adds to the
formidableness of Blackstone Edge is that on the one hand
you have a vast precipice almost the whole way both as one
ascends and descends and in some places the precipice is on
either hand; this hill took me up much tyme to gaine the top
and alsoe to descend it and put me in mind of the description
of the Alps in Italy, where the clouds drive all about and as
it were below them, which descends lower into mists then
into raines, and soe tho' on the top it hold snow and haile
falling on the passengers which at length the lower they go
comes into raine and so into sun-shine at the foote of those
valleys fruitful the sunshine and singing of birds; this was
the account my Father[17] gave of those Alps when he passed
them and I could not but think this carryed some resemblance
tho' in little, yet a proportion to that.

From the foot of this Blackstone Edge I went to Rochdale
4 mile, a pretty neate town built all stone; here I went to an
acquaintances house Mrs. Taylor and was civilly entertained;
here is a good large Meeteing place well filled—these parts
Religion does better flourish than in places where they have
better advantages—here I observ'd the grounds were all enclosed with quicksetts cut smoothe and as even on fine green
bancks and as well kept as for a garden, and so most of my
way to Manchester I rode between such hedges, its a thing

---

[17] As her father died when Celia Fiennes was seven, this must have been
one of her few memories of him. He would have seen the Alps when visiting
Geneva in his youth, see Introduction, p. xvii.

remarked by most their great curiosity in this kind, 8 mile.

Manchester[18] looks exceedingly well at the entrance, very substantiall buildings, the houses are not very lofty but mostly of brick and stone, the old houses are timber work, there is a very large Church all stone and stands high soe that walking round the Church yard you see the whole town; there is good carving in wood in the Quire of the Church and severall little Chappells, wherein are some little Monuments; there is one that was the founder of the Colledge and Library where hangs his picture, for just by the Church is the Colledge [Chetham Hospital], which is a pretty neate building with a large space for the boys to play in and a good garden walled in; there are 60 Blew Coate boys in it, I saw their appartments and was in the cellar and dranck of their beer which was very good I alsoe saw the kitchen and saw their bread cutting for their supper and their piggins[19] for their beer; there is a Cloyster round a Court; in it is a large roome called a parlour and over it a large roome for the Judges to eate in, and also for the roomes for heareing and dispatching their buissness; there is a large Library 2 long walls full of books on each side there is alsoe the globes at the end and maps, there is alsoe a long whispering trumpet and there I saw the skinn of the Rattle Snake 6 foote long, with many other Curiositys, their anatomy of a man wired together, a jaw of a sherk; there was a very fine clock and weather glass; out of the Library there are leads on which one has the sight of the town which is large as alsoe the other town that lyes below it called Salfor [Salford], and is divided from this by the river Uvall [Irwell] over which is a stone bridge with many arches.

Salfor has only a little Chappell of Ease and is belonging to

---

[18] The population of Manchester was reckoned over 50,000 by Defoe, who thought it bigger than Norwich; but this must be a gross exaggeration as Manchester (with Salford) was only 84,000 in the 1801 census. Defoe was trying to strengthen his protest against Manchester's having no member of Parliament and no municipal corporation. It was "the greatest meer village in England" and "the chiefest magistrate is but a constable". (Op. cit., ii, 261–2.)

[19] A piggin was a drinking vessel, often made of wood.

the Parish of Manchester; there is another river called the Shark [Irk], which runs into the Uval [Irwell]; the Market place is large it takes up two streetes length when the Market is kept for their Linnen Cloth Cotten Tickings Incles[20], which is the manufacture of the town; here is a very fine schoole for young Gentlewomen as good as any in London and musick and danceing, and things are very plenty here this is a thriveing place.

Thence I went a very pleasant roade much on the Downs mostly champion ground some few enclosures; I went by Dunum [Dunham Massey] the Earle of Warringtons[21] house which stands in a very fine parcke, it stands low but appeared very well to sight, its old fashion building which appeares more in the inside and the furniture, old but good gardens walled in: I also passed by severall Gentlemens seates one [Vale Royal] was Mr. Chalmonlys [Cholmondeley] another [Tabley Old Hall] Mr. Listers [Leicester] surrounded with good walks and shady trees in rows and severall large pooles of water some containeing severall acres; I passed over two or three stone bridges cross little rivers so to Norwitch [Northwich] which is 14 mile; I entred Cheshire 3 mile before I came to the town, its not very large, its full of Salt works the brine pitts being all here and about and so they make all things convenient to follow the makeing the salt, so that the town is full of smoak from the salterns on all sides; they have within these few yeares found in their brine pitts a hard Rocky salt that lookes cleer like suger candy, and its taste shews it to be Salt, they call this Rock salt;[22] it will make very good brine with fresh water to use quickly, this they carry to the water side into Wales and by those rivers that are flow'd with the tyde and soe they boile these pieces of rock

[20] An Inkle is a kind of linen tape, or the thread or yarn from which it was made.

[21] George Booth, second Earl of Warrington (1675–1758), author of a pamphlet advocating divorce for incompatibility of temper, was a remote connection of Celia Fiennes. His grandfather, George first Baron Delamere, had married Catherine, daughter of Celia's Aunt Bridget (née Fiennes) and of her husband the fourth Earl of Lincoln.

[22] This was the rock salt on the Marbury estate, on which Celia Fiennes held a mortgage. See Introduction, p. xxi.

in some of the salt water when the tyde's in, which produces as strong and good salt as the others; thence I went to Sandy Head 3 mile farther; there was 12 salterns together at Nor-witch—all the witches are places they make salt, in Nantwitch [Nantwich] and Droctwitch [Droitwich] they make salt, for at each place they have the salt hills where the brine pits springs; this is not farre from the place whence they digg the mill stones.

From Sandy Lane Head where I baited to Whitchurch is 16 long miles, over a long heath for 4 or 5 mile then to Bestonwood [Beeston] and came by Beston Castle [Beeston Castle] on a very high hill the walls remaineing round it, which I left a little on my right hand just at the foote of the hill and so I crossed the great Road which comes from Nant-witch to Chester being then just the midd way to either being 7 mile to each; and here I think I may say was the only tyme I had reason to suspect I was engaged with some Highway men; 2 fellows all on a suddain from the wood fell into the road, they look'd truss'd up with great coates and as it were bundles about them which I believe was pistolls, but they dogg'd me one before the other behind and would often look back to each other and frequently justle my horse out of the way to get between one of my servants horses and mine, and when they first came up to us did disown their know-ledge of the way and would often stay a little behind and talke together then come up againe, but the Providence of God so order'd it as there was men at work in the fields hay make-ing, and it being market day at Whitchurch as I drew neer to that in 3 or 4 mile was continually met with some of the market people, so they at last called each other off and soe left us and turned back; but as they rode with us 3 or 4 miles at last they described the places we should come by, and a high pillar finely painted in the road about 3 mile off of Whitchurch which accordingly we saw as we pass'd on, which shew'd them noe strangers to the road as they at first pretended.

I passed over a little brooke a mile before I came to Whit-church which entred me into Shropshire, this is a large market town, here are two very fine gardens one belongs to an apothecary full of all fruites and greens, the other was at the Crown Inn where I staid, it was exceeding neate with oring and lemmon trees mirtle striped and gilded holly trees box and filleroy [phillyrea] finely cut and firrs and Merumsuracum [Marum Syriacum] which makes the fine snuff, and fine flowers, all things almost in a little tract of garden ground.[23]

From thence its 14 mile to Shrewsbury and pretty level way, the miles were long and the wind blew very cold, I went on a Caussey 2 or 3 miles to the town so that in the winter the way is bad and deep but on the Causey; the town stands low, the spires of 2 of the Churches stand high and appear eminent above the town, there is the remaines of a Castle the walls and battlements and some towers which I walked round, from whence had the whole view of the town which is walled round with battlements and walks round some of which I went on; its here the fine river Severn encompasses the greatest part of the town and twines and twists its self about; its not very broad here, but its very deep and is esteemed the finest river in England to carry such a depth of water for 80 or more miles together ere it runns into the sea which is at Bristol; this comes out of Wales Ross and Monmouthshire[24] and here it turns about and comes to the town; on each side there are 3 bridges over it in the town, one of them that I walked over had some few houses built on it, as London Bridge, at one end of it; its pleasant to walk by the river there is just by it the Councill house an old building; here are three free Schooles together all built of free stone, 3 large roomes to teach the children with severall masters; the first has 150£ a year the second 100 the third 50£ a year and teach children from reading English till fit for the University, and its free for children not only of the town but for all over England if they exceed not the numbers; here is a very fine Market Cross of stone carv'd, in another place

[23] A marginal note here reads "The Stratum Stone found in the coal pitts being powdered and boyled in water make[s] good pitch".
[24] The Severn is never near Ross or Monmouthshire. Celia Fiennes may have confused it with the Wye.

there is an Exchequor or Hall for the towns affaires, there is alsoe a Hall for the Welsh manufacture.[25]

There is a Water house which supplys the town through pipes with water, but its drawn up with horses and it seemes not to be a good and easye way, so they intend to make it with a water Engine in the town; there are many good houses but mostly old buildings, timber, there is some remaines of a great Abbey and just by it the great Church but nothing fine nor worth notice save the Abbey Gardens with gravell walks set full of all sorts of greens orange and lemmon trees: I had a paper of their flowers were very fine, there was alsoe firrs myrtles and hollys of all sorts and a greenhouse full of all sorts of Curiosityes of flowers and greens, there was the aloes plant; out of this went another Garden much larger with severall fine grass walks kept exactly cut and roled for Company to walke in; every Wednesday most of the town the Ladyes and Gentlemen walk there as in St. James's Parke and there are abundance of people of quality lives in Shrewsbury more than in any town except Nottingham;[26] its true there are noe fine houses but there are many large old houses that are convenient and stately, and its a pleasant town to live in and great plenty which makes it cheap living; this is very near bordering on Wales and was reckon'd formerly one of the Welsh Countys as was Herifordshire; here is a very good Schoole for young Gentlewomen for learning work and behaviour and musick.

From Shrewsbury I went through the great faire which was just kept that day there, full of all sorts of things and all the roade for 10 mile at least I met the people and commoditys going to the faire; 2 mile thence I passed over the River Cern [Tern] on a large stone bridge: this is deep and joyns the Severn and soe I rode by the great hill called the Reeke [Wrekin] noted for the highest piece of ground in England—but it must be by those that only live in the heart of the kingdom and about London, for there are much higher

[25] So much Welsh was spoken here that "on a market day you would think you were in Wales". (Defoe, op. cit., ii, 75.)

[26] For the gaiety of Shrewsbury in this period see Farquhar's *The Recruiting Officer*, written 1706.

hills in the north and west, and alsoe not 40 mile distant from it Manborn [Malvern] hills seems vastly higher; this hill stands just by it self a round hill and does raise its head much above the hills neare it, and on the one side does looke a great steep down; but still my thoughts of the fells in Cumberland and Westmoreland are soe farr beyond it in height that this would not be mentioned there; it is seen 20 mile off and soe may many other hills, but when I rode just under it I was full convinc'd its height was not in competition with those in other parts that I have seen; there are great hills all about which I pass'd over full of Coale Pitts; here I came into the Whatling [Watling] Streete which is one of the great roads of England which divided the land into so many kingdoms under the Saxons (the Streete the Foss).[27]

The roads are pretty good but the miles are long; from Shrewsbury to the Reeke [Wrekin] is 9 mile from thence to Sir Thomas Patsells house[28] 10 mile more, here I went to see his Gardens which are talk'd off as the finest and best kept; the house is old and low, if the Gentleman had lived he did design a new house, its now his sons who is an infant; before you come to the house for a quarter of a mile you ride between fine cut hedges and the nearer the approach the finer still, they are very high and cut smoothe and even just like the hedges at Astrop Waters; and of each side beyond are woods, some regular rows some in its native rudeness, with ponds beyond in grounds beneath it; the end of this walke you enter a large gate of open iron grates with as many more iron grates on each side as the breadth of the gate, opposite to this is just such another that opens into those grounds I first mention'd, and fore right there is a large pitched Court with some open iron gates and grates at each end, that gives the Visto quite across through to other rows of trees which runs up all about the severall avenues.

In this Court stands two dyals between which is an open gate and pallasadoes the whole breadth of the front of this

[27] Celia Fiennes probably means Ermine Street and Fosse Way.
[28] This must be Patshull Park, belonging to Sir John Astley, who was one year old when he succeeded his father in 1688. (H.A.T.)

iron work which leads to the inner court, and on the other side just in front is another large gate, carv'd iron with pillars brick and stone and flower potts, and on each side to take the whole breadth of the house to which it faces and soe give the sight of the garden is open pallisadoes, and a little beyond are two more such open pallisadoes that are corner ways and discovers the Groves whose walks looks every way, so that to stand in this outward Court you may see the house and Court full of Statues in grass-plotts with a broad pav'd walke to the house; in the middle on the one side are flower gardens and the parke, the other side other grounds with rows of trees and by it very handsome stables and coach houses and then in the front this large opening to this garden where is a fountaine allwayes playing, very high the water, the gravel walkes and fine flowers and greens of all sorts in potts and on the borders; this gate I mention'd had brick pillars with stone heads on which stood a Turky Cock on each, cut in stone and painted proper; the grove I mentioned is the finest I ever saw, there are six walks thro' it and just in the middle you look twelve wayes which discovers as many severall prospects either to the house or entrance or fountaines or gardens or fields; the Grove it self is peculiar, being composed of all sorts of greens that hold their verdure and beauty all the yeare, and flourishes most in the winter season, when all other garden beautys fades, for Firrs (both Silver Scots Noroway) Cyprus Yew Bays, etc., the severall squares being set full of these like a Maze; they are compassed round each square with a hedge of Lawrell about a yard high cut exactly smooth and even, there are also Box trees in the middle; there are two other large Gardens with gravell walkes and grass-plotts full of stone statues; the stone is taken out of the quarrys about this country which is not a very firme stone and so the weather cracks them.

In one of these Gardens just the side of the house, into which it opens with glass doors, and just over against it is a large Avery of birds with branches of trees stuck into the ground; by it is a little summer-house neatly painted, beyond this is another Garden with a broad gravel walke quite round; in the middle is a long as well as large fountaine or pond which is called a sheete of water, at the four corners are seates, shelter'd behind and on the top and sides with boards painted, on which you sit secured from the weather and looks on the water, which has 348 lead pipes at the brims of it, which takes in the sides and ends, and with the turning a sluce they streame at once into the fountaine which looks well and makes a pleaseing sound; if those pipes were but turned in a bow it would cast the water in an arch, and so would augment the beauty of the prospect; there are 2 large Images stands in the midst that cast out water 4 sea horses all casting out water; in the other Gardens there were little figures which bedewed the borders with their showers, this large pond I spoke of before is very deep and good fish encreasing in it, there is another great pond in a ground beyond which lyes to view thro' those open pallasadoes and is stored with much good fish.

Thence I went to Aubery [Autherley] 2 miles a little Market town, thence to Panckeridge [Penkridge] and passed through some parcks which belongs to some gentlemens seate; I went by one Mr. Peirpoynts, and Sir Walter Rochlys [Wrottesley] house which stands on a hill in a thicket of trees, and soe came againe to the Whatling-streete [Watling Street] way, and soe over Kankewood [Cannock Wood] to Woolsly [Wolseley], in all 14 mile farther.

9. THROUGH WORCESTER, GLOUCESTER, BRISTOL TO WELLS AND TAUNTON

FROM WOOSLY to Haywood Parke 2 mile and home againe 2 mile; from Woolsley to Kank town [Cannock] 6 mile thence to Woolverhampton 6 mile; I went more in sight of Sir Walter Rochly [Wrottesley] which stands very finely on a hill and woods by it lookes very stately, these miles are very long thro' lanes; I passed by a fine house Prestwitch [Prestwood], Mr. Philip Folies [Foley] a pretty seate; in a parke a mile beyond there is another house of the same

Gentlemans; here we had the inconveniency of meeteing the Sheriffs of Staffordshire just going to provide for the reception of the Judges and Officers of the Assizes, whose coaches and Retinue meeteing our Company which was encreased with Cosen Fiennes's[1] coach and horsemen which made us difficult to pass each other in the hollow wayes and lanes; thence to the Seven Starres where we baited; thence 2 miles farther we entred out of Staffordshire into Worcestershire, to Broad water [Broadwaters] a place where are severall fullers and dyers mills; thence on the right hand are forging mills for iron works which belong to Mr. Thomas Folie [Foley]; there is a rocky hill in which is a Roome cut out in the rocks.

On the left hand you goe 7 mile to Ambusly [Ombersley] a very sad heavy way all sand, you goe just at Kederminster [Kidderminster] town end, which is a large town much employ'd about the worstead trade spinning and weaving; we also rode by Sir John Packingtons' house [Westwood] on the left hand on the hill just by Droitwitch, where are the 3 salt springs divided by a fresh spring that runs by it; of this salt water they boyle much salt that turns to good account.

All the way from the Seven Starrs where we baited to Ambusly [Ombersley] the road was full of the Electers of the Parliament men coming from the choice of the Knights of the Shire, which spake as they were affected, some for one some for another, and some were larger in their judgments than others, telling their reason much according to the good liquors operation and of these people all the publick houses were filled that it was a hard matter to get Lodging or Entertainment; we entered Worcester town next day just as the cerimony of the Election was performing and soe they declared it in favour of Mr. Welsh [Walsh][3] and Sir John Packington.

[1] This may be William, son of Celia's Uncle John, or his brother Laurence, who became fifth Viscount Saye and Sele in 1710. William died in 1700.
[2] Sir John Packington was the Tory squire who has been wrongly taken for the original of Sir Roger de Coverley.
[3] William Walsh, the poet. See Johnson's *Lives of the Poets*, vol. i. He was a friend of Pope, and is grossly over-praised in the concluding lines of the *Essay on Criticism*.

Four miles more to this town—from Broad water in all is 11 mile—Worcester town which is washed by the river Severn; its a large Citty, 12 Churches, the streetes most of them broad, the buildings some of them are very good and lofty; its encompass'd with a wall which has 4 gates that are very strong; the Market place is large; there is a Guildhall besides the Market house which stands on pillars of stone; the Cathedrall stands in a large yard pitch'd, its a lofty magnificent building the Quire has good wood carv'd and a pretty organ; there is one tombstone stands in the middle of the Quire by the railes on which lyes the Effigies of King John; the left side of the alter is Prince Arthurs tomb of plaine marble in a fine Chappell which is made all of stone finely carv'd both the inside and the outside is very curyously carv'd in all sorts of works and arms, beasts and flowers; under it lyes the statues of severall Bishops, beyond this are two tombstones with the figure of the body in their proper dress of 2 Saxon Bishops on the pavement;[4] the painting of the windows are good and they are pretty large and lofty tho' nothing comparable to the Cathedrall at York; the tower is high and about the middle of it you may walk round the inside and look down into the body of the Church just as it is in York; just against the pulpit in the body of the Church is a little organ to set the Psalme, the font is all of white marble and a carv'd cover of wood.

From Worcester we pass'd a large stone bridge over the Severn on which were many Barges that were tow'd up by the strength of men 6 or 8 at a tyme; the water just by the town encompasses a little piece of ground full of willows and so makes it an island, part of which turns Mills; thence I went 4 mile where I cross the River Thames [Teme] on a stone bridge; this runs to Whitborne [Whitbourne], and is a very rapid streame especially after raines, which just before we begun our Journey had fallen, and made the roads which

---

[4] Prince Arthur, who died in 1502, was the eldest son of Henry VII. The two Bishops were St. Oswald and St. Wulfstan. According to Defoe, King John was buried between them, "believing that they should help him *up* at the last call. . . . But I can hardly think the king himself so ignorant, whatever the people might be in those days of superstition". (Op. cit., ii, 44.)

are all lanes full of stones and up hills and down soe steep
that with the raines the waters stood or else ran down the
hills, which made it exceeding bad for travelling; when we
had gone 7 mile at a little Parish you enter out of Worcester
into Herriffordshire and soe 7 mile farther to Stretton
Grandsom [Stretton Grandison] and New House my Cos'n
Fiennes's;[5] this is the worst way I ever went in Worcester
or Herrifordshire—its allwayes a deep sand and soe in the
winter and with muck is bad way, but this being in August it
was strange and being so stony made it more difficult to travell.

From thence I went to Stoake [Stoke Edith][6] 4 miles,
where I saw Mr. Folies [Foley] new house which was building and will be very fine when compleated; there is to be
3 flat fronts to the gardens sides, the right wing of the house
is the severall appartments for the family, 2 drawing roomes
and bed chambers and closets opening both on a terrass of
free stone pavements each end, and the middle there is stone
stepps goes down on each side with half paces to the
garden, which is by more stepps descending one below
another; the other wing is to the other garden and are to
be roomes of state which lookes towards Herrifford town:
this is to be coupled together with a large hall which composes the front and is of stone work, the rest is brick only
coyn'd with stone and the windows stone, and is in forme of
a halfe moone each side with arches to the severall offices and
stables; to this front which is to be the entrance large opening iron spike gates which lookes into their Grounds and
Meddowes below it of a great length with rows of trees to
the river; the roofe is cover'd with slatt which shines and
very much represents lead, its adorn'd round the edges with
stone figures and flower potts; there is a noble Parck and
woods behind; it will be very fine when finished, now I saw
it only in the outside shell and plattform.

Thence I returned to Newhouse 4 mile; then I went to
Canaan Froom [Canon Frome] a mile, and one mile back

---

[5] William or Laurence, sons of Colonel John Fiennes.

[6] Stoke Edith, the home of Paul Foley, was nearly complete. On her previous visit Celia Fiennes had only seen it "staked out".

which was 2 mile more; then to Stretton four tymes and back which was 8 mile; then from New house to Aldbery [Alders End] 5 mile, thence to Marlow [Marcle] 3 mile and there entred Gloucestershire; they are pretty long miles and in the winter deep way though now it was pretty good travelling; its 8 mile beyond to Glocester [Gloucester] town (tho' in most places near London this would be reckon'd 20 miles) you may see the town 4 miles off.

Glocester town lyes all along on the bancks of the Severn and soe look'd like a very huge place being stretch'd out in length, its a low moist place therefore one must travel on Causseys which are here in good repaire; I pass'd over a bridge where two armes of the river meetes where the tyde is very high and rowles in the sand in many places and causes those Whirles or Hurricanes that will come on storms with great impetuosity; thence I proceeded over another bridge into the town whose streetes are very well pitch'd large and cleane; there is a faire Market place and Hall for the assizes which happened just as we came there, soe had the worst Entertainment and noe accomodation but in a private house—things ought not to be deare here but Strangers are allwayes imposed on and at such a publick tyme alsoe they make their advantages—here is a very large good Key on the river; they are supply'd with coales by the shipps and barges which makes it plentifull, they carry it on sledgs thro' the town, its the great Warwickshire coale I saw unloading; here they follow knitting, stockings gloves wastcoates and peticoates and sleeves all of cotten, and others spinn the cottens.

The Cathedrall or Minster is large lofty and very neate, the Quire pretty; at the entrance there is a seate over head for the Bishop to sit in to hear the sermon preached in the body of the Church, and therefore the organs in the Quire was on one side which used to be at the entrance; there was a tomb stone in the middle with a statue of Duke Roberts[7] second son to William the Conquerours son, with his legs across, as is the manner of all those that went to the holy warre—

[7] Robert of Normandy, actually the eldest son of William the Conqueror.

this is painted and resembles marble tho' it is but wood and soe light as by one finger you may move it up, there is an iron grate over it; at the alter the painting is soe fine that the tapistry and pillars and figure of Moses and Aaron soe much to the life you would at least think it Carv'd; there are 12 Chappells all stone finely carv'd on the walls and rooffs, the windows are pretty large and high with very good paintings, there is a large window just over the alter, but between it and the alter is a hollow walled in, on each side, which is a Whispering place;[8] speake never so low just in the wall at one end the person at the other end shall heare it plaine, tho' those which stand by you shall not heare you speake, its the wall carrys the voyce—this seems not quite soe wonderfull as I have heard for the large roome in Mountague House (soe remarkable for fine painting) I have been in it and when the doores are shutt its so well suited in the walls you cannot tell where to find the doore if a stranger, and its a large roome every way; I saw a Lady stand at one corner and turn her self to the wall and whisper'd, the voice came very cleer and plaine to the Company that stood at the crosse corner of the roome soe that it could not be carry'd by the side wall, it must be the arch overhead which was a great height.

But to return to the Church: the tower was 203 stepps, the large bell I stood upright in but it was not so bigg as the great Tom of Lincoln, this bell at Glocester is raised by ten and rung by 6 men; on the tower leads you have a prospect of the whole town, gardens and buildings and grounds beyond, and the river Severn in its twistings and windings; here are the fine Lamprys taken in great quantetys in their season of which they make pyes and potts and convey them to London or else where, such a present being fitt for a king; this and the Charr fish are equally rare and valuable; here are very good Cloysters finely adorn'd with fretwork, here is the Colledge and Library but not stored with many books; I think this was all the remarkables in Glocester.

[8] Defoe held that "since there is now the like in the church of St. Paul, the wonder is much abated". (Op. cit., ii, 41.) Sir William Brereton, another Puritan, alleged that the priests had exploited the "wonder" to frighten penitents and extort confessions. (*Travels*, ed. 1844, 179–182.)

From thence I went in Company all this while with my Cos'n Filmer and family;[9] we came to Nymphsffield after haueing ascended a very steep narrow and stony hill 10 mile to Nympsfield, all bad way, but the 20 mile afterwards made up for its badness for these were exceeding good wayes: 2 mile to Cold harbour thence 15 to Landsdon: long but bowling green way; here I passed by Babington [Badminton][10] the Duke of Beaufforts house, stands in a Parke on an advanc'd ground with rows of trees on all sides which runns a good length and you may stand on the leads and look 12 wayes down to the parishes and grounds beyond all thro' glides or visto of trees; the Gardens are very fine and Water works.

On Landsdon [Lansdown] Summersetshire begins, which is a very pleasant hill for to ride on for aire and prospect; I went 3 mile over it which leads to the Bath down a vast steep descent of a stony narrow way, as is all the wayes down into the town; the Bath is a pretty place full of good houses all for the accomodation of the Company that resort thither to drink or bathe in the summer; the streetes are faire and well pitch'd, they carry most things on sledges and the company use all the morning the Chaires of Bayes [baize] to carry them to the Bath, soe they have the Chaire or Sedan to carry them in visits; there is a very fine Hall which is set on stone pillars which they use for the balls and dancing, this is the only new thing since I was at the Bath before except the fine adornments on the Cross in the Cross Bath, fine carving of stone with the English arms and saints and cupids according to the phancye and religion of King James the Seconds Queen Mary of Modina, as part of her thanks and acknowledgments to the Saints or Virgin Mary for the

[9] Thomas Filmer, husband of Celia's cousin Susanna, daughter of Colonel John Fiennes.
[10] The Duke of Beaufort at Badminton had a "princely way of living". He presided over some two hundred persons, excluding women, at dinner every day; and brewed his own beer from "malt sun-dried upon the leads of his house. Those are large, and the lanthorn is in the centre of an asterisk of glades, cut through the wood of all the country round. . . . Divers of the gentlemen cut their trees and hedges to humour his vistos; and some planted their hills in his line, for compliment, at their own charge." (*Lives of the Norths*, i, 271-7.)

Welsh Prince she imposed on us;[11] and from the Bath I went westward to Bristol over Landsdown 10 mile and passed thro' Kingswood, and was met with a great many horses passing and returning loaden with coals dug just thereabout; they give 12 pence a horse load which carryes two bushells, it makes very good fires, this is the cakeing coale.

Bristol lyes low in a bottom the greatest part of the town, tho' one end of it you have a pretty rise of ground; there are 19 Parish Churches beside the Cathedrall which has nothing fine or curious in it; the buildings of the town are pretty high most of timber work, the streetes are narrow and something darkish, because the roomes on the upper storys are more jutting out, soe contracts the streete and the light; the suburbs are better buildings and more spacious streetes; there are at one place as you enter the town 2 almshouses 6 men and 6 women apiece at each, there is alsoe at another part of the town a noble almshouse more like a gentlemans house that is all of stone work, a handsome court with gates and pallisadoes before four grass plotts divided by paved walks and a walk round the same; the one side is for the women the other for the men, the middle building is 2 kitchins for either and a middle roome in common for washing and brewing, over all is a Chappell; they have gardens behind it with all things convenient, they have their coales and 3 shillings per weeke allowed to each to maintaine them; this is for decayed tradesmen and wives that have lived well, its set up and allowed to by Mr. Coleson [Edward Colston] a merchant in London.

This town is a very great tradeing citty as most in England, and is esteemed the largest next London; the river Aven, that is flowed up by the sea into the Severn and soe up the Aven to the town, beares shipps and barges up to the key, where I saw the harbour was full of shipps carrying coales and all sorts of commodityes to other parts; the Bridge

---

[11] An allusion to the view, held by most Whigs, that the Prince of Wales (afterwards the Old Pretender) was not legitimate but was smuggled into the palace in a warming pan. The ornaments to the Cross Bath were erected in honour of Queen Mary of Modena's visit in 1687, which puts the date of Celia Fiennes's previous visit in or before that year.

is built over with houses just as London Bridge is,[12] but its not so bigg or long, there are 4 large arches here; they have little boates which are called Wherryes such as we use on the Thames, soe they use them here to convey persons from place to place; and in many places there are signes to many houses that are not Publick houses just as it is in London; the streetes are well pitch'd and preserved by their useing sleds to carry all things about.[13]

There is a very faire Market place and an Exchange set on stone pillars; in another place there is a very high and magnificent Cross built all of the stone or sort of marble of the country, its in the manner of Coventry Cross, a piramedy form running up of a great height with severall divisions in niches where is King Johns Effigy and severall other Kings round and adorned with armes and figures of beasts and birds and flowers, great part of it gilt and painted, and soe terminates in a spire on the top; the lower part is white like marble; just by the water side is a long rope yard which is encompass'd with trees on either side which are lofty and shady, therefore its made choice of for the Company of the town to take the diversion of walking in the evening; this compasses round a large space of ground which is called the Marsh, a green ground; there[14] was noe remaines of the Castle; there are 12 gates to the Citty, there is a very large conduit by the key finely carv'd all stone, this conveys the water about the town but all the water has a brackish taste.

There is one Church [? St. Mary Redcliffe] which is an entire worke all of stone, noe timbers but the rafters and beames belonging to the roofe and the seates they sit in, the

[12] It was an exact copy of the original London Bridge, and had been built in 1247. It was taken down in 1761.

[13] The sleds were used instead of wheeled traffic because of the underground vaults. Some held that the object was to avoid disturbing the stores of "Bristol milk". Pepys had been entertained with "plenty of brave wine, and above all Bristol milk." (June 13th, 1668.) "Though as many elephants are fed as cows grased within the walls of this city, yet great plenty of this metaphorical milk, whereby *xeres* or *sherry sack* is intended. Some will have it called milk because . . . such wine is the first moisture given infants in this city." (Fuller, *Worthies III*, 115.) Actually the vaults were sewers, a rarity then much admired. (See Mundy, *Travels*, iv, 8-9 and Speed, *Great Britaine*, 1631, p. 23.)

[14] The area round Queen Street. March Street still exists. Pepys speaks of "Marsh Street where our girl was born". (June 13th, 1668.)

leads are very high and large and very neate kept, the tower 150 stepps up, on which the whole Citty is discover'd which by reason of the good gardens and grounds within its walls is a very large tract of ground in the whole; there you see the Colledge Green in which stands the Cathedrall and the Doctors houses which are not very fine built of stone; there are some few monuments in this Church with good carvings of stone round the tombs and some Effigies; there are 8 bells in this Church, there is 2 men goes to the ringing the biggest bell.

From thence I went 2 miles to the hott spring of water which lookes exceeding cleer and is as warm as new milk and much of that sweetness; this is just by St. Vincents Rocks that are great clifts which seeme as bounds to the river Aven [Avon] this channell was hewn out of those rocks[15] they digg the Bristol Diamonds which look very bright and sparkling and in their native rudeness have a great lustre and are pointed and like the diamond cutting; I had a piece just as it came out of the rock with the rock on the back side, and it appeared to me as a cluster of diamonds polish'd and irregularly cut; some of these are hard and will endure the cutting and pollishing by art and soe they make rings and earings of them; the harder the stone is the more valuable, which differences the true diamond, that will bear the fire or the greatest force, and cannot be divided nor cut but by some of it self diamond dust, being the only way they can cut diamonds that it self is capable of impressing carracters on glass; here I ferry'd over the Avon that comes up to the town with a great tyde in two parts; about 6 mile off it joyns the Severn which now begins to swell into a vast river of 7 mile over, before it enters the sea.

[15] "But what was most stupendious to me was the rock of St. Vincent . . . the precipice whereoff is equal to anything of that nature I have seenc in the most confragose cataracts of the Alpes, the river gliding betweene them at an extraordinary depth. Here we went searching for diamonds, and to the Hot Wells at its foote." (Evelyn, *Diary*, June 27th, 1654.)

"Were this rock of raw diamonds removed into the East Indies, and placed where the beams of the sun might sufficiently concoct them; probably in some hundreds of years they would be ripened into an orient perfection." (Fuller, *Worthies III*, 114.)

Then I went to Aston [Ashton Court] a mile from the water side thro' a fine park, an old large house, and thence I passed over large downs and saw 2 other good houses built of stone with towers on the top and severall rows of trees leading to them which made them appear very fine; soe to Oakey Hole [Wookey Hole] which from the water side where I ferry'd is esteemed but 15 long mile (its the same distance from Bristole but I would not goe back to the town, but twere better I had for I made it at least 17 mile that way).

Oacky Hole [Wookey Hole] is a large cavity under ground like Poole Hole in Darbyshire only this seemes to be a great hill above it; its full of great rocks and stones lying in it just as if they were hewen out of a quarry and laid down all in the ground; the wall and roofe is all a rocky stone, there is a lofty space they call the Hall and another the Parlour and another the Kitchen; the entrance of each one out of another is with greate stooping under rocks that hang down almost to touch the ground; beyond this is a Cistern allwayes full of water, it looks cleer to the bottom which is all full of stones as is the sides, just like candy or like the branches they put in the boyling of copperace for the copperice to crust about it, this in the same manner so that the water congeales here into stone and does as it were bud or grow out one stone out of another; where ever this water drops it does not weare the rock in hollow as some other such subterranian caves does, but it hardens and does encrease the stone and that in a roundness as if it candy'd as it fell, which I am of opinion it does, so it makes the rocks grow and meete each other in some places.

They fancy many Resemblances in the rocks, as in one place an organ, and in another 2 little babys, and in another part a head which they call the Porters head, and another a shape like a dog; they phancy one of the rocks resembles a woman with a great belly which the country people call the Witch which made this cavity under ground for her enchantments; the rocks are glistering and shine like diamonds, and some you climbe over where one meetes with the congealed drops of water just like iceicles hanging down; some of the stone is white like alabaster and glisters like mettle; you walke for the most part in the large spaces called the Roomes on a sandy floore the roofe so lofty one can scarce discern the top and carry's a great eccho, soe that takeing up a great stone as much as a man can heave up to his head and letting it fall gives a report like a Cannon, which they frequently trye and call the Shooteing the Cannons; at the farther end you come to a water call'd the Well, its of a greate depth and compass tho' by the light of the candles you may discern the rock encompassing it as a wall round; these hollows are generally very cold and damp by reason of the waters distilling continually, which is very cold as ice almost when I put my hand into the Cistern.

These roads are full of hills and those, some of them, high ridge of hills, which does discover a vast prospect all wayes; behind me I saw a great valley full of inclosures and lessar hills by which you ascend these heights which are all very fruitfull and woody; also I could see the Severn when encreased to its breadth of 7 mile over, and there it disembogues into the sea; then it gave me a prospect forward of as large a vale replenish'd with fruitefull hills and trees and good ground; thence I could discern Glassenbury [Glastonbury] tower, this was Maiden Hill, just beyond the little town of same name, and soe by degrees descending from a higher to a lower hill, which had its ascents as well as its descents, which makes the miles seem and are indeed long tracts of ground.

From Ocley Hole I went to Wells which was on an even ground one mile farther; this Wells is what must be reckoned halfe a Citty, this and the Bath makeing up but one Bishops See; here are two Churches with the Cathedrall; the Cathedral has the greatest curiosity for carv'd work in stone, the West Front[16] is full of all sorts of figures, the 12 apostles, the King and Queen with angells and figures of all forms as thick one to another as can be, and soe almost all round the Church;

[16] Defoe calls it "one complete draught of imagery, very fine, and yet very ancient". (Op. cit., i, 276–7.)

the assizes was in the town which filled it like a faire, and little stands for selling things was in all the streetes; there I saw the Town Hall—the streetes are well pitch'd—and a large market place and shambles; the Bishops Pallace is in a park moated round, nothing worth notice in it; St. Andrews Well which gives name to the town bubbles up so quick a spring and becomes the head of two little rivers which encreases a little way of[f] into good rivers.

Thence I went to Glassenbury, 4 miles a pretty levell way till just you come to the town; then I ascended a stony hill and went just by the tower[17] which is on a green round riseing ground, there is only a little tower remaines like a Beacon; it had Bells formerly in it, and some superstition observ'd there but now its broken down on one side; from this I descended a very steep stony way into the town; Glassenbury tho' in ancient tymes was a renowned place where was founded the first monastery, its now a ragged poor place and the Abbey has only the Kitchen remaining in it, which is a distinct building round like a pigeon house all stone;[18] the walls of the Abby here and there appeares, and some little places and the cellar or vault which if they cast a stone into the place it gives a great echo, and the country people sayes its the Devil set there on a tun of money, which makes that noise least they should take it away from him; there is the Holly Thorn[19] growing on a chimney; this the superstitious covet much and have gott some of it for their gardens and soe have almost quite spoiled it, which did grow quite round a chimney tunnell in the stone; here is a very pretty Church, a good tower well carv'd all stone 160

[17] The tower of St. Michael's Chapel on Glastonbury Tor.

[18] Traditionally it was built all of stone because the King had said he would come and set fire to the Abbot's kitchen. (See Mundy, op. cit., iv, 4 and Hammond, *Western Counties*, 79.)

[19] The holy thorn (supposedly imported by Joseph of Arimathea) blossomed sometimes on Christmas Day (which then fell on our January 7th). It was destroyed by Cromwell's soldiers but an offshoot had previously been planted in a tavern garden, and it will have been this one that Celia Fiennes saw. It was upon the original thorn that Sir William Brereton had cut his initials in 1635, although he admitted that "the tree and bark is much decayed (as I conceive) by this practise of those that visit it". (*Travels*, ed. 1844, p. 174.)

stepps up; walking in the tower I could have a prospect of the whole place which appeared very ragged and decayed; the Church is neate, there is the Effigie of the Abbot on a tombstone carved all about with Eschuteons of a Camell, and round it an inscription or motto in old Latin and an old Caracter; it was phancy of his Stewards who was a very faithfull dilligent servant, and as he made use of those creatures in his masters service that were strong and industrious, so the motto described his services under that resemblance; the Effigee was very curious and with rings on the fingers, but in Monmouths tyme the soldiers defaced it much.

From thence to Taunton 16 long miles through many small places and scattering houses, through lanes full of stones and, by the great raines just before, full of wet and dirt, I passed over a large common or bottom of deep black land which is bad for the rider but good for the abider, as the proverb is; this was 2 or 3 mile long and pass'd and repass'd a river as it twin'd about at least ten tymes over stone bridges; this river comes from Bridgewater 7 mile, the tyde comes up beyond Bridgewater even within 3 mile of Taunton, its flowed by the tyde which brings up the barges with coale to this place, after having pass'd a large common which on either hand leads a great waye good rich land with ditches and willow trees all for feeding cattle, and here at this little place where the boates unlade the coale the packhorses comes, and takes it in sacks and so carryes it to the places all about; this is the Sea coale brought from Bristole, the horses carry 2 bushell at a tyme which at the place cost 18d. and when its brought to Taunton cost 2 shillings; the roads were full of these carryers going and returning.

Taunton is a large town haveing houses of all sorts of buildings both brick and stone but mostly timber and plaister; its a very neate place and looks substantial as a place of good trade; you meete all sorts of country women wrapp'd up in the manteles called West Country rockets [rochets], a large mantle doubled together of a sort of serge, some are linsywolsey, and a deep fringe or fag at the lower end; these hang down some to their feete some only just below the wast, in the summer they are all in white garments of this sort, in the winter they are in red ones; I call them garments because they never go out without them and this is the universal fashion in Sommerset and Devonshire and Cornwall; here is a good Market Cross well carv'd and a large Market House on pillars for the corn; I was in the largest Church, it was mending, it was pretty large, the alter stood table ways in the middle of the Chancell; there was one good stone statue stood in the wall the Effigie was very tall in a ruff and long black dress like some Religious with his gloves and book in his hand; there were severall little monuments with inscriptions round them; they have encompass'd the Church-yard with a new brick wall and handsom iron gates; there is a large space called the Castle yard and some remaines of the Castle walls and buildings, which is fitted up for a good dwelling house.

10. THROUGH DEVONSHIRE TO LAND'S END

FROM THENCE I went to Wellington (they call it but 5 mile but its a long 7 tho' the way was pretty good) this is a Little Market town: thence to Culimton [Cullompton] 11 mile more, but indeed these were very long miles; the hostler at Tanton [Taunton] did say, tho' they were reckon'd but 16 miles it really was a good 20 miles, and I am much of that mind; I mostly pass'd through lanes, I entred into Devonshire 5 mile off from Wellington just on a high Ridge of hills which discovers a vast prospect on each side full of inclosures and lesser hills, which is the description of most part of the West; you could see large tracts of grounds full of enclosures, good grass and corn beset with quicksetts and hedge rows, and these lesser hills, which are scarce perceivable on the ridge of the uppermost yet the least of them have a steep ascent and descent to pass them.

Culimton [Cullompton] is a good little Market town, a Market Cross and another set on stone pillars (such a one was at Wellington but on brick work pillars); here was a large Meeteing of neer 4 or 500 people, they have a very good Minister but a young man, I was glad to see soe many tho' they were but of the meaner sort, for indeed its the poor receive the Gospell, and there are in most of the market towns in the West very good Meeteings; this little place was one continued long streete, but few houses that struck out of the streete.

From thence 10 mile to Exetter up hills and down as before till one attaines those uppermost ridges of all which discovers the whole valley, then you sometymes goe a mile or two on a Down till the brow of the hill begins in a descent on the other side; this Citty appears to view 2 mile distant from one of those heights, and also the River Ex which runs to Topshum [Topsham] where the shipps comes up to the barre; this is 7 mile by water, from which they are attempting to make navigeable to the town which will be of mighty advantage to have shipps come up close to the town to take in their serges, which now they are forced to send to Topshum on horses by land which is about 4 mile by land; they had just agreed with a man that was to accomplish this work for which they were to give 5 or 6000£, who had made a beginning on it.

Exeter is a town very well built the streets are well pitch'd spacious noble streetes and a vast trade is carryd on; as Norwitch is for coapes callamanco and damaske soe this is for Serges—there is an increadible quantety of them made and sold in the town; their market day is Fryday which supplys with all things like a faire almost; the markets for meate fowle fish garden things and the dairy produce takes up 3 whole streetes, besides the large Market house set on stone pillars which runs a great length on which they lay their packs of serges, just by it is another walke within pillars which is for the yarne; the whole town and country is employ'd for at least 20 mile round in spinning, weaveing, dressing, and scouring, fulling and drying of the serges, it turns the most money in a weeke of anything in England, one weeke with another there is 10000 pound paid in ready money, sometymes 15000 pound; the weavers brings in their serges and must have their money which they employ to provide them yarne to goe to work againe; there is alsoe a Square Court with penthouses round where the Malters are with mault, oat meal, but the serge is the chief manufacture; there is a prodigious quantety of their serges they never bring into the market but are in hired roomes which are noted for it, for it would be impossible to have it altogether.

The carryers I met going with it as thick all entring into town, with their loaded horses, they bring them all just from the loome and soe they are put into the fulling-mills, but first they will clean and scour their roomes with them—which by the way gives noe pleasing perfume to a roome, the oyle and grease, and I should think it would rather foull a roome than cleanse it because of the oyle—but I perceive its otherwise esteemed by them, which will send to their acquaintances that are tuckers[1] the dayes the serges comes in for a rowle to clean their house, this I was an eye witness of; then they lay them in soack in vrine [urine] then they soape them and soe put them into the fulling-mills and soe worke them in the mills drye till they are thick enough, then they turne water into them and so scower them; the mill does draw out and gather in the serges, its a pretty divertion to see it, a sort of huge notch'd timbers like great teeth, one would thinke it should injure the serges but it does not, the mills draws in with such a great violence that if one stands neere it, and it catch a bitt of your garments it would be ready to draw in the person even in a trice; when they are thus scour'd they drye them in racks strained out, which are as thick set one by another as will permitt the dresser to pass between, and huge large fields occupy'd this way almost all round the town which is to the river side; then when drye they burle them picking out all knotts, then fold them with a paper between every fold and so sett them on an iron plaite and screw down the press on them, which has another iron plaite on the top under which is a furnace of fire of coales, this is the hott press; then they fold them exceeding exact and then

---

[1] I.e. fullers or cloth-finishers.

press them in a cold press; some they dye but the most are
sent up for London white.

I saw the severall fatts [vats] they were a dying in, of
black, yellow, blew, and green—which two last coullours
are dipp'd in the same fatt, that which makes it differ is what
they were dipp'd in before, which makes them either green
or blew; they hang the serges on a great beame or great pole
on the top of the fatt and so keep turning it from one to
another, as one turns it off into the fatt the other rowles it
out of it, soe they do it backwards and forwards till its
tinged deep enough of the coullour; their furnace that keepes
their dye panns boyling is all under that roome, made of
coale fires; there was in a roome by it self a fatt for the scarlet,
that being a very chargeable dye noe waste must be allow'd
in that; indeed I think they make as fine a coullour as their
Bow dies [dyes] are in London; these rolers I spake off; two
men does continually role on and off the pieces of serges till
dipp'd enough, the length of these pieces are or should hold
out 26 yards.

This Citty does exceedingly resemble London for, besides
these buildings I mention'd for the severall Markets, there is
an Exchange full of shops like our Exchanges are, only its
but one walke along as was the Exchange at Salisbury House
in the Strand; there is also a very large space railed in just by
the Cathedrall, with walks round it, which is called the
Exchange for Merchants, that constantly meete twice a day
just as they do in London; there are 17 Churches in the Citty
and 4 in the subburbs; there is some remaines of the Castle
walls, they make use of the rooms within side for the assizes;
there is the two barrs besides, being large rooms with seates
and places convenient, and jury roome; here is a large walke
at the entrance between rowes of pillars; there is besides this
just at the market place a Guild Hall the entrance of which
is a large place set on stone pillars, beyond which are the
roomes for the session or any town affaires to be adjusted;
behind this building there is a vast Cistern which holds
upwards of 600 hodsheads of water which supplyes by pipes
the whole Citty, this Cistern is replenish'd from the river

which is on purpose turned into a little channell by it self to turn the mill and fills the Engine that casts the water into the truncks which convey it to this Cistern; the Water Engine is like those at Islington at Darby as I have seen, and is what now they make use of in diverse places either to supply them with water or to draine a marsh or overplus of water.

The river X [Exe] is a fine streame; they have made severall bays or wires [weirs] above the bridge which casts the water into many channells for the conveniencys of turning all their mills, by which meanes they have composed a little island, for at the end it againe returns into its own united channell; those wires makes great falls into the water it comes with great violence, here they catch the salmon as they leap, with speares; the first of these bayes is a very great one; there is one below the bridge which must be taken away when the navigation is compleate, for they will need all their water together to fill it to a depth to carry the shipps, for just by the bridge is the key design'd, or that which now is already they will enlarge to that place; just by this key is the Custome house, an open space below with rows of pillars which they lay in goods just as its unladen out of the shipps in case of wet, just by are severall little roomes for Land-waiters, etc., then you ascend up a handsome pair of staires into a large roome full of desks and little partitions for the writers and accountants, its was full of books and files of paper, by it are two other roomes which are used in the same way when there is a greate deale of bussiness; there are severall good Conduites to supply the Citty with water besides that Cistern, there is alsoe a very fine Market Cross.

The Cathedral at Exettor is preserv'd in its outside adornments beyond most I have seen, there remaining more of the fine carv'd worke in stone the figures and nitches full and in proportion, tho' indeed I cannot say it has that great curiosity of work and variety as the great Church at Wells; its a lofty building in the inside the largest pair of organs[2] I have ever

[2] Actually one organ, but "the two side columns, that carry the tower, are lined with organ pipes, and are as columns themselves". (*Lives of the Norths*, i, 246.) Celia Fiennes adds a marginal note, "The great pipe 15 inches diameter is two more than the celebrated one at Coln [Cologne]".

seen with fine carving of wood which runs up a great height and made a magnificent appearance; the Quire is very neate but the Bishops seate or throne was exceeding, and very high, and the carving very fine, and took up a great compass, full of all variety of figures, something like the worke over the Arch-Bishops throne in St. Pauls London, but this was larger if not so curious; there was severall good Monuments and Effigies of Bishops, there was one of a Judge and his Lady that was very curious their garments embroyder'd all marble and gilt and painted; there was a very large good Library in which was a press that had an anatomy of a woman; the tower is 167 steps up on which I had a view of the whole town which is generally well built; I saw the Bishops Pallace and Garden; there is a long walke as well as broad enclosed with rows of lofty trees which made it shady and very pleasant, which went along by the ditch and banck on which the town wall stands; there are 5 gates to the town; there is alsoe another long walke within shady trees on the other side of the town, which leads to the grounds where the drying frames are set up for the serges.

From thence I pass'd the bridge across the River Ex [Exe] to Chedly [Chudleigh], which was 9 mile, mostly lanes and a continual going up hill and down, some of them pretty steep hills, and all these lesser hills as I have observ'd rises higher and higher till it advances you upon the high ridge, which discovers to view the great valleys below full of those lesser hills and inclosures, with quicksett hedges and trees, and rich land; but the roads are not to be seen, being all along in lanes cover'd over with the shelter of the hedges and trees; then when I was on the top hill I went 3 or 4 miles on an open down which brought me to the edge of another such a ridge, which was by some steps to be descended, as it was gained, by the lesser hills one below another till I came to the bottom; and then I had about 2 or 3 mile along on a plaine or common, which for the most part are a little moorish [marshy] by reason of their receiving the water that draines from the severall great hills on either side, and so then I am to rise up another such a range of hills, and as neer as I could compute in my rideing it was 6 or 7 mile between one high ridge of hills to that over against it, whereas were there a bridge over from one top to the other it could not be 2 mile distant; but this does give them the advantage of severall acres of land by reason of the many hills, which if drawn out on plaines as in some other parts would appear much vaster tracts of land; on these hills as I said one can discern little besides inclosures hedges and trees, rarely can see houses unless you are just descending to them, they allwayes are placed in holes as it were, and you have a precipice to go down to come at them; the lanes are full of stones and dirt for the most part, because they are so close the sun and wind cannot come at them, soe that in many places you travell on Causeys which are uneven also for want of a continued repaire.

From Chedly [Chudleigh] to Ashburton is 11 mile more, in all 20 mile from Exeter, the roads being much the same as before; this Ashburton is a poor little town, bad was the best Inn; its a Market town and here are a great many Descenters and those of the most considerable persons in the town, there was a Presbiterian an Anabaptist and Quakers meeting.

Thence I went for Plymouth 24 long miles, and here the roades contracts and the lanes are exceeding narrow and so cover'd up you can see little about, an army might be marching undiscover'd by any body, for when you are on those heights that shews a vast country about, you cannot see one road; the wayes now became so difficult that one could scarcely pass by each other, even the single horses, and so dirty in many places and just a track for one horses feete, and the banks on either side so neer, and were they not well secured and mended with stones struck close like a drye wall every where when they discover the bancks to breake and molder down which else would be in danger of swallowing up the way quite, for on these bancks which are some of them naturall rocks and quarrys others mended with such stone or slate struck edgewayes to secure them, for the quicksetts and trees that grow on these bancks loosen the mold and so makes it molder downe sometymes.

I pass'd through severall little places and over some stone bridges; the waters are pretty broad soe these are 4 or 5 arches most bridges, all stone; the running of the waters is with a huge rushing by reason of the stones which lye in the water, some of them great rocks which gives some interruption to the current which finding another way either by its sides or mounting over part of it causes the frothing of the water and the noise, the rivers being full of stones bigger or less.

About 4 or 5 mile from Ashburton I came to a little place called Dean and at the end of it ascended a very steep hill, all rock almost and so it was like so many steps up; this is called Dean Clapperhill, it was an untoward place but not soe formidable to me as the people of the place where I lay described it, haveing gone much worse hills in the North; all along on the road where the lanes are a little broader you ride by rowes of trees on each side set and kept exactly even and cut, the tops being for shade and beauty, and they in exact forme, as if a grove to some house; at first I thought it was neer some houses, till the frequency and length proved the contrary, for there are very few if any houses neare the road, unless the little villages you passe through; this country being almost full of stone the streetes and roades too have a naturall sort of paveing or pitching, tho' uneven; all their carriages are here on the backs of horses with sort of hookes like yoakes stands upon each side of a good heigth, which are the receptacles of their goods, either wood furse or lime or coal or corn or hay or straw, or what else they convey from place to place; and I cannot see how two such horses can pass each other or indeed in some places how any horse can pass by each other, and yet these are the roads that are all here abouts; some little corners may jutt out that one may a little get out of the way of each other, but this but seldom.

Two mile from Plymouth we come to the river Plym just by a little town [Plympton] all built of stone and the tyleing is all slatt, which with the lime its cemented with makes it look white like snow, and in the sun shineing on the slatt it glisters; here I came in sight on the right hand of a very large house [Boringdon] built all with this sort of stone which is a sort of marble; even all quarryes are and some fine marble this house look'd very finely in a thicket of trees like a grove and was on the side of a hill, and led just down to the head of the river Plym which is fill'd with the tyde from the sea; and here I cross'd it on a stone bridge, soe I rode 2 miles mostly by the river, which encreases and is a fine broad streame and at the town which is its mouth it falls into the sea; the sea here runs into severall creekes, one place it runs up to the Dock and Milbrook another arm of the sea goes up to Saltash and Port Eliot.

Plymouth is 2 Parishes called the old town and the new, the houses all built of this marble and the slatt at the top lookes like lead and glisters in the sun; there are noe great houses in the town; the streetes are good and clean, there is a great many tho' some are but narrow; they are mostly inhabitted with seamen and those which have affaires on the sea, for here up to the town there is a depth of water for shipps of the first rate to ride; its great sea and dangerous, by reason of the severall poynts of land between which the sea runs up a great way, and there are severall little islands alsoe, all which beares the severall tydes hard one against the other; there are two keyes [Hamoaze and Catwater] the one is a broad space which leads you up into the broad streete and is used in manner of an exchange for the merchants meeteing, for in this streete alsoe is a fine stone Crosse and alsoe a long Market House set on stone pillars; there are severall good Cunduits to convey the water to the town, which conveyance the famous Sir Francis Drake (which did encompass the world in Queen Elizabeths days and landed safe at Plymouth) he gave this to the town; there are two Churches in the town but nothing fine; I was in the best and saw only King Charles the First Picture at length at prayer just as its cut on the frontispiece of the Irenicum,[3] this picture was drawn and given the Church when he was in his troubles for some piece of service shown him; the alter stands in the Chancell or railed place, but it stands table wise the length and not up against the wall; the font was of marble and indeed soe is all

[3] The *Eikon Basilike* must be meant.

buildings here, for their stone is all a sort of marble, some coarser, some finer; there are 4 large Meetings for the Descenters in the town takeing in the Quakers and Anabaptists.

The mouth of the river just at the town is a very good harbour for shipps; the Dock yards are about 2 mile from the town, by boate you goe to it the nearest way; its one of the best in England, a great many good shipps built there, and the great depth of water which comes up to it, tho' it runs up for 2 mile between the land, which also shelters the shipps; there is a great deale of buildings on the Dock, a very good house for the Masters and severall lesser ones and house for their cordage and makeing ropes, and all sorts of things required in building or refitting ships; it lookes like a little town the buildings are so many, and all of marble with fine slate on the rooffs, and at a little distance it makes all the houses shew as if they were cover'd with snow and glisters in the sunn which adds to their beauty.

The fine and only thing in Plymouth town is the Cittadell, or Castle, which stands very high above the town, the walls and battlements round it with all their works and plattforms are in very good repair and lookes nobly, all marble full of towers with stone balls on the tops and gilt on the top, the entrance being by an ascent up a hill looks very noble over 2 drawbridges, and gates, which are marble, as is the whole well carv'd, the gate with armory and statues all gilt and on the top 7 gold balls; the buildings within are very neate, a large appartment for the Governour with others that are less for the severall officers; there is a long building alsoe which is the arsnell [arsenal] for the arms and amunition, and just by it a round building well secured which was for the powder; round the works is the plattform for the Gunns which are well mounted and very well kept; walking round I had the view of all the town and alsoe part off the main Ocean, in which are some islands: there is St. Nicholas Island[4] with a fort in it—there it was Harry Martin one of the

---

[4] Henry Marten, the regicide judge, was imprisoned in several places, but not here. Probably Celia Fiennes has confused him with Major-General John Lambert.

Kings Judges was banished dureing life—there you can just discover a light house which is building on a meer rock in the middle of the sea;[5] this is 7 leagues off it will be of great advantage for the guide of the shipps that pass that way; from this you have a good refflection on the great care and provision the wise God makes for all persons and things in his Creation, that there should be in some places, where there is any difficulty, rocks even in the midst of the deep which can be made use of for a constant guide and mark for the passengers on their voyages; but the Earth is full of the goodness of the Lord and soe is this Great Sea wherein are inumerable beings created and preserv'd by the same Almighty hand, whose is the Earth and all things there in, he is Lord of all.

From the plattform I could see the Dock and also just against it I saw Mount Edgecomb [Mount Edgcumbe] a seate of Sir Richard Edgcomes [Edgcumbe]; it stands on the side of a hill all bedeck'd with woods which are divided into severall rowes of trees in walks, the house being all of this white marble; its built round a Court so the four sides are alike, at the corners of it are towers which with the Lanthorne or Cupilow in the middle lookes well; the house is not very lofty nor the windows high but it looked like a very uniforme neate building and pretty large; there is a long walke from one part of the front down to the waterside, which is on a descent guarded with shady rowes of trees; there is a fine terrass walled in at the water side with open gates in the middle, and a sumer house at each end from whence a wall is drawn round the house and gardens, and a large parck the walls of which I rode by a good while; so that altogether and its scituation makes it esteemed by me the finest seat I have seen, and might be more rightly named Mount Pleasant.[6]

[5] The first Eddystone lighthouse, designed by Henry Winstanley (see page 62) in 1696. He and his workmen had been captured by the French in 1697, but Louis XIV had agreed to exchange Winstanley as a benefactor to humanity at large. (Luttrell, op. cit., iv, 251.) Winstanley perished with the lighthouse in the Great Storm of November, 1703.

[6] Fuller reports that Medina Sidonia, commander of the Armada, "was so affected at the sight of this house (though but beholding it at a distance, from the sea) that he resolved it for his own possession in the partage of this kingdom . . . which they pre-conquered in their hopes and expectation." *Worthies I*, pp. 303–4.

From Plymouth I went 1 mile to Cribly [Cremyll] Ferry which is a very hazardous passage, by reason of 3 tydes meeting; had I known the Danger before I should not have been very willing to have gone it, not but this is the constant way all people goe, and saved severall miles rideing; I was at least an hour going over, it was about a mile but indeed in some places, notwithstanding there was 5 men row'd and I sett my own men to row alsoe I do believe we made not a step of way for almost a quarter of an hour, but blessed be God I came safely over; but those ferry boates are soe wet and then the sea and wind is allwayes cold to be upon, that I never faile to catch cold in a ferry-boate as I did this day, haveing 2 more ferrys to cross tho' none soe bad or halfe soe long as this; thence to Milbrooke [Millbrook] 2 mile and went all along by the water and had the full view of the Dock-yards.

Here I entred into Cornwall and soe passed over many very steep stony hills tho' here I had some 2 or 3 miles of exceeding good way on the downs, and then I came to the steep precipices great rocky hills; ever and anon I came down to the sea and rode by its side on the sand, then mounted up againe on the hills which carryed me along mostly in sight of the South sea; sometymes I was in lanes full of rowes of trees and then I came down a very steep stony hill to Louu [Looe], 13 mile, and here I cross'd a little arme of the sea on a bridge of 14 arches; this is a pretty bigg seaport, a great many little houses all of stone, from whence I was to ascend a very stormy and steep hill, much worse and 3 tymes as long as Dean Clapper hill, and soe I continued up and down hill.

Here indeed I met with more inclosed ground and soe had more lanes and a deeper clay road, which by the raine the night before had made it very dirty and full of water; in many places in the road there are many holes and sloughs where ever there is clay ground, and when by raines they are filled with water its difficult to shun danger; here my horse was quite down in one of these holes full of water but by the good hand of God's Providence which has allwayes been with me ever a present help in tyme of need, for giving him a good strap he flounc'd up againe, tho' he had gotten quite down his head and all, yet did retrieve his feete and gott cleer off the place with me on his back.

Soe I came to Hoile [Hall Farm], 8 mile more, they are very long miles the farther West, but you have the pleasure of rideing as if in a grove in most places, the regular rowes of trees on each side the roade as if it were an entrance into some Gentlemans ground to his house, the cut hedges and trees; at Hoile [Hall Farm] I ferryed over againe cross an arme of the sea, here it was not broad but exceeding deep, this is the South sea which runs into many little creekes for severall miles into the land, which is all the rivers they have; I observed this to be exceeding salt, and as green as ever I saw the sea when I have been a league or two out from the land, which shews it must be very deep and great tides; this Hoile [Fowey] is a narrow stony town the streetes very close, and as I descended a great steep into the town soe I ascended one off it up a stony long hill farre worse and full of shelves and rocks and 3 tymes as long as Dean Clapperhill, which I name because when I was there they would have frighted me with its terribleness as the most inaccessible place as ever was and none like it, and my opinion is that it was but one or two steps to other places forty steps, and them with more hazard than this of Dean Clapper.

Well to pass on I went over some little heath ground, but mostly lanes and those stony and dirty 3 mile and halfe to Parr [Par]; here I ferry'd over againe, not but when the tyde is out you may ford it; thence I went over the heath and commons by the tinn mines, 3 miles and halfe to St. Austins [St. Austell] which is a little Market town where I lay, but their houses are like barnes up to the top of the house; here was a pretty good dineing-roome and chamber within it, and very neate country women; my Landlady brought me one of the West Country tarts, this was the first I met with, though I had asked for them in many places in Sommerset and Devonshire, its an apple pye with a custard all on the top, its the most acceptable entertainment that could be made me; they scald their creame and milk in most parts of those countrys and so its a sort of clouted creame as we call it, with a little sugar, and soe put on the top of the apple pye; I was much pleased with my supper tho' not with the custome of the country, which is a universall smoaking[7] both men women and children have all their pipes of tobacco in their mouths and soe sit round the fire smoaking, which was not delightfull to me when I went down to talke with my Landlady for information of any matter and customs amongst them; I must say they are as comely sort of women as I have seen any where tho' in ordinary dress, good black eyes and crafty enough and very neate.

Halfe a mile from hence they blow their tin which I went to see: they take the oar [ore] and pound it in a stamping mill which resembles the paper mills, and when its fine as the finest sand, some of which I saw and took, this they fling into a furnace and with it coale to make the fire, so it burns together and makes a violent heate and fierce flame, the mettle by the fire being seperated from the coale and its own drosse, being heavy falls down to a trench made to receive it, at the furnace hole below; this liquid mettle I saw them shovel up with an iron shovel and soe pour it into molds in which it cooles and soe they take it thence in sort of wedges or piggs I think they call them; its a fine mettle thus in its first melting looks like silver, I had a piece poured out and made cold for to take with me; the oare as its just dug lookes like the thunderstones, a greenish hue full of pin-dust; this seemes to containe its full description, the shineing part is white.

I went a mile farther on the hills and soe came where they were digging in the Tinn mines, there was at least 20 mines all in sight which employs a great many people at work,

---

[7] Every traveller mentions this West Country habit, although we may suspect a "leg-pull" in what M. "Jorevin de Rocheford" was told, "that when the children went to school, they carried in their satchels with their books a pipe of tobacco, which their mother took care to fill early in the morning, it serving them instead of a breakfast; and that at the accustomed hour every one laid aside his book to light his pipe, the master smoking with them, and teaching them how to hold their pipes, and draw in the tobacco; thus habituating them to it from their youth, believing it absolutely necessary for a man's health". (Op. cit., 583.)

almost night and day, but constantly all and every day in-cludeing the Lords day which they are forced to, to prevent their mines being overflowed with water; more than 1000 men are taken up about them, few mines but had then almost 20 men and boys attending it either down in the mines digging and carrying the oare to the little bucket which con-veys it up, or else others are draineing the water and looking to the engines that are draineing it, and those above are attending the drawing up the oare in a sort of windless as is to a well; two men keeps turning bringing up one and letting down another, they are much like the leather buckets they use in London to put out fire which hang up in churches and great mens halls; they have a great labour and great expence to draine the mines of the water with mills that horses turn and now they have the mills or water engines that are turned by the water, which is convey'd on frames of timber and truncks to hold the water, which falls down on the wheeles, as an over shott mill—and these are the sort that turns the water into the severall towns I have seen about London Darby and Exeter, and many places more; they do five tymes more good than the mills they use to turn with horses, but then they are much more chargeable; those mines do require a great deale of timber to support them and to make all these engines and mills, which makes fewell very scarce here; they burn mostly turffs which is an unpleasant smell, it makes one smell as if smoaked like bacon; this oar as said is made fine powder in a stamping mill which is like the paper mills, only these are pounded drye and noe water let into them as is to the raggs to work them into a paste; the mills are all turned with a little streame or channell of water you may step over; indeed they have noe other mills but such in all the country, I saw not a windmill all over Cornwall or Devonshire tho' they have wind and hills enough, and it may be its too bleake for them.

In the Tinn mines there is stone dug out and a sort of spar something like what I have seen in the Lead mines at Darbyshire but it seemed more sollid and hard it shines and lookes like mother of pearle; they alsoe digg out stones as cleer as Christal which is called Cornish Diamonds—I saw one as bigg as my two fists, very cleer and like some pieces of Chrystal my father brought from the Alps in Italy which I have got by me, I got one of those pieces of their Cornish Diamonds as long as halfe my finger, which had three or four flatt sides with edges, the top was sharpe and so hard as it would cut a letter on glass.

Thence I went to Tregna [Tregony], 6 miles good way, and passed by 100 mines, some on which they were at work, others that were lost by the waters overwhelming them; I crossed the water on a long stone bridge and so through dirty stony lanes 3 mile and then I came into a broad coach rode [road] which I have not seen since I left Exeter; so I went 3 mile more to Mr. Bescawens[8] Trygoltny [Tregoth-nan] a Relation of mine; his house stands on a high hill in the middle of a parke with severall rows of trees with woods beyond it; the house is built all of white stone like the rough coarse marble and cover'd with slate; they use much lime in their cement which makes both walls and cover look very white; there is a Court walled round with open iron gates and barrs; the entrance is up a few stone steps into a large high hall and so to a passage that leads foreright up a good stair-case; on the right side is a large common parlour for constant eating in, from whence goes a little roome for smoaking that has a back way into the kitchin, and on the left hand is a great parlour and drawing roome wanscoated all very well, but plaine, the great parlour is Cedar, out of that is the drawing-roome, which is hung with pictures of the family; that goes into the garden which has gravel walks round and across, but the squares are full of goosebery and shrub-trees and looks more like a kitchen garden as Lady Mary Bescawen told me, out of which is another garden and orchard which is something like a grove, green walks with rows of fruit trees; its capable of being a fine place with some charge, the roomes above are new modell'd, 3 roomes wans-

---

[8] Hugh Boscawen (d. 1701) widower of Margaret, daughter of Celia's Aunt Bridget (née Fiennes) and of the fourth Earl of Lincoln. Lady Margaret Boscawen had died in 1688.

coated and hung as the new way is, and the beds made up well, one red damaske, another green, another wrought, some of the Ladyes own work and well made up which is her own roome with a dressing-roome by it; there is a dressing roome and a roome for a servant just by the best chamber; there are two other good roomes nualter'd with old hangings to the bottom on wrought work of the first Ladyes Lady Margets work, that was my Cos'n German; within that roome was a servants roome and back staires there was just such another apartment on the other side; between all from the staires a broad passage leads to a Balcony over the entrance which look'd very pleasantly over the parke, but in the Cupulo on the Leads I could see a vast way at least 20 mile round, for this house stands very high to the land side; eastward and the south was the Great Ocean which runns into Falmouth thats the best harbour for shipps in that road; 6 mile from this place westward was to Truro, and the north to the hills full of Copper mines.

Here I was very civily entertained; from thence I returned back, intending not to go to the Lands End which was 30 miles farther, for feare of the raines that fell in the night which made me doubt what travelling I should have; soe to St Culomb [St Columb Major] I went a pretty long 12 mile; here I met with many rowes of elm trees which I have not found in any country except Wiltshire, these were mostly soe, tho' there were alsoe ashes and oakes; the hedges were hazelthorne and holly but to see soe many good rowes of trees on the road is surpriseing, and lookes like the entrance to some Gentlemans house, and I cannot tell but some of them were soe, tho' a mile off from the house.

The next day finding it faire weather on the change of the moone I alter'd my resolution, and soe went for the Lands End by Redruth 18 mile mostly over heath and downs which was very bleake and full of mines; here I came by the Copper mines, which have the same order in the digging and draining tho' here it seemes dryer and I believe not quite soe annoy'd with water; the oar is something as the tinn only this looks blackish or rather a purple colour and the glistering part is yellow as the other was white; they do not melt it here but ship it off to Bristol by the North Sea, which I rode in sight of, and is not above 2 or 3 mile from hence; which supplyes them with coales for their fewell at easyer rates than the other side, Plymouth and the South Sea, because since the warre they could not double the poynt at the Lands End being so neer France, the pirats or privateers met them; indeed at St Ives they do melt a little but nothing that is considerable, thats 10 mile from Redruth which is a little Market town; here they carry all their things on horses backs, soe that of a market day which was Fryday you see a great number of horses little of size which they call Cornish Cavelys; they are well made and strong and will trip along as light on the stony road without injury to themselves, whereas my horses went so heavy that they wore their shoes immediately thinn and off—but here I met with a very good smith that shooed the horses as well as they do in London, and that is not common in the country, but here I found it soe and at a place in Westmoreland by the fells a smith made good shoes and set them on very well.

From Redruth I went to Pensands [Penzance] 15 mile, and passed by the ruines of great fortification or Castle on a high hill about 3 mile from Redruth and passed to Haile [Hayle], and soe went by the sea side a great way, it being spring tide it was a full sea; just over against it there was a Church which was almost sunck into the sands [St. Gwithian's Chapel] being a very sandy place, so I went up pretty high hills and over some heath or common, on which a great storme of haile and raine met me, and drove fiercely on me but the wind soone dry'd my dust coate; here I came by a very good grove of trees which I thought was by some Gentlemans house, but found it some farmers.

The people here are very ill guides, and know but little from home, only to some market town they frequent, but will be very solicitous to know where you goe, and how farre, and from whence you came, and where is the abode; then I came in sight of the hill in Cornwall called the Mount [St. Michael's Mount] its on a rock in the sea which at the flowing tyde is an island but at low water one can goe over the sands almost just to it; its but a little way from Market Due [Marazion] a little market town which is about 2 mile from Penzants [Penzance] and you may walke or ride to it all on the sands when the tyde's out; its a fine rock, and very high, severall little houses for fisher men in the sides of it just by the water; at the top is a pretty good house where the Govenour lives sometymes, Sir Hook his name is; there is a tower on the top on which is a flag; there is a chaire or throne on the top from whence they can discover a great way at sea and here they put up Lights to direct shipps.

Pensands [Penzance] is rightly named being all sands about it; it lies just as a shore to the maine south ocean which comes from the Lizard, and being on the side of a hill with a high hill all round the side to the landward, it lookes soe snugg and warme and truely it needs shelter haveing the sea on the other side and little or no fewell: turff and furse and ferne; they have little or noe wood and noe coale which differences it from Darbyshire, otherwise this and to the Lands End is stone and barren as Darbyshire; I was surprised to find my supper boyling on a fire allwayes supply'd with a bush of furse and that to be the only fewell to dress a joynt of meat and broth, and told them they could not roast me anything, but they have a little wood for such occasions but its scarce and dear—which is a strange thing that the shipps should not supply them, they told me it must be all brought round the Land End, and since the warre they could not have it—this town is two parishes, one Church in the town and a little Chapple, and another Church belonging to the other parish which is a mile distance, there is alsoe a good Meeteing place.

There is a good Key and a good Harbour for the shipps to ride, by meanes of the point of land which runns into the sea in a neck or compass which shelters it from the maine, and answers the Lizard Point which you see very plaine, a point of land looks like a double hill one above the other that runns a good way into the sea; the Lands End is 10 mile farther, pretty good way but much up hills and down, pretty steep and narrow lanes, but its not shelter'd with trees or hedg rows this being rather desart and like the Peake Country in Darbyshire, dry stone walls and the hills full of stones; but it is in most places better land and yeilds good corne both wheate barley and oates and some rhye; about 2 mile from the Lands End I came in sight of the maine occan on both sides, the south and north sea, and soe rode in its view till I saw them joyn'd at the poynt, and saw the Island of Sily [Scilly] which is 7 leagues off the Lands End; they tell me that in a cleer day those in the Island can discern the people on the maine as they goe up the hill to Church, they can describe their clothes; this Church and little parish which is called Church town is about a mile from the poynt, the houses are but poor cottages like barns to look on, much like those in Scotland—but to doe my own Country its right the inside of their little cottages are clean and plaister'd, and such as you might comfortably eate and drink there, and for curiosity sake I dranck there, and met with very good bottled ale.

The Lands End terminates in a poynt or peak of great rocks which runs a good way into the sea, I clamber'd over them as farre as safety permitted me;[9] there are abundance of rocks and sholes of stones stands up in the sea, a mile off some, and soe here and there some quite to the shore, which they name by severall names of Knights and Ladies roled up in mantles from some old tradition or fiction the poets advance, description of the amours of some great persons, but these many rocks and stones which lookes like the Needles in the Isle of Wight makes it hazardous for shipps to double the poynt especially in stormy weather; here at the Lands End they are but a little way off of France 2 dayes saile at farthest convey them to Haure De Grace [Havre] in France,[10] but the peace being but newly entred into with the French I was not willing to venture, at least by my self, into a Forreign Kingdom, and being then at the end of the land

[9] She did not put her foot into the sea, as Defoe did here and at Dover, the South Foreland, Lowestoft, Selsey and John o' Groats. (Op. cit., i, 254.)

[10] Land's End is 250 miles west of Havre; the nearest French port is Brest. The Peace of Ryswick had been signed a year before (September, 1697).

my horses leggs could not carry me through the deep and so return'd againe to Pensands [Penzance] 10 mile more, and soe came in view of both the seas and saw the Lizard Point and Pensands, the Mount in Cornwall which looked very fine in the broad day the sunn shineing on the rocke in the sea.

11. FROM LAND'S END TO NEWTON TONEY

THEN I continued my returne from Pensands to Hailing [Hayle], and now the tide was down, and so much land appeared which lay under water before, and I might have forded quite a crosse, many that know the country do but I tooke the safer way round by the bridge; here is abundance of very good fish, tho' they are so ill supplyed at Pensands because they carry it all up the country east and southward; this is an arme of the north sea which runs in a greate way into the land, its a large bay when the sea comes in, and upon the next hill I ascended from it could discover it more plaine to be a deep water and the supply of the maine ocean; just by here lay some ships and I perceived as I went (there being a storme) it seemed very tempestious and is a hazardous place in the high tides, so I came to Redruth.

I perceive they are very bleake in these countryes especially to this north ocean and the winds so troublesome they are forced to spin straw and so make a caul or net worke to lay over their thatch on their ricks and out houses, with waites of stones round to defend the thatch from being blown away by the greate winds; not but they have a better way of thatching their houses with reeds and so close that when its well done will last twenty yeares, but what I mention of braces or bands of straw is on their rickes which only is to hold a yeare; these places as in some other parts, indeed all over Cornwall and Devonshire, they have their carryages on horses backes; this being the time of harvest (tho' later in the yeare than usuall being the middle of September) but I had the advantage of seeing their harvest bringing in, which is on a horse's backe with sort of crookes of wood like yokes on either side, two or three on a side stands up in which they stow the corne and so tie it with cords, but they cannot so equally poise it but the going of the horse is like to cast it down sometimes on the one side and sometimes on the other, for they load them from the neck to the taile and pretty high and are forced to support it with their hands; so to a horse they have two people and the women leads and supports them as well as the men, and goe through thick and thinn; sometymes I have met with half a score horses thus loaded, they are indeed but little horses, their Cavelles as they call them, and soe may not be able to draw a cart, otherwise I am sure 3 or 4 horses might draw 3 tymes as much as 4 horses does carry, and where it is open ground and roads broad, which in some places here it was, I wondred at their labour in this kind, for the men and women themselves toiled like their horses—but the common observation of custom being as a second nature people are very hardly convinc'd or brought off from, tho' never soe inconvenient.

From Redruth I went to Truro 8 mile which is a pretty little town and seaport, formerly was esteemed the best town in Cornwall now is the second next Lanstone [Launceston]; its just by the Copper and Tinn mines and lies down in a bottom, pretty steep ascent, as most of the towns in these countrys, that you would be afraid of tumbling with nose and head foremost; the town is built of stone, a good pretty Church built all stone and carv'd on the outside, it stands in the middle of the town and just by there is the Market House on stone pillars and hall on the top, there is alsoe a pretty good key; this was formerly a great tradeing town and flourish'd in all things but now as there is in all places their rise and period, soe this which is become a ruinated disregarded place.

Here is a very good Meeteing, but I was hindred by the raine the Lords day else should have come to hearing, and so was forced to stay where I could hear but one Sermon at the Church, but by it saw the fashion of the country being obliged to go a mile to the parish Church over some grounds which are divided by such stiles and bridges uncommon and I never saw any such before; they are severall stones fixed across and so are like a grate or large steps over a ditch that is full of mudd or water, and over this just in the middle is a great stone fixed side wayes which is the style to be clambered over; these I find are the fences and guards of their grounds one from another and indeed they are very troublesome and dangerous for strangers and children; I heard a pretty good Sermon but that which was my greatest pleasure was the good Landlady I had; she was but an ordinary plaine woman but she was as understanding in the best things as most, the experience of reall religion and her quiet submision and self resignation to the will of God in all things, and especially in the placeing her in a remoteness, to the best advantages of hearing and being in such a publick employment which she desired and aimed at the discharging soe as to adorn the Gospel of her Lord and Saviour and the care of her children; indeed I was much pleased and edify'd by her conversation, and that pitch of soul resignation to the will of God, and thankfulness that God enabled and owned her therein, was an attainment few reach that have greater advantages of learning and knowing the mind of God; but this plainly led me to see that as God himself teacheth soe as none teacheth like him, soe he can discover himself to those immediately that have not the opportunity of seeing him in his sanctuary, and therefore to him we must address for help in this or any duty he calls us to, both in the use of what meanes he appoynts, as alsoe for success and blessing on it.

From Truro which is 9 mile from Fallmouth [Falmouth] and 4 mile from Trygolny [Tregothnan] which was the place I was at before with my Relation, that would have engaged my stay with them a few dayes or weekes to have given me the diversion of the country and to have heard the Cornish Nightingales, as they call them (the Cornish Cough [Chough] a sort of Jackdaw if I mistake not) a little black bird which makes them a visit about Michaelmas [Sept. 29th], and gives them the diversion of the notes which is a rough sort of musick not unlike the bird I take them for, so I believe they

by way of jest put on the Cornish Gentlemen by calling them
Nightingales; but the season of the year enclined to raine, and
the dayes declineing I was affraid to delay my return, and
these parts not abounding with much accomodation for
horses, theirs being a hard sort of cattle, and live much on
grass or furses of which they have the most and it will make
them very fatt being little hardy horses, and as they jest on
themselves, do not love the taste of oates and hay because
they never permit them to know the taste of it; but my horses
could not live so especially on journeys, of which I had given
them a pretty exercise, and their new oates and hay suited
not their stomach; I could get noe beanes for them till I came
back to St Columbe [St Columb Major] againe, which from
Truro by St Mitchel [Mitchell] was 12 miles mostly lanes
and long miles; as I observed before I saw noe windmills all
these countrys over they have only the mills which are over-
shott and a little rivulet of water you may step over turns
them, which are the mills for grinding their corn and their
oar or what else; from St Culombe I went to Way Bridge
[Wadebridge] 6 long miles; there was a river which was
flowed up by the tyde a greate way up into the land, it came
from the north sea it was broad, the bridge had 17 arches.

Thence to Comblefford [Camelford] over steep hills 9 mile
more, some of this way was over Commons of black moorish
ground full of sloughs, the lanes are deffended with bancks
wherein are stones, some great rocks others slaty stones such
as they use for tileing; Combleford was a little market town
but it was very indifferent accomodations, but the raines that
night and next morning made me take up there, till about 10
oclock in the morning it then made a shew of cleering up,
made me willing to seek a better lodging; 2 mile from this
place is a large standing water called Dosen Mere Poole, in a
black moorish ground and is fed by no rivers except the
little rivolets from some high hills, yet seemes allwayes full
without diminution and flows with the wind, is stored with
good fish and people living near it take the pleasure in a
boate to goe about it, there is alsoe good wildfowle about it;
it seemes to be such a water as the mer at Whitlesome

[Whittlesey] in Huntingtonshire by Stilton, its fresh water and what supply it has must be the rivolets that must come from the south sea, being that way ward towards Plymouth; as I travelled I came in sight of a great mountaine esteemed the second highest hill in England, supposeing the account Black Comb in Cumberland the first—but really I have seen soe many great and high hills I cannot attribute preheminence to either of these, tho' this did look very great and tall—but I thinke its better said the highest hill in each county.

I travelled 4 pretty long miles much in lanes and then came into a Common where I cross'd the great roads,[1] which on the right hand leads a way to Plymouth and the south sea the left hand to Bastable [Barnstaple] and the north sea which conveys the stone or rather marble which they take from hence at Bole [Delabole Quarries] remarkable Quarrys for a black stone exceeding hard and glossy like marble very dureable for pavements; this they send to all parts in tyme of peace and London takes off much of it.

Here I rode over a Common or Down 4 mile long in sight of the north sea and saw Hartly Poynt [Hartland Point], which is the Earle of Baths just by his fine house called Stow, his fine stables of horses and gardens; there I discern'd the Poynt very plaine and just by I saw the Isle of Lundy which formerly belonged to my Grandfather William Lord Viscount Say and Seale[2] which does abound with fish and rabbets and all sorts of fowles; one bird that lives partly in the water and partly out and so may be called an amphibious creature, its true that one foote is like a turky the other a gooses foote, it lays its egg in a place the Sun shines on and sets it so exactly upright on the small end, and there it remaines till taken up and all the art and skill of persons cannot

[1] The topography is not quite clear. She had not reached the main Plymouth-Barnstaple road. At her cross-roads the right-hand road led east to Launceston. The "great mountain" was probably Brown Willy, near Camelford. She could hardly have seen High Willhays, the highest point on Dartmoor, until she had reached Launceston.

[2] "Old Subtlety" had acquired Lundy during the Civil War, more or less by right of conquest. He had retired there after the execution of the king, and, according to Dorothy Osborne, was thought to be writing "a romance". (*Letters*, October 2nd, 1653.) The island was the rightful property of the Grenviles.

set it up soe againe to abide;[3] here I met with some showers
which by fits or storms held me to Lanston [Launceston] 4
mile more; these 12 mile from Cambleford [Camelford] was
not little ones and what with the wet and dirty lanes in many
places I made it a tedious journey; I could see none of the
town till just I was, as you may say, ready to tumble into it,
there being a vast steep to descend to which the town
seemed in a bottom yet I was forced to ascend a pretty good
hill into the place.

Lanston [Launceston] is the chief town in Cornwall where
the assizes are kept; I should have remarked at the Lands
End that Pensands was the last Corporation in England, soe
this is one of the last great towns tho' noe Citty, for Cornwall is in the Diocess of Devonshire which is Exeter, there
is a great ascent up into the Castle which looks very great
and in good repaire, the walls and towers round it, its true
there is but a part of it remaines the round tower or fort
being still standing and makes a good appearance; the town
is encompass'd with walls and gates, its pretty large, tho' you
cannot discover the whole town, being up and down in soe
many hills; the streetes themselves are very steep unless it be
at the Market Place where is a long and handsome space set
on stone pillars with the Town Hall on the top, which has a
large Lanthorne or Cupilo in the middle where hangs a bell
for a clock with a dyal to the streete; there is in this place 2
or 3 good houses built after the London form by some
Lawyers, else the whole town is old houses of timber work;
at a little distance from the town on a high hill I looked
back and had the full prospect of the whole town which was
of a pretty large extent.

A mile beyond I crossed on a stone bridge over a river
and entred into Devonshire againe, and pass'd through
mostly lanes which were stony and dirty by reason of the
raines that fell the night before and this day, which was the
wettest day I had in all my summers travells hitherto, having

---

[3] The bird is thought by one authority to have been the Great Auk, but
controversy has raged around this point. (L.R.W. Lloyd, *Lundy, its History
and Natural History*, p. 210.)

had noe more than a shower in a day, and that not above 3
tymes in all except when I came to Exeter; as I came down
from Taunton there was small raine most of the afternoon,
but this day was much worse, so that by that tyme I came
through lanes and some commons to Oakingham [Oke-
hampton] which was 15 mile I was very wet; this was a little
market town and I met with a very good Inn and accomodation, very good chamber and bed, and came in by 5 of the
clock so had a good tyme to take off my wet cloathes and be
well dryed and warme to eate my supper, and rested very
well without sustaining the least damage by the wet; I should
have remark'd that these roads were much up and down hill
thro' enclosed lands and woods in the same manner the other
part of Cornwall and Devonshire was, gaineing by degrees
the upper grounds by one hill to another and so descending
them in like manner; these raines fully convinced me of the
need of so many great stone bridges whose arches were soe
high, that I have wonder'd at it because the waters seemed
shallow streames but they were so swelled by one night and
dayes raine that they came up pretty near the arches, and ran
in most places with such rapidity, and look'd so thick and
troubled, as if they would clear all before them; this causes
great floods and the lower grounds are overwhelm'd for a
season after such raines, so that had I not put on and gotten
beyond Lanston [Launceston] that day there would have
been noe moveing for me till the flouds, which hourly encreased, were run off.

Next day I went to Cochen Well [Crockern Well] 10 mile,
mostly good open way except a hill or two which were steep
and stony; tho' this was the longer way and about, yet by
reason of the former raines it was the safest, for the lower way
was run over by the waters, which are land flouds from the
swelling brookes which are up in a few hours and are sunck
in the same tyme again; the wayes were somewhat dirty.

Thence to Exeter 10 mile more, but this was the basest
way you can goe, and made much worse by these raines, but
its narrow lanes full of stones and loose ground clay, and
now exceeding slippery by the raines; a quarter of a mile on

this side of the town I stood on a high banke from whence
the prospect of the Citty of Exeter was very pleasant, could
see it to great advantage, the Cathedrall and other Churches
spires encompass with the whole town which in generall is
well built, with the good bridge over the Ex, which is a fine
river on whose bancks are severall rows of trees all below the
town; the walks all about it augments the beauty of the Citty;
from whence I went to Topsham 3 mile, which is a little
market place a very good key; hither they convey on horses
their Serges and soe load their shipps which comes to this
place all for London; thence I saw Starre Cross [Starcross]
where the great shipps ride and there they build some shipps;
this was up the river, 5 or 6 miles up the river, but the tide
being out could not goe and it was ten mile by land and their
miles are soe long here I would not goe it, seeing almost as
well the shipps that lay there as if at the place.

Thence I returned to Exeter 3 mile where I had been very
kindly entertained by Mr. Goswill and his wife (which was
one my brother Sir Edmund Harrison did employ in buying
Serges);[4] from Exeter I went to Honiton 15 mile, all fine
gravell way the best road I have met withall in the West;
here it is they make the fine Bonelace in imitation of the
Antwerp and Flanders lace, and indeed I think its as fine, it
only will not wash so fine which must be the fault in the
thread; Honiton is a pretty large place, a good Market house,
near it a good Church with a round tower and spire which
was very high and a little peculiar in its forme, somewhat like
a pigeon house rooffe; here is a very large Meeteing of
Descenters.

Thence I went to Axminster 7 mile more, but not soe good
way being much in lanes, stony and dirty, and pretty much
up and down hills, like the other parts of these countys:
beyond Axminster where I passed over the river Ax on a
pretty large bridge I came to Somersetshire againe (this
Axminster is a little market town) and the London Road by

[4] The Exeter serges were a major English export to the Continent. Sir
Edmund Harrison sold them in 1699 at Leghorn. (Cal. S. P. Dom., 1699–
1700, p. 151.) See also Introduction, pp. xxviii and xxxix.

Chard, but I struck out of that road 2 mile off the town to Liegh [Leigh], which was 4 mile from Axminster, to a Relations house Mr. Hendleys[5] [Henley] which stands on a hill; but its such an enclosed country and narrow lanes you cannot see a bow shott before you, and such up and down steep hills; its an old house a large court with open gates that enter you into a passage on the right hand, a good parlour new wanscoated, next that a kitchen and pantrys leads into a court where all the offices are and stable and coach houses; on the left side of the passage at the entrance is a large old hall with a great halfe pace at the upper end with 2 chimneys in the hall, this leades into a passage on the left hand and so through to another parlour with good old fashion carved wanscoate; the roomes are low; out of the passage leads up a paire of staires to 3 or 4 roomes all low, and but one well furnish'd, then out of same passage below is a doore into the garden, which are one lower than the other, with stone stepps; its capable of being very handsome if made with open grates to let one out to see the orchards and woods beyond, they were a turffing the walks and make- ing banks in order to it; the house alsoe is capable of altera- tion to a good house if the windows were made lower and the roomes fitted with wanscoate and good furniture; just to the front there is design'd a visto to be cut thro' the wood to the water side, which will be very fine being on a descent.

About a mile from hence is one Mr. Predueax [Prideaux] house [Forde Abbey] a fine old house and well furnish'd but they permitt none to see it, soe I saw it not, only drove by it to see my Cozens little girle at nurse, and soe returned home againe a mile; and then from Liegh [Leigh] I went through narrow stony lanes up hills and down, which steeps causes the water on raines to trill down on the low ground, that for a few hours or a day there will be noe passing in the bottom; which happen'd while I was at Liegh, one nights raine put the cattle in the meddows swimming and hindred

---

[5] This may be Henry Henley of Colway, who married Catharine, daughter of Celia's Aunt Margaret Holt (née Whitehead). It may, however, be his uncle or a cousin. Colway and Leigh belonged to the same family. (Hutchins, *Dorset*, iv, 420.)

us from going to Church, the water would have came over
the windows of the Coach; these stony lanes I passed till I
came to the great road which comes from Lime [Lyme], here
I entred into Dorsetshire and soe went through a little town
called Maiden Newton eight mile more, and soe thence to
Dorchester town 6 mile more, all a fine hard gravel way and
much on the downs, this is good ground much for sheep;[6]
thence I went to Blandford 12 long miles, thro' Piddle town
[Puddletown], Milborn [Milborne], and Whitchurch, there
I staid with my relation Cos'n Collier, Husys, and Fussells;[7]
thence to Salisbury 18 mile; when I had passed 6 mile I came
through a gate which brought me into Wiltshire and soe over
the downs to Salisbury and from thence to Newton-tony 7
miles.

[6] Dorchester was the centre of very famous pastures. The narrators of
Cosimo of Tuscany's tour (1669) reported that "in a circuit of three miles
round Dorchester, they reckoned 40,000 head of oxen and sheep". (*Travels
of Cosmo III*, tr. 1821, p. 147.)

[7] Collier of Puddletrenthide, related by marriage to the Cullifords, i.e.
to Celia's maternal grandmother. There were several Husseys in this part of
the country (see Hutchins, *Dorset*) but the Fussells I cannot trace.

12. FROM NEWTON TONEY THROUGH WINDSOR TO LONDON

I WENT from Newtontony [Newton Toney] to Sarum and
home againe 3 tymes which made it 42 miles in all; then to
Wallop 4 miles and home again 4 miles; and to Grattly
[Grately] twice and back again 12 mile; and to Cholderton
twice 4 mile; to Allington and home 2 mile more, then to
London.

From Newtontony to Winchester 15 mile, there I went to
see a Relation Mrs. Horne[1] thence Alsford [Alresford] 8
mile; the little raines I had in the morning before I left
Newtontony made the wayes very slippery, and it being
mostly on chaulk way, a little before I came to Alsford

[1] Alice, daughter of Celia's Uncle John Fiennes, had married John Horn
of Winchester. After his death she married Sir John St. Barbe, widower of
Celia's cousin Honor (née Norton). She outlived both husbands and died in
1734.

forceing my horse out of the hollow way his feete failed, and he could noe wayes recover himself and so I was shott off his neck upon the bank, but noe harm I bless God, and as soone as he could role himself up stood stock still by me, which I looked on as a great mercy—indeed mercy and truth allwayes have attended me; the next day I went to Alton 10 miles, thence Farnum [Farnham] 9 miles more, this proved a very wet day; after an hours rideing in the morning it never ceased more or less to raine, which made me put in at Farnum and stay all the day after; I came in at noone but then it began to raine much faster and soe continued; thence next day I went over the Forrest in sight of Fairly [Farnham] Castle which is the Bishop of Winchesters Pallace, it lookes nobly on a hill; thence to Bagshott 9 mile, thence to Winsor [Windsor] over the Forrest 7 long miles, this way most clay deep way, the worse by reason of the raines and full of sloughs.

About a mile off Windsor Castle[2] appeares standing on a hill much after the manner of Durham, with the walls and battlements round, only that is all stone and this is but partly soe, and the rest brick plaister'd over in imitation of stone, which does not look so well; it is a pretty great ascent to the town which is well built something suitable to London by reason of its affinity to the Court; and I saw the Cathedrall or St. Georges Church which is very fine built all stone and carved on the outside; severall cloysters leads to the Doctors houses, its a lofty noble building; the Quire is properly St. Georges Chappel whose rooff is very high and carved very curiously, all free stone, so is the rest of the Church; there hangs up the Banners and Ensignes of honour belonging to the severall Knights of the honourable Order of the Blew Garter, their complement is 26; there was one void at this tyme by the death of the Earle of Peterborough;[3] there is a greate cerimony in their inauguration; their seates are of wanscoate carved which are all quite round the Quire with

---

[2] The royal apartments at Windsor had been largely rebuilt by Charles II. The new part was in brick.

[3] The second Earl of Peterborough died in June, 1697.

each Garters and Coate armours and Banners on the top; and when they are installed their garments are blew velvet in shape like the coapes, lined with white sattin or silk, that and their blew Garter in which hangs a George on horse-back besett with jewels, and a Diamond Garter put on their right leg, which is performed by 2 of the former knights of the order, which is given them by the king that is the Principal of that order; then they have an oath given them to maintain the Rights and Cerimonyes of said order, and soe are seated in their Seate; there are great fees paid by each new Knight to the officers to the Poore Knights of Windsor, whose seates are just under the seates of the Knights of the Garter, 18 Poore Knights of Windsor which have houses provided for them[4] about the Cloyster and 40£ per annum each besides their perquisits at such tymes; there are alsoe 18 singing men and petty Cannons, those that are preachers has houses and 30£ per annum each, but the others have but 22£ each a yeare and houses to live in, these all have their fees at the installment of each Knight of the Garter and of this order are severall Princes and Great men both here and in forreign parts.

There is a very large fine organ at the entrance of the Quire, the alter is crimson velvet striped with gold tissue large candlesticks and basons gilt; at the installment there is a great deale of plaite set out which belongs to the Chappel, over the alter is a painting of Christ and his twelve apostles at the passover supper very naturally drawn, and over it a large window full of fine paintings, the history of the testa-ment; the Quire is paved all with black and white marble under which is a large vault for the Royal family, there lyes King Henry the 8th and King Charles the First etc.: there is in the Church a tombe and vault of the Duke of Norfolks familly with steele carvings all about it very curious and, to add to its rarity, it may be all taken piece by piece and put up in a box, its a very large thing and great variety of work, this is on the right side of the alter.

[4] Celia Fiennes has confused the Knights' quarters (which had no cloister) with those of the Minor Canons or Vicars Choral. (H.A.T.)

There is, in a little Chappel by, a very fine monument with two large statues in alabaster painted and gilt all at length in their garments and round the tomb-stone are the statues of their children, 7 daughters (four of them were twinns and soe represented being put together) and 3 sonnes all alabaster, and there is a role of matt under the head of the Lord and Lady that was so naturall looked like real matt, this was Lord Earle Lincolns[5] tomb; there is another monument of the Earle of Rutlands[6] the first of the family which was Earle 100 year since, it was in the year ano: dom: 1513, there is round that 6 sonns six daughters, with carvings of other images holding their coates of armes; there is another monument which is of the old Duke off Beaufort, who was base son to King Edward the 4th[7] and therefore there is a barr of reproach across the English arms which he beares; there is another statue of white marble in a leaneing posture almost lyeing quite along and they say its very like his Effigie, this was the Bishop of Chichester; there is another Bishops Effigie in the wall, just to the waste, of alabaster; there is a Chappel in which are prayers at 8 of the clock at night; there is a white marble font; the rooff of the Quire is very curious carv'd stone and soe thinn to the leads one might grasp it between thumb and finger and yet so well fixt as to be very strong.

From thence I proceeded on to the Castle which is the finest pallace the king has, especially now Whitehall is burnt[8] but that was old buildings and unless it were the Banqueting House and the apartment which our good Queen Mary beautifyed for herself, that was never soe well as Winsor; you enter in through a gate, on the right hand is a tower which is built with redouts and walks round it as

[5] The Elizabethan Lord High Admiral, not one of the later Earls who were Celia Fiennes' near relations.

[6] This was George Manners, Lord Roos, father of the first Earl of Rutland.

[7] The Beaufort family were John of Gaunt's bastards, not Edward IV's. They were Dukes of Somerset, but not of Beaufort. One descendant, the Earl of Worcester, was buried at Windsor. A yet more remote descendant became Duke of Beaufort in 1682 and was still alive. (H.A.T.)

[8] Whitehall was burnt on January 2nd, 1698. (See Evelyn, *Diary* and Luttrell, op. cit., iv, 328.) Inigo Jones's Banqueting Hall alone survived.

was Durham Castle; its 120 stepps up, where is the Gaurd roome hung with armes, thence a dineing roome the Duke of Norfolks appartment a drawing-roome and two bed chambers, one with a half bedstead as the new mode, dimity with fine shades of worstead works well made up, there are good Pictures; the next roome has such a bed but that is fine Indian quilting and embroidery of silk; the tower on the leads is as many stepps more, I walked round it and could see a great prospect of the whole town and Winsor Forrest, the country round to Kensington; I could see Lord of Hollands house and rowes of trees and to Harrow of the Hill, and to Shooters Hill beyond London; and the town of Winsor looked very well, there were severall noblemens houses Duke St Albans and fine gardens [Burfield Lodge]; just by it is the Lord Guidolphins [Godolphin] house and gardens, there I could see the fine walk [the Long Walk] or rather road planted with trees, of a huge length into the Forrest, which King Charles made for his going out in divertion of shooteing; and here I could see the river Thames which twists and turns it self round the meddowes and grounds; upon this tower which is most tymes moist, all in the walls grows the best maiden haire, both white and black, which is an herb much esteemed for coughs and to put into drinks for consumptions.

Thence I proceeded on to a large Court like the Quaderangle at Christ Church College in Oxford or Trinity in Cambridge, in the middle of which is a statue of King Charles the Second on horseback all of brass and is railed in with iron spikes; round this Court are the buildings which are the severall appartments of the Lords of the Bed Chamber and the Ladies, alsoe one side is the Lodgings belonging to the Princess Ann of Denmarke[9] which are all of stone and well built and beautify'd; in the middle you enter a large pair of iron gates finely carv'd into a paved large space supported with severall rows of stone pillars and ascending up large staires which enters you into the Queens Gaurd Chamber hung full of armoury, which is so exactly set, the Pikes set

[9] Later, of course, Queen Anne.

up like pillars and such distances, the Muskets laid a long one above the other, the Boxes for the Powder, and the edge of the cornish [cornice] is Pistols set as thick as they can be set, and above it are Drums and Helmets and back and breast armour; the chimney piece is of the same, Swords in the middle there poynts turned outward, with a round of little Pistolls set close to compass them and at each corner a sett of Pistolls set close in quarter circle—its all exactly uniforme and very handsome.[10]

Next into a noble Hall which has very fine paintings, this is the Standard for Curiosity in all places you see painting, its done by the same hand [Verrio] did the paintings att Windsor; the top is full of all sort of varietys, in the middle is King Charles's picture, the sides are all descriptions of Battles and between each picture in the pillars is the George and Blew Garter and Starre; at the upper end is the large picture of St. George encountering the Dragon and at the lower end is the picture of the King[11] that first instituted this order of the Blew Garter and is putting it on himself on his son who was just returned victor from some considerable Battle.

I should have noted in my remarks of the Cerimonyes off that order that when any dies and a Garter drops they make a solemn offering up of all their Ensignes of honour to the Church and then take them down and pay some fees as well as their Entrance into it.

From this roome I entred into the Chappel under the gallery or closet the King and Queen sets in at prayers, this was supported by four Brass Gyants or else painted like brass; this seate of the Kings looks into the Chappel, its crimson velvet all the inside and cannopy, with the cloth which hung over before it all alike richly embroyder'd with gold fring; this is the house Chappel and is exceeding beautifull, the paintings of the rooffe and the sides wich is the

---

[10] This armour was arranged by Prince Rupert, while Constable of the Castle (1668). His military career was then over, and he had dabbled in mezzotint engraving, but had still to fight a number of naval battles in the Dutch war.

[11] Edward III.

history off Christs miracles, his Life, and the good he did in healing all distempers which are described at large here and lookes very lively; there is alsoe the most exactest workmanship in the wood carving, which is (as the painting) the pattern and masterpiece of all such work both in figures fruitages beasts birds flowers all sorts, soe thinn the wood and all white natural wood without varnish; this adorns the pillars and void spaces between the paintings, here is a great qualiety so much for quantety; there was a pretty alter at the upper end and two gallerys for the musick.

Thence I went up staires into a large dineing-roome, damaske chaires and window curtaines wanscoated and severall fine pictures; the rooffe of this was well painted also but they are soe lofty its enough to breake ones neck to looke on them; thence into a Gallery full of pictures with a large looking-glass at the end; thence into the drawing roome where is the large branch of silver and the sconces round the roome of silver, silver table and stands and glass frames and chaire frames; next is the Queenes Chamber of State all Indian Embroidery on white sattin being presented to her by the Company [East India Company] on it is great plumes of white feathers; there is very good tapistry hangings full of gold and silver but they are large old figures; here's a silver table and stands and glass frame; there was a raile set across at the beds feete which reach each side of the roome made of sweate [sweet] wood frames and open wires in the middle, and was to be doubled together in leaves as a screen; this was instead of the raile use to be quite round the king and queens beds to keep off companyes coming near them.

Thence into an anty-roome through a little gallery or passage, thence into the Kings dressing roome almost all glass, the chimney piece is full of great stone heads, in nitches or hollow made for them, of some Emperour; the windows of all the roomes are large sarshes as big as a good looking-glass and are all diamond cut round the edges, the height of the windows makes them looke narrow; thence into the Kings constant bed chamber being one of the halfe bedsteads of crimson and green damaske inside and outside the same hangings, and chaires and window curtaines the same; it was lofty and full, with good fringe and there was such another screen or raile at the feete of the bed that tooke the length of the roome as in the Queens chamber; here was tables stands glass frames gilt gold fine carving on the chimney pieces both here and in the Queens appartment.

The next was the Chamber of State which is noble indeed very lofty and painted on the roofe as they all are; the bed was green velvet strip'd down very thick with gold orrice lace of my hands breadth, and round the bottom 3 such orrices and gold fring all round it and gold tassells, so was the cornish [cornice]; the inside was the same; at the head-piece was like curtaines fringed round with gold and tyed back with gold strings and tassells as it were tyed back, and soe hung down in the middle where was the Crown and Sypher [Cipher] embroyder'd; the hangings the same and such another screen acrosse the roome, to secure the bed from the common; next this is the Drawing-roome of State, the cannopy and throne and the part behind is all green velvet richly embroyder'd with silver and gold of high emboss'd work, and some curiously wrought like needlework that you can scarce see the ground or stuff its wrought on, and the Crown of crimson velvet embroyder'd just over the Chaire or Throne of State, the footstoole the same, which was all set on a half pace or part raised above the rest as the manner is with a fine carpet over it; the cannopy was so rich and curled up and in some places soe full it looked very glorious and was newly made to give audience to the French Embassadour to shew the grandeur and magnificence of the British Monarch—some of these foolerys are requisite sometymes to create admiration and regard to keep up the state of a kingdom and nation.

Thence I went into the Common Audience Roome where was a throne on such a raised space with a carpet, this throne and canopy and the back with stooles and chaires was crimson and gold coullour'd figured velvet; out of this I came into a large roome for people to wait in, painted with black and white and gold, description of some fights and men in armour, thence into the Kings Guard Chamber which is deckt as the Queens, the walls being adorned with the severall armes put in exact order, only in the pillars or spaces here they hang the Bandaleers which holds their powder; in the mantlepiece there was noe difference, but in the middle was the starre and soe set about with the pistols and swords; thence I descended large staires of stone and soe through a court back to the walk of pillars and soe through the large iron gate into the courts one without another all built round.

Winsor town lookes well, the streetes large the Market Cross on stone pillars and a large Hall on the top, from thence the streete runs along to the bridge[12] over the Thames and there you enter Buckinghamshire and a quarter of a mile off, tho' indeed there is building all along, there is Eaton Colledge, a good stone building carved on the outside; its round a square, there is at the front a large schoole roome; 400 Schollars[13] and 8 Fellows which have 400£ a piece yearely, the Master has 1000£, he payes all the ushers in number seven; there is alsoe an Under Master for the Little Schollars; this was founded by King Edward the Confessour[14] and endowed so richly by him; and on the same foundation is the revenue of the Cathedrall and the Poore Knights which goe in a peculiar black gown like fryers, all their salleryes and the repaire of the Cathedrall is taken care off by the same foundation with the Colledge—not but there is a little Chappel to the Colledge with in it self for every dayes prayers—the Chappel and Schoole room takes up two sides of the square, the two others is the Lodging for the Fellows and for the Schollars, then the middle there is an arch which leads to the Cloyster and soe into their kitchen and cellars which are very convenient and high but pretty old; just by is the great Hall in which they eate, the Schollars and Fellows and Masters should eate with them: this is the same foundation as Kings Colledge in Cambridge so that those Schollars

[12] A wooden bridge, as were all the Thames bridges between London and Oxford.
[13] Technically 70 Scholars, the rest would be Oppidans.
[14] It was, of course, founded by King Henry VI.

that are fitt to be removed to the University at the Election are sped to Kings Colledge in Cambridge and so are advanced as they can get friends into Fellowshipps to either.

From Windsor I went to the ferry 3 mile and rode in sight of the Castle on this side, which is all the Kings and Queens appartments, and lookes very noble, the walls round with the battlements and gilt balls and other adornments; here I ferry over the Thames and so went a nearer way which is a private road made for the kings coaches, and so to Colebrooke [Colnbrook] 3 mile more, thence to Houndslow-heath and so to London 12 mile more; then I went to Bednall [Bethnal] Green 4 mile and home again 4 mile; and here ends my Long Journey this summer, in which I had but 3 dayes of wet except some refreshing showers sometymes, and I thinke that was not above 4 in all the way; and it was in all above 1551 miles and many of them long miles, in all which way and tyme I desire with thankfullness to own the good providence of God protecting me from all hazard or dangerous accident.

PART IV

LONDON AND THE LATER JOURNEYS
(*c.* 1701-1703)

1. LONDON AND THE LORD MAYOR'S SHOW

It cannot be thought amiss here to add some remarke on the metropolis of England, London, whose scituation [is] on so noble a river as the Thames (which emptyes it at the Boy [Buoy] of the Nore, being there joyned with the Medway another very fine river alsoe, and falls there into the sea which is about 30 miles from London) and is an ebbing flowing river as farre as Sheen beyond London; this is very comodious for shipps,[1] which did come up just to the bridge, but from carelessness the river is choaked up that obliges the shipps to come to an anchor at Blackwall; all along this river are severall docks for building shipps of the biggest burden; six miles from the town the last yeare was built the Royal Souveraign[2] which is our greatest ship.

London joyned with Westminster, which are two great cittyes but now with building so joyned it makes up but one vast building with all its subburbs, and has in the walls ninety-seven parishes, without the walls 16 parishes, 15 subburbs, Surrey, Middlesex, 7 parishes in Westminster.[3]

[1] Defoe once counted 2,000 sea-going vessels in the Pool of London. (Op. cit., i, 348.)

[2] The *Royal Sovereign*, built at Woolwich, went into service June 1st, 1702 (Cal. S. P. Dom., 1702-3. Cf. Sir George Rooke's *Journal* (Navy Records Society), pp. 147 and 149). She carried 100 guns, and 780 men (Chamberlayne, *Magnae Britanniae Notitia*). She replaced the old *Royal Sovereign* built in 1637 out of Ship Money. The life of a man-of-war was often three-quarters of a century, and Charles II had employed ships which had fought against the Armada.

[3] The population of London at this period has been variously estimated at between 600,000 and 1,000,000, the population of England being perhaps 5½ million, and certainly not more than 7 million. (See J. N. L. Baker in *Historical Geography of England*, ed. Darby.) The open country between London and Westminster had only just been built over, and during Anne's reign it was still possible to shoot woodcock where Regent Street now stands. (*Gentleman's Magazine*, 1785.)

London is the Citty properly for trade, Westminster for the Court; the first is divided into 24 wards, to each which there is an Alderman, and themselves consist of Common Council men and all Freemen of the Citty, and have power to choose these Aldermen and make their own orders and to maintain their own priviledges; all Freemen or Livery men of this Citty hath a right to choose their Sherriffs, of which every yeare there is two, one for Middlesex the other the Corporation, but both are joyned and officiate together in all matters of juries, justice or ceremonies, and to maintaine all rights.

These Freemen alsoe have their voyce in choice of their Lord Major [Mayor] which is done every yeare with this sollemnity, the Sheriffs being chosen and sworne at Mid summer, the Michaelmas after the Lord Major is chosen and sworne; the evening before (which is Simon and Judes day) is a feast called Calveshead Feast.[4] Next day the old Lord Major comes to meete the new one, and with him on his left hand is conducted on horse back in all their gowns of scarlet cloth lined with furr; all the aldermen in like robes only differenc'd as their station, those of them which have been Lord Majors weare a gold chaine ever after, but those that have not passed the Chaire weare none; the Lord Major is allwayes one of the Aldermen and he has a great gold chaine round his neck, the Sheriffs also weare a gold chaine round their neck that yeare. Thus on horseback they proceed two and two with all their officers; the Lord Major has his Sword Bearer which walkes before him with the Sword in an embroyder'd sheath, he weares a great velvet cap of crimson, the bottom and the top of furr or such like standing up like a turbant or great bowle in forme of a great open pye, this is called the Cap of Maintenance; this is the Lord Majors chiefe officer, he holds his place dureing his Life and has 1500£ a yeare allowed him for his table which in all things is as good as Lord Major's, and he entertaines all people at it, yet he himself must officiate at the Lord Majors

---

[4] Not to be confused with the famous Whig ceremonial at which the calf's head was symbolical of Charles I. (See *The Calveshead Club* or *The Republican Unmasked*, 1703.)

table to see all things in order, and comes in at sett tymes accordingly to performe them and bring the Lord Majors Compliments to the Companyes; he thus walkes before the Lord Major with the Water Bayliff beareing a Gold Mace, and a Serjeant another, to the waterside.

At Fleete Ditch they enter the Barges which are all very curiously adorned, and thus he is conducted, the river being full of Barges belonging to the severall Companyes of London, adorned with streamers and their armes and fine musick, and have sack to drinke and little cakes as bigg as a crown piece; they come to Westminster Staires where they land and are conducted, the Lord Majors traines being borne up (as well the old as new Lord Major) they enter Westminster Hall and are conducted to the severall Courts of Justice where there is severall ceremonyes perform'd; the new Lord Major is presented to the King or those deputed to act under him and there is sworne,[5] all which being over they are conducted back to their Barges, and soe to the staires [where] they took barge, where they are received by some of the nobility deputed by the King, [who] make some little speech of compliment and give the Lord Major and Aldermen a treate of wine and sweet meates passant.

They mount on horseback and returne, only the new Lord Major takes the right hand, and haveing by the Sheriffs invited the King and Court to dinner (which sometymes they accept but mostly refuse because it puts the Citty to a vast charge) they being then conducted through the Citty with greate acclamations, their own habits and trappings of their horses being very fine, and they haveing all the severall Companyes of the Citty, which walke in their order and gowns with pagents to most or many of their Companyes, which are a sort of Stages covered and carryed by men and on the top many men and boys acting the respective Trades or Employments of each Company, some in shipps for the Merchants; and whatever Company the new Lord Major is off his pageant is the finest and that Company has the pre-

[5] At this point, for some reason, there is a gap of nearly a page in both manuscripts. It is possible that a drawing or picture had once been pasted in.

cedency that yeare of all the Companyes except the Mercers Company, which allwayes is the first and esteemed the greatest; and when there is a Lord Major of that Company their pageant is a maiden queen on a throne, crowned and with royal robes and scepter and most richly dressed, with severall ladyes dressed, her attendants, all on the same pageant and with a cannopy over her head and drawn in an open chariot with 9 horses (the horses goe 3 abreast) very finely accouter'd and pages that ride them all, with plumes of feathers; after being drawn through the Citty she is invited by the Lord Major to a dinner provided on purpose for her, and soe many rich Batchelors are appointed to entertaine her (that is a ranck among the Freemen); she has her traine bore up and is presented to Lady Majoris [Mayoress] that salutes her, as doth the Aldermens Ladyes, all which are conducted in their coaches to Guildhall.[6] The new Lady Majoress richly habited has her traine borne up, and introduced by one of the officers; the Sheriffs Ladyes likewise weares gold chaines that yeare, the Lady Majoress does wear it ever after, as doe all the Aldermens Ladyes whose husbands have been Lord Majors; and as I said before the Lord Majors must be Aldermen and must have served as a Sherriff before, and allwayes the King confers knighthood on the person that is chosen to be Sheriff unless he were a knight before; there is also every year chosen a Chamberlain of the Citty and a Bridgmaster.

In Guild Hall there are severall long tables plentyfully furnished with all sorts of varietyes suiteable to the season, with fine desserts off sweetemeates, jellys which in pyramidyes stand all the tyme; the hott meate is brought in first and second courses. The Lord Major and Lady Majoress sitt at the upper end, but in case the Court is there then the Lord Major has one table, the Lady another, and the old Lady

---

[6] Celia Fiennes omits the noonday fireworks, the "squibs and serpents" and "the burning perriwigs" described by Misson, possibly because "this is only to amuse the Cockneys" (*Memoirs and Observations*, trans. J. Ozell, 1719, pp. 187–8). She omits for more obvious reasons the quite unprintable horseplay indulged in by the mob on these occasions and described with gusto by Ned Ward in his *London Spy* (ed. Straus, 297–302).

Majoress is set at the left hand of the new Lady, and the Aldermens Ladyes at her right hand according to their senioritys, after which they retire into a gallery where is danceing the whole evening.

All this yeare Lord or Lady Majoress goe no where but with their officers to attend them; and the old Lord Major and Lady Majoress has their traines bore up to Guild Hall and after dinner return without it.

The whole affaires of the Citty are managed by the Lord Major and Court of Aldermen and Common Councill men, he is obliged to take care of justice and right; he does during his yeare invite each Company with all their Masters Wardens and Officers twice—the last tyme all their wives alsoe—the Sherriffs doe the like; each person brings their gift, two, three guinneas, some more, and according to their gift at the last entertainment they have a silver spoon double gilt, either weighing soe many ounces and soe many as they give guinneas many tymes in the yeare; those that would shew particular respect will go dine with them and bring presents without haveing spoones; but these dinners and invitations are at their pleasure, not as a custom.

All offices falling vacant in the Majoralty acrue to Lord Major to dispose off; there are 24 Companyes which have each severall officers, as Masters, Wardens etc., and doe meete to fix and maintaine their priviledges; they doe walke at the Lord Majors day and make sumptuous feasts at each Hall appertaineing to their Company, which is at the charge of the Masters and Wardens which are officers chosen new every yeare; they have great stocks and lands belonging to their Companyes common stock, and which does maintaine Schooles and Hospitalls and such like, which from tyme to tyme are encreased by severall Benefactors and Legacyes, some of which are greate—as in the Mercers Company which have lands to a great value for such ends.

There are severall feasts which Lord Majors and Sherriffs are absolutely obliged to make at their first entrance into their offices, two dayes following each other, and the first day of the terme to all the judges, and 3 dayes at Easter, going to hear a sermon at St. Brides each day, and then to inspect the severall Charityes and Hospitalls that all be kept in due order and provided for; Bedlam is one Charity of the Citty for care of lunitick persons in Moore Fields, a great house and building, and revenue for officers doctors and physick for them and all necessarys. The Lord Major and Sherriffs attends the King at all tymes to represent the publick affaires of the Citty and receive his orders, they alsoe officiate at the proclaiming any new King or Queen[7] or to declare peace or warr, which is done in greate solemnity by the King at Arms and severall of the nobillity in coaches or on horseback, and the officers of the kings household.

King Williams return after the peace was concluded with France and the Confederates,[8] the Kings entry was in this manner: the Lord Major in crimson velvet gown with a long traine, on horseback, attended by all his officers, the Sword Bearer and Water Baily very well dress'd; the Common Hunt was clad in green velvet; thus with all the aldermen in their scarlet gowns, they proceeding to receive the King just at the end of Southwark on the borders of Kent, the Lord Major carrying a scepter with a crown of pearle on the top. The King was attended thus: first all his soldiers and officers marched in ranke, the Aldermen and Lord Major and officers, then all the Nobillity in their coaches, and the Bishops and Judges, then the first coach of the King with his Household, then the Guards of his body, and then the coach where in the King was, which was a very rich and costly thing, all the fring rich gold, the glass very large, the standards and all outwork like beaten gold, drawn by 8 very fine white horses with massy gold harness and trappings, the French Kings present to our King when the peace was concluded, the first article of which was owning King William King of England. After the Kings coach a troope of Guards de corps, then the third coach of the Kings with his Household, and other coaches with severall officers of

[7] "When the King dies", wrote Misson, "the Mayor is the chief man in the Kingdom till the succession is proclaim'd". (Op. cit., 189.)

[8] The King's entry was made on November 16th, 1697 (see Luttrell, op. cit., iv, 306) after the Peace of Ryswick.

the Household; then as the King passed Southwarke the Baily presented him his mace, he returned it with the usuall ceremony and grattification; then at the bridge the Lord Major demands his place and the sword, which is to march as Captain of the Kings guards just imediately before the Kings own coach, which accordingly was given him, and he returns the said scepter to the proper officers, who bear that and all the maces before him; and he bare headed beares the sword on horseback just before the Kings coach. At the same tyme the Water Baily rides in the middle of the guards as their officer and is on horseback, two men like pages leading it, (soe is Lord Majors) in this order; they proceeding through the Citty, which from the Royal Exchange on each side had placed the Traine Bands of the Citty with their officers, next them the 24 Companyes of the Citty in their order, and marks of their Honour and privilidges, which reached to the Conduite in Cheapside, all which paid their respective homage and duty to the King, who receiv'd it very kind and obligeingly, as he did the generall joy and acclamations which proceeded from thousands which were spectators; at Pauls Schoole the Schollars made him a speech and thus he was conducted to his own pallace at Whitehall.

But before I leave the Citty of London I must describe its building and treasure; the Government as I said was Lord Major, Aldermen, Sherriffs, Recorder, and Chamberlaine, and other officers as Common Serjeant, and other Serjeants, Sword Bearers, Water Bayly, Common Cryer, and the Town Clerke; all these with many other officers has considerable saleryes and endure their life (except the Chamberlaine thats annually chosen, tho' mostly is in the same person againe); those others are in the Lord Majors dispose and brings a greate advantage to him if any dye in his Majoralty. There is alsoe many considerable perquisitts belonging to him to support the honnour; the Citty plaite is kept for each; notwithstanding, in the year it costs them more many tymes than they receive, and in the whole I have had it from one that had been at the charge said it was above 8000£ in the year.

There is as I said great Publick Stock in the Citty by which they have raised sumptuous Buildings, the Royal Exchange for one, a large space of ground enclosed round with cloysters and open arches on which are built many walkes of shopps of all trades; the middle space below was design'd and is used for the merchants to meete to concert their buisness and trade and bills, which is all open and on the top of these piaza's are the effigies in stone of most of our kings and queens since the Conquest which were anoynted crowned heads, from whence this Exchange takes its name Royal.[9] In the midst of it stands in stone work on a pedestal the effigies of King Charles the Second railed in with iron spikes. There is alsoe at the Bridge a Great Monument[10] of stone worke (as is the Exchange) this is of a great height 300 stepps up and on the top gives the view of the whole town; this was sett up in memory of Gods putting a check to the rageing flame which by the plotts and contrivance of the Papists was lighted; there is a large inscription on it all round mentioning it, and alsoe of the Popish Plott and the Gun Powder Treason and all by the Papists.

The Bridge[11] is a stately building all stone with 18 arches most of them bigg enough to admit a large barge to pass it; its so broade that two coaches drives a breast, and there is on each side houses and shopps just like any large streete in the Citty, of which there are many and well built, even and lofty, most has 5 if not 6 degrees; most of the Halls belonging to

[9] The Royal Exchange was built 1669–70 on the north side of Cornhill, at a cost of £80,000, and burnt down in 1838. The statue of Charles II by Grinling Gibbons survived the fire. According to Misson "they justly observe that this is the richest spot of ground for its bigness in the whole world, since it contains but three-quarters of an acre, or very little more, and brings in an annual revenue of 50,000 livres, or 4,000 pounds sterling". (Op. cit., 76.)

[10] The Monument is 202 feet high. The inscription attributing the Great Fire to the Papists was erased by James II, but restored and cut deeper after the Revolution. Ned Ward alleges that the City authorities embezzled £2,000 out of the £3,000 subscribed, and he therefore exclaims " 'tis a Monument to the City's shame, the orphans' grief, the Protestants' pride and the Papists' scandal, and only serves as a high-crowned hat, to cover the head of the old fellow that shows it." (*The London Spy*, ed. Hayward, p. 47.)

[11] Some houses on London Bridge had been burnt in the Great Fire, and had been replaced. The Bridge itself dated from *c.* 1200 and had nineteen arches. The houses survived till 1758.

each Company are large and magnificent buildings, as alsoe
the Churches very fine and lofty of stone work. The greate
Cathedrall is St. Pauls which was a vast building but burnt
by fire, has since by the Citty been built up, or rather a tax
on coales[12] which brings all to pay for it in London; it now
is almost finish'd and very magnificent, the Quire with
curious carved work in wood; the Arch Bishops seate and
the Bishop of Londons and Lord Majors is very finely
carv'd and adorned, the alter alsoe with velvet and gold; on
the right side is placed a large crimson velvet elbow chaire
which is for the Dean; this is all finished (with a sweet
organ) but the body of the church which is to be closed on
the top with a large Cupilo[13] is not quite done.

There was formerly in the Citty severall houses of the
noblemens with large gardens and out houses and great
attendances, but of late are pulled down and built into
streetes and squares and called by the names of the noble-
men, and this is the practise by almost all even just to
the Court excepting one or two;[14] Northumberland[15] and
Bedford House,[16] and Lord Mountagues house[17] indeed has
been new built and is very fine; one roome in the middle of
the building is of a surpriseing height curiously painted and
very large, yet soe contrived that speake very low to the

[12] The coal tax (1s. 6d. a chaldron) was lucrative. Defoe claimed that
London consumed three-quarters of a million tons a year and that the
colliers were arriving 500–700 at a time. (Op. cit., i, 346.) These figures
appear to be only a slight exaggeration. (See Nef, *Rise of the British Coal
Industry*, ii, 381–2.)

[13] The Choir of St. Paul's was opened for service in December, 1697; the
Dome was completed in 1710 and the whole Cathedral reported finished in
1717. The dilatoriness of the workmen in the later stages became notorious.
(See Ned Ward, op. cit., passim.) When Vanbrugh asked the Duchess of
Marlborough for £300 a year for seeing to the maintenance of Blenheim, she
said that Wren had been "content to be dragged up in a basket three or four
times a week to the top of St. Paul's, and at a great hazard, for £200 a year".

[14] Most had ceased to live there but a notable exception had been Shaftesbury, who lived in Aldersgate Street, where he was in touch with his two
allies, the City merchants and the London mob.

[15] In Northumberland Avenue, now demolished; it belonged in this period
to the "Proud Duke" of Somerset through his marriage to the heiress of the
Percies.

[16] It had been pulled down by Macky's time. (Op. cit. i, 202.)

[17] On the present site of the British Museum. It was burnt down in 1685,
and rebuilt by the French architect Puget.

wall or wanscoate in one corner and it should be heard with
advantage in the very opposite corner across—this I heard
Myself.

2. WESTMINSTER AND THE ROYAL FUNERALS AND CORONATIONS

AND THIS leads me to the Citty of Westminster in which are
many of these Noblemens houses built into very fine squares;
the Kings pallace was a most magnificent building all of
freestone, with appartments suiteable to the court of a King,
in which was a large roome called the Banqueting-roome
which was fitted for and used in all publick solemnityes and
audiences of ambassadours etc.; this is the only thing left
of the vast building which by accident or carelessness, if not
designe, has laid it in ashes[1] together with exceeding rich
furniture of antiquity, as alsoe the greate and good Queen
Mary's Closet and curious treasures; this has all along the
prospect of the Thames on one side and a large Parke on the
other, walled in, which is full of very fine walkes and rowes
of trees, ponds and curious birds, deer and some fine cows;
in this Parke stands another pallace, St. James, which is very
well and was built for some of the royal familly as the Duke
of Yorke or Prince of Wales; there is at Whitehall in the
privy garden a large pond with a spout of water of a vast
height; this of St. James is little but daily building adding
may make it greate; there is alsoe one Nobleman's house in
this, Parke House,[2] which is a very curious building.

[1] Whitehall Palace was burnt on January 2nd, 1698 (see Evelyn, *Diary*)
supposedly through the carelessness of a Dutch chambermaid. The banqueting hall by Inigo Jones alone survived. Misson had called the old palace
nothing but "a great heap of bricks and a confus'd parcel of ordinary houses"
(op. cit., 360) and the Swiss Muralt "a heap of ill-built houses which were not
intended to join" (*Letters*, trans. 1726, p. 76) while the Italian courtiers of
Cosimo de Medici had found "nothing in its exterior from which you could
suppose it to be the habitation of the king". (*Travels of Cosmo III*, 367.)

[2] In a marginal note, written after the main account was complete, Celia
Fiennes says "Arlington, now the Duke of Buckinghams being new built".
Arlington House was pulled down in 1703 and replaced by Buckingham
House, which in turn was replaced by Buckingham Palace. John Sheffield,
Earl of Mulgrave and Marquis of Normanby, was only created Duke of
Buckingham in March, 1703.

Just by this Parke you enter another much larger, Hide-Parke, which is for rideing on horseback but mostly for the coaches, there being a Ring[3] railed in, round which a gravel way that would admitt of twelve if not more rowes of coaches, which the Gentry to take the aire and see each other comes and drives round and round; one row going contrary to each other affords a pleasing diversion; the rest of the Parke is green and full of deer, there are large ponds with fish and fowle; the whole length of this Parke there is a high causey of a good breadth, 3 coaches may pass, and on each side are rowes of posts on which are Glasses—cases for Lamps which are lighted in the evening[4] and appeares very fine as well as safe for the passenger. This is only a private roade the King had which reaches to Kensington, where for aire our great King William bought a house[5] and fitted it for a retirement with pretty gardens; besides these the King has a pallace in the Strand[6] with fine gardens all to the Thames river, this appertaines to the Queen Dowager while she lives—in this place was that cruel barbarous Murder of Sir Edmund Berry Godfrey by the Papists.[7]

Westminster is remarkable for haveing in it the ancient large Abbey which is a most magnificent building of stone finely graved, and within is adorned with severall monu-

[3] The "Ring" in Hyde Park was a great resort for the fashionable. "Jorevin de Rocheford" called it "the common walk and jaunt for the coaches of London, where we plainly perceive that the English ladies are very handsome, and that they know it very well" (*Description of England* in Grose *Antiq. Repert.* iv, 566). "When", wrote Misson, "they have turn'd for some time round one way, they face about and turn t'other. So rowls the World." (Op. cit., 126.) Cf. *Grammont's Memoirs*, chap. vii.

[4] A scheme, invented by Edward Heming in 1684 for lighting London with a lamp outside every tenth house, was theoretically in operation. (See Misson, op. cit., 172, cf. Macaulay, *History*, ed. 1849 i. 361.) But the causeway to Kensington was the only road that was actually well lighted. (Macky, op. cit., i, 87–8.)

[5] The germ of Kensington Palace. King William had to sleep away from London's coal-smoke because of his asthma. (Macky, op. cit., i, 87; Muralt, op. cit., 77.)

[6] Old Somerset House built by Protector Somerset. The Queen Mother was still Catharine of Braganza, who lived till 1705, but had not resided in England since 1693.

[7] Sir E. B. Godfrey was actually found dead on Primrose Hill, but the body was taken to Somerset House, to become the pivot of the "Popish Plot".

ments of our Kings and Queens and great personages; in
Harry the Sevenths Chapple layes our great and good as well
as ever glorious King William, and Queen Mary his Royal
Consort and joinctly on the throne of these kingdoms,
whome noe tyme can ever obliterate the memory of, their
being Englands deliverers in Gods hands from popery and
slavery which King James by the King of Frances power
was involving us in.

This Abby alsoe is the place where the sollemnityes of the
Kings interrments and corronations are performed, of which
shall give a perticular: at the Death of a Prince, which I have
been a mournfull spectator or hearer of two of the most
renowned that ever was, King William and Queen Marys;[8]
the Queen dying before the King he omitted noe ceremony
of respect to her memory and remains, which lay in State
in Whitehall in a bed of purple velvet all open, the cannopy
the same with rich gold fring, the middle being the armes
of England curiously painted and gilt, the head piece embroyder'd richly with a crown and cyphers of her name, a
cusheon of purple velvet at the head on which was the
Imperiall Crown and Scepter and Globe, and at the feete
another such a cusheon with the Sword and Gauntlets, on
the corps which was rowled in lead, and over it a coffin
cover'd with purple velvet with the crown, and gilt in
moldings very curious; a pall on all of a very rich tissue of
gold and silver, ruffled round about with purple velvet
which hung down on the ground, which was a halfe pace
[dais] railed as the manner of the princes beds are; this in a
roome hung with purple velvet, full of large wax tapers, and
at the 4 corners of the bed stood 4 of the Ladyes of the Bed
Chamber—Countesses—with vailes; these were at severall
tymes relieved by others of the same.

The anty chamber hung with purple cloth, and there
attended four of the Maids of Honnour, all in vailes, and the
Gentlemen of the Bed Chamber; pages [in] another roome

[8] William died March 10th, 1702; Mary died December 28th, 1694. Her
lying-in-state was on February 21st and 22nd, 1695, and her funeral on
March 5th, 1695.

all in black, the staires all below the same. The Queen dyeing while the Parliament sate, the King gave mourning to them (500) and cloakes, which attended thus: their Speaker haveing his traine bore up, then the Lord Major the same, and attended by the Aldermen and officers all in black, and the Judges; then the officers of the Houshold, then the Guards, then the Gentleman Master of the Horse led the Queens led horse cover'd up with purple velvet; next came the open chariot made as the bed was, the cannopy the same all purple velvet, a high arch'd teister ruffled, with the rich fring and pall, which was supported by six of the first Dukes of the Realme that were not in office; this chariot was drawn by the Queens own 6 horses covered up with purple velvet and at the head and feete was laid the emblems of her dignity, the Crown and Scepter on a cushion at the head, and Globe and the Sword and Gauntlets at the feete; after which the first Dutchess in England, Dutchess of Summerset, as chief mourner walked being supported by these Lords, the Lord President of the Councill and the Lord Privy Seale, she haveing a vaile over her face, and her traine of 6 yards length being bore up by the next Dutches assisted by four young ladyes; after which two and two the Ladies followed and Lords, all long traines according to their ranke, the Bishops likewise, all on foote on black cloth strained on boards, from Whitehall to Westminster Abby where was a sermon, in which tyme the body of the Queen was reposed in a masulium [mausoleum] in form of a bed with black velvet and silver fringe round, and hanging in arches, and at the four corners was tapers and in the middle a bason supported by cupids or cherubims shoulders, in which was one entire great lamp burning the whole tyme.

Then after the service of burial which is done with solemn and mournfull musick and singing, the sound of a drum unbraced, the breakeing of all the white staves of those that were the officers of the Queen, and flinging in the keys of the rest of the offices devoted by that badge into the tomb; they seale it up and soe returne in same order they went. There is allwayes a High Steward made for all solemnityes of the

Kings and Queens, and he is only soe for that day, and he goes just before the led horse. The pages also lead all the horses that draws the chariot, and the Yeaumen of the Guard walks on each side, and the Gentlemen Pensioners, the guards on horseback being set in ranke on each side all the way. This is the manner of publick funeralls but if it be Kings then the ladyes attend not.

The next Ceremonys is the crowning the Kings and Queens of England which is done in this manner as I have seen it: the Prince by letters summons all the Nobility to be ready to attend them such a day—its usually on St. Georges Day— by the Earle Marshall at Westminster Hall, another greate building which containes the Parliament Houses [and] the Courts of Justice and Requests, all which shall describe hereafter. But as I said they being come to this Westminster Hall, the Dean of Westminster Abbey with Prebends etc. comes with the Crown, Scepter, Swords and Orb and all the Regalias, it being in their custody, which are all put on the table; the Prince does appoynt these all to be carryed by severall Lords; then there being blew cloth spread from the Hall to the Abby (which is all railed in and lined with foote and horse guards) the Procession beginns thus: first four drums two and two, as is the whole procession, these beate the March; then the 6 Chancery Clerkes, then the Chaplaines that have Dignityes, then the Aldermen of London and the Masters in Chancery, the Solicitor Generall, the Attorney General, then the Gentlemen of the Privy Chamber; next the Judges, then the Children of the Kings Chappel, then the Choir of Westminster, then the Gentlemen of the Chapple; next the Prebends of Westminster, then the Master of the Jewel House, then goes the Privy Councellors that are not Peers of the realme, then two Pursuivants goes.

Next them goes the Barronesses in crimson velvet robes lined with earmine, and cut waved in a long traine lined with white sarsnet, the sleeves were open to the shoulder, tyed up there with silver cords and tassells hanging down to the wast, the sleeves being fringed with silver, under which fine point or lace sleeves and ruffles, with gloves laced or with ribon gold and white, their peticoates were white, some tissue laced with gold or silver, and their stomatchers some were all diamonds; over all they had mantles of the same crimson velvet lined with earmine and fastened to the shoulder, on which there was a broad earmine like a cape reaching to the waste powder'd with rowes according to their degree, the Barroness 2 rows, the Viscountess 2 rows and halfe, the Countesses 3 rowes, the Marchoness 3 rows and a halfe, the Dutchesses 4 rows, the Queen 6; these all having long traines suiteable to their robes and were in length as their degree: the Barronesses had their traines 2 yards and a quarter drawing on the ground, the Viscountess 2 yards and halfe, the Marchionesses 2 yards 3 quarters, the Dutchess 3 yards drawing on the ground. Their heads were dress'd with much haire and long locks full of diamonds—some perfect peakes of bows of diamonds as was the Countess of Pembrook—their heads so dress'd as a space left for their coronets to be set, all the rest is filled with haire, jewells and gold, and white small ribon, or gold thinn lace, in form of a peake, and gold gause on their rowles; they have also diamond necklaces and jewels on their habitts. Each carry their corronets in their hands which does also distinguish their dignityes: the Barrons is a velvet cap with a coronet of gold, with six great pearles or what resembles them a white gilding in that form; the Viscounts coronet is a gold set with 16 pearles of like sort set very close each other; the Earles coronet is of gold with spikes, on the tops of which are laid pearles which stands at a distance, and have leaves at the frame; the Marquess's coronet is gold alsoe with spikes of leaves of the same at distances, between which are those pearles, much lower just proceeding from the frame; the Dukes are a double row of leaves, the one standing up at distances, the others between, low by the frame.

The Dukes, Marquess's, Earles, Viscounts, and Barrons are differenced as the ladyes are by their rows of earmine on their mantles—they all being clad with rich vests under their robes, and trimm'd gloves of lace or fringe, fine linnen, and carry their coronets in their hands; only those that are

Knights of the Garter weare a chaine of gold SS on their shoulders upon their earmine cape, and have their George hanging to it, their Starr on the breast of their robes and a diamond Garter on their leg with blew ribon.

In this manner habited proceeds the Barronesses and Barrons; then the Bishops that sit in the Parliament as peeres, their habit is lawn sleeves and black, their capps are flatt like a 4 square trencher put on cornerwise; after which went a Pursuivant, then in same order the Viscountesses and next the Viscounts; then two Heraulds, then in same order the Countesses and next the Earles; then a Herauld, then in the same order the Marchionesses, next the Marquisses; then two Heraulds, then in the same order the Dutchesses, next them the Dukes, then two Kings at Armes, after which the Lord Privy Seale, next him Lord President of the Councill; then the Archbishops which are esteemed in higher rank than the Dukes, then a Duke which is of the Royal family with their traine bore up (Prince George of Denmarke being Royal Consort to Queen Ann walked so, haveing his traine bore by the Vice-Chamberlaine, the Prince is Duke of Cumberland which is the first Duke) next goe two personages in robes of state, but of an antique forme, velvet and earmine with hatts of gold tissues, personateing the two Dukes of Acquitaine and Normandy which belongs to the English Crown.

Next them went the Lord which bore St. Edmunds Staff, with a Lord that bore the Gold Spurrs, another Lord with the Scepter Royal, 3 other Lords following with the Sword of Justice, the Curtana Sword of Mercy, and another poynted sword; next which Sir Garter King at Armes between my Lord Major and the Usher of the Black Rod; (these Heraulds dress in coates full of the Kings armes all about with gildings, and hang short with long sleeves and sleeves hanging behind alsoe); next the Lord High Chamberlaine single, then next an Earle beares the Sword of State between the Earle Marshall and the Lord High Constable, made for that dayes solemnity; next goes an Earle beareing the Scepter of the Dove, next that a Duke carrying the Globe Orb, next went a Duke with the Crown, which must be Lord High Steward for that dayes solemnity, next which went a Bishop with the Bible between two other Bishops that carryed the Pattent and the Challice, which last appertaines to the Dean of Westminster (who is always a Bishop)[9] to carry.

Next this the cannopys, and in case there is a King then his Consort goes before him in this manner, under a cannopy of cloth of gold borne up by 8 Barrons of the Cinque Ports, and is supported by two Bishops, and her coronet or crown is alsoe carryed by a Lord before, and alsoe a silver rod by another Lord, which when she returns she holds in one hand, and the little scepter. Her traine is bore up by the first Duchess of the Realme assisted by 4 maiden daughters of Earles, and her robes ought to be only crimson velvet (but King James's Queen would have purple) but never changes them as doth a Queen that is regent in her self the principal, as Queen Ann and her sister Queen Mary joinct in the throne with King William. All which in some things makes a difference as shall show, for the Queen Consort (as King James's Queen was) was not anoynted nor sworne unless as a subject to the King, and walked thus before him, after which the King came under another cannopy of gold tissue supported by 8 more of the Barrons of the Cinque-Ports; he leaned on two Bishops, his traine borne up by the Lord which is Master of his Robes assisted by four Lords sonns— these cannopyes have silver staves for each person to hold them up by.

In the case of King William and Queen Mary that were set joynctly on the throne, anoynted both and sworne by the coronation oath, they likewise walked both under one of these canopyes, made very large, supported by the 16 Barrons; and on the outside of each went a Bishop on whome they leaned, leading each other; and their traines were bore, the Kings by the Lord which is Master of the Robes, the Queen by the first Dutchess and young ladies; and soe their throne was entire two seates and their cannopyes one at the

---

[9] In Celia Fiennes' day the Deanery of Westminster was held in conjunction with the Bishopric of Rochester.

table; but now as in case of our present Majesty Queen Ann I saw her thus; her cannopy was large bore by the sixteen, and she because of lameness of the gout had an elbow chaire of crimson velvet with a low back, by which meanes her mantle and robe was cast over it and bore by the Lord Master of the Robes and the first Dutchess, with 4 maiden ladies, Earles daughters, on each side, richly dress'd in cloth of gold or silver, laced with the same, [and] long traines, dressed in their haire full of jewells; after which followed four of the Ladies of the Bedchamber as were not Peeresses, in such gowns of cloth of gold or silver laced, with long traines, richly dress'd in fine linnen, and jewells in their hair, and embroider'd on their gowns. The Queens traine was 6 yards long, the mantle suitable of crimson velvet with earmine as the other of the nobility, only the rowes of powdering exceeded, being six rows of powdering; her robe under was of gold tissue, very rich embroydery of jewells about it, her peticoate the same of gold tissue with gold and silver lace, between rowes of diamonds embroyder'd, her linnen fine; the Queen being principall of the Order of the Garter had a row of Gold SS about her shoulders, the Georges which are allwayes set with diamonds and tyed with a blew ribon; her head was well dress'd with diamonds mixed in the haire which at the least motion brill'd and flamed; she wore a crimson velvet cap with earmine under the circlet, which was set with diamonds, and on the middle a sprig of diamond drops transparent hung in form of a plume of feathers, for this cap is the Prince of Wales's Cap, which, till after the coronation that makes them legall king or queen they weare.

Thus to the Quire doore she came, then leaveing the cannopy (the chaire she left at the Abby doore) she is conducted to the Alter, which was finely deck'd with gold tissue carpet and fine linnen, on the top all the plaite of the Abby set, the velvet cushions to place the Crown and all the Regallias on; she made her offering at the Alter, a pound weight or wedge of gold. Here the Dean of Westminster and the Prebends which assists the Archbishop in the cerimonyes are arrayed in very rich coapes and mitres, black velvet embroyder'd with gold starrs, or else tissue of gold and silver. Then the Littany and prayers are sung and repeated by two Bishops, with a small organ, then the Queen, being seated on a green velvet chair faceing the pulpit, attends the tyme of the sermon, which was by the Archbishop of York; which being ended the Queen arose and returned thanks for the Archbishops sermon; [she] is shewed to the people by saying a form, Will you take this to be your Souveraigne to be over you?—thus I saw the Queen turn her face to the four sides of the church, then the coronation oath is repeated to her, which she distinctly answered each article, which oath is very large in three articles, relateing to all priviledges of the Church and State to which she promised to be the security and to maintaine all to us; then she kiss'd the Bible, then a Bible was presented to her to maintaine the true Protestant religion.

Then she being on a little throne by the Alter, cover'd all with cloth of gold, she has the Spurrs of Gold brought her and they toutch her heele, then the Sword of State is presented her which she offers up on the alter, which a Lord appoynted for it redeemes the sword for 100 shillings, and draws it out and beares it naked all the day; after the other Swords are brought and presented her, which she delivers to the several officers, then the Ring is put on her finger to witness she is married to the Kingdom, then the Orb I saw brought and presented to her and the Scepters. Then she was anoynted in this manner: there was a cloth of silver twilight embroyder'd, held a little shaddowing over her head; I saw the Bishop bring the oyle in a spoone, soe annoynted the palmes of her hands, her breast and her forehead, last of all the top of her head, haveing taken off the Prince of Wales's Cap and the haire being cutt off close at the top, the oyle was poured on and with a fine cloth all dryed againe.[10] Then last of all the Archbishops held the Crown over her head, which

[10] William III had been reduced to greater nudity. "They took off his peruke, his robe, and his wastecoat; and as he was now in his shirt quite to the waste, some of the gentlemen of his Privy Chamber held up a Cloth of Gold to keep him from the cold," (Misson, op. cit., 53.)

Crown was made on purpose for this cerimony vastly rich in diamonds, the borders and the globe part very thick sett with vast diamonds, the cross on the top with all diamonds which flamed at the least motion; (this is worth a vast summe, but being only made for this cerimony and pulled to pieces againe, its only soe much for the hire of such jewells that made it); this I saw was fix'd on the Queens head with Huzza's and sound of Drumms Trumpets and Gunns, and at the same tyme all the Peeres and Peeresses put on their coronets on their heads—there are divers forms of speech that belong to each cerimony.

The Queen after this goes to the Alter and there I saw her receive the Sacrament, I saw the Deane bring her the bread and wine; then she is conducted with her Crown on, her Globe and Scepter in her hand, and seated on the Royal throne of the Kingdom which is of gold finely wrought, high back and armes set on a theatre of severall steps, assent rises on four sides to it; she being thus seated is followed with a second Huzza and sound of Drums and Trumpets and Gunns, then all the Lords and Bishops pay their homage to her; the eldest of each ranke swears fidelity to her in his own name and in the name of all his ranck; they all singly come and touch her Crown and some kiss her right cheeke—they may all do soe—she kisses the Bishops. All this while anthems are sung and the Medals are cast about by the Treasurer of the Houshold; after which the Queen arose and went and made her second offering, sate down on the throne on which she was annoynted and crown'd; thereafter an anthem is sung proper for the tyme, after which the Queen retired into King Edwards Chappel to private prayer.

Which being ended, and her crimson velvet mantle being taken off and one of purple velvet made just the same put on, in the same manner they returned, each one in his station, only the Lords that carryed the Regalias now tooke their places as peers with the rest; the Queen walked to the doore of the Abby with obligeing lookes and bows to all that saluted her and were spectatours, which were prodigious numbers in scaffolds built in the Abbey and all the streetes on each side reaching to Westminster Hall, where the Queen againe quitted her chaire which was carryed by four men; the whole procession being, both going and comeing, attended by the Gentlemen Pensioners clad in scarlet cloth with gold lace, holding halberds with gold tops like pick-axes; these make a lane for the Queen to pass, and follow two and two, next them the Groomes of the Bed Chamber, then the Captaine of the guards went between the Captaine of the pensioners band and the Captaine of the yeaumen, and were attended by their officers and yeamen.

The Queen being come up to her table, which was on a great rise of stepps, she was seated on her throne which was under a fine cannopy. When King James was crown'd he sate soe and at his left hand sate his Queen under another cannopy, but King William and Queen Mary being both principalls sate under one large cannopy on one large throne; but our present Queen should have sate alone, as she did in the upper end under the cannopy, but she sent and did invite Prince George her Consort to dine with her; so he came and at her request tooke his seate at her left hand without the cannopy. The first course was served in just before the Queen came in; when that was taken away the second was served in, being ushered in by the Earle Marshall, Lord High Steward, and Lord High Chamberlaine on horseback, their horses being finely dress'd and managed, and the Cookes came up with their point aprons and towells about their shoulders of poynt;[11] after which comes up the Lord High Steward againe on horseback, with the other two Lords, and acquaints the King or Queen there is their Champion without, ready to encounter or combate with any that should pretend to dispute their legal title to the Crown of these Kingdomes, after which he is conducted in on horseback by the Earle Marshall and the Lord High Steward, and they come up to the stepps of the throne, and there the Champion (all dress'd in armour cap-a-pe) declares his readyness to combate with any that should oppose the Right of their Majestyes, and there upon throws down his guantlet which

[11] Lace made with a needle, not with bobbins.

is giving challenge, after which the King or Queen drinks to him in a gold cup with a cover, the same which is carryed to the Champion and he drinks, and then he retires back and carrys it away, being his due, as is the best horse in the kings stable, the best suite of armour in the armory—this belongs to Sir John Dimmocks familly[12] that hath a yearly salery from the Crown—my Lord Major here officiates as the Kings Butler, and hath for a reward such another cup of gold, covered; and thus the ceremony ends and they all retire; Westminster Hall is as full of spectatours sitting on scaffolds on each side, under which are severall long tables spread and full of all varietyes prepared for the Lords and Ladies, others for the Judges, Aldermen etc.

When there is a Rideing Coronation they proceed on from the Abbey when a King is crowned, all on horseback thro' the Citty in the same order as at the Entry at the Peace, quite to the Tower, all richly dress'd and their horses with fine trappings, led on both sides by each Lords pages; and when its a King only, then only the Lords attend, as in the Coronation of King Charles the Second, but at Queen Elizabeths the Ladies alsoe attended to the Tower, which is at the utmost extremity of the Citty of London, where the Governour presents the King with the Keyes which he returns againe and after some other cerimonyes and makeing some Knights of the Bath—either six or eight I cannot tell which; these are an order that prefferr such a knight above all other knights, but is not so high as a Barronet and it alsoe expires at their death, descending not to the son; they wear a scarlet ribon round their shoulders, athwart the right shoulder like a belt; then they all return back to the pallace; usually the Rideing Coronation holds two dayes.

The Tower is built just by the Thames, thereon many gunns are placed all round, its built of free stone, four towers; in one is the amunition and powder, called the White Tower, which is kept very secure with 6 keyes which are kept by six persons; in another part the Coynage is, where they refine, melt, form, stamp and engrave all the money, which is

[12] It still does.

304

managed by severall over which there is the Comptroler of the Mint; in another part is kept severall lyons which are named by the names of the kings, and it has been observ'd that when a king has dyed the lion of the name has alsoe dyed; there are other strange creatures kept there, leopards, eagles etc. which have been brought from forreign parts;[13] in another place is kept the Crowns and all the Regalias, as orb, scepters, swords; the Crown that is made on purpose to crown a prince is pulled to pieces againe, and they only reserve an old large crown of King Harry the Seventh in form of a ducall coronet, and the Crown which is used for the passing of bills, of which here after; this hath large pearles on the cross, and an emerauld on the top of the head, which closes the bands which goes every way of the sides to the round frame full of diamonds and saphyr's and rubies, which the frame at the bottom is also enchased with; this large emerauld is as bigg as an egg all transparent and well cut; the Globe is alsoe sett with diamonds representing the lines on the celestial globe; the middle or body of the Tower is full of armour of all sorts and placed in each roome with great curiosity like a furniture on the walls and kept very bright and fine.

[13] The Tower Zoo was kept till 1834 where the Refreshment Rooms are now.

3. THE COURTS OF JUSTICE

And now I shall return to the Hall att Westminster where are all the Courts of Justice kept. There are severall parts out of the Hall for the Court of the Kings Bench for tryal of all causes by jurys (Grand Juryes and Petty Jurys) to manage which there is a Lord Chief Justice and three other Judges his assistants, where matters are heard by Councellors; attornys and solicitors are the under officers which prepare the breviates [briefs] and buissness into form, for those lawyers that are Councellors to plead the cause in the Court; all these formerly were but few in number, when buissness was not delayed but brought to a quick issue and persons had matters decided quicker, but now they are increased extreamly and consequently buisness lengthened out for their profit.

There is alsoe another Court of the Common Pleas, to which is another Chiefe Justice, the first is call'd the Lord Chiefe Justice of the Kings Bench Court, the other the Lord Chiefe Justice of the Common Pleas—he hath alsoe three Judges assistants; this Court is in something the same nature managed as the former, only the matters of life and death are not here tryed or determined, that belongs to the Kings Bench. There is alsoe the Exchequer Chamber which is another Court managed by a Lord Chiefe Baron and 3 other Barrons assistants, which are all judges, and all first sergeants, and in this manner are fitted, having been entred at such an age into any of the Inns of Court of which there are many in the town, Lincolns-Inn, Grays-Inn, Furnifulls-Inn, Clemens Inn, Cliffords-Inn and others.

The Temples likewise are such, where they are students in the law and goe to hear causes and are trained up in that learning which is grounded on our Laws, the Magna Charta Law of the whole kingdom by which all matters are or may be decided; after soe many yeares studdy and being thus entred they are called to the barr—that is, to plead as Councellors and Barristers in these Courts, and out of such that have been thus Barristers many yeares they commence Serjeants, and are made in this manner the first day of a terme; they walk two and two in their gowns from the Temple to Westminster Hall where each that is designed for Serjeants stand with their back to the Barr of the Court at a little distance, the puny [puisne] judge on the Bench sayes to the Lord Chief Justice, my Lord I think I spye a Brother; the Lord Chief Justice replies, truly Brother I thinke its soe indeed, send and bring him up to be examined whether capable or well quallify'd; which is done, and after severall questions he is sworn and has a coiffe put on his head, which is a black satten cap with a white lace or edge round the bottom, and thus he is received into their number and soe returned; the first year he weares a two coloured gowne, tauny one half and purple the other, so does his servants. They have a feast and pay their fees, which is considerable, all to maintain the Court.

Out of such as are Sergeants the King makes Judges and gives them salleryes; all the Judges doe weare scarlet robes lined with furr; these twelve Judges sitt in the House of Lords on wooll packs, not as peers but as councellors to informe the House of what is their former Laws, and to decide matters that come before them if relating to the Law, and soe are only their officers and cannot put on their caps without permission of the Lords.

There is alsoe another Court for justice which is called the Court of Equity or Chancery—the other Courts properly judge of the matters of right by Law, this, as to the Equitty of it—which is managed by a Lord Chancellor or a Lord Keeper, which is not in soe high a station nor at so vast expence, but answers the ends of the other as to the buissness—[he] is called Lord Keeper because he keepes the Great Seale of England which makes all authentick that passes it; this sometymes is managed in commision by three, but many tymes by one single person, he allwayes sitts in the House of Lords alsoe and is the Speaker of the House of Lords; under him there is the Master of the Roles [Rolls] which is his deputy and in the others absence acts in the Court as Chiefe; this Court keeps all the records and statutes; there are two registers belongs to it with six Masters which are alsoe the under justices, and six clerks which have all their respective offices and enter all things; under them is the 60 clerks and other under writers.

This formerly was the best Court to relieve the subject but now is as corrupt as any and as dilatory; the causes in the Chancery are heard and refferr'd to some of the Masters and they report the matter againe, and soe from the notion of this being a Court of Equitty and so gives liberty for persons to make all the allegation and reasons in their cause, which much delayes the dispatch, which formerly was of a very good advantage to prevent a huddling up a cause without allowing tyme for the partys to produce their evidences or right, but now by that meanes is soe ill managed that it admitts of heareing, reheareing, over and over on the least motion of the contrary party, that will pretend to offer new reason, matter for delaying judgment, that by this it accrues great advantage to the Lawyers that have all their fees each motion, and may be so continued many yeares to sometyme the ruin of the plaintiffs and deffendants; a small gratuiety obteine an order to delay till the next terme and so to another.

There are four termes in a yeare, one at Easter, another at Midsumer, and at Michael-mas, and Candle-mass, at which tymes these Courts of Justice are open for tryal of the Causes belonging to their Courts, and holds a fortnight or more, one three weekes, another a month, one 5 weekes; but there are sealeing dayes which hold much longer and this between Easter and Midsumer terme joyns the tymes; the last terme is the shortest but the seales hold longer; after this is the Long Vacation being the heate of the weather and tyme of harvest,[1] in which tyme alsoe are the Assizes in all the Countys in England; for at the end of the Midsummer terme the Judges takes the Circuites assigned each, usual the Lord Chiefe Justice of England, which is of the Kings Bench, chuses the Home Circuit which is the County adjacent all about London, which is a less fatigue and more easily perform'd; two judges must goe in each Circuite and in all places the one sitts on the Bench of Life and Death, the other on buisness de-nise-prises [nisi prius], and soe they exchange in all the places they come, the judge that was on the Life and Death at one County, in the next takes the barr of the nais prisse [nisi prius] and so on. There is one called the Northern Circuit which is a long one and takes in Wales; there is the Western Circuite alsoe: this takes up 6 of the 12 Judges and Barrons.

But all this while there must be two at least left in London to heare and attend the sessions of the Old Bayly which is

---

[1] The Inns of Court term, like that of the Universities, ends in time for the young men to go home and help with the hay harvest. The Long Vacation lasts until the corn harvest is safely in.

kept once a month, both of Life and Death and Common Pleas: In all these sessions at the Old Bayly the Lord Major is the judge and sitts as such, but leaves the management of the Law to the Chiefe Justice or Judges which ought to be two; there is the Recorder of the Citty also (another justice) who after the judge has summon'd the evidence does alsoe summ it up, and this is in all the tryals at the Kings Bench alsoe, here the Sword Bearer is an officer alsoe and Common Cryer, and alsoe the two Sherriffs attends, they impanell the Jury and their office is so necessary that at the death of a Sherriff (as happened last yeare) the buissness of the terme happening then stood still till another was chosen and sworne. The Recorder of the Citty is allwayes knighted and soe is the Chamberlaine of the Citty.

Now in the Assizes in all the Countyes of England, the Sherriff of the County comes to the edge of the County and receives the Judges from the hand of the Sherriff of the next County, and conducts him to the County town attended with the Gentry; and there is a large house in the town hired for that tyme for the Judge, and all the Sherriffs officers attends him, and he in person; alsoe he sends the Judge a present, the first night, of meate and wine and gives him one dinner; its usual that the Judges are entertained most of the tyme by the Bishop, Major [Mayor] and best gentlemen, its seldom they stay more than a weeke in a place unless [they] have great deale of buisness or that one of the Judges should be sick so that the other must supply both barrs one after another. There are Lawyers that allwayes do follow the Judges, some Serjeant which people make use of in their Causes and joyne with them some of their own country lawyers; there are two of these Assizes in a year, the other is in the winter, besides which in each County they have Quarterly Sessions to which all Constables of that precinct repaires, and the titheing men with their presentments and complaints to punish and relieve in petty matters which the Justice of Peace are judges off, and if they have a matter before them beyond their decision they bind them over to the Asizes and there to prosecute them.

The manner of Criminalls punishment after Condemnation: which if it be for fellony or treason their condemnation of the first is to be hanged, and they are drawn in a cart from their prisons (where they had been confined all the tyme after they were taken) I say they are drawn in a cart with their coffin tyed to them and halters about their necks, there is alsoe a Divine with them that is allwayes appointed to be with them in the prison to prepare them for their death by makeing them sencible of their crimes and all their sins, and to confess and repent of them; these do accompany them to the place of execution which is generally through the Citty to a place appoynted for it called Tiburn [Tyburn];[2] there after they have prayed and spoken to the people the Minister does exhort them to repent and to forgive all the world, the Executioner then desires him to pardon him, and so the halter is put on and he is cast off, being hung on a gibbet till dead, then cut down and buried unless it be for murder; then usually his body is hung up in chaines at a cross high road in view of all, to deterre others.

For high treason they are drawn in a sledge to their execution without any coffine, for their condemnation when hang'd to be taken down before quite dead and to be opened; they take out their heart and say, this is the heart of a traytor, and so his body is cutt in quarters and hung up on the top of the great gates of the City, which are the places of their prison, some gate houses for debters, others for

----

[2] Tyburn stood where the Marble Arch is now—thus originating the term " to go West". Misson calls it "about a quarter of a league from the suburbs of London". His description is more gruesome than that of Celia Fiennes. The executioner "gives the horse a lash with his whip, away goes the cart, and there swing my Gentlemen kicking in the air. The hangman does not give himself the trouble to put them out of their pain; but some of their friends or relations do it for them: they pull the dying person by the legs and beat his breast, to dispatch him as soon as possible. The English are people that laugh at the delicacy of other nations, who make it such a mighty matter to be hanged. . . . Sometimes the girls dress in white, with great silk scarves, and carry baskets full of flowers and oranges, scattering these favours all the way they go; but to represent these things as they really are, I must needs own that if a pretty many of these people dress thus gayly and go to it with such an air of indifference, there are others that go slovenly enough, and with very dismal phizzes". (Op. cit., 123-5.) About this time victims began to go to execution dressed in shrouds, to deprive the hangman of their clothes, his perquisite.

fellons and traytors; in case its a woman which is a traytor then she is condemned to be burnt; all at their execution have liberty to speake, and in case they are sencible of and repent of their crimes they do declare it and bewaile it and warne others from doing the like, but if they are hard'nd they persist in the denying it to the last. Now as I said the Law condemns all thus to be executed, but if it be great persons they obtaine leave of the king they may be beheaded, which is done on a scaffold erected on purpose in manner of a stage, and the persons brought in coaches with Ministers do as the former; then when they have ended their prayers and speech they lay down their head on a block and stretch out their bodies; the Executioner strikes off their heads with an ax or sword made on purpose, and if it be for treason take the head and hold it up saying this is the head of a traytor; and such great persons, especially those that can pay well for it, have their heads sewed on againe and so buried.

The Prison in London for great persons is in the Tower where are appartments for that purpose; there is in all the County towns Jailes maintained at the publick charge, besides which there are houses for correction of lesser faults, as Bride-wells to correct lazy and idle persons and to set them to work, and alsoe stocks and pillorys to punish them for their lesser faults; the Pilory indeed is to punish perjur'd persons, which is a greate crime; there is alsoe whipping, some at a carts taile, and for some crimes they are burnt in the hand or cheeke as a brand of their evil,[3] and if found againe to trans-gress, that marke serves as a greater witness to their con-demnation; some alsoe are banish'd out of the Kings domi-nions dureing life[4] and should such return they must be executed without any other tryal—under which we may speake of out laweryes: a person for treason or fellony ab-sconding into another kingdom, after a process at law by which he is summon'd to come and take his tryal, and he

[3] For thefts of less than one shilling in value.
[4] A euphemism for transportation to the Colonies. Not all the early immigrants to America were Pilgrim Fathers.

refuses, then he is outlaw'd and all his estate forfeited to the King, and if ever he be taken in the Kings dominions he is immediately executed with out any farther tryal; and its usual if such a one be known to be in a kingdom of our allies to make a demand of him by the ambassadour, and such a state takes care either to deliver him up or else to expel him their dominions by proclamation, that none harbour such a one but deliver up to the government.

Here is noe wracks or tortures nor noe slaves made, only such as are banish'd, sometymes its into our forreign plantations there to worke; we have also prisons for debtors and some of which are privilidge places, as the Kings Bench the Marshalsea and Fleete, which persons entring themselves prisoners there cannot further be prosecuted, but continue there prisoners dureing life, and out of the term tymes hire a keeper of the prison to go allwayes with him as a jaylor; but the Chief Master must have good security to produce him every term else he will be lyable to pay his debts, so its only for such as are debtors, and indeed its a sad thing they should be so suffer'd and that there should be places of refuge for such. There is one good act to relieve persons that are confined, it may be, out of malice and spleen to keep them allwayes so, but by this act any such can sue out his Habeas Corpus and soe be brought the first day of the terme either to a tryal or give bail and soe be let out, and so may answere.

Besides this there are in most Lordships, Courts kept, which are Courts Barrons and was at first the only jurisdiction, by each gentleman held, all misdemeanours punished, and by them informed up to the higher courts of Kings Bench or Chancery, and alsoe had all their own privelidges maintained amongst their tennants and neighbours, and consisted of a Court Lite [Leet] also which ran in the same nature with their Session Courts.

These our Laws are esteemed the best in the world, we haveing two distinct parts, one Comon Law which is singular to our nation and are managed in these Sessions, Assizes, Kings Bench, and Common Pleas, and Ex-chequor; the other is the Civil Law which is the only sort of Law in any other Kingdom, of which the Chancery, the Arches which is under the Archbishop and by his appoyntment to the severall Judges of that Court that are all Civillians, matters of equitty, all probats of wills, which in the Arches are made and recorded; this is in a place in the Citty, the Doctors Commons, where is this court of Arches and Prorogative Court is, which consists of Doctors, Chancelours, Proctors, Suragats [Surrogates], which do the offices of Councellours Attorney and Solicitours at Common Law; there are registers also from this at London. All the Bishops courts are kept in each Citty, managed by Chancelours which are lay men, and the Suragats, also the Bishops deputyes, the Proctors, and Parolers, which summons all to it, and there are four in a year in each County; from hence are given out Licenses for marriages, here are the Cannon Laws of the Church explain'd and defended, all Church officers punish'd and examin'd, here are proceeding on information all persons that infringe the Church Rites, and formerly all that were vitious and corrupt in their practices, even of the Clergy also, and receiv'd suspension or some punishment due to the crime, as Excommunication; but evil men and governours corrupt and change wholesome laws to evil, so of late these laws have been put in execution against tender consciences that could not comply to some forms prescrib'd in the Litturgy of the Church of England, and they have been excommunicated; after which they are turned over to the Lay Chancellour and so prosecuted at Common Law, because the Spiritual courts and men will not pretend to use the sword of punishment, but while they have turned its edge thus against the tender consciences scrupleing the forms of worship in the Church of England, they have left punishing the enormous crimes of their parishoners, nay of their Clergy also, to the scandal of Protestants. Indeed blessed be God that since King William and Queen Mary of happy memory weilded the scepter, and Liberty for such Descenters have been establish'd by an Act of Parliament, of which Houses shall now speak of.

313

4. PARLIAMENT AND THE CONSTITUTION

OUR KINGDOM is governed by Laws made and establish'd pursuant to the first Constitutions and Magna-Charta, from which is derived all the Charters full of priviledges to each Corporation in the Kingdom, suiteable to their customs and well being of each; these Laws are made and are not truely authentick if not enacted and pass'd by our three States which is King, Lords and Commons,[1] which can make Laws for all cases provided they are for the good of the whole and do not tend to subvert our originall contract grounded on our Magna Charta or fundamental laws of the land, which Constitution is by all the world esteemed the best, if kept on each ones basis, a tripple foundation, and when the King exerts not his prerogative beyond its limitts to the oppressing his peoples priviledges, nor the people exorbitant and tumultuous in the standing or running up their power and priviledges to cloud and bind up the hands of the prince; but if it goes in an equal and just footeing, the people (whose is the purse and strength) will maintaine the King and his Councellours, and they will do the best offices to the King from the people, and so the King might allwayes reigne in his peoples hearts by love, as well as over them, and they yeild duty and obedience to him, and securely repose in him that should so studdy to preserve them in all their privilidges and trade, which would procure us honour and admiration to the whole world, and continue us too greate for enemyes to invade or molest us, and so great as to have all seeke to be our allies, and those that were so would find a secure trust and faithfull friends in us; but alas! its too sadly to be bemoaned, the best and sweetest wine turns soonest sour, so we by folly faction and wickedness have endeavour'd our own ruin, and were it not for Gods providentiall care and miraculous works we should at this day been a people left

---

[1] The three estates are of course Lords Spiritual, Lords Temporal, and Commons. The mistake made by Celia Fiennes is still almost universal.

to utter dispaire, haveing only the agraveteing thoughts of our once happy Constitution to lament its losse the more.

To go on: the Parliament which in Westminster Hall has appartments, the one for the House of Lords[2] and called the Upper House, where all the Lords which are not Papists and which are of age do sitt in their order on benches covered with scarlet cloth; the Bishops likewise sitt as peers of the realme and have voices in all causes but in bloud,[3] the sanguinary laws and decision thereon; its said they may sitt, but they from their order in the Church alwayes go out, but they first make their claime that they might continue,[4] but all other of the Lords if absent can give their proxy to another Lord and desire him to give his voice in matters debateable in his absence, and any such Lord chuses another that he knows to be of his own sentiments, or should give him account at any case he should differ that may have the absent Lords real consent, which has happened that a Lord has given his own voice one way and the proxy voice another as the absent Lord shall direct, but this is seldome, and this is permitted because sickness or extraordinary buissness of their own, the Kings, or the peoples, may require his absence; now the Lords which are peeres of the realme are born Councellors to the King and are looked on as such; its true tho' at all tymes they may and should give the King their advice, yet the King has power and do make choice of a Privy Councill, which consist of Lords temporall and spirituall, which are the Bishops, and also out of some of the Commons of England which are the Gentry; all Privy Councellors while so are Justices of the Peace in all Countys.

In this House of Lords the judges as I said before sitts but

[2] A marginal note here says "The House of peeres one of the estates in the kingdom", repeating the mistake above.

[3] By Canon Law the bishops could not vote if the sentence might involve death or mutilation. It depended, wrote Misson, "upon a certain ridiculous maxim, that the Church loves not blood". (Op. cit., 20.)

[4] Celia Fiennes originally wrote, "These bishops have noe power to send or leave a proxy in the hand of any other to act or give their voice in their absence, they lose it." She erased this, however, and wrote against it "this a mistake". It was.

have noe vote. The Lord Chancellor or Keeper of the Seale sitts and is Speaker to that house, but if he be noe peer (which sometymes happens and is at this tyme in Right,[5] Lord Keeper of the Seale) then I say he has no voice in any matter and serves them only as their servant or officer, to put questions, to count their voice on their dividing on a matter, to make a speech to them from the King, and to present anything to the King, and he sitts on a wool-pack and just under the throne where the King sitts when there (which is seldome but to pass bills).

On each side of the throne is two stooles, that on the right hand is for the Prince of Wales if any is, that on the left to the first Duke, prince of the blood royal or kings brother that is heir more remote; behind the throne is a place for the noblemens sonns (minors) to be, to give them opportunity to heare and instruct them in the Laws of England; in the middle of the roome is tables with bookes and records, and there sitts the Secretarys of State which are two, these with some under them take the minutes of what is debated and resolved. The Lords do form Law agreable to the Fundamentall Laws in which the judges advise them; they thus form a bill, which being in all poynts examined, all objections answered, and being well amended and passed three tymes, being read and agreed, is carryed down to the Lower House which consists of the Commons of England,[6] chosen by a precept from the Crown to all the Sherriffs of the Countys to chuse amongst themselves two of each Corporation or Burrough, and two for each County which are called Knights of the Shire, to represent them in this assembly; all that are free-holders of a County has a voice to choose; the Corporations and Burroughs chuse by their freemen also, but because of the peculiar customs and priviledges in each place it makes some variation; those that have most of voices which are legal to chuse, the Bailiff or Major of the place or Sherriffs return up to the Crown office, from whence the

---

[5] "Right" is corrected to "Wright" in the fair copy. She means Sir Nathan Wright, Lord Keeper from 1700–1705.

[6] Here a marginal note reads "Second Estate of the House of Commons 500 men is the number". It was actually 513.

precept came, the name of such persons so chosen to sitt in the Parliament.

This was an excellent Constitution and order when kept to its order that none were chosen but the Gentlemen of the shire or town living there, or else the Chiefe of their Corporation that lived there, by which meanes they were fully instructed what was for the weale and good of each place they serv'd for, and so could promote designes for their advantage and trade and represent their grievances to be redress'd; they also know the strength and riches of the nation and soe could with a more equal hand lay the taxes on all answerable to their ability; but instead of this the nation is so corrupted that what with hopes of prefferrment at Court or being skreen'd by their priviledges from paying their debts, which is thus: dureing the sessions or forty dayes before or after, such as are parliament men cannot be arrested or troubled for money they owe (the reason at first was well grounded that these persons were known to be, and in case a troublesome person had money due and had been delay'd by some extraordinary cause, that this troublesome person might find such a one at the Parliament House might lay him in prison and so hinder the buissness of the nation); but this is abused to a great prejudice of the subject, men run out of their estates strive to get into the Parliament to be skreen'd from their creditors; and how can those that are worth little or nothing be good disposers of the kingdom, treasure or priviledges, or stand up for them; but by this there is such bribeing, by debauching by drinke and giving them money, that instead of the parliament men which use to be chosen to be the countrys representatives and servants, to whome they allowed soe much a day for their expences in London from their homes while attending the parliament, that now those that would be parliament men spend prodigious summs of money to be chosen—some to serve for Knights of the Shire have spent 1000 and 1500£, and for Corporation and Burroughs in proportion, so that they come in with design to be bribed by the Court or anybody that has any buisness before them, that so they may be reemburs'd and may gaine more—

some place at least they expect, and these care little for the good of the nation, being for the most part perfect strangers to the places for whome they serve, and consequently to all their circumstances, and so can appeare for none of them to their advantage; indeed its their own gaine they mainly aime and pursue, for they have in their power to form good laws suiteable to the Fundamentall and explanatory of such with additionalls to them, tending to the enlargeing as well as secureing their priviledges; such Laws being brought in manner of a Bill is read three tymes three severall dayes, so as all the members might or should have tyme to heare debate consider and amend it; and every member of this House of Commons that are so chosen and have met and take the oathes required of allegiance, they come up to the House of Lords, where the King meetes them and desires them to chuse a Speaker for themselves out of their own number, which they do and come and present him to the King for his approbation; which done the King makes them a speech and tells them what is requisite to be done relateing to the Crown, to foreign things, if any warre or any breach of peace, any injury from whence, what is necessary to be done thereon, if any want of money which they only can supply, the reasons of its wants, his promise well and faithfully to dispose it; he exhorts them to rectifye disorders in practice and soe dismisses them.

This Speaker of theirs is the Kings officer dureing his being Speaker and has a sallery and must keep a great table; the King gives him one thousand pound presently to fitt him in his equipage, he always goes in coach or a foote haveing a mace carry'd before him, he has the advantage of all bills brought into the House a certainty for each, he has the advantage of all the votes printed, to sell them, he sitts in a chaire above all the rest of the House to give him advantage to see or heare any member that speakes; he is to put all questions, to count the voices of noes and yeas on the division of the House; there are many Comittees in this House as well as in the Lords House, appoynted by the whole to inspect severall buissness, and to form bills on such buissness to

be brought in to the House; if it be a matter of great conse-
quence there may be a Comittee of the whole House which
is only thus, the Speaker leaves his chaire and they resolve
themselves into such a Committee and debate matters, and
for that tyme choose a Chairman for the Committee; then
the Speaker reasumes the chaire and this Chaireman of the
Comittee reports the debate of that Committee to the Speaker
and whole House. When there is a full house, which may be
never was, there is 500 as I said before.

When they have pass'd a Bill thrice through the House with
approbation they send it up to the Lords, and if they pass it
three tymes also without amendment then it is ingross'd,
haveing been pass'd the two States, and so lyes ready to pass
the last which is the Kings consent;[7] but if either the bills
sent down by the Lords are amended by the Comons, and
when brought up to the Lords againe and they like not those
amendments then they cast out the bill, so likewise any bill
sent up by the Commons for the Lords assent in case they
make amendments which the Comons like not then they
cast out their bill; but if each other agree to the amendments
or pass the bills without amendment through both Houses,
then they are engross'd and prepared for the Royal assent,
the third State of our government which is in this manner:
the King sends to the House of Lords to attend him in their
own House, with their robes, which are scarlet cloth with
earmine and rows of earmine with gold galloone on each
row, the rows are encreassed to each dignity; and here the
Bishops weare robes which are scarlet also, but they have
about their neck a large cape which hangs to their waste all
round of a furr that lookes like lambskinns, it hangs like the
capes of the cloakes the shepheards weare in the open plaine
downes. The King enters, or the Queen as now it is—but I
saw King William pass bills, in his royal robes of purple
lined earmine, with rows of earmine, and the Crown on his
head which was the crown I spake of that had great pearles

---

[7] Here a marginal note reads "3rd Estate of the kingdom"—an unortho-
dox description of the royal assent, even as the third and final stage in a bill's
becoming law.

on the cross and saphires rubies and emeraulds—the Scepter in their hand; the Usher of the Black Rod is sent to the House of Comõns to attend the King in the House of Lords, which they do, with their Speaker, that brings up such bills which are so prepared and holds them in his hand, one by one presenting them to the King, who touches them with the Scepter and sayes, "je le veux bien"[8] and so to all of them one by one; which done, if there be any thing necessary to be told them, the King either speakes to them or else orders the Lord Chancellour or Lord Keeper to acquaint them of any thing in the Kings name, if its the Kings pleasure to prorogue them for a few dayes weekes or months; then that putts an end to that session till the tyme prefix'd, and at that tyme they must meete againe without summons, and if they are not to meete so soone, the King issues out a proclaimation that its his pleasure the parliament should be prorogued so much longer; these prorogations allwayes puts an end to all debates and all bills which are not finished and brought the King to pass, so that at their meeteing againe they must begin the things they would have, or were about the last tyme, anew; this prorogation is in the Kings power and is often done for ten dayes only to put a stop to heates and debate in the Houses, and also to put an end to something that is not lik'd by the government; true indeed they may begin the same things at their next meeteing, but if it be for the great and absolute service of the nation they may, but its contrived in another method so as not openly to confront our governours, tho' too often we have seen it in our dayes against our glorious truely great King William, whose wisdom and compassion for our good pass'd it by and forgave it.

Now in some cases the King may and does call the Parliament by a proclaimation to sitt, before the tyme of the prorogation be expired which takes it off; the Parliament does often adjourn themselves, as every night so sometymes for a weeke, but still the Parliament is look'd on as in sitting and so buisness is not interrupted, but goes on from day to day as they appoint it; the King may also adjourn them and the

[8] "Le Roi le veult."

two Houses may be adjourned together, but sometymes they may adjourn seperately, for one may adjourn themselves and the other continue to act within themselves; its also in the Kings power to dissolve the Parliament, which puts a finall end to all their buisness which was not finished and brought to the King to pass, it also disperses the members of the House of Commons to be noe more representatives of the nation till another Parliament be summon'd and the nation make new choices, which sometymes and in some places falls on the old members. It is in the Kings prerogative thus to call and disolve parliaments,[9] to declare warre or peace [or] making alliances, but the Kings ought not nor do rightly undertake any such thing but by the advice of his standing Privy Councill, which I have spoken before; and so his proclaimations allwayes runs, by and with the advice of his Privy Councill he does so and so, to which he joyns the Great Councill of the nation which is his two Houses of Parliament, Lords spiritual and temporall and Commons of England, when great matters are in agitation as that of peace or warre, which is in the constitution of the government, and strengthened by this, that the sinnews of warre is in the people, for without them no money is to be had; they give the taxes and subsidies for such expences, nay the very revenue is given by them to the King or Queen only dureing the then prince's life, and must be asked of them that succeed at the death of their predecessour, at the death of such that is in the throne.

Formerly the Parliaments of course was dissolved, all offices even to a Justice of Peace was vacant, but our wise King William, contriveing only our good, not only laid a scheme which if be followed will carry on all the confederacys and designes against the common enemy of mankind, but also as farre as he could to secure our peace, which was by obtaining an Act of Parliament[10] that the Parliament in being when the King died, or else the Parliament but just then

[9] Here a marginal note reads "A Parliament ought to sitt but 3 year and so a new one the which was by an act of parliament ordained King Charles the Seconds tyme." She means the Triennial Act of 1694.
[10] The Act of Settlement, 1701.

dissolv'd by the King, after he dies should assemble together to take care of the government and to act under the
next prince for six months, and till that tyme all offices should
remain as they were, unless the next heir should before that
full tyme were expired should make any change of places;
this thing made the loss of his death less felt immediately
and our Queen Ann found a quiet easye ascention into the
throne.

There was also at the same tyme an Act to settle the succession in the Protestant Line, and just before our Heroe
resign'd his life crown and throne he pass'd an Act to secure
us more firmly against any Popish successour or pretended
heirs to the Crown, by an abjuration oath to be taken by all
subjects of any Prince thats a Papist, which confirms the
Acts of Parliament in years past which made a Papist prince
unable to be King or Queen of England, because a Papest;
so this engages the subjects to abjure all such or any of their
abbettors or pretenders; this was a great pleasure to our
dying King to leave us with all the security possible to enjoy
what he came to save us in, and give us, and what he had
fought to obtaine for us, Liberty in religion and priviledges.
I pray God we do not by our provokeing sinns move his
anger not only to take from us our Benefactor and Deliverer,
but also our said valuable blessings and priviledges, the
Gospel Light and being a Free Nation.

I should have said when the King comes in his robes to the
Parliament and all the Lords have theirs, so if there be any
Prince of Wales he is also in his, and weares his Prince of
Wales Cap with a branch of diamonds in forme of a plume of
feathers; he sitts in the House of Lords often—he may allwayes—to hear debates and to vote, and he does present
them to the King any of their addresses they desire, which he
is attended with some of the Lords which are the Privy
Councellors; they bring back the Kings answere. The like is
observ'd by the House of Commons, if they have any
address or any petition to the King they desire some of their
members which are of the Privy Councill to move the King
when the House shall attend him or her, which they knowing

do it and their Speaker is their mouth; so when they would have a conferrence with the House of Lords they send to them to meete them in the Painted Chamber or Lobby of their House; so does the Lords send to the Commons when they would have a conferrence with them; these things are so well adjusted and so for the common good that if rightly maintain'd in their proper places would be a happy Constitution.

All Acts of Parliament so pass'd are printed, but the records of them are kept in the journalls of the Parliament by the Clerke of the Parliament; to him are added in the House of Commons also scribes or secretaryes which record and take minutes also: now it is on these Laws that all Causes are tryed, for there are Laws made of all sorts both what relates to religious matters as well as humaine; true indeed as to points of religion for rectifying matters as to the orders and Church government, that is debated and agreed by a Convocation, which is allwayes summoned at the same tyme a Parliament is chosen, which consists of two houses also, the Bishops and Deanes, and off the inferior Clergy, and is managed by way of debates and disputation, which have a Moderatour and Prolocutors; here they endeavour to reforme any abuse in the Church, any deffect in their Cannon Laws, and to explaine those Laws; and if they should find as in our first Reformation was great deffect in our religion not agreable to the word of God, they form it into a bill or petition which is presented the King in way of an address, he being owned as head and supreame under Christ over these Churches and realmes; so this is to request his care of it which the King does by laying it before the Houses of Parliament who enacts laws to secure our religion, and reforme evil both in doctrine and practise by their Acts duely pass'd—as I said before the Archbishop's chiefe of this Convocation house.

Next I will proceed to give some short account of Tryalls on our Laws which is thus. Every free man of England being oppress'd comes in due form of Law to demand his right, which being heard by the Judges and a Jury of his own fellow subjects—his country men—they give their verdict in the matter as they thinke most just according to the Statutes and Laws, and so the right between man and man which does vary from the different customs of each County or precinct; this Jury are twelve men all sworne on the Bible solemnly to do justice, not out of feare, fraud or malice, favour or affection to injure any man, and the first man is their foreman and speakes for the rest, either acquit or condemns the person, which is in Life or Death, so determining other Causes the same manner; and these twelve men must all be agreed in their verdict, which is after they have heard all can be witness'd or alleadged on all sides, which verdict the Judges also must pronounce on the Causes as they have brought it in. Now those suites of Law as well as causes of Life and Death are brought in by bill to the Grand-jury, which are twenty four and these all of the best Gentry and many of them Justices of Peace, they examine the matter and if they find it (that is by any Act of Parliament) is pleadable or to be enquired into, they draw it up into an indictment and so its sent into the Court to be tryed by the Petty Jury, after whose verdict and the Judges pronouncing it, the matter must be at an end and taken out of that Court. Sometymes indeed if the subject is oppress'd he may appeale to another Court thats higher, as from the Sessions to the Assizes, thence to the Kings Bench, thence to the Chancery, or the Parliament House—which when a matter has there been debated and decided there can be noe more done in it, because they are the makers of the Laws so best able to interpret: sometymes in these other Courts a Jury brings in a matter speciall, that is, leaves it on the Judges to determine being a matter of Law, then the Judges must consult and do it all of them together.

All persons are tryed by those of their own ranke, a Commoner of England is tryed by a Jury of Commoners in all cases and of Life and Death, a Peer of England is tryed by his Peers, and in case it is not the tyme of the Parliament sitting, then by a bill of oyer and terminer issued out, there is 12 Peers are impannell'd as a jury; but I must mention one thing as to the Petty Juryes of Commoners, a person which is tryed for his life may challenge some of those which are brought to be sworne for his Jury, that is except against them to such a number without giving reason, but if he exceeds that number he must give reason for such exception, either to be a man he had injured or one which had former malice or one related to the persons who either is dead or injured; for our Laws condemn to death murther, fellony, treasons—by this order you see its justice and care—then in matters of Life and Death the witness for the King are sworne, but the witness for the prisoners are not sworne but only examined to declare the truth.

But to returne to the tryals of a Peer which by such a jury is tryed; but in case the House of Lords the Parliament is sitting, then they prepare Westminster Hall for the tryal, the House of Comons manage the evidence and prosecute them, and the House of Lords are the Judges and Jury in this manner if it be for life or death, which is grounded on a statute either against murther, treason or fellony, and so the arraignment is read and the Councill for both sides;[11] the House of Commons produces their evidence and witness and the King constitutes a Lord High Steward for that day, or in case the tryal be long he must be continued till the tryall finishes; he beares a white staff as badge of his great office which indeed is the greatest officer in England and for the tyme can act for the King, so above him; he is usually the person that is Lord Chancellor, if he being a peer, which all-wayes is; there he sitts as Judge to whome the other peeres of the whole House of Lords are joyn'd, and after a full examination on both sides, and the criminall haveing had full leave to cleer himself, then the Lord High Steward askes the Lords one by one (beginning with the puny Lord, so to the highest) "in honour, my Lord such-a-one, do you thinke my Lord that is prisoner at the Barre is guilty or not guilty?" —to which each Lord stands up and answeres for himself either, so as he judges, "guilty upon my honour", or else

---

[11] She is describing an Impeachment. The Commons are not the accusers in other cases tried by the Lord High Steward's Court.

"not guilty upon my honour", and so it goes from one to all; in this manner the Lord High Steward marks down to each Lords name his answere, and at the last reckons them up so many Guiltyes, so many Not Guiltyes, then he adds his own thought to the side he thinks best (but usualy he is so crafty as to add to the side of the majority) which being done he pronounces the verdict as the majority said, either Guilty or not; now this verdict the Lords give thus on their honour is equivalent to the oath the commoners take that serve in Juryes, for the peeres take no oath in these matters, otherwise than so; now in case the matter against a peer be only a Law matter of nuise-prise [nisi prius], then the matter being debated and the answere by the Lord made in his deffence read, and Councell pleading, then the Lord High Steward askes each Lord in same order as before, but in this forme, "in the matter which has been debated before your Lordships concerning the Lord at the Barre with his deffence, whether his deffence be sufficient to cleer him or not, what sayes your Lordships? Content or not content on your honour?" they all answere as they are affected or understand the matter "content", or else "not content", which are fixed to each name and so reckon'd up, and the majority carrys it either to quitt or not to quitt him, to which the Lord High Steward adds his as he pleases also; after which they shew the High Steward a respect as a king; he is serv'd on the knee and drinkes some wine and when that is done he breakes his white staff and so pulls off his hatt; when he was the High Steward he had all the maces carry'd before him all the officers attending. But in case there be no Chancellour, only a Lord Keeper as at present is, which is no peer of the realme, then he has not vote with the Lords, only count up the votes and declares them which has the majority, without the addition of his, haveing none; and he is only substituted the deputy steward for the day and so sitts, but on a wool sack as he does in the House of Lords, and is only their speaker and officer and must aske leave for himself and the Judges to put on their caps before they might do it; now the High Steward sitts in the throne of justice under a cannopy but I see this Lord Keeper only sate on a wool sack at the foote of the throne which stood empty behind him; he had noe compliment paid him more than at another tyme, being only as the Speaker to the House of Lords and so their officer.

There are severall great officers of the Court, as Lord Treasurer which takes account of all the Kings revenues—this sometymes is in commision between 3 or more; there is also the High Admirall of England that has the command of all the shipps and stores, this sometymes is in Comission also of 3 or more, under whome are the Vice Admirall and Rear Admirall; also under the Treasurer are severall officers; in tyme of Warre there is usually Generalisimo which has the greatest power over all the kingdom; there is also two principal Secretaryes of State which write all things, the Kings Letters etc., and relateing to the government, maintain all Inteligences in the kingdom and abroad; there is also a Master of the Generall Post Office that has all the under masters and officers of the posts both for forreign letters and inland letters.

There are also Governours as Lord Lieutenant of Ireland —that sometymes is held in commission;[12] there is also Lords Justices there, all which have their salleryes ariseing out of the same kingdom. There is also to all our forreign plantations Governours sent from England and their salleryes arise from the plantation. The Kings Revenues arise from the Customs of goods exported and imported, from the Excise on all liquors that are made in England and sold, besides which there is a considerable revenue from lands belonging to the Crown, tho' that is much lessen'd by the severall donations of our kings for many yeares to their favourites; out of those revenues all the Civil List is maintain'd, which is the Judges salleries, the great officers, the household of the king; there is another great revenue in the Post Office besides; at all extraordinary occasions of the marriage of any of our princess's their portion, or any warre, then the Parliament raises taxes on the nation on land, on trade, additional

---

[12] In 1697 it was held in Commission by the Marquis of Winchester, the Earl of Galway and Viscount Villiers.

customs, and also on the excise, encreasing that; under the Civil List is the expences of the Court, the Guards, and also the Ambassadors which are sent by the king into forreign kingdoms to treate matters for each others good; their expences while there are allowed and so of all envoyes or Consulls which are lesser Embassadours; there is also the maintaining the navy, building shipps, the wood of which indeed is out of the King's Forest.

There remaines now only in what manner the Kings or Queenes of England give publick audience to forreigne ambassadours either when they come in their first entrance or at the tyme of their takeing leave; but first I may give account of our Bishops and Gentry: there is 26 Bishopricks with the two Archbishops Canterbury and York and there are as many Cittyes and Cathedralls which in my travells have described; all these Bishopricks are held of the Crown and are given by the King, to whome is due the first fruites which is one yeares income of the Bishopricks; they are held for life, true indeed they admit of being removed from one Bishoprick to another for advancement, nay they may forfeit their Bishoprick by not being qualify'd, if they will not sweare to be faithfull to the government, and so they may be suspended, as in the case of severall in the last Revolution would not sweare to King William and Queen Mary and so now refuse also to sweare to her present Majesty Queen Ann.[13] These Bishops are only Barrons in themselves, their wives have noe honnour thereby nor their children; but for all Peeres of England theirs is hereditary from father to son and their ladies partake of it, nay the honour descends on a daughter in default of male issue; the Peeres must first be made Barrons by which they hold all their priviledges— Barrons of England—which is from the King by patent; all his children are called the Honourable adding the Christian name to their sirname, and this remaines to daughters when marry'd; by this patent or another of the same they may be created Viscount, Earles, Marquesses, Dukes, and if they are Dukes their patent expresses all the four other titles;

[13] The Non Jurors.

alsoe Viscounts children are the same with Barrons; and Earle's, Marquess, and Duke's are called, the daughters Lady, by their Christian names, before and after marriage, unless they marry a Barron then they lose that name and are called a Barroness and so loses their place; the eldest son of an Earle is called Lord by his fathers title of Barron, the Eldest son of a Marquiss is called Earle by the title of his fathers Earledome, and all Marquiss's younger sons are called Lord by their Christian name added to their sirname; so the same of Dukes children, the eldest son is called Marquiss; now if any Dowager to a Lord marry a Private Gentleman she in Law is sullied and has lost her peeress, so if a Dutchess or Marquess or Countess or Viscountess marry a Barron or either of the degrees which was below her, she looses it and is only called as the Lady of the present peer she has marry'd now: though these titles be given the noblemens sons and daughters its not that they are really soe, for in our Law they are only called and esteemed in the first ranke of Gentlemen, and so take place before all Gentlemen whatsoever. The lower titles made by patents by the king is Barronets, and is differenc'd only from a Knight by takeing place of all Knights and that it is hereditary and goes from father to son; a Knight only is for his own life and the King makes them thus: any Gentleman that is to be made a Knight kneeles down and the King draws his sword asking him his Christian name, layes the sword on his head and shoulder, and bids him rise up Sir Such-a-one, as for example Sir James Bateman[14] our last Sherriff, etc. These severall titles and patents pays great fees to the severall officers according to the ranke, a Duke cost £1000—so in proportion. The same manner the Knights of the Garter are made as other knights nevertheless it may be to those which were dukes before; their installment is at Windsor Castle, in this manner: the herraulds which [I] have mentioned several tymes before as a part and management of all the cerimony, and also the persons that studdy all matters of honours and are the recorders of all the titles in England, and all their coates of armour, and knows

[14] Sir James Bateman became Sheriff of London in 1702.

and keepes each in their ranke at all Cerimonyes, and gives out their armes for eschuteons at every bodyes funeralls; they have an office just by Doctors Commons by StPauls Cathedrall. There is one Principal King at Armes[15] and 3 if not more other King at Armes and other under-herraulds and sergeants, which all weare coates with the kings armes all aboute it; these as I say officiate at the installing, for they record it and add the blew garter about such a Lords atchievement: the Cerimony I have in part described together with the account of Windsor.[16]

[15] An addendum in the manuscript says "St. George, Garter"; she is referring either to Sir Thomas St. George, Garter King-at-Arms, who died in March, 1703, or to his brother Henry, who succeeded him and died in 1704. (See Noble, *History of the College of Arms*, pp. 331–3.)

[16] A marginal note added here reads "Soe that a King of England as will be the man off his people as Sir William Temple told King Charles, should be the happyest monarch in the world; but he that sought more by an arbitrary sway of his scepter would be nothing at all. King Charles answer: 'I will be the man off my people'—which had he made good he and we had been happy."

5. "ANOTHER JOURNEY FROM WILTSHIRE TO LONDON BY MALBROUGH"

MAULBERY [MARLBOROUGH] is in view at some distance from the adjacent hills and lookes very fine, with a good river that turns many mills; its buildings are good and compact, one very large streete where stands the Market place and Town Hall and at each end the two Churches; its of a great length includeing the two parishes and the town stands it self on a high hill; beyond one of the Churches is the Duke of Sommersets house[1] has been a great rambling building but now most pulled down and newly building; they were painting it, good appartments for what is done, but none furnish'd, and its but one wing is built with drawing dineing roomes and bed chambers with closets and dressing-roomes and two

[1] The Duke's house is now the nucleus of Marlborough College. He was Charles Seymour, sixth Duke of Somerset (1662–1748), "the Proud Duke" (see Introduction, p, xxxiii) who made his two daughters stand guard over him while he took his afternoon nap and, on waking to find one of them sitting down, docked £20,000 from her inheritance. (*Memoirs of the Kit-Cat Club*, p. 13.)

stair cases and some roomes above, which is to have another such a wing on the other side and joyn'd with a greate hall; the only curious thing is out of the bowling green; you go many stepps down into a grass-walke with quick sett hedges cut low, this leads to the foote of the Mount and that you ascend from the left hand by an casye ascent bounded by such quick set hedges cut low, and soe you rise by degrees in 4 rounds bounded by the low cutt hedge and on the top is with same hedge cut in works, and from thence you have a prospect of the town and country round and two parishes two mile off in view, and the low grounds are water'd with ditches and this mount is encompass'd about with such a cannal which emptys its self into a fish pond, then it empts it self into the river; there is a house built over the fish pond to keep the fish in; at the foote of the mount as I began out of a green walke on the left hand to ascend it so on the right hand leads to another such a walk quite round by the cannall to the other side of the bowling green; in the midst of the top of the mount was a house built and pond, but thats fallen down; halfe way down is a seate opposite to the dwelling house which is brick'd; Maulbery [Marlborough] is one of the towns in Wiltshire the quarter sessions is kept in.

Its 8 mile to Hungerford over Savernack [Savernake] Forrest where is many deer; from Hungerford to Newbury in Barkshire 7 mile all very deep way, 15 mile thence to Reading in Barkshire flatt way, but the vale is heavy sand for 3 or 4 mile; Reading is the shire town its pretty large, accomodated for travellers being a great Road to Glocester and the West Country but it is very dear.[2]

[2] This is the point at which the smaller manuscript (Southey's MS.) ends. What follows may be an appendix added, at a later date, to the main text of the journal.

6. FROM LONDON THROUGH NORTHAMPTON TO WOLSELEY

FROM LONDON to Rusbery [Wyrardisbury] 18 mile by Stanes [Staines], pretty house and gardens, in sight of Windsor in

Buckinghamshire, thence Uxbridge 7 mile pretty good way; thence Amersham 9 mile all in the Alesbury [Aylesbury] road, thence Barkminstead [Berkhamsted] 6 long miles steep hills into Hartfordshire, a good market town, good inns; thence Dunstable 7 or 9 long miles steep hills, thence Arsly [Arlesey] in Bedfordshire 10 mile, which I entered at Astick [Astwick] 2 mile from Arsly, 2 good houses old of the Edwards and Browns, but this was base way narrow and lanes rooty and long; thence Bedford town 9 miles good way, a village in a mile or two distance, Hanlow [Henlow] Clifton Sheford [Shefford] Checkston [Chicksands] and Bedford the great road comes in good way thence Turvoy [Turvey] 5 mile belonging to the Earle of Peterborough[1] where he was.

They make much bonelace in these towns; in the Church are fine tombs and monuments of that familly, the first with two ladyes on each side the higher one in a widdows dress, all marble finely gilt and painted on a bed and rowles of matt very naturall at their head and feete; there was another and the lady dyed in childbed, the child by her, costly carved and gilt and 4 beddmen [bedesmen] at the feete; he allowed for four old mens maintenance; by it another and his lady all rich marble gilt and painted.

Here I enter Buckinghamshire againe, over the bridge, so to Northampton 10 mile over a pretty good road and entred the shire within 4 mile off the town; I describe nothing more of Northampton, but the Church was finish'd,[2] the entrance with a breast wall and paved, and stepps within round 3 sides of the Church, which was begun when I was there before; so I proceeded on to Litchfield [Lichfield] to Creek [Crick] 10 [miles] very good way, as exactly straight as a line the Whatling [Watling] Streete way, but it was deep heavy ground as in all these rich countrys; I passed between two

<hr />

[1] Charles Mordaunt, third Earl of Peterborough (1658–1735) the future victor of Barcelona. He was not only the most unduly neglected of all very great British soldiers, but a most versatile and enigmatic man. At this time he was engaged in translating Demosthenes, in collaboration with his political and personal enemy Lord Somers.

[2] The West Portico of All Saints' Church was finished in 1701 (*Victoria County History, Northamptonshire*, iii, 49).

noble seates Homby [Holdenby] on the right hand on the
side of a hill in woods, stone buildings with towers almost
like a Castle old built, the rows of trees exact on each side
and avenues, which is Earle of Fevershams;[3] the other on
the left hand lay low within a thicket of wood on all sides
but the front where it appear'd like a Princes Court of brick
and stone very fine [Althorp], Lord Sunderlands,[4] with a
large Parke wall'd in of a good extent; thus I went to a Bridge
not very large of stone but it is the boundary of three
countys.

I pass'd from Northampton [shire] into Leicestershire with
Warwickshire on my left hand, and so went to a rich land
here it lookes of a redder earth; I came to Cross wayes[5]
where was a Latterworth hand poynting 4 wayes to Coventry, Leicester, London, and Litchfield and something farther
to High Crosse which is esteemed the middle off England,
where the two great Roads meete that divides the kingdom
in the Saxons tyme in 4 parts, the Whatling [Watling]
Streete on which still I continued, and the Fosse Way; thus
to a little place called Smockington fitted for inns on a road
very comodious; here I lay in Warwickshire and my equipage in Leicestershire 10 mile, thence 6 to Anderton [Ather-
stone] and Talmouth [Tamworth] 7 where I enter Staffordshire, soe Litchfield 6 mile thence Woolsly [Wolseley] eight.

From thence to Budsworth [Beaudesert] Lord Pagets in a
fine parke, large coale mines about it, 4 miles; the house is
old but the front very regular, 3 juttings out large compass
windows, a good little parlour out of the hall another large
one with drawing roome and bed chamber and good back

[3] Holdenby or Holmby House was Elizabethan, and it was there that the
Scots "sold" Charles I to the Parliamentary Commissioners in 1647. The Earl
of Feversham was the naturalized Frenchman, Louis Duras, a good soldier
who commanded the Royal troops at Sedgemoor.
[4] Charles Spencer, third Earl of Sunderland (1674–1722) Marlborough's
son-in-law and a great Whig statesman. Althorp, being "disposed after the
Italian manner", was one of the few English houses to meet with the approval
of Cosimo of Tuscany's courtiers in 1669. It "may be said to be the best
planned and best arranged country seat in the kingdom; for though there be
many which surpass it in size, none are superior to it in symmetrical elegance."
(*Travels of Cosmo III*, tr, 1821, p. 250.)
[5] Possibly Cross-in-hand, two miles west of Lutterworth.

staires and entrys large light fit for attendance; then you go up and enter a dineing roome drawing roome and chamber, a long gallery that is the length of the house and broad and which adds to its greatness; the end opens doores on a terrass out in the garden of same breadth and length up to an orchard or wilderness which lookes very nobly; here at each end is two good Chambers of State, lofty, with anty chambers and for servants, and back staires; there are many very good roomes of a second rate which if well furnish'd would look well; the leads are a greate many stepps up, on the top a large Cupulo of windows, and the walls round the leads are so high a person of a middle stature cannot look over them scarce when on tiptoe, which is a great lessening of its beauty which would give a large prospect round of the country of 10 or 12 mile off; there is an addition of new wall on the battlements which is visible, so its likely it was from some accident from the leads enduced the walls being built higher; this Lord has a greate Command and Royalty in the country; the Kank forrest [Cannock Chase] of 20 mile is his, most of the Gentlemen in the country pay him chiefe rent and some hold right in some of their land by waiteing on him on some solemn feast dayes in the yeare and bring up his dinner and waite on him as he eates, if then in the country; but these things are better wav'd then sought and is not done few tymes in an age to keep up the custom.

7. FROM WOLSELEY THROUGH WORCESTERSHIRE TO NEWTON TONEY

From Woolsly [Wolseley] after an 8 weekes stay I went to Wolverhampton 11 long mile, then to Churchill near Sturbridge [Stourbridge] 9 or 10 mile farther, by the many Glass houses where they blow broad glass but they were not at work on that sort when I was there; at Church hill was at a farmer like Gentlemans a new pretty house of brick but wanted furniture and cleaneing and good order, but a hearty

Mr. and Mrs.; the hill is pretty high and gives a greate view of the country which most belongs to Mr. Foley, Tom of 10,000£,[1] large comõnage; there he has a little Lodge new brick his own house is 6 or 10 mile, thence all within his own ground and has great iron works and mines, this is within two mile of Kederminster [Kidderminster] as farre on the other side to Sturbridge [Stourbridge]; thence I went to Worcester town, a sandy way and here are in some places quicksand as at. . . . [blank in both MSS].

This is a 10 long mile to Worcester but pretty flatt way for the most part, thence to New house 12 or 14 the basest way for hills a stony narrow hollow wayes very difficult to pass; I went from New house to Stoake [Stoke Edith] four miles, Mr. Foleys the Speakers son, has a very fine pile of building, the wing to Herreford being now up in the shell, which is all for state, great parlour drawing roome and bed-chambers, with their appendixes, and back staires and a great stair case with chambers over for state; this is entred into out of the greate hall the middle of the house raiseing many stepps out of the Court, the entrance which on each side as buildings uniform for coach house stables dairy out houses; the wing to the garden side is finish'd being their appart-ment, a pretty staircase that two easily go up, light from the skye, iron railes and barristers, this from an arch isle below, which goes to the kitchen, and hath a doore into this front Court, and into the gate backward tho' not visible on the garden side by the disguise of painting; from this you ascend these staires to the dineing roome which is even to the great hall and must enter from it when finish'd; out of this on the right hand was Mr. Paul Folies [Foley] the fathers studdy, long and large, with back staires and a servants roome; on the left hand is a drawing room, beyond his Ladys bed chamber closet and servants roome, and next it are these staires of iron railes that goes up to the next stage which is over this same wing and is the appartment of the young Mr.

---

[1] This was the younger Thomas Foley of Witley Court, grandson of the great ironmaster, and nephew of Paul Foley of Stoke Edith. Paul Foley had died in 1699.

Folie [Thomas Foley] and his Lady which now is the heir and in possession.

There is their chamber, her fine closet, a servants roome, and a large studdy for him, there is also two large chambers for strangers which takes the whole wing over the dineing roome and studdy, there is also a little roome at the end for strangers, opposite to Mr. Folies roome, which lookes to the front; this dineing roome is what they eate in allwayes is well wanscoated; there is a fountaine bason just faceing the balcony doore that leads to a terrass paved with black and white marble and iron palisadoes, it has a long space and broad for walking, and two enclosed on each side by same iron work a step up or two these doores from the Ladies closet and the studdy; out on them in the middle goes the staires two wayes all iron work and meete halfe way and joyne in the next descent on gravel which is in a halfe moon, and so design'd to be left in a low place with a cascade beneath and the gravel walke and grass walks to go by it and beyond it in many rows of trees, the walled gardens and walks one below another; this terrass gives a vast prospect of the country it being scituated on the ascent of a hill, many rows of trees in meadows below it adds to its beauty, being all within his own ground; he has a great estate and a great parke up above it, with great woods; the adornment of the rooffe is flower potts and figures globes and scallop shells; it will be noble compleate buildings and deserves 10000£ a yeare to live like it.

The offices are all below and even with the first entrance of the front; what is finished is neate good wanscoate and tapistry, there is two or three damaske beds and one velvet one what they had before, so noe new furniture, but the best wing noe doubt will be finely finish'd and furnish'd; the prospect is large, and indeed to view—at least in the summer and in drye tyme—Herrifordshire is like a fruitfull garden; near Richards Castle is the Bone well, a fountain alway full of fish and froggs bones tho' often cleared of them yet still renewed.

From Newhouse I came over Maubern [Malvern] Hills

336

which are like the Alps, and have had much wet, the roads deep and difficult; to Upton in Worcester 10 mile where I pass the Severn on a stone bridge, here it is not broad; thence Pursha [Pershore] 5 mile, thence Esham [Evesham] 4 and Weston [Weston-sub-Edge] 4 in Glocestershire to my Cos'n [Pharamus] Fiennes; thence to Morton Hindmost [Moreton-in-the-Marsh] up a vast stony high hazardous hill of neare two mile long ascending all the way from Weston —this is in sight of Cambden [Chipping Campden]; so to Morton 6 miles, down as steep a stony hill 2 mile before I came to my Aunts;[2] thence to Broughton in Oxfordshire passing by 4 Shires Stone (Warwick, Worcester, Glocester and Oxfordshire) and so by Kingston; thence to Oxford 18; Abbington [Abingdon] where is a fine Town Hall for the Judges two barrs and all seates aboute set on stone pillars, the staires to the top is about 100, the leads fine and gives a large prospect all about; there is halfe way the staires a place to go in and in gallerys round company may stand to heare causes all above the Judges heads—this is Buckinghamshire; then to Newbery [Newbury] by Market Hillsly [Ilsley] its 16 miles, Barkshire, which town has been famous for whipps, and presents a King or Queen when they pass through it with one of great price and also with a purse of gold; from thence to Way hill through lanes and woods 14 mile this is in Hampshire; thence to Newton-tony in Wiltshire 6 mile.

[2] Susanna (née Cobb) second wife and now widow of Celia's uncle Richard Fiennes, who had died in 1674.

8. EPSOM

SOME ACCOUNT of Epsome in Surrey about ten miles from London; its on clay and gravel the waters are from Alum: the Well is large without bason or pavement on the bottom, it covered over with timber and is so darke you can scarce looke down into it, for which cause I do dislike it; its not a quick spring and very often is dranke drye, and to make up the defficiency the people do often carry water from common wells to fill this in a morning (this they have been found out in) which makes the water weake and of little opperation unless you can have it first from the well before they can have put in any other;[1] the usual way of drinking them is by turning them with a little milk; there is a walk of trees by it but not very pleasant, there is a house built, in which the well is, and that is paved with brick to walke in in the wet weather, and where people have carrawayes sweetemeates and tea etc., but it look'd so dark and unpleasant, more like a dungeon that I would not chuse to drinke it there, and most people drink it at home; there are severall good buildings in Epsome for lodgings and good gardens behind them for walking.

There is a good house of the Lord Bartlets [Berkeley] in a parke at the end of the town lookes very well; the greatest pleasure of Epsom is either Banstead Downs[2] where is good aire and good rideing for coaches and horses with a pleasant view of the country, or else Box Hill which is 6 or 7 miles off and is the continuation of the ridge of hills [the North Downs] I mentioned by Maidstone; its a greate height and shows you a vast precipice down on the farther side and such a vast vale full of woods enclosures and little towns; there is a very good river that runs by a little town called Darken [Dorking] just at the foote of this hill, very famous for good troutts and great store of fish; on this hill the top is cover'd with box, whence its name proceeds, and there is other wood but its all cutt in long private walks very shady and pleasant and this is a great diversion to the Company and would be more frequented if nearer Epsom town.

[1] More fraudulence was soon to follow, as in 1706 the Wells were ruined by one Livingstone, who built the Assembly Rooms and sank a new well, which proved inefficacious and discredited the old one. (*Some Particulars Relating to the History of Epsom by An Inhabitant*, 1825, p. 65.)

[2] For the amenities of Epsom, see Introduction, p. xxvi, cf. Macky's *Journey through England*, i, 138–158 and John Toland, *A New Description of Epsom*, 1711. Defoe has a lyrical passage on Banstead Downs, "covered with coaches and ladies, an innumerable company of horsemen, as well gentlemen as citizens, . . . the racers flying over the course, as if they either touched not, or felt not, the ground they ran upon; I think no sight, except that of a victorious army, under the command of a Protestant King of Great Britain, could exceed it". (Op. cit., i, 159.)

About 4 mile off is Sir Robert Howards[3] house [Ashtead Park] which I went to see; its a square building the yards and offices very convenient about it and severall gardens walled in; all the windows are sarshes and large squares of glass, I observ'd they are double sashes to make the house the warmer for it stands pretty bleake; its a brick building; you enter a hall which opens to the garden, thence to two parlours drawing-roomes and good staires; there are abundance of pictures, above is a dineing roome and drawing roome with very good tapistry hangings of long standing, there is severall bed chambers well furnish'd good damaske beds and hangings and window curtaines of the same, and so neatly kept folded up in clean sheetes pinn'd about the beds and hangings; there are severall other good beds and furniture, one roome all the bed and hangings are of a fine damaske made of worsted it lookes pretty and with a gloss like camlett of a light ash coullour; there are good pictures of the family Sir Roberts Son and Lady which was a Daughter of the Newport house with her Children in a very large picture; there is fine adornements of glass on the chimney and fine marble chimney-pieces, some closets with inlaid floores, its all very neate and fine with the severall courts at the entrance; this I thinke was all remarkable at Epsome which is 14 mile to London.

[3] Sir Robert Howard built Ashtead House in 1684 out of his gains as Auditor of the Exchequer. He was also a dramatist and one of Dryden's collaborators.

9. FROM LONDON THROUGH BEDFORD TO BROUGHTON CASTLE

ANOTHER JOURNEY to Broughton in Oxfordshire my Brothers and now my Nephews house, the Lord Say and Seale: I went by Hartfordshire and Bedford; from London to Ware 20 mile, thence to Hitching [Hitchin] 14 miles, most in lanes and deep land; in the winter bad roads but very good land good corn the wheate look'd well, but grass and summer corn wanted rain being a drye spring; thence to Bedford town 12 mile more, these miles are longer than those about London and much in lanes and woods.

Bedford town is an old building its wash'd by the river Ouse which comes from Buckingham and is here broader than in most places till it reaches Yorke,[1] its stored with very good fish, and those which have gardens on its brinke keepes sort of trunck or what they call them (its a receptacle of wood of a pretty size full of holes to let the water in and out) here they keep fish they catch as pike perch tench etc., so they have it readye for their use; this is of mighty advantage especially for the Publick houses, you see the fish taken out fresh for supper or dinner; the river runns twineing about and runns into severall notches of ground which is sett full of willows, and many little boates chained to the sides belonging to the people of the town for their diversion; it runns by a ground which is made into a fine bowling-green, its upon a hill and a pretty ascent from the river that is besett with willows all round beneath; the bowling green is well kept with seates and summer houses in it for the use of the Town and Country Gentlemen of which many resort to it especially the Market dayes; at the entrance of the town you pass over the river on a bridge which has a gate on it and some houses: this river beares barges; these truncks or baskets which keepes the fish are fastned by chaines to the sides of the banks in each mans garden.

There is nothing worth notice in the town, severall streetes small and old, the middle streete which runns from the bridge is pretty broad wherein stands the Market place and House which is on severall stone pillars and raill'd in; there is above it roomes which were design'd for the session and publick buissness of the town by the Lord Russell[2] that built it, but his untimely death, being beheaded, put a stop to its finishing; they now put it to noe use but spinning, haveing begun to set up the woollen worke, but its just in its infancy;

[1] This Ouse flows into the Wash; Celia Fiennes has confused it with the Yorkshire Ouse.
[2] Lord William Russell, the Whig "Martyr", executed in 1683 after the Rye House Plot.

over this is the top which is flatt rooff'd leaded and railed in from thence you see the whole town and country round.

There is a pretty many Gentry about the country neare neighbours, and many live in the town tho' in such old houses; from thence I went to Asply [Aspley Guise] 8 mile where the earth turns wood into stone and had a picce of it, it seemes its only one sort of wood the Aldertree which turns so, and lay or drive a paile or stake into the ground there, in seven yeares its petrify'd into stone.

From thence to Ouborn [Woburn] which is 3 mile more; here is the Duke of Bedfords house which I had seen before with the fine gardens and parke, so proceeded on to Dunstable 9 miles farther, where I staid and dined with my kinswoman my aunt Woolsley's Daughter marry'd to a Doctor of Physick Dr Marsh, and from thence I went to Laighton Buserd [Leighton Buzzard] and thence to Whinslow [Winslow] about 12 mile; this is in Buckinghamshire; thence to Broughton in Oxfordshire 17 mile and staid a weeke and then returned through Oxfford Citty 18 mile and so to London 48 mile more.

10. "A FURTHER DESCRIPTION OF EPSOME, HAMPTON COURT AND WINDSOR"

EPSOM IS 15 miles from London, there are great curiositys in cut hedges and trees almost before all doores; they have trees in rows which they cut up smooth and about 3 or 4 yards up they lay frames of wood in manner of a penthouse, so plat the branches on it and cut it smooth; they leave the stem of the tree to run up and then cut it clear to the top which they cut in round heads; there are severall good houses in or about Epsham [Epsom] Sir Robert Howards [Ashtead] (which I have described) Mr. Wessells now Mr. Scawens[1] [Carshalton]; there is Lord Baltimores[2] in Wood-

[1] William Scawen, a great business magnate, was a "Hamburg Merchant" and a Director of the East India Company.
[2] Lord Baltimore, a Catholic but a Whig, had acquired Woodcote Park from the Minn family. Evelyn, whose brother Richard married Elizabeth Minn, had visited there for the wedding.

cut Green [Woodcote] encompass'd with a wall at the entrance, a breast wall with pallisadoes, large courts one within the other, and a back way to the stables where is a pretty horse pond; the house is old but low, tho' large run over much ground; in front 6 windows, and in the top just in the middle 12 chimneys in a row, being 3 and 3 below joyning back to back, and 3 and 3 above the others, looke into a court which is built round; as I drove by the side saw broad chimneys on the end and at due distance on the side on both ends the sides of a court which is terminated in a building on which is a lead with railes and barristers.

That house[3] [Durdans] which is now Lord Guilfords at another side of Epsham lookes nobly in a fine park pailed round, severall rows of trees in the front of all sorts, lofty and some cut piramidy some suger loafe or rather like a mushroom-top; the front has 6 large windows and the doore which is glass, as many on the next story; you enter by a large court which is on the left side stable court, to the right into the gardens fore right you enter a broad tarass railed in paved with stone, you enter a noble lofty hall, plaine but neate painted white; on the right is a little parlour the lesser hall hung with armes, a butlers office with bedchambers and closets, thence goes the kitchen, schullery, bakeing-room, laundry into a court of all the offices and the stable yard; out of the little parlour goes into a pretty Chappel which has a balcony closet looking into it for the Lord and Lady.

The left hand of the hall led into a great parlour which runnes to the end of the house and makes the front, and short again into another great parlour or dineing-roome which makes the end front of the house; this also opens into the staircase, it leads on to a drawing-roome closet bed chamber two dressing roomes, which with the great staircase makes up the front backward and the other end front, which lookes into the stable yard and a garden railed in with a large pond or cannall; the back front goes out into a garden

---

[3] Durdans had been built by Lord Berkeley, largely out of the materials of Nonsuch Palace, when it was broken up and sold. It belonged now to the second Baron Guildford (son of the Judge). Later it passed to Frederick Prince of Wales and eventually to Lord Rosebery.

or court with gravel walks round and a crosse which cuts
it into 4 grass-plotts, where are brass statues, and leads out
through fine iron carved gates as at the front out into the
highway; the right end front of the house is into the garden;
out of both of the great parlours and drawing roome two
entrances at an equal distance upon gravell walks; this garden
is gravell'd round the two middle walks run up to a double
mount which cast the garden into 3 long grass walks which
also are very broad, with 3 flower potts, there are two degrees of stepps to each of these gravell walks, the first lands
on a gravell that turns in a 3 side square which shapes the
upper mount, the long gravell walke to the right hand runns
acrosse the mount to a thicket that enters the grove and is
lost, the other to the left runns up the whole length of the
grove up to white gates and open views into the parke;
the two ends of the little square gravel walke round the first
mount terminates on the right in same thicket or grove and
has only for show a carved frame as a gate, with wood
carv'd like cage work painted white with an arch entrance
in the middle for form sake, to make it look uniforme to
the like on the left, which leads to a walk as long as the
gravell up to the wall and is directly arbour-like, high trees
cut up to the top and with heads which close in an arch; in
the middle is long white seates.

There are two or three lesser walks which run across it to
the right into the grove and lost in the maze, to the left to
another long walk which leads to a grotto and runs parrallel
with the gravel walke to the top; you enter a space paved
and open arch'd round in seates like a court, and thence you
enter the grotto, an arch entirely dark, but at the entrance it
is so large as 6 arched seates, and between carv'd stone very
fine of all sorts of flowers figures fruites, the pillars or peers
pretty broad; this ran up to a sumerhouse at the end, which
is grown over with greens cut smooth, windows all round,
below this is a broad green walke, which begins at the first
garden, and so continues round with the wall quite to that
broad gravel-walke and is continued by the wall quite encompassing the maze, in which are some slaunt cut wayes,

and it terminates in the other side of the first garden just by a garden railed in, in which is a large pond square, in nature of a cannall, the bank green cut fine and borders for flowers and greens, and a breast wall to the first garden, on which are flower potts on the upper mount, all the grass and bank even cut, stands 4 flower potts painted blew some red on the 3 divisions the gravell, cut out as on the margin.

From the hall you go to the staircase, there is also a doore out of the second parlour, this is noble and lofty, all plain wanscoate only the halfe paces inlaid; the first is a window the whole height, 13 large pannells in length 5 in breadth, which lookes into one of the courts where the pond is and stable yard; the next half pace leads you on the left hand to the private appartment, that is not so lofty, over the least hall to an anty room thence a dineing roome soe drawing roome 5 bed chambers and closetts; the last closett goes into a balcony which runs across the middle of said lofty window and looks into the staircase; out of the eating or dineing roome goes a closet for the Ladyes into the Chappell with very good back staires up to the top roomes; the great staires continues up to the gallery and turns in a long halfe pace which enters it at two doores in equal distances; its a lofty large as well as long roome, noe painting or frettwork; at each end are severall handsome bed chambers and closetts but none furnish'd but the private appartment, as pladd chamlet damaske neatly made up, not new, glass sconces and over the chimney looking glasses in frames; the parke is fine but not stock'd which when it is and house furnish'd will be a noble seate.

There is another house[4] of Mr. Ruths [Rooth] who married Lady Dennagall [Donegal] is new and neate, the entrance is a space the breadth of the court and front, rail'd in an opening in the middle with sort of wicket, two such at each end with heavye latches to pull up and the gates swings both wayes; there is a brick wall with peers and breast high,

[4] The house was in New Inn Lane (see Toland, op. cit., in *Misc. Works*, ii, p. 96). Mrs. Rooth (née Jane Itchingham) born 1645, had married Lord Donegal almost as a child and been widowed in 1678. She then married Richard Rooth and died in 1712.

and iron pallisadoes of a good breadth each side the gate, which is carv'd iron work with a Deer on the top of a Cypher and an Oaken Tree cut a top; the two first peers are with great flower potts those on the peeres each side the iron works lesser flower potts; beyond are the gates into the coach yard which with the stables is a neate pile of buildings by it self; just on the other side is such a building, the kitchen and offices and little laundry court, and here is the back entrance through a long brick entry, open on one side but a wall to the court side and house, and enters into a passage that leads to a little hall brick't with roomes for the buttler and a batheing roome; by it is a large hall paved with stone and thence is one way into the garden; under the staires and balcony that descends from the dineing roome in the first passage are staires which brings to a space that turns up to the great staires and roomes.

The front entrance is into a handsome court, one large paved walke in the middle between grass, the borders round of flowers the wall with trees; you ascend some stepps to a broad terrass, paved and with a breast wall sett with flower potts; this is the breadth of the house and at each end two large white seates with arches over the head; the middle you enter, a step or two to this space which leads to the staires, on the left to a little parlour wanscoted, white in veines and gold mouldings, a neat booffett furnish'd with glasses and china for the table, a cistern below into which the water turn'd from a cock, and a hole at bottom to let it out at pleasure; within this roome was a large closet or musick room, on the other side was a dineing room with a balcony door which has staires to the garden in a round with half paces and iron railes; thence is a drawing-roome beyond that a closet that comes out into a little passage to the staircase which is large and makes the fourth part of the house; they are wanscoate varnish'd and the lower step or two larger and the other end is in a turn; the half paces are strip'd, the wood put with the graine, the next slip against the graine, which makes it looke pretty as if inlaid.

You enter one roome hung with crosstitch in silks, the bed

the same lined with yellow and white strip'd sattin, window curtaines white silk damaske with furbellows of callicoe printed flowers, the chaires crosstitch, and two stooles of yellow mohaire with crostitch true lover knotts in straps along and a cross, an elbow chaire tentstitch, glasses over all the chimneys and marble pieces; the windows in all the roomes had cusheons; the next roome was Lady Dennagalls [Donegal] chamber and closet hung with very rich tapistry, the bed crimson damaske lined with white India sattin with gold and crimson flowers printed, the chaires, one red damaske the other crostitch and tentstitch very rich, soe round the roome; the closet green damaske chaires and many fine pictures under glasses of tentstitch sattinstitch gumm and straw-work, also India flowers birds etc.; the roome over the little parlour was Mrs. Ruths [Rooth] a pladd bed lined with Indian callicoe and an India carpet on the bed, within was her closet; over this are good garretts and staires to the leads which shews you all about the town.

The first garden is square the walls full of trees and nail'd neate, an apricock, peach, plumb, necktarine, which spread, but not very high, between each is a cherry stript up to the top and spreads then composeing an arch over the others, there are borders of flowers round and a handsome gravel round, the grass plott is large, in the middle a little gravel in an oval or round where is a large fountain of stone full of stone images to spout the water; this garden is the breadth of the dwelling-house, the dineing roome and drawing roome looke into it.

Out of this (which is fenced by a breast wall with iron pallasadoes painted blew with gilt topps) you ascend severall stepps through an iron-work'd gate to a ground divided into long grass walks severall of which ascends the hill, and between the ground improv'd with dwarfe trees of fruite and flowers and greenes in all shapes, intermixt with beds of strawberyes for ornament and use, thus to another bank with stepps to a green cross walke and then more trees and devices; thence to two mounts cut smoothe, between is a cannall, these mounts are severall stepps up under which are ice

houses, they are a square flatt on the top fenced with banks
round and seates, beyond which is a summer house in a tree
which shews a great way off the country; there are low cut
hedges on each bank, and painted sticks with gilt tops in the
greens and flower potts and thus is one terrass above another
—over their stables are chambers for the men, over the
kitchen and dairy and buttery and scullery are roomes for
laundry and for the maids.

Sir Thomas Cookes house has such an enclosed walk before the gate with such swinging gates at each end and a
larger in the middle, without it is a row of oakes with thick
heads which makes it very shady; you enter a close gate into
a court with a broad paved walk between two large grass-
plotts besett with green cyprus yew and holly in piramids,
and two large statues in the middle, the wall cloath'd with
box holly filleroy cut even, the front is two juttings out at the
ends, flatt in the middle like a half Roman H; you rise a step
or two into a good hall pav'd with black and white marble,
the sides painted black and white resembling nitches or arches
for seates; on the right hand is a good dineing-roome wanscoated oake without varnish the pannell large, and within a
drawing roome, which lookes into the garden wanscoated;
over right another square one; between these runs an entry,
wherein are closets and the butlers office, to the kitchen and
offices into the stable coach yard and into a laundry court;
in the middle fronting the entrance is a door into the garden;
just by is a servants hall and way to the cellars under; the
great staires noble and lofty all wanscoate, hung with very
good pictures, above in the rooffe is frettwork and an oval
curiously painted with angells and figures.

Here are two very good appartments bed chambers dressing-roomes closets and presses, besides there are two other
good chambers with closets, and one large roome, the frame
of the chimney piece carv'd with all variety of fruites herbes
etc., painted proper and all hollow work, very good pictures
in all the roomes over chimneys and doores all fix'd into the
wanscoate, noe furniture, there is a very good pair of back
staires goes hence up to the garret's, one very large, 6 other

347

besides little room; there you ascend into a Cupilow, windows round shews a vast prospect of the place; from thence you may descend another such a good pair of back staires to the kitchen; the garden is in forme as Mr. Ruths first flatt but larger, with a larger fountaine walled in with free stone a pedistal with little Cupids and Dolphins and Shells on which are Images and on the top a Crown made all to spout out water; the walls full of fruite, in the middle you ascend severall stepps to a bank, on which are iron painted pallasadoes with gilt tops, gates the same, here is a large square with green walks and gravell and ovall in the middle with devices of little paths of gravell to cut the grass into shapes squares and 3 squares,[4a] in the middle stands a Gladiator on a pedistal and on the walls are Cupids at each riseing of the walls for the banks; on the left side is a summer house with paints of the seasons of the yeare, thence into another garden for kitchen stuff and hott beds with convenient houses neat, from this great flatt you ascend severall stepps at three places equal distance and then long green walks between borders of strawberies dwarf trees and some with green squares sett with cyprus mirtle yew holly cut fine and flowers, thus three severall bancks, the spaces so adorn'd, then you pass on to a long green walke; the right side or end is a fine summer house, the bank all along guarded with dwarffe trees; the other to the field side rowes of tall walnutts with quick sett hedges cutt; this carryes on not only the breadth of the house but the length of the whole ground which is for the other garden for use, and just at the end of the pleasure garden begins a large and long pond or cannall the length of the walke, which is its bank cut fine, there is another great pond on the right side of the house, and two more in the grounds belonging to it on the left.

Mrs. Steeven has a very pretty neate house and gardens, before the doore is a part railed in as before, only this is close at each end with high wall and seates; in the middle is a gate which leads to the gate of the court, grass walled round, a broad pavement to the house and round stepps 4 or 5; you

[4a] I.e. triangles.

enter into a passage which leads to a little parlour thence a step or two down to an entry which leads away to a little court or passage which runs to the streete and back to the garden.

On one side is a building, a summer parlour for a still-roome with brick kitchen and offices and coach house and stables with chambers over for the men; there is in the first parlour a large closet, on the left is a large parlour and drawing-roome all very neate and well wanscoated; under the staircase is a little roome for a butler thence the staires to the cellars, this is between the back staires (which are very good and light and wanscoated up to the garrets) and the great staires which are very handsome painted white, the rooffe an oval of Cupids; here are two handsome chambers with dressing-roomes and light and dark closets and presses; next floore is to such appartments againe; over all are three good garrets and two roomes for stores and it is sash'd up to the top with low windows to sit in; every corner is improved for cupboards and necessarys, and the doores to them made suiteable to the wanscoate; the garden goes out opposite to the entrance the walls full of all fruite neately kept, here are six grass walks three and three, guarded with dwarfe fruite trees, a large gravell walk round by the wall, and gravell between each grass walke, the front is a breast wall with a yew hedge cut neate, and iron pallisadoes painted and gilt tops with gates leading to another garden of grass cut in shapes and knotts with flowers and all sorts of greens cut in shapes, with paths of gravel to form them, on the left side a coddling hedge secured a walke of orange and lemmon trees in perfection, this is closed with a green house all the breadth of this garden, through which you enter another of flowers; thence into orchard and kitchen garden, which is cast in exact forms to look neate, in the green garden was large alloes plants and all sorts of perpetualls as well as annualls.

There are abundance of houses built of brick, with fine gardens and courts with open gates and railes to view, which are used as lodgings for the Company; and now the Wells are built about and a large light roome to walk in brick'd, and a pump put on the Well, a coffee house and two roomes for gameing, and shops for sweetmeates and fruite; Monday morning is their day the Company meete, and then they have some little diversion, as raceing of boyes, or rabbets, or piggs; in the evening the Company meete in the Greenes, first in the Upper Green, many steps up, where are Gentlemen bowling, Ladyes walking, the benches round to sitt, there are little shopps, and a gameing or danceing-roome; the same man at the Wells keepes it, sells coffee there also;[5] the Lower Green is not far off, just in the heart of the town, its a much neater Green and warmer, the whole side of this is a very large roome with large sashe windows to the Green with cusheons in the windows and seates all along; there are two hazard-boards; at the end is a Milliner and China-shop, this is belonging to the great tavern or eateing house, and all the length of this roome to the street ward is a piaza wall, and a row of trees cutt and platted together as the fashion of the place with tops running up a top with heads, the Crosse in the streete has a good Clock.

On the hill where is the race posts, they have made a Ring as in Hide [Hyde] Parke, and they come in coaches and drive round, but it is only Lords day nights, and some nights there has been 40 coaches and six which are the Gentlemen in the county round, and 20 and 2 horses the Company in the town; Epsham [Epsom] shall be clutter'd with Company from Satturday to Tuesday and then they many times goe, being so neare London, so come againe on more Satturdays.

From Epsham [Epsom] I went to Banstead where the parson of the Parish has diverted himself in his garden these fifty yeares, is now old and doates, but has curious hedges, one Garden with grass plotts and earth walks, cut and wedd, his grass plotts has stones of divers formes and sizes, which he names Gods and Goddesses, and hedges and arbours of thorn soe neately cut and in all figures in great rounds; one is a large arbour, you enter a straite passage as unto a cell but within a roome, round that by a narrow entry you come to a

---

[5] Coffee was introduced into England *c.* 1650, and Coffee Houses had immediately become the height of fashion.

large square with trees and seates all quick sett hedges cut
fine; one is a tree which the ivy has covered and there are
staires up directly upright and on the top is an eight square
bench round, the green grows up close about it cut even,
this he calls Tenneriff being in that form; next it is another
tree, there is a flatt and on it is a table or stoole on which is a
great white stone in form of some statue thats Apolo with 9
stones round less, the Muses, this is Parnassus; there are
severall heads painted which are named Mogul, Grand
Seignior, Cham of Tartary, Zarr of Muscovy, placed in
severall places; another garden is grass plotts with yews and
holly lawrells, round this on the bank is sett stones very
thick, some very much bigger for officers, this is the whole
Confederate army and their Generalls;[6] here is a trumpeter,
Hercules and Bacchus, and a hedge of lawrell 7 foote broad;
here are also two trees cover'd with ivy and thorne, cut
smooth and made in fashion of two great pillars, for
Hercules pillars, there is in the middle some platted together
and makes a cover to a seate below, and there is a Rose cut
out—you may talk as under the Rose; in his house he has
many curiosetyes of stones, one like a brick of bread another
like a shoulder of mutton, a piece of wood from an old tree
as like a mounteer capp[7] with a button on the top, another
like a fur-bellow'd peticoate, another stone like an apple
paired and a piece cut out and grown deadish, its said this is
petrify'd into stone as the moss in Knarsborough and the
wood at Apsley [Aspley] in Bedfordshire, here were many
shells, birds, Indian shoes, bootes, purses, etc.[8]

From Epsham [Epsom] to Leatherhead 3 mile, we pass by
Sir Robert Howards which I have described [Ashtead Park];
here is a little town where they make much leather and other
little trades, many butchers which supply Epsham, here it is
that the water which sinks away at Swallow Hole at Mole

[6] Our Allies in the War of the Spanish Succession. One of the Generals
would have been Prince Eugene of Savoy.
[7] A montero was a Spanish hunter's cap with a spherical crown and a flap.
[8] Here a couplet, written with apparent irrelevance in the margin, reads:
"Some for an acre more of land
Oftymes take a fool by the hand."

under Box Hill which is 7 mile off and here it bubbles up in twenty places from a hill and composes a great river half a mile off, over which a long bridge of 14 great arches of stone by their height shews sometimes the water to be very deep; a little farther its so deep as cannot be forded; here the channell is not so broad only four large arches; we goe over thence a mile and halfe to Mr. Moores[9] fine house on a hill [Fetcham Park] its built with brick and stone coyned, and the windows stone, nine sashes to the garden; the jutting out in the middle is three windows; the top is in a peak painted frisco [fresco] and a cornish [cornice] round; on each side a low building each end like wings with same cornish leaded and flower potts on it which are the offices, on one side lead to a summer house and backward to the private entrance, a court that you ascend by steps of stone iron barristers with turnings and halfe paces, to the part of the house in constant use; the front in the entrance is as the garden only here are but eight windows, only two in the middle jutting, the top, and that here you see not those two low wings.

You enter by the Church yard, noe great court or roome for it, a very little court which on the right hand leads into the garden on a banck green walke to a seate or summer house finely painted stands on four pillars, within this leads into a gravel walk which goes round the first garden; the summer house you might pass through to the same green banck walk which leads to a broad grass walk on the right hand up the hill near a quarter of a mile each side planted with trees, and the ground some for kitchen gardens orchards hott beds, the top of the hill has two white seates and a summer house, this has white open gates large as the walk; here is a very fine pond runs across the breadth of the gardens and orchards; the garden at the house is all flatt much in grass walks and bancks sett with green, most yews; there is a great gravel walk to the fountain from the middle of the house which is filled by a long cannall as broad as the walk,

[9] Surrey was already becoming the haunt of company directors. Arthur Moore, a Commissioner of Trade and Plantations, was a Director of the South Sea Company. (See Defoe, op. cit., i, 146–7.)

at the farther end is a trion [triton] gilt with a horn which can blow the water 20 yards; here are seates on the bancks, and the ground round it much in grass walks with dwarfe [greens];[10] at the founttaine is jetts of water; on one side is a large carvd summerhouse painted green in which were two marble tables of dark marble, you pass'd through to gravel walks, a stone step or two opposite to it, from two or three such stone stepps a brass figure of a Black Moore [Blackamoor] large very naturall with a great dish on his head like a shield; from these comes slaunt gravel walks to the house on each side; beyond the fountain garden is two iron work gates with an arch in the middle for entrance with a doore, one to another garden, the other into a little garden that is to the road; there is by the road a little farther near the house a lower garden with a breast wall to this garden which you looke over and has another great pond which serves the house; this is with physick and pott herbs and little flowers; all the water which fills these ponds is brought a mile and half from Leatherhead up the hill which was a vast expence: the two end fronts of the house is with middle juttings, but four windows, the rooff a peake and all with friscow [fresco] work all sash windows; its said to be finely finish'd and furnish'd but I saw it not in the inside, only one ground bedchamber which was an Indian attlass[11] white very fine; the ground for many acres is planted in manner of a park.

The Commons all about Epsham [Epsom] is very good aire and shews the country like a landskip, woods, plains, inclosures, and great ponds.

Thence to Hampton Court by Kingston 6 mile, all by the park, the palace enters just by the Thames, on the gate is Lyon Unicorn and flower potts the Starre and Garter and Draggon the Thistle and Rose carv'd; here is a space where the stables on one side and houses for suttlers for to provide for the servants; the front is in a demy-circle, at the gates four towers of brick, beyond the halfe moone are two straite buildings in which are gates at the ends, two such brick

10 The bottom line of a manuscript page has been torn off here.
11 Atlas was a silk satin made in the East.

towers, soe you enter through those four towers, the guard court on the left goes to the old buildings; on the right you enter a long paved entry, on one side are lodgings, at the end are cloysters round a court which has a large fountaine in grass and at each corner a painted post for balls or statues, the grass is planted round with lawrell and yew filleroy [phillyrea] and cyprus cut a round head and a piramid; the cloysters lead to the royal staircase which is very lofty and spacious, with arches for seates, the steps, iron railes carv'd and gilt, the wall black and gold painted with armory like a wanscoate, over that is curious paintings the twelve Cæsars, over that the banquet of the Gods all at length, with Ceres over the side board with plenty; the rooffe is angells and cherubins, the front on the halfe pace is Julian and the spectre that appear'd to him, in a tent of green, the curtain drawn soe bold as if real with gold fringe; here you enter the guard-chamber adorn'd with Pikes, Halberts, Bionnetts,[12] Daggers and Pistolls, and Gunns with Bandeleers or Pouches for ammunition all set in workes and figures about the wanscoate, over the chimney Pistolls and Daggers sett like the Starre in the Garter.

Thence you go into an anty-room hung with tapestry, thence into the Common Audience roome where was a throne and cannopy crimson damaske with gold fringe the form the same round the roome; here was King Charles the Firsts picture on horse back over the mantlepiece; all the rooffes of the roomes are curiously painted with different storyes, out of this you enter the grand State Roome which has King Williams picture at length on the mantlepiece, fine pictures over all doores, and carvings in wood, the throne and cannopy here was scarlet velvet with rich gold orrice and window curtains; thence into the dineing roome where hangs in the middle a chrystall branch for candles, its hung with

[12] The guardroom was built in the reign of William III and the bayonets also must have been of recent date. "Plug" bayonets, which fitted inside the muzzle and prevented firing, had been used by the French in 1647 and were issued to British troops in 1672—at first to cavalry. Their use was largely responsible for the defeat at Killiecrankie (1689) which induced the defeated General Mackay to invent the Ring bayonet, used until displaced in 1805 by Sir John Moore's Clip bayonet.

tapistry, I think its here the Queen of Bohemias picture is over the chimney piece, Sophia's mother;[13] the window curtaines flower'd crimson damaske with gold fringe; thence the drawing roome which has a silver branch in the middle and sconces and Queen Marys picture, here is crimson velvet; out of this is the Presence chamber, with a low screen across the roome to keep company off the bed, which is scarlet velvet with gold orrice and hung with fine tapistry; out of the bedchamber goes the dressing roome hung with yellow damaske and chaires the same; here was the Queen Mother Dutchess of Yorks picture over the chimney: here is a doore into the private lodgings where there is 2 bed chambers one Indian embroydery the other a mixt damaske, and closets and antyroome to the galleryes and backstaires.

Out of the dressing-roome is the Queens closet, the hangings, chaires, stooles and screen the same, all of satten stitch done in worsteads, beasts, birds, images and fruites all wrought very finely by Queen Mary and her Maids of Honour; from thence into a large long gallery wanscoated and pictures of all the Roman Warrs on one side, the other side was large lofty windows, two marble tables in two peers with two great open jarrs on each side each table, two such at the end the same for to put potts of orange and mirtle trees in, the window curtaines and couches or formes all green and white rich damaske.

Out of this into a long gallery, plain wanscoate without any adornment, which is for people to waite in either of the servants of the houshold or who waites in buissness of the ordinary sort, and here are doores that lead to the back staires and to private lodgings; this leads at the end into the part was design'd for the Kings side, into a noble gallery with curious pictures of the Scriptures painted by the Carthusion,[14] the King of France offer'd 3000 pound apiece

[13] Elizabeth, daughter of James I, the "Winter Queen" of Bohemia and wife of Frederick Elector Palatine. Her daughter the Electress Sophia, mother of George I, and sister of Prince Rupert, died in 1714. Had she lived a few months longer, she would have been Queen of England.

[14] The pictures were Raphael's cartoons; the "Roman Warrs" mentioned above must be Mantegna's "Triumph of Julius Caesar".

for them or indeed any money; here are green and white damaske window-curtaines and couches as the other was; this leads to roomes not finished, in the same number as on the Queen's side, one is begun to be painted on the top; the sides of the walls are painted just like pieces of tapestry; here is Prince Georges[15] picture at length, with his dukall corronet and an anchor, as High Admirall; and thus to the other roomes to the guard roome and royal staircase as on the Queens side, but none here finish'd.

The leads gives a vast sight all about of the parke and gardens, the front of the house to the garden has four large stone figures, Hercules, Jupiter, Mars, Neptune; there is a long Cannall runs from the front a great way and a large founttaine next the house in the first garden, with a broad gravell and a cross which cutts the grass plotts into four, which are cutt into flower deluces [fleur de lys] and severall devices, with paths of gravell, borders of mould in which are greens of all sorts, piramids and then round interchangeable; beyond this is another space as large with a round space with a large stone figure and severall less figures of brass in the little squares and strapps [strips] of grass which was form'd by cross and round gravell-walks; there is two broad gravell walks runns aslaunt like two wings from the first garden as it were parrallel with the cannall and these terminate in a wood, which has a glide throw [through] trees cut aslant agreable to the walks to give the view quite to Hampton town.

The Stepps out of the house is ⌷ to goe 3 wayes down; there is at the two sides of the house gardens; their form is much like this the front the Steps suppose as thus[16] the other for all flowers hot beds shady arbours and private walks with cut hedges the one side; this looks into the grounds and park and has a less fountain; out of the cloysters you enter the private appartment under the chambers of the private lodgings, where is an anty-room full of cane chaires;

---

[15] Prince George of Denmark, Consort of Queen Anne.
[16] There is a gap in the manuscript here, to leave room for a drawing, which apparently was once pasted in.

next is the constant dineing-roome where are hung all the
pictures of the Ladyes of the Bed Chamber in Queen Maryes
time that were drawn by Nellor [Kneller] and were then
hung in the Water Gallery before that was pulled down;[17]
within this is a drawing room with pictures—I think here
was the old Queen Mother[18] with some of her Children over
the Chimney—this appartment goes out into a tarress walk
of gravel and so into the flower garden on the right side of
the house which has the private and shady walks, fine aloes,
paricantha, mirtles orranges and oliantas [oleander] etc.; in
the cloysters are two very handsome back-staires for the
Kings or Queens to come to this private appartment or to
the gardens or the Chappel of stone, which with handsome
spaces to each set of degrees hung on their own work as to
one side, and with iron railes painted blew and gold; there
is also two or three private stone staires hung the same way
with iron railes that are narrower, runs up to the leads and
lead to severall of the Maids of Honours appartments and
the lodgings to the Household; the Chappel is refitting; the
rooff is fretwork painted and gilded, so is the Queens closet
and galleryes on each side for her Ladies, the rooffe and alter
the same with the crown in the old form like a corronet shape
as K[ing] H[enry's] great old crown is; the pillars are carv'd
like stone but are all of wanscoate as are the seates without
paint or varnish.

From Hampton Court to Kingston by the Thames where
I cross'd it and soe to Staines; then I had the Thames on the
other side till I came almost to Windsor; I drove by some of
the Forest and the Parke, came in another way into town by
the Castle across King Charles's Walk cut up in the Forrest;
having seen the Castle, only was in the Queen's Chappel
which have describ'd already, so shall only add what I remark'd not before, as in the Castle yard is a little box the
Queen has bought of Lord Godolphins (the garden joyns to

[17] The Water Gallery along the river side had been fitted temporarily in
1690 for Queen Mary's accommodation. Work on Hampton Court had been
stopped by William on Queen Mary's death in 1694, but resumed in 1699.
(H.A.T.)
[18] Queen Henrietta Maria.

the Duke of St. Albans[19] [Burfield Lodge]) for a little re-
treate out of the Palace; you enter a brick court, on the left is
a little guard roome, on the right a row of roomes with
chambers over them for the kitchen and pastry[20] and but-
teryes and a little garden pailed in; then you go on and on
the left hand enter the house; into an entry on the left is a
little parlour for the Ladies of Honour to dine in, beyond
that back staires pantry and a cistern or place to wash things
in, by that is the guard roome under it the cellars.

On the right hand is a large anty roome for persons to
waite where are marble tables in the peeres between the windows, white damaske window-curtaines and cane chaires;
next it is the dineing roome some stepps down where was
red silk curtaines, chaires and stooles and benches round the
roome all red silk, with same coulloured orrice lace; here was
a white marble table behind the doore as a side board and a
clap table under the large looking-glass between the windows; next this was a drawing roome; both these roomes
were hung with small image tapistry very lively and fresh,
here was crimson damaske window-curtaines, chaires and
stooles; the next was what was Prince George's dressing-
roome, hung and window curtaines chaires and stooles all
with yellow damaske, with marble chimney pieces—as all
the roomes have of differing coullours, black white grey
rance etc.—large looking-glasses; all the roomes in all the
house is plain unvarnished oake wanscoate which lookes
very neate; within the dressing roome is a closet on one
hand, the other side is a closet that leads to a little place with
a seate of easement of marble with sluces of water to wash
all down; there is a back doore in the dressing roome to a
little anty roome, with presses and little wanscoate tables for
tea, cards, or writeing; so to a back staires, the Queen's
appartment is over it; from the greate staire at the entrance
of the house lands you in a passage that enters the anty
roome, is crimson damaske curtains great chaire and stooles
and benches the same next it; the Presence roome here is

[19] The Duke of St. Albans was the son of Charles II by Nell Gwyn.
[20] A Pastry was a pastry kitchen (see O.E.D.).

figured crimson velvet window curtaines chaires and stooles; here is the Queen Anne Wife to King James the First at length in her rideing habit by her horse and three or four couple of hounds; these were hung with fine tapistry as the two below.

Next this was the Queen's bed chamber, hung the bed window-curtaines the same all rich crimson damaske; here was the screen round the bed as the manner is to all the Souveraignes beds, over the chimney was Prince Georges picture and by the side of the bed was the Duke of Glocesters[21] in an oval; thence into a dressing-roome hung with divers coulloured flower'd sattin chaires and stooles, the same fine flower'd muslin window curtaines, a fine little high screen burnt jappan of 4 leaves, another chimney screen with 4 leaves of the stone work in figures Indian; out of this was the Queens closet just over Prince Georges, but that was lock'd; the other side was a little waiting roome to just such marble seates of easement with the sluces of water as that below was in the Queens bedchamber; overright the entrance of the dressing-roome was another little closet with the tea equipage and under that was such a little tea roome within the drawing roome; here in the dressing roome was a back way to a little waiting passage with presses and such little wanscoate tables, this leads to the back staires where there is one bedchamber; the Queen's Appartment fronts the garden out of the drawing roome, you come on a terrass of gravell then descend stepps down a green banck to a large green space that has 4 bench seates painted white, behind them is a green bank and a large space of green on either end fill'd with trees—lawrells filleroy [phillyrea] cyprus yews, heads and pirramids, and mirtles; this is fenced with iron palasadoes painted, to another garden cut in squares and figures with all sorts of flowers and greens which has at the end a cut hedge and leads on to a sort of orchard with dwarfe trees; these gardens and orchards is in gravel walks and long green walks, in variety as such a thing in miniature can admitt.

I drove through another part of the Forrest of Windsor to

---

[21] The Duke of Gloucester was the only one of Princess Anne's children to survive infancy, but he never lived to be Prince of Wales.

see a race run by two footemen an English and Scotch, the former a taller bigger man than the other; the ground measur'd and cut even in a round was almost four mile, they were to run it round so often as to make up 22 mile, which was the distance between Chareing Cross and Windsor Cross; that was five times quite round and so farre as made up the odd miles and measure; they ran a round in 25 minutes; I saw them run the first three rounds and halfe another in an hour and seventeene minutes, and they finish'd it in two hours and a halfe, the English gain'd the second round the start and kept it at the same distance the five rounds and then the Scotch-man came up to him and got before him to the post; the Englishman fell down within a few yards of the post; many hundred pounds were won and lost about it, they ran both very neately but my judgment gave it the Scotch man because he seem'd to save himself to the last push.[22]

I drove home by a fine house [Cranbourne Lodge] of Lord Rawnelaughs[23] [Ranelagh] 14 windows in the front a square building (much gardening and curious they say, but that Ladyes pride is none must see them) and soe drove a fine gravell road cut with rows of trees: in a mile you come to a broad open way to Windsor on the left hand, on the right to a little house of the Dutchess off Marlbroughs [Windsor Lodge] which is very exact gardens and fountaines cut hedges and groves pailed in, from this house is the fine gravell walke continued very broad between high rows of trees on one hand a fine grove of straite trees.

[22] Since this passage is quoted in Southey's *Omniana* (see Introduction, p. xiii) Southey must have seen the larger MS., in which alone it appears, as well as the smaller MS. which is known to have been owned by him.

[23] Richard Jones, first Earl of Ranelagh (1636–1712), a friend of Charles II, was detected in 1702 in gross peculation as Paymaster General of the Forces, but escaped prosecution. He had bought Cranbourne in 1700, and built extensively there since, a fact which helps to date the writing of this passage. According to Macky, he "had originally no great estate, yet hath spent more money, built more fine houses, and laid out more on household-furniture and gardening, than any other nobleman in England; he is a great epicure, and prodigious expensive . . . several Parliaments have been calling him to an account, yet he escapes with the punishment only of losing his place . . . he is a bold man, and very happy in jests and repartees, and hath often turned the humour of the House of Commons, when they have designed to have been very severe". (*Memoirs of the Secret Services*, ed. 1733, p. 82.)

This is three mile to Windsor all a clear visto to the Castle to that which is King Charles's Walke for Shooting which you enter by a broad pallasadoe fences the whole breadth of the road, so at the other end which is a mile and goes out into the road which comes from Hampton Court, which you cross into the yards and courts that lead up into the Castle, where is the Cathedral [St. George's Chapel].

APPENDIX

CELIA FIENNES' WILL

OWING TO the closure, during the war and for some time after, of the relevant department in Somerset House, it was notpossible to obtain the Will of Celia Fiennes until the Introduction was already in print. Since the Will is informative and highly characteristic, this short appendix is devoted to it.

The Will is dated November 6th 1738 and there are three Codicils, the last added three months before her death. One of the witnesses was the younger Daniel Defoe, which proves that he had not, as has been thought, already left the country.[1] Celia Fiennes is living at Hackney, apparently in a house of her own, near her niece Jane King (née Harrison) who is appointed executrix. Celia Fiennes, however, has her main establishment at Barnet, although her house there seems to have been let. She may well be the "Mistress Fiennes" who endowed the Nonconformist chapel at Wood Street, Barnet, in 1709;[2] she has already "given them a table cloth and pewter plate for the Communion".

The Will opens by stating that—at seventy-six—she is sound in mind and "in perfect health, praised be my good God, but . . . increasing in infirmitys of body and sudden seisures". There follows a lengthy passage commending her soul to her "Creatour". Next she provides in some detail for her burial at Newton Toney, "without ostentation only put into a leaden coffin", with no memorial beyond an inscription on her father's monument. "I forbid all escutcheons or bearers". All is to "be as privat as can be a hearse and one coach and to go out early in the morning and goe the backside of the Town to the Western roade".

---

[1] See W. Wilson, *Life of Daniel Defoe*, 1830. Vol. iii, p. 462.
[2] W. Urwick, *Nonconformity in Hertfordshire*, p. 270.

She records "a great diminution of the temporal estate both as to the sinking my substance in a great measure and by depredations on my lands that little but annuitys remain which conclude at death". This is the occasion of her making a new will "but not in the least [of] repining or reflection for my good God gives and has power to take away when he sees good and he still affords me a sufficiency". Apart from her two houses, the only lands she now owns appear to be her "Marshlands".

She wishes to continue a charity (the income from £40) with which she has been charged by a deceased friend to "purchase bread for to be distributed to the prisoners at Ludgate and White Chappell". Almost all the rest is a long list of personal possessions and a few small monetary bequests assigned to her surviving relatives, to her friends (especially her doctor, Justinian Morse of Barnet) and to her servants. One manservant William Butcher had formerly been with her fifteen years and is to have £50; so is her personal maid Mrs. Cecilia Whithall. Other servants remembered include a "cookmaide" and four other women. The residual estate is "to be paid into the fund for country ministers of the descenting denomination".

Celia Fiennes apologises for the relatively small value of what she is leaving to her nieces and, perhaps for that reason, she is careful to specify what handsome wedding presents they had from her in more prosperous days—"a diamond necklace of 48 large diamonds", "my dressing plate and a buckle of 16 large diamonds", "my diamond ring with the crown", "a large pearl necklace", "a large silver salver and a pearl necklace of three rows". The possessions they are now to inherit include "my ring sett with diamonds and rubie to be worn by her not altered" and "my diamond earings to be worn by her for my sake", while a nephew receives "my repeating clock for his closet to remind him time passes".

Celia Fiennes' jewellery includes a "ring of emarals and haire", buckles, "taggs" and "colets" of diamonds, a gold watch, seven mourning rings and "my little locket the christal a little crakt". Among the furniture we hear of "Japan" and "tortishell" cabinets, of a "seatee of Irish stitch", an ebony couch, an "easy chair English stitch", "my other easy chair on wheels" and two "square stools that have hook and staples to hang on to the chair as a couch".

The pictures include two portraits of her "grandfather Say and Seale", one "set in gold" and one "in square ebony", together with her father "set in gold in minature". The few books specified are devotional or theological but there is also "my book of archbishops in a red leather with gold". Her executors are instructed to dispose only of "books but what have anybodys name on the frontispiece". There is more detail as to clothes and linen. Mention is made of "my sable muff and tippet and the furr in the box to make it up", "my blake silk Mantua and coat", "my green damask and peices of the same", "my unwattered tabby mourning", "my blew and gold atlas", "my scarlet", "my velvet" and several "wraught gowns". We hear too of "stitch pillows and quilt" and "8 Irish stitch coushons". "Let my washer woman have my cotton night gown and one paire of my ordinary couch sheets and ordinary apron". Other items specified include a "Japan tea chest", "my silver warming pan", a "copper brass stove" and "my Dutch lamp and kettle copper". Lastly, the plate—a "silver cup and cover with the coronet", a "single large silver plaite", "2 silver spoons with C.F.", besides silver "tea kettle", canisters, coffee pot and nutmeg box, 6 gilt tea spoons and a "case of knife fork spoon and gold thimble". There is "other plaite", unspecified, which is to be divided. Celia Fiennes must have remained unrepentantly modernist to the end, for she adds "let but the canisters be sold being old".

The Will is a most detailed one but contains no reference to any manuscript account of her journeys.

INDEX